SAGE, SAINT AND SOPHIST

SAGE, SAINT AND SOPHIST

Holy men and their associates
in the Early Roman Empire

Graham Anderson

London and New York

First published 1994
by Routledge
11 New Fetter Lane, London EC4P 4EE

Simultaneously published in the USA and Canada
by Routledge
29 West 35th Street, New York, NY 10001

© 1994 Graham Anderson

Typeset in Garamond by
Florencetype Limited, Kewstoke, Avon
Printed and bound in Great Britain by
T J Press (Padstow) Ltd, Padstow, Cornwall

British Library Cataloguing in Publication Data
A catalogue record for this book is available from the British Library.

Library of Congress Cataloging in Publication Data
Applied for

ISBN 0-415-02372-6

For Alf and Margaret Smyth

CONTENTS

CONTENTS

PREFACE

This book sets out to study the careers and social relationships of an assortment of religious activists in the first three centuries of the Roman Empire. They range from familiar figures such as Jesus Christ and Apollonius of Tyana to the puzzling Peregrinus Proteus, who immolated himself after an Olympic Games, or the Secundus, who defied an emperor with an oath of silence. My object is to bring the climate of belief in these centuries more clearly within the framework of Roman social history. I have set out to examine what we can make out of the career patterns of holy men, their techniques of revelation and persuasion, their relations with patrons, populace and one another; and the growth of cults of individuals. In particular I have been interested in the overlap between a number of categories traditionally divided: the cultural environment of the period made it easy for doctor and medicine man to form part of a single spectrum; so do philosopher, religious antiquarian and magician, or Hellenic intellectual and oriental sage. The result is that most individuals are more complex than is allowed by the sources.

Existing studies of holy men have emerged piecemeal, and an integrated view of their activities for the early Imperial period is lacking. Yet holy men were expected to advise on hygiene during an epidemic, sedate the local rapist, bring down the price of corn, or issue warnings to the Emperor. They were expected to command some brand of wisdom to enable them to make dramatic revelations; and they required and exercised a 'publicity machine' of patrons and supporters to further their ends. The activities of such figures contributed to the climate in later antiquity in which theurgy eventually came to oust pagan philosophy, and monastic saints could take political initiatives. Holy men have remained too long on the fringe of Roman 'senatorial' history as colourful eccentrics and

ix

fringe revolutionaries. Instead they deserve to be recognised as an essential part of the cultural and religious history of the Empire throughout its existence. Charismatic figures have to be all things to all men: this study is about what such 'all things' turned out to be in an early Imperial context. I hope to suggest why it was that such figures commanded the material and spiritual influence they did; or how widespread the tide of irrationalism of the fourth century was in the first three.

The breadth and scope of the subject has imposed some economies. I have attempted to illustrate rather than exhaust, and have been frugal, relatively speaking, with scholarly apparatus. This is not a book about 'the Gospel of Mark and pagan miracle-workers' as so many attempts to survey the field run the risk of becoming; neither is it about the sociology of ancient magic. It is a necessarily eclectic book about a variety of figures themselves eclectic enough to be different from most of their fellow men. It is about the sort of men who were likely to be taken for supermen, and how they were likely to go about it. In a large number of instances I have abandoned detailed discussion of specific episodes in favour of a subsequent series of studies, provisionally entitled *Horresco Referens: Studies in Literature and the Occult in Antiquity*.

My interest in this field has developed from an early interest in ancient religion and in Lucian's reaction to it; it has continued over the years through interests in Apollonius of Tyana and pagan cultural history. Over a long period a number of debts have accumulated: to Alan Galloway and Dermot Ryan, who introduced me to biblical scholarship, and to John Court, who maintained my interest in it; to Ludwig Bieler, who introduced me to the unfamiliar world of early hagiography nearly forty years after his own landmark gave the subject its focus; to Howard Kee, who patiently read the heresies of someone who must have appeared to him as a latter-day Celsus, and contributed constructive criticism from a perspective very different from my own; to my wife, who put up with these exotic intruders; to Geraldine Beare, who compiled the index, and to Richard Stoneman and his staff, who awaited the manuscript for longer than some await the Second Coming. And to the two dedicatees, for their long and supportive friendship over so many years.

Graham Anderson
University of Kent at Canterbury

ABBREVIATIONS

ABSA	*Annual of the British School at Athens*
AJ	*Antiquitates Iudaicae*
AJPh	*American Journal of Philology*
ANRW	*Aufstieg und Niedergang der römischen Welt*
BG	*Bellum Gallicum*
BJ	*Bellum Iudaicum*
BSOAS	*Bulletin of the School of Oriental and African Studies*
BZ	*Byzantinische Zeitschrift*
CMC	*Codex Manichaeus Colognensis*
CRAI	*Comptes rendus de l'Académie des Inscriptions et Belles-Lettres*
EM	*Epigraphical Museum in Athens*
HA	*Historia Animalium*
HE	*Historia Ecclesiastica*
HSCP	*Harvard Studies in Classical Philology*
IG	*Inscriptiones Graecae*
IGRRP	*Inscriptiones Graecae ad Res Romanas Pertinentes*
JAC	*Jahrbuch für Antike und Christentum*
JHS	*Journal of Hellenic Studies*
JJS	*Journal of Jewish Studies*
JRS	*Journal of Roman Studies*
LCL	*Loeb Classical Library*
NA	*Noctes Atticae*
NH	*Naturalis Historia*
PCPS	*Proceedings of the Cambridge Philological Society*
PE	*Praeparatio Evangelica*
PG	*Patrologia Graeca*
PGM	*Papyri Graeci Magici*

ABBREVIATIONS

PIR	*Prosopographia Imperii Romani*
PL	*Patrologia Latina*
RE	*Realencyclopädie der classischen Altertumswissenschaft*
RHR	*Revue de l'Histoire des Religions*
SHA	*Scriptores Historiae Augustae*
SPG	*Scriptores Physiognomonici Graeci*
TAPhA	*Transactions and Proceedings of the American Philological Association*
VA	*Vita Apollonii Tyanensis*
VPS	*Vitae Philosophorum Sophistarumque*
VS	*Vitae Sophistarum*
WS	*Wiener Studien*
YCS	*Yale Classical Studies*
ZDMG	*Zeitschrift der Deutschen Morganländischen Gesellschaft*
ZPE	*Zeitschrift für Papyrologie und Epigraphik*

1

CONCEPTS
The holy man and his milieux

Four years before the Jewish War, according to Josephus,

A man by the name of Jeshua son of Ananias, an ordinary
rustic fellow, came to the feast at which all Jews are accustomed to set up tabernacles to God. And in the Temple he
suddenly began to shout 'A voice from the east, a voice from
the west, a voice from the four winds, a voice against
Jerusalem and the sanctuary, a voice against bridegrooms and
brides, a voice against the whole people!'. Day and night he
would wander all the alleyways with this cry. Some of the
leading citizens took exception to these words of ill-omen,
seized hold of the fellow and gave him a savage beating. But he
did not say a word to defend himself, nor did he divulge
anything in private to his persecutors; he just kept shouting
the same tirade as before. The Jewish authorities, concluding
that some more supernatural force had incited him – as was
indeed the case – brought him before the Roman procurator.
There, though flogged till his flesh was torn to ribbons, he
neither begged for mercy nor shed tears, but lowering his
voice to its most mournful register responded to every blow
with 'Woe to Jerusalem'.

The procurator, Albinus, actually had Jeshua acquitted as manic but
harmless; he had no sooner pronounced woe to himself when he
was killed during the siege.[1] The brief adventure of Jeshua is a useful
starting-point, since he illustrates in short compass so many of the
typical features of an early Imperial holy man. He has access to
some information, supernaturally inspired according to Josephus,
and arguably fulfilled. He delivers his message in a prominent time
and place. He engenders opposition (and belated interest and

1

support, since he is regarded as right); he engages the attention of
the authorities in an indecisive way, and he has a spectacular death.
If Jeshua was unfortunately deranged and insignificant, at least he is
intelligible in the context in which Josephus presents him: we expect
prophets of doom in a context of national emergency. But a century
and a half later the curious inhabitants of Moesia and Thrace could
not so easily have expected the following:

> A little before this same *daimōn*, declaring himself to
> be Alexander of Macedon, and like him in appearance and
> accoutrement, set off from the Danube region, after somehow
> or other making his appearance there, and made his way
> though Moesia and Thrace performing Bacchic rites; he was
> accompanied by four hundred men equipped with Bacchic
> wands and faunskins, but they did no harm. All in Thrace at
> the time agreed that bed and board were laid on for him at
> public expense. And no one – no governor, soldier, procurator
> or local magistrate – dared to confront or contradict him, and
> he travelled as far as Byzantium as if in some solemn pro-
> cession, travelling by day, as announced in advance. From
> there he made his way over to the Chalcedon region, carried
> out some rites at night, buried a wooden horse, and
> disappeared.[2]

In the end one might feel disappointment that this exotic traveller
did not claim to be the transmigration of Achilles or Odysseus for
good measure. But Dio Cassius' sketch, while not explaining the
phenomenon he sets out to describe, at least gives us a portrait
which raises the typical questions we shall want to ask about any
given holy man, ancient or modern. The first such question is 'Who
do you think you are?'. This particular holy man might have
answered 'I am Dionysus, and/or Alexander the Great; and I am a
daimōn'. He would certainly have had to have been a supernatural
superman at the least to be a return version of Alexander, dead for
nearly five-and-a-half centuries. Next we must ask what would have
been the effect on his audience. Alexander, a world-conqueror,
might have been expected to worry the secular powers; he would
have been someone likely to say 'my kingdom is of this world, and I
am going to claim it back'. But the claim to be the god Dionysus
would have been more subtle and compelling. Educated rulers in
antiquity knew only too well what had happened to King Pentheus
when he had opposed the will of Dionysus and tried to imprison the

god: he had gone mad and was torn limb from limb. Passing through Thrace, the stamping-ground of Dionysus, this new *daimōn* might not have been unduly surprised to find no further opposition. We might also be tempted to ask how anyone could have 'pulled off a stunt' on anything like this scale. Obviously with such an entourage he would have had the opportunity for some forward planning of his campaign, and we are not surprised to find him duly announced in advance; thus is raised the question of how holy men conduct their day-to-day operations. We then have to ask what was the point of the whole exercise: the wooden horse seems to evoke some reference to Troy – until we reflect that this rite does not seem actually to have taken place at Troy, and that Plato's myth of Gyges knows of a buried horse in a quite different context.[3] In the end we seem none the wiser, and not untypically either: holy men have the capacity to arouse expectation, but to keep even their closest followers guessing.

In the period we are dealing with, the early Roman Empire, we expect to find a large number of figures whose activities can be related to those of Jeshua or the pseudo-Alexander: figures who may not always fit readily into the framework of established religions, but who have some distinctive contribution to offer. It is a measure of the controversy they engender that the term 'holy man' itself may not always be the most readily applied to all of them. There is an obvious overlap between the alliterating labels 'sage' 'saint' and 'sophist' in our title: 'sages' include a variety of wise men, from Persian magi, through Greek philosophers of any sect who claim interest or expertise in the divine, down to the local village wise man;[4] 'saint' in turn need not be an exclusively Christian term, and the concept readily includes pagan holy men; 'sophist' is a still more treacherous term, most commonly applied in our period to rhetorical virtuosi; but in its connotation 'expert', usually with a high media profile, it can be applied to a religious expert or virtuoso as well. Lucian, a satirist both fascinated and repelled by the activities of holy men, can use it both of Jesus Christ and of a mercenary Palestinian exorcist.[5]

In general I have sought for the broadest possible framework and the most flexible kind of label. This has led me to regard as a holy man anyone who can reasonably be called 'a virtuoso religious activist'. Even in such an attempt at definition it is well to recognise that all three terms are contestable. Many men one would wish to include fall short of complete virtuosity, from Simon Magus, reputed to have had a bad fall when he tried to fly,[6] to humble priests of Atargatis struggling for a dishonest subsistence in rural Greece with a one-line oracle.[7] And 'religious' covers a broad spectrum which may well include those who criticise or even deny the gods, as well as figures normally regarded as philosophers who propagate views about them;[8] while 'activist' is not perhaps the right word for a hypochondriac who proclaims the virtues of Asclepius from a litter in a temple-precinct for more than a decade.[9] Our sub-title 'and their associates' is equally flexible, and is intended to cover the social context – imitators, rivals, clients, patrons, and any other associates who can throw light on what holy men did. By nature such a formulation will embrace self-seeking villains as well as those who are perceived as sincerely and divinely motivated, and there is likely to be no consensus ancient or modern as to how to separate them in a historically conclusive way.

THE RELIGIOUS ENVIRONMENT

The religious frameworks we are dealing with are not always easily characterised either. 'Paganism' as it comes to be regarded from the perspective of emergent Christianity embraces any number of cults of deities, with any number of priests and religious functionaries.[10] Judaism in turn is the exclusive cult of one such deity, Yahweh, again with his priesthoods, prophets, and a wide variety of religious sects and political pressure groups;[11] and Christianity with its gradually developing heresies centres on a figure who might originally have been perceived as a single holy man operating in a Jewish context.[12] The term 'holy man' can be reasonably applied to any 'cult worker' in all three contexts: it could be applied to those who held priesthoods of, say, the Imperial cult, or to those who belonged to a strongly committed Jewish sect such as the Pharisees, or indeed to the initiator of some new but influential Christian heresy. But in practice the restrictions of the evidence tend to force us to concentrate on those who attain special prominence either through their own efforts or those of others. One tends to think of late antique holy men as Syrian or Egyptian monks practising ascetic virtuosity in their respective deserts; but at least some pagan holy men had already achieved substantial recognition also. And the Jewish Jeshua for his part might be said to have attained the most poignant prominence with the least real effort. In fact there had been nothing specifically 'religious' about his message 'Woe to

Jerusalem!', though any wider perspective of the tradition of Hebrew prophecy would easily accommodate him in the ranks of 'apocalyptic prophets'.[13] With modern perceptions of mental illness it is easy to dismiss him as the village idiot in an urban context, whose message is so vague as to be easily construed as fulfilled by the siege of Jerusalem. But any number of other such figures elude identification: the silent figures who played their part in the operations of the oracle of Abonouteichos;[14] the now silent proto-Christian opponents of Paul in Second Corinthians;[15] or at the other end of the scale the anonymous and often unwitting con-men who might sell dream-interpretations in any market-place.[16] Nor can any categories be confined to the silent and socially *déclassés*. It would be impossible to talk of holy men without recognising that a distinguished religious antiquarian such as Plutarch himself held a priesthood and was seriously concerned with the justification of oracles, or that a philosophical sophist such as Dio of Prusa could disseminate what he describes as a Persian conception of divinity to a remote Greek community on the Black Sea Coast.

Traditional paganism is not easy to characterise: it is accommodating to anything but the most exclusively monotheist divine manifestation, and to any means of coming to terms with it. Cults had their priests, and by no means all cults had professional priesthoods, so that the phenomenon of the lay priest was commonplace and easily allowed the concept of the religious freelance.[17] So did the standard institutions for consultation of the gods: if a god's wish was not immediately intelligible through prayer or oracle, one would consult anyone competent to interpret – or trust the person who could supply a satisfactory answer.[18] Moreover, the traditional modes of communication by the gods – visions, dreams, or oracles – allowed any individual to experience a call to worship the gods in his own way and encourage others to follow.[19] The proliferating mystery cults of the Early Empire offered initiations, discipleships, priesthoods and further knowledge, protection and even identification with the divine.[20]

The nature of the philosophical schools offered a further context for the operations of holy men, and an often quite substantial area of overlap. A life professionally devoted to philosophy found room for a wisdom devoted to the gods, and a capacity to give advice about them. This is especially and indeed increasingly true of the Platonism which came to dominate the schools from the second century AD onwards.[21] Most major schools found no difficulty in accommodating the concept of the holy or divine man: even Epicureans could see a divinity in their founder, while Stoic, Cynic or Pythagorean[22] versions of the species are readily encountered. In practice Stoicism was able to accommodate divine beliefs as diverse as monotheism, the traditional Graeco-Roman pantheon, and astrological determinism; and to relate all of them to the concept of an active life of civic concern.[23] Cynicism on the other hand operated at a more popular and predominantly anti-intellectual level, but a Cynic would have had Heracles as his model, and his basic practical ideals of self-sufficiency and independence would have fitted him for a life of roving iconoclasm which could have claimed in turn to be a different sort of holiness.[24] In practice the *Kynikos tropos* allowed a life little different from that of the Christian disciples in the Synoptic Gospels.[25] As to Pythagoreanism, it was able to satisfy the dual appetite for mystical discipleship and an ascetic regime, with its abstinence from animal products and sacrifices, and a pure worship of a still traditional pantheon.[26] It is unsurprising that it should have been the sect associated with that archetypal holy man, Apollonius of Tyana, whatever he was really like.[27]

The two linked monotheistic systems of Judaism and Christianity also provided a cultural and religious crucible for the articulate individualist. The Judaism of the early Imperial period had a rich texture of sects, pressure groups and parties, with the ascetic desert-dwelling apocalyptic community of the Essenes as characteristic a part as the purifying Pharisees or their Sadducee rivals: either of the latter groups could provide the High Priest, but it was the last which constituted the aristocratic religious establishment. Political radicals could seek identification with the Zealots devoted to the overthrow of Roman rule in Palestine.[28] The whole religious tradition of Israel had looked back to a succession of traditionally charismatic figures, embodied in the patriarchs from Abraham to Moses; and a priestly establishment which had co-existed with a prophetic tradition ever since the foundation of the Israelite kingdom.[29] Moreover Palestine was not totally insulated from the outside world of both the surrounding Greek-speaking *oikoumenē*, the legacy of the Empire of Alexander the Great, and the Roman Empire which took possession of it.[30] In these circumstances it is no surprise to find charismatic individuals such as John the Baptist and Jesus Christ, both Galileans from a 'mixed' Jewish-Hellenist area,[31] or Paul, a Pharisee from a Hellenistic city with Roman citizenship.[32] Furthermore, Judaism was not static; after the fall of

Jerusalem in AD 70 a predominantly Pharisaic and rabbinical tone comes to pervade the surviving Palestinian Judaism.[33]

With the emergence of Christianity as a new force, the potential for new factions, new identities, and new sub-cults proliferated. It was well into the second century AD before the Christian pheno-menon comes close enough to the idea of a church to designate its dissidents systematically as heretics and schismatics.[34] Any Gnostic deviant, or any outspoken enemy of Paul, might claim in some meaningful sense to be a holy man. And outside the familiar terri-tory of religious cults and Judaeo-Christian monotheism there is a more exotic fringe which could at least supply some of the inspi-ration for more familiar holy men.[35] The Indian Brahmans were at least dimly perceived in the Early Empire, though often enough through a curtain of literary décor that goes back to the traditions of their encounter with Alexander the Great;[36] gymnosophists were reported to exist between Egypt and Ethiopia, and Apollonius of Tyana is presented as having visited both.[37] One hears also of supposedly shamanistic figures to the north: the tradition of Abaris and his kind still surfaces in the second century AD, when Lucian presents Greek philosophers as convinced of the supernatural ('when I saw the Hyperborean flying . . . ').[38] Nor was the far west free of the presence of religio-magical figures who could be vari-ously perceived as philosophers or magicians: the Druids are copiously reported, and only their suppression on the grounds of human sacrifice prevents their engaging the patronage of those in search of more ancient and exotic wisdom.[39] Any boundary region of the Empire could produce the impression of religious virtuosity, and inevitably the sense of *omne ignotum pro magnifico* – the awe of the unknown.

To a greater or lesser degree the idea of a sacred functionary can be linked to the traditional priesthoods of traditional deities: the fact that so many such functionaries can also be linked with political life in the cities of the Empire does not necessarily detract from sacred duties and divine connexions.[40] By the end of the Republic Rome had acquired a variety of priesthoods, sacred fraternities, and official diviners with a variety of functions and different conditions of tenure.[41] Moreover, the strongly archaising sense of identity in the resurgent Greek cities of the Eastern Empire could give rise to a determination to preserve traditional priesthoods as far as possible in their ancient form.[42]

On the other hand the spread of foreign cults brought an element of diversity which pagan accommodation did little to check: Apuleius gives us an arresting picture of some wandering priests of the Syrian Atargatis in Greece itself:[43] or Plotinus expects to encounter his personal demon in the Temple of the Egyptian Isis in Rome itself.[44] In total contrast again is the religious variety possible in the Jewish Diaspora, where communities detached from the situation in Palestine itself might find themselves more accommodating to the religious life of the Greek and other communities surrounding them.[45]

RELIGIOUS ENVIRONMENT: OTHER FORCES

If we cannot too closely define holy men, still less can we be clear about the market for them. There was no lack of those who could challenge any given holy man with the rebuke 'Is your revelation really necessary?'; but still they appear.[46] We can survey the larger historical forces of the early Empire and supply a kaleidoscope of contexts against which any given religious activist has to be seen. It is necessary to recognise a moral climate in which there were ills of society to be put right and regulation of the social order required.[47] 'The poor you have with you always' was a sentiment as familiar to the sceptical Lucian as it was to Jesus Christ,[48] and there is a general consensus among early Imperial moralists on what one might aim for in this mortal life – the virtues of simple life and common man, freedom from fears, tensions and strife through this or that moral code or set of values, or through simple pragmatism. Such needs called for moral advice, moral instruction, and in general for 'consultants' in the art of living.[49] Not all of these need be religious; but a religious framework of belief was a potent adjunct to such needs. Epictetus stresses as readily as Paul the need to regard nothing as one's own possession, and yield everything to the deity, or presents his addressees as slaves of righteousness;[50] and he is just as likely as Jesus Christ or Paul to advocate the giving up of physical desires and ambitions.[51]

Also a part of this moral universe is the quest for personal security, identity and salvation. Healing the sick is the most obviously immediate need. I have indigestion: Asclepius tells me to moderate my diet. Great is Asclepius when I am healed.[52] And if I am well a god can earn his living by protecting me from disease.[53] Nor is there any limit to the degree of immunisation I can undergo. But if I am well, I can still suffer: there will be basic human anxieties, regardless of the current state of society. Shall I get married? Should I change jobs? Is it wise to sail?[54] And besides the information itself, there will be a need for interpretation ('Is the god really telling me to do such-and-such?'). When the god tells me to kiss my mother three times, does he mean my own mother, or mother earth? But information sought might be more sophisticated ('When Pythagoras told us not to sacrifice living things, what did he mean us to sacrifice instead?'). And there are always more subtle and persistent anxieties which will plague the neurotic, as any page of Aristides' personal religious diaries, the so-called *Sacred Tales*, will reveal. The priest's words to 'Lucius of Madaura' are familiar, that the goddess Isis will provide him with a protection from the buffetings of Fortune, and a salvation from 'servile pleasures'.[55] In a Hellenistic milieu where institutions and rulers might seem all too remote, the offer of protection was not to be lightly rejected.

Nor are simple human needs the only matter of concern: whatever one's own religious base, the world may be felt to be in the grip not only of Fortune or some similar force of instability but also of demonic powers.[56] These are common to Graeco-Roman and Judaeo-Christian experience: intermediate forces are felt to exist between gods and men, and may be maleficent, yet capable of mastery by some means or other. Such a belief had obvious propensity for popular acceptance within a polytheistic system, but had also enjoyed intellectual respectability as well: Middle Platonism espoused the notion of demons responsible for the day-to-day operations of Providence, and the philosophers who discuss good and evil spirits in Plutarch or Lucian are perfectly serious about their existence.[57] It follows that the philosopher or religious operator who can understand or better still control such forces through superior strength, intellect or divine power itself will be highly valued. Demon control is necessary, and calls for proven expertise.

In addition to aspirations for meaning in life and freedom from its ills, a larger belief might intervene: this is that the world may be moving towards a new order in which some single figure will emerge to bring the present world-order to an end. Such belief had a natural receptacle in the Jewish world, with its deep and well-founded dissatisfaction with first Hellenistic then Roman domination.[58] And it found a central place in the early Christian scheme of things with the identification of Jesus Christ rightly or wrongly and by whomsoever with the Jewish Messiah. But it was hardly incompatible with trends in later Greek philosophy either. The notion that matter was corrupted and that a divine redeemer would come to free the human soul from bondage in matter found a natural enough expression in a world where Platonism in particular had an increasingly prominent role in intellectual life, and where that Platonism was versatile enough to be constantly updated.[59]

One factor applies across the ancient world as a whole: there was never any total exclusion of new religious forces or manifestations, or of those who might aspire to control them. Gods or numinous forces must communicate their will as they please, and it is up to man to listen; if someone should announce himself as 'Ialdabaoth son of Beelzebub' or the like, then the assumption will be that he will increase the sum of human happiness or a further insurance against disaster. If he says 'I am the mouthpiece of Ialdabaoth son of Beelzebub' he will not have lessened his claim to a hearing, provided that he can show some command over some demons, however defined or undefined.[60] In the second century we find the anti-Christian Celsus complaining that in Palestine and Syria there are many

> who go begging both inside and outside temples, some of
> them gathering crowds and frequenting cities or camps, and
> these men are of course urged to prophesy. It is routine for
> them to be ready with 'I am a god', or 'a son of a god' or 'a
> divine spirit'; and 'I have come, for the universe is already
> perishing, and you, men, will die because of your wrongdo-
> ing. But I want to save you, and you shall see me once again
> returning with heavenly power. Happy is the man who has
> worshipped me on this occasion. Against all the rest, in town
> and country alike, I shall cast eternal fire. And men who are
> unaware of the impending punishments will repent in vain and
> wail, but those I have persuaded I shall protect forever'.[61]

Celsus' generalisation is designed to 'level down' Jesus Christ to a type of charlatan familiar enough in his own time. But it also draws attention to what we can identify as a routine. These holy men have a claim of authority, a venue and a means of putting across a message; they have a social relevance, and can conjure up a potent threat. They are operators (in a neutral sense) and mediators able to act on society. And they can combine in quite succinct form the call for moral indignation, personal salvation, and divine judgement.

The role of mediator is specially important. Antique religion saw no need to 'cut out the middleman'. The Hellenistic world on the contrary felt a political distancing of men from the centres of power in the material world; the same forces are at work in the spiritual world, where gods can be distant and communication difficult.[62] One might send sophists from one's city to the Emperor; one can equally readily send intercessors from one's city to the gods or their oracles.[63] Nor is there much to jam the channels of communication. There were few voices in antiquity outside Judaism and Christianity to say 'x is the only god and I am his prophet'. But gods or their intercessors had to 'get it right', and they were judged on results. A polytheistic culture had little time for divine forces which had taken early retirement on the job:[64] gods had to work for their sacrificial sustenance towards the welfare of mankind.

But there is always a market too for the novel and alternative. Tacitus ruefully remarks on the appearance of early Christians in Rome 'into which all things horrific and unseemly congregate and become popular' (*quo cuncta undique atrocia aut pudenda confluunt celebranturque*); while the Acts-author makes a point of observing the love of novelty in Athens. And Lucian time and again emphasises the appetite of his second-century fellow-men for revelation.[65] There may also be a certain visual impact to a holy man: a bread riot is in progress, and a Roman governor is in danger of being lynched: a Pythagorean vowed to silence dramatically appears, and by communicating to the parties in writing asserts his authority over the situation.[66] Or a holy man has it announced that he will set fire to himself on such and such a day,[67] or take on a rival and see who can kill and raise the dead.[68] There will be a good slanging match and someone may even get hurt.

MODELS OF HOLINESS

There is nothing specifically new about the operations of holy men. Because of the particular literary appeal of the *Iliad*, it is easy to lose sight of the initial situation, in which not one but two holy men are involved. A priest of Apollo in effect brings down a sacred curse on the Greeks at Troy in revenge for a personal slight; and a religious consultant interprets the facts to Agamemnon. What is more, both these operators are highly effective, irrespective of the consequences to their clients: Chryses does procure a plague,[69] and Calchas prescribes the correct action for averting it. Religious tension and patronage are also at work: Calchas invokes the protection of Achilles from the consequences of a religious ruling to protect himself against Agamemnon, who duly brings up his unfortunate past record.[70]

Moreover, it is not uncommon to identify a holy man with reference to some standard set by illustrious predecessors: when in the second century AD Alexander of Abonouteichos had established his oracle with great success, 'there was a disquisition between two wise idiots about him, as to whether he had the soul of Pythagoras because of his golden thigh, or another soul like it'.[71] Similarly, when Jesus Christ was carrying out a combination of preaching and healing:

> he asked the disciples 'Who do the crowds say I am?' And they replied, 'Some say John the Baptist, others Elijah, others again one of the ancient prophets'. And he asked them, 'But who do you say?' And Peter replied 'God's anointed one'.[72]

Both passages illustrate the natural tendency to translate a new religious phenomenon into terms of the familiar, and to be at least divided in drawing conclusions about it.

One figure stands pre-eminent on the Greek side as the paradigm of the holy man: Pythagoras.[73] Already too far removed from memory to be easily recoverable, he is none the less the subject of at least three biographies by men of Imperial date not unknown for their 'theosophical' interests: Apollonius of Tyana,[74] Porphyry, and Iamblichus.[75] His life, at least as the last conceives it, includes an association with a Thracian Abaris who recognises Apollo in Pythagoras himself and enables the latter to deflect plagues and hurricanes from cities by means of a golden arrow which also served as a mode of travel.[76] Shipwrecks could be foretold, storms stilled,[77] snakes driven from the countryside, oxen spoken to,[78] or predictions made, to say nothing of such feats as bilocation.[79] Pythagoras is given a wide range of wisdom garnered from Egypt and Babylon,[80] and it could be translated into political terms when he confronted the tyrant of Agrigentum.[81] A revived Pythagoreanism, of whatever sort, we are at least aware of in the first two centuries AD: Seneca the Younger abandoned a flirtation with Pythagorean regimen under one Sotion,[82] and that was before the supposed efflorescence of the supposed arch-Pythagorean Apollonius.

Apart from Pythagoras the philosophical tradition enabled other spiritual advisers to lead the holy man in a similar direction. The philosophical cults of the martyred Socrates could present the picture of a man who claimed to be advised by a personal *daimōn*,[83] which in itself was a proper subject of serious philosophical investigation, and helps to point the path that will lead in due course to Neo-Platonic mysticism.

Nor is the interest and involvement of Graeco-Roman intellectuals in the irrational fringe a new phenomenon of the Empire. Nigidius Figulus in the late Roman Republic is already established as a figure with an authoritative status in occult art. We find Cicero addressing him as *uni omnium doctissimo et sanctissimo* ('most learned and holy of all') – the kind of appellation that would still fit Plotinus several centuries on.[84] He is attributed with a successful horoscope on the birth of the future Emperor Augustus in 63 BC;[85] on a more mundane level we find him tracing a lost sum of money, allegedly with the help of boys inspired by incantation;[86] or demonstrating the viability of astrology even in the case of twins by using the potter's wheel to represent the speed of heavenly bodies. A summary of Nigidius' known output shows the general direction of his interest: a *de Augurio Privato* and a *de Extis*, a *Sphaera* giving the legends behind the zodiacal signs, and nineteen books on the gods, not excluding Persian and Etruscan materials.[87]

The Near East had provided priestly sages since the earliest Egyptian and Sumerian times. Apart from the lore of the 'Chaldaeans' themselves, there was a strong Hebraic tradition of religious virtuosity, parts of which were readily accessible to the Mediterranean world. Elijah offers a suitable paradigm for the Old Testament prophet.[88] He is able to live in hiding and threaten King Ahab with drought; he is sustained miraculously by the self-replenishing oil and meal of a widow who shelters him, and he revives her dead child. He himself is later sustained still more miraculously in the desert. He can threaten the King and challenge the rival prophets of Baal to a rain-making contest: he himself has a friend in high places, the King's chamberlain Obadiah, who has rescued prophets of Yahweh from the massacre instituted by the King's wife Jezebel. He can condemn the king for taking forcible possession of land through a murder by Jezebel, and Ahab's sick son and successor for turning to Baalzebub. He divides waters for himself and Elisha, and goes up to heaven in a whirlwind.

Besides the prophetic paradigm as such, the Old Testament and intertestmentary literature produces a number of different expectations of a future Messiah or anointed one.[89] The identities are highly flexible, varying from a Davidic King and conqueror of the Gentiles, through priestly and prophetic figures to Messiahs of esoteric speculation, including one to be anointed by a successor of Elijah, and not to be conscious of his destiny until such anointing should take place. The variety of such identities made it relatively easy for outstanding radical figures to identify with at least one of them, or to redefine the parameters still further.

Besides the prophets one other figure stands out as a contributor to the tradition of holy men: Moses.[90] Philo at the beginning of our period and Gregory of Nyssa after the end of it left Greek *Lives* of this central figure in Judaic tradition, as the mediator of the Torah itself to the Israelite nation in the desert. It is not too difficult to see how the biblical presentation of his life accorded with the likely career patterns of holy men. Adopted as a foundling into an Egyptian royal house,[91] he turns against his roots with a murder and exile;[92] he threatens the Egyptians with plagues, and organises a mass movement into the desert, where he finds the wherewithal for survival.[93] He produces legal codes with divine authority, and finally has no known burial site.[94] Small wonder that a first-century Jewish charismatic should claim to divide the Jordan,[95] or that Paul should have been mistaken for an Egyptian who led yet another mass exodus in the desert.[96]

From one of a number of allusions in Gregory of Nyssa it is not hard to see the attraction of Moses for the connoisseur of holy men: 'For the story tells us that Moses, outside the visible world and within the invisible shrines (so the cloud indicates) learned the divine mysteries and through his own knowledge of God explained them to the people'.[97] Here is the ideal authority for anyone with something in the future to reveal. There is no surprise in the way that the same author fits the life of Moses to highlights of his more modern hero, Gregory Thaumaturgus.[98] The latter is hailed as the Moses of our times, because of his Egyptian learning, his miracles with water, and his encouragement of his people from a distance.[99] Nor is this merely a fourth-century Christian surge of interest in the patriarch. Philo in the first century had already been able to invest the model with a thoroughly Greek garb of wide-ranging *paideia* under Greek teachers – not leaving out Assyrian letters or Chaldaean science, to say nothing of Egyptian symbolism:

> Naturally therefore those close to him and everyone else were amazed, as if struck by a new phenomenon: they wondered at the nature of the soul that dwelt in his body like an image in its shrine, as to whether it was human or divine or a mixture of

the two: it was so unlike those of most men, but soared above and was exalted to a higher plane.[100]

When Moses could be a good Platonist, it is clear that a holy man can be redefined for some new age of his own or the perception of others. And it is to such perceptions that we must now turn.

2

VIEWPOINTS
Perceptions and perspectives

Whatever a holy man's inspiration, real or supposed, we are continually dependent for our own picture of his activities on the way
our sources perceive him. But the materials we have are disparate,
and we must be aware of their limitations. In the first place it is
obvious that Roman historians of the early Empire had relatively
little use for holy men, prophets, or the like.[1] Such figures will
appear in order to set the seal on the fate of an emperor, but that is
likely to be the limit of Tacitus' or Dio Cassius' interest in them.
Tacitus' notice of the earliest Roman persecution of Christians in
AD 64 affords only the briefest mention of Christ ('Christus, the
source of their name, had been executed in Tiberius' reign by the
procurator of Judea, Pontius Pilate'). The mention of Christ seems
prompted by the need to explain the still relatively unfamiliar term
'Christian' itself.[2] While the cataloguing of portents of momentous
events was enshrined in historiographical tradition, it was quite
routine to provide a list of happenings with little or no mention of
those consulted to interpret them ('and soothsayers followed with
an interpretation that a different head was being prepared for
human affairs').[3] Tacitus balances the evidence neatly enough,
though his own sceptical disposition is apparent elsewhere:

> When I hear this and other stories like it I am unsure whether
> human affairs are moved by the unalterable necessity of fate,
> or by sheer chance. For on this question you will find the
> wisest of the ancients and their followers at odds. Many are
> convinced that heaven is unconcerned with our human births
> and deaths, and that the human condition itself is of no
> concern to the gods. . . . But to most men however it seems
> inevitable that each individual's destiny is predestined from

birth; and that some events turn out different from what was foretold because of the deceits of ignorant predictors; hence belief in the science of prediction is discredited in spite of the clear proofs of it from ancient and modern times alike.[4]

The context of this passage is singlemindedly political, occasioned by considerations of the Emperor Tiberius' prophecy of the Imperial destiny of Galba, and prompting mention of Thrasyllus' son's prediction of Nero's reign.[5]

On the other hand Dio Cassius and the biographer Suetonius are inclined to be less agnostic: Dio himself had compiled a work on the portents which heralded the accession of Septimius Severus;[6] and both relay the story of a man who foretold the death of Domitian:

> (Askletarion) did not deny having declared openly what he had foretold by his art. So Domitian asked him what manner of death awaited him. When Askletarion replied that he himself would shortly be torn to pieces by dogs, the emperor killed him without delay, but also gave orders for his funeral rites to be conducted with the utmost decision, to confound the rashness of prediction. But while this was being done, it came about that a sudden wind-storm scattered the pyre and dogs tore apart the astrologer's half-burnt corpse.[7]

Nor is Dio inclined to discount the incredible enough story of Apollonius' simultaneous prophecy of the death of Domitian from halfway across the Empire:

> I have one more fact amazing even to mention . . . . One Apollonius of Tyana on the very day and at the very hour when Domitian was being assassinated (as was afterwards precisely established by events in both places) climbed up onto a lofty rock at Ephesus (or perhaps some other place) and having called the people together he made his proclamation: 'Good, Stephanus! Well done, Stephanus! Strike the foul murderer! You have smitten, you have wounded, you have slain!'. This really did happen as I have described, however often anyone may doubt it.[8]

However sophisticated, serious historians in antiquity are never wholly exempt from the parameters of current belief. When Dio had been describing the eruption of Vesuvius of AD 79 he put it as follows:

This was what happened. Great numbers of enormous men, taller than any human being – resembling the giants as painters depict them – manifested themselves at one moment on the mountain, at another in the land round about, and in the cities too, wandering about on the earth day and night and also flitting about through the air . . . . Some supposed that the giants were rising up again in revolt, for at this time too many of their forms would appear in the smoke, and in addition a trumpet-like sound was heard.[9]

The picture is not quite beyond the bounds of possibility: any semblance can be momentarily generated by a cloud, and few in these situations would have had time for dispassionate scientific observation; only a belief in the existence of supernatural figures in the first place is necessary in order to enable an observer to interpret the phenomena as described.

But however orthodox Greek or Roman historians might view our subject, the range of works by Josephus offers a far more sympathetic context against which holy men may be seen in operation. For a start, Josephus is a Jew and able to witness at first hand the complex religious context of the first century AD in Palestine; he is the only figure with pretensions to historiography to have first-hand participation in holiness.[10] And on the other hand many of his asides on holy men as such are not obviously coloured by the disingenuousness so apparent in his interpretation of political events – except when he describes the operation of his own prophecy of the rise of Vespasian, and that in itself may count at least as how Josephus wished and would have expected 'sacred' actions of his own to be viewed.[11] Whether or not he really believed in his prophetic powers except in retrospect is beyond recovery.

It is rather in the materials for the private history of the Empire that holy men begin to appear in any degree of detail. And here much of our evidence is highly subjective. One is either for holy men or against them, and the result may be either wholesale eulogy or uncompromising polemic. At the other extreme from formal historiography come the various narratives written to support or commemorate holy men themselves. These include not only such works as gospels and acts, canonical or apocryphal,[12] martyrologies and the like, as well as the culturally more ambitious works inspired by them, such as Philostratus' *Life of Apollonius of Tyana*;[13] in each case they will have been written at a considerable distance from most if not all of the events in question, though they may include or purport to include eyewitness information. But their aim is primarily to present what is acceptable to their authors and public rather than biography or history as we should conceive them. The canonic gospels in particular one assumes to be addressed to Christian communities in an evolving church with specific needs and viewpoints; and they are related ultimately to what their authors wish and expect such believers to believe. As such they may offer a specific and objective record of certain religious attitudes, aspirations and assumptions; but they cannot be made to go far beyond such a record. In including resurrection-narratives in gospels written most probably upwards of forty years after the death of Jesus Christ, three of the four evangelists attest to a belief which they accept and wish to transmit, that such a resurrection appeared to them to have taken place. But it can prove little more than that.

The Synoptic problem has much light to offer on attitudes and viewpoints in the making. In passages where Matthew and Luke agree almost verbatim but in consistently less detail than Mark, then it will be clear enough that they can have no independent authority; while any alterations they do make can throw light upon the redactors themselves. It seems ominous for early views of Jesus Christ that both redactors had to 'correct' the prophecy of resurrection 'after three days' to 'on the third day' – a day shorter: the fact has to be faced that in terms of the expectation of the original Mark-author Jesus Christ may have come back too soon.[14]

Such narratives often have an inbuilt tendency to dismiss any opposition to their central figure. It is a matter of no concern to the writers of the Synoptic Gospels, for example, that the Gadarene demoniac sets off a herd of swine into the sea, or that Jesus Christ is subsequently driven out of the region.[15] In one respect, however, sacred texts seem reliable on principle: they do not knowingly score 'own goals' against their subject. It follows that information which with different moral perspectives seems detrimental to Apollonius of Tyana or Jesus Christ, for instance, should be authentic, otherwise it would not be included at all. Hence Apollonius' command to stone a beggar[16] or Jesus Christ's utterance of what might be reasonably construed as a racist remark against the Syrophoenician woman has to be treated as authentic;[17] likewise reports that something approaching techniques of intimidation were used by the earliest Christian missionaries acting on instruction.[18]

One technical or quasi-technical term continues to recur in all such discussion: aretalogy, a catalogue of the 'virtues', 'powers' or miracles of the holy man.[19] The term has a great deal of convenience for the kind of substance that provides much of the central material and justification of gospel narratives and other biographical works relating to holy men. But it acquires a more treacherous life of its own if it is made to represent a notional literary form which then influences by its pre-existence the whole shape of gospels and acts, Christian or pagan.[20] It has to be constantly borne in mind that much of the literary shape of our material in each case is determined by the kind, quantity and immediate source of material actually available. A writer may have been influenced particularly by the fact that his holy man is only just beginning to recede from popular memory. The kind of material available to him at such a time may well be already acquiring overtones of the miraculous. The other material that can be added to the base will also be incidental, such as chance sayings, chance correspondence, or the text or substance of addresses. When these are added together, and fused with any literary ambitions or theological perspectives of an author, the results are almost bound to be diverse, resembling one another only as unsatisfactory attempts to enlarge a central achronological catalogue of miracles. We may call that or its central part *aretai* if we wish. But the operation comes close to definition in terms of itself and for its own sake. Authors do not in general set down to write an aretalogy. They try to piece together what they can about whom they must, in what will only pass for a crude attempt at biographical order.

As well as the normal tasks of evaluating historical sources in relation to one another, the historian who touches on hagiography, pagan or Christian, has to be ever alert to the problem of reconstructing the basis of a tradition. There is often the temptation to be just too sceptical, and to fail to look for a conceivable basis of truth underneath a layer of pious admiration. It is not always wise to dismiss this or that alleged miracle as impossible and therefore invented, or no less indolently dismiss it as the product of the state of mind of collective consciousness of late antiquity. Often a solution may lie in quite simple adjustments of one's own angle of vision. Take the following fairly typical instance from Athanasius' *Life of Antony*:

But once again the enemy (i.e. Satan), seeing his zeal and

20

wanting to impede it, laid in his path the phantom of a huge silver dish. But Antony, knowing the cunning of the hater of goodness, stood and looked at the dish and accused the devil in it, saying 'Where did a dish in the desert come from? This way has not been travelled, nor is there a trace of travellers here. Since it is so very large, it could not have been missed when lost, but the person who lost it would have found it again when he came back to look (hence no one else would have done so), since this place is desert. This is a trick on the part of the devil. You will not stop my enthusiasm this way, Devil! Take this with you and go to hell!'. And the moment Antony said this, it disappeared like smoke from a fire.[21]

The importance of this passage is not that it is fiction, since it is objectively possible to go into a desert and see something *that can be interpreted* as a silver dish. The point is that the modern Western traveller will more than likely be inclined to describe Antony's large silver dish as a mirage of bright water. What the historian has to ask is why Antony or his reporter would have described it as one of these objects rather than the other. It is the predisposition to see demonic temptations rather than neutral objects which will determine the saint's choice: there is not very much temptation to be resisted in longing for a drink of water.

A similar situation arises over a famous miracle attributed to Gregory Thaumaturgus: the saint is supposed to have dried up a lake in order to settle a dispute over ownership between two brothers: the site of the lake, now ordinary land, is still exhibited. One will not doubt that Gregory was capable of procuring such a result, the drying up of the lake. Whether it could have been done overnight as his biographers, presumably oral sources, might have claimed, is another matter. The real point of such an exercise must have been to persuade the disputing parties that half the land was more valuable as cultivable land than the lake would have been for its fishing: the holy man may have been less of a miracle-monger than a rural development officer.[22] But throughout texts with a hagiographical texture one is conscious of authors viewing their material with an uncritical eye. When Antony presents himself after twenty years of solitude in the desert, eyewitnesses are struck by the exact similarity of his appearance after so long an absence – a similarity not one of them will have been in a position to determine objectively after such an interval.[23] But a journalistic piety dictates their response.

These perspectives must also be borne in mind in all matters to do with dreams, visions and similar experiences. Eusebius' presentation of the arrival of Bishop Alexander in Jerusalem will serve as an example: the subject's own calling to be co-Bishop of Jerusalem with the ageing Narcissus is dictated by a nocturnal vision, to leave his see in Cappadocia and visit the city; it is confirmed by a second, collective vision by the congregation in Jerusalem itself, which appeared at night 'with the clearest voice to the most zealous of them' to go out and welcome him as their bishop.[24] But even Eusebius indicates that Alexander's purpose in visiting Jerusalem was really as a pilgrim; the interpretation of his arrival as the opportunity to detain a younger bishop may well have occurred independently to a number of people; but their expression of this notion as a God-given vision must by now be seen as a cliché of hagiography. From the Book of Acts onwards, the Holy Spirit acts as the divine prompter, as ready to stamp good ideas with divine inspiration as the demon of Socrates almost half a millennium before.[25]

At the same time a hagiographical source can communicate something of the personalities and ethos of those involved, as when the late antique Western nun Egeria marvels at the spectacle of the desert monks, and well conveys the outlook of at least one spiritual tourist:[26]

> So then this turned out beyond my hopes, and I was really pleased, that we saw the holy genuine monks of Mesopotamia there: though I hadn't thought I would really see them, not because it is impossible for God to grant this to me as well – since he saw fit to grant me everything else – but because I had heard that they do not come down from their dwellings except at Easter and on (this martyr's feast-day), because they are the kind who actually perform many miracles; and since I did not know what month this martyr's feast-day I mentioned was. And so by God's prompting it turned out that on that day I had not even hoped to be present, I arrived there. I actually stayed there, then, for two days because of the martyr's feast and had a sight of these holy men, who brought themselves to grant me a willing audience and spoke to me, something I did not deserve. For they themselves immediately after the mar-

tyr's feast were not seen there, but while it was still night they made for the desert and each returned to his cell there.

In Egeria's thought-world divine providence synchronises the tourist attractions with her own personal timetable.

It is seldom that we have independent doublets of the same episode to act as a control, and where we do they serve less as a means of getting to 'the facts' than of illuminating the perceptions of the sources. There is a good instance in the account of the death of John the Baptist in Mark's Gospel and in Josephus.[27] The latter notes that Herod had designs on his brother's wife; his wife discovers them and causes hostilities on the part of her father Arethas. The defeat of Herod's army is seen as a revenge for his execution of John the Baptist, a good man whom Herod had seen as too powerful.[28] The Mark-author by contrast knows nothing of any political explanation, but centres on John's opposition to the marriage of Herod and his brother's wife. John is imprisoned by a reluctant Herod, and killed only as the result of an oriental tale of the 'fatal promise' type, when Salome asks for his head.[29] In the first place the Mark-author has most probably been responsible for a serious factual error: Herod's brother is given as Philip, in all probability a confusion with his son-in-law.[30] But beyond that the two texts may represent complementary perceptions: the gospel tradition gives John military clients, and he is not the man to have around in times of a border war; on the other hand an ascetic holy man is certainly likely to condemn Herod's behaviour with Herodias as immoral; political hindsight and scandalmongery are not incompatible.

More promising in the sense that they may have a less immediately propagandist message are documents which can be classed as letters and diaries. A careful study of some of the vignettes in the second-century sophist Aelius Aristides will serve to show from time to time some suspect operations, naively revealed by a neurotic and pompous devotee. Asclepius convinces Aristides that he is to die within two days of his consultation. He establishes his bona fides with the patient by observations on the next day, state of the weather, position of the charioteer constellation, and the like. Then he gives instructions *inter alia* for a sacrifice to Asclepius. Aristides is also to yield up a part of his body – instead of the whole – and instead of the part of his body, a ring. He feels that divine harmony is restored, and registers his mixture of hope and fear.[31] But through Aristides' perceptions Asclepius' operations amount to salvation. In fact the god, or more specifically his unscrupulous agents, appear to have used accessible information to extract a valuable present from a client. On another occasion Aristides is ordered to take a particular prescription:[32] he is amazed to find that on reciting details to the temple doctor Asclepiacus he himself is able to supply it from something brought in that very morning.[33]

But here too the evidence can be treacherous: an infamous case is Paul's presentation of a visit to Jerusalem to come to terms with the Christian community there over the problem of imposing Judaic practices on Gentiles. Paul emphasises that this took place 'at a private meeting with the people who counted'. In Acts 15 the scenario for what appears to be the same occasion is presented as the so-called Apostolic Council. One notes ingenious attempts to save the integrity of the two texts.[34] But it is difficult to escape from the very real possibility that *both* are subject to embellishment, in opposite directions: the Acts-author wants to make the event 'important' by making it an assembly, while Paul wishes to emphasise his intimacy with the leaders of the Jerusalem church, whose standing he emphasises more than once.

Much of the rest of our material is blatantly refutatory in character: it is intended to counteract the supposed propaganda of other parties whose motives the writer is prepared to impugn, and it may avail itself of all the rhetorical weaponry of the unscrupulous persuader. Tertullian writes of the Gnosticising Marcion:

> Now these contemptible cuttle-fish – it was to symbolize such people that the law excluded that sort of fish among others from permissible foods – as soon as they become aware that they are being exposed, they vomit up darkness mixed up with their blasphemy, and so distract the immediate attention of everyone by asserting and reiterating those statements which cast a cloud over the Creator's Goodness, radiant as it is.[35]

Marcion might indeed be guilty of obfuscation, though scarcely more so than the texture of Tertullian's style of polemic: all that the latter is likely to prove is the synthesis of literary sophistication and anger that Marcion's sometimes dualist views of God are likely to generate. Similar reserve is needed when sifting the sceptical Lucian's view of Alexander of Abonouteichos:

> Such then was his outward appearance; but his soul and his

mind – O Heracles Forfender! O Zeus Averter of Mischief! O twin Brethren, our Saviours! May it be the fortune of our enemies and ill-wishers to encounter and have to do with the like of him! In understanding, quick-wittedness and penetration he was far beyond everyone else; and activity of the mind, readiness to learn, retentiveness, natural aptitude for studies – all these qualities were his, in every case to the full. But he made the worst possible use of them, and with these noble instruments at his service soon became the most perfect rascal of all those who had been notorious far and wide for villainy, surpassing the Cercopes, surpassing Eurybatus or Phrynondas, or Aristodemus or Sostratus.[36]

Clearly much of the passage is as hysterical as it is rhetorical: Lucian makes out his enemy to be an arch-villain, and many of the subsequent charges are typical of ancient polemic, some of them at least next to impossible to substantiate, for Lucian no less than for us. But the centre of this passage, the 'good' qualities perverted by Alexander, are plausible enough: few holy men could expect to survive for long without a certain astuteness and versatility; though perhaps again Lucian might be felt to be enhancing these qualities in turn in order to enhance the sheer villainy of his subject. Some of the rest of Lucian's polemic is difficult to evaluate even when he is reporting what seem to be facts. We are told that Alexander was in league with one Coconnas who acts as his agent and partner in crime.[37] But how much does Lucian know, and how much does he have to infer? The question has to be reiterated for almost every reported fact, and in many cases the answers must remain in the balance.

Among the most interesting cases are those where the man himself is a rhetorician giving an account of his own actions. Dio Chrysostom[38] and Apuleius[39] were both rhetorical entertainers and philosophers: both had occult interests, and both were versatile enough to be able to answer any criticism levelled against them. In fact the urbanity of holy men was a feature: for Lucian, Alexander's suave personality was part of his hypocritical act.[40]

In general a high veneer of education in the sources is not in itself a guarantee of their integrity. That of the *Life of Apollonius of Tyana* is particularly open to question. There is a repeatedly tendentious tone, and one notes how many of the most rhetorically expansive episodes tend to occur in the kind of situations least subject to

25

verification, such as private audiences with emperors or dialogues with Brahmans in India. Yet disqualification of his chief witness Damis would still leave a substantial caucus of material about an itinerant religious consultant who operates impressively in the Eastern Mediterranean in the late first century AD.[41]

In some cases we can assemble sources whose effect is neatly complementary. For several overlapping decades in the second century AD we have two usefully contrasting kinds of evidence. Lucian's pamphlet against the oracle-monger Alexander of Abonouteichos can be used in conjunction with the so-called *Sacred Tales* of Aelius Aristides, the persistent client of the shrine of Asclepius at Pergamum; we can thus see the phenomenon of healing oracles through the double perspective of the sceptic and the satisfied customer. Where both come close to agreement is in their evocation of the thought-world of Aristides himself, willing to ascribe every other event in life, however trivial, to the benevolence of an all-powerful Providence. And Aristides' evidence can readily be supported by the attitudes revealed in inscriptions from other grateful clients of Asclepius: the god can be credited with the cure of pregnancies three to five years on end;[42] or settle for a free cure from stones of a boy who offers him ten dice in return.[43]

We can usefully discuss definitions and profiles of holy men with reference to several figures not always so considered. It is a commonplace in the literature of holy men to include Jesus of Nazareth, but what of Saul of Tarsus? The stereotypes imposed by facile labelling will make Paul an apostle, a missionary, a theologian, or a founder of Christianity. But they will tend to exclude him from the kind of categorisation that will bring him into the company of desert ascetics or stylite saints. They will also tend to stress Paul's profile, largely self-generated, as that of a tireless worker for a self-evidently justifying cause, rather than as just one itinerant religious activist among hordes; and one moreover who may have resorted to amulets,[44] who was mistaken for a god,[45] and whose legendary elaborations include the affair of Paul and a talking lion.[46] The significance for Christianity of letters to early Christian communities has tended to consolidate a reputation which owes a great deal to the subsequent history of the church. We are used to seeing holy men very vaguely, and at a respectable distance, in no specific context; Paul we know too closely and too well in one particular activity, and in a context too easily unquestioned. We have to guard against a curious and unstated principle: the more a late antique figure commits himself to writing, the more he is likely to be seen as a writer and a rational intellectual, not capable of the actions that are the stuff of hagiography.

Sometimes the profile of holy men can only be dimly discerned by means of scattered and enigmatic hints. Paul's opponents in Second Corinthians are recoverable only from his own attack, but it is not too long before the gibes have the makings of a familiar picture. These men are designated 'superapostles', of impressive physical appearance and perhaps furnished with letters of recommendation;[47] they have a rhetorical skill, including the ability to show themselves superior to others in the art;[48] they have a professional attitude to financial support by their admirers.[49] And besides their Jewish pedigree they probably purvey reports of mystical or apocalyptic revelation, possibly even performing miracles.[50]

Sometimes the available material furnishes only just enough to place such figures in their social and cultural context. Artemidorus, the second-century author of an *Oneirocritica*, tells us that his home-town on his mother's side was Daldis in Lydia, and that it was at the instigation of the local deity there that he composed his book. He has described himself as 'of Ephesus'.[51] In order to produce a thorough work of research he visited cities and festivals in Greece, Asia and Italy, and the largest and most populous islands,[52] and did not hesitate to draw on the experience of interpreters in the market-place.[53] The dedicatee of the first three books is one Claudius Maximus, whom it has long been attractive to identify with the philosophic essayist Maximus of Tyre. Artemidorus mentions dreams of Plutarch, Aristides 'the pleader', Fronto 'the arthritic' and Philagrus the rhetor.[54] Even if any or all of these match the obvious candidates, it may not mean that they were clients of Artemidorus himself. But it does seem of some significance that even his contemporary, the eminent physician Galen, was prepared to use cures prescribed in dreams and attest to their efficacy.[55] The fourth and fifth books are dedicated to Artemidorus' son, to whom he gives a good deal of professional advice: a succession from father to son is possible, or at least an informed interest which might entail actual practice on the son's account.[56] Either way a (none too reputable) figure begins to emerge.

MEDICINE, MIRACLE AND MAGIC

A further matter of different perspectives lies in the views available
in our period on medicine, miracle and magic. If a patient is healed
in anything more than the most routinely professional medical
context it is possible to regard the event as a triumph of medicine
itself, within the fairly narrow limits of ancient medical practice; as
a matter of divine or demonic intervention, since a deity or divinity
has willed it to happen; or as a simple matter of its being brought
about by magic, however this last is defined or understood.[57] It is
tempting to try to separate these categories too firmly, and to see
medicine and magic as reputable and disreputable faces of Graeco-
Roman culture, with miracle as a matter for Judaeo-Christian charismatics.[58] But such distinctions may not always work in practice.
For a start, Graeco-Roman medicine and magic are diverse
phenomena in themselves,[59] and both can be connected very firmly
with divine operations, with doctors allied closely to Asclepius.[60]
Miracle is claimed readily enough outside Judaic contexts, as
Lucian's *Philopseudes* readily attests, while there is considerable
subjectivity over the claims of miracle and magic. Miracle is a term
of approval applicable to the work of one's friends, while magic in
many but by no means all cases turns out to be the work of one's
enemies.[61] And all three can be allied to other ends or regarded as
inseparable from them, as when miracles are presented as indicators
of a New Age ushered in by Jesus Christ.[62]

SAINT AND SCOUNDREL: PERCEPTIONS
AND PERSPECTIVES

Within such flexible parameters the student of holy men will not
range very far before encountering contrary perceptions of the same
figures. Apart from the contrasting figures of Jesus Christ encountered in the Synoptic Gospels and in John's Gospel, the same figure
appears in pagan or Jewish sources from a number of different
perspectives. For Suetonius he is evidently just another Jewish
agitator (*impulsore Chresto*);[63] for Lucian he is treated with a
mixture of spiritual snobbery and contempt, again a fairly standard
intellectual view of Christianity from the outside in the age of the
second-century apologists;[64] or in later Jewish polemic which in
turn influences Celsus he is seen as an illegitimate villain.[65] It is
difficult to separate knowable facts from prejudice or propaganda.

Suetonius is clearly not interested in Jesus, and seems even to confuse a title with a name; Lucian is obviously interested in discrediting Peregrinus as someone who has used the Christians, rather than an objective witness; while Jewish sources after AD 70 might well see in Jesus Christ an impostor to Messiahship who had engineered the destruction of the temple without fulfilling the apocalyptic aspirations of the Jewish people against Rome. Lucian and Suetonius contribute to the historical picture only a clue to their own perceptions: Jewish views of Jesus hostile to the gospel accounts are a different matter far less lightly dismissible, as they may contain discreditable truths which the gospel writers would naturally wish to omit. In this case we know enough to establish a limited range of possible viewpoints; in many other cases we do not have even that. We can perhaps be content with the generalisation that holy men by nature are not exempt from contemporary and subsequent controversy and divergent judgement. They are independent of social and religious status to the extent of being divisive by nature in political terms.

Nor need it always be possible to see who is a charlatan and who is not. Sometimes the answer is only too obvious: the man who announces that the world will end when a stork descends from a tree on the Campus Martius disproves his own claims to prophetic powers when he himself falls out of the tree along with his stork.[66] The man who was allegedly burned for teaching Libyan parrots to proclaim his own godhead might be cited as a comparable case: but he might have claimed that any divine impulse to learn the language of birds, or to teach them the language of men, was a gift from some higher power, and who is then to contradict him?[67] 'By their works shall ye know them' is the Christian reflex for discrediting false prophets and charlatans: but it would be unwise on the other hand to presume that because Alexander of Abonouteichos invented and marketed a highly successful new god that he was the self-seeking villain through and through that Lucian makes him out to be.[68] The impulse to announce a new deity can always be divinely attributed: old gods may wish to extend their influence through a new subsidiary – that in effect is what the God of Jesus Christ is often enough announced as doing. Some works that Alexander claims to do, such as resurrections from the dead, would unquestionably have qualified as good works, if he could have stopped the burial alive of even one corpse wrongly diagnosed as dead. And we can hardly deny that Alexander advanced the standing of his community – as a no less resourceful Irish priest within the last decade was able to do for the shrine at Knock; it is difficult to decide whether such gestures can be construed as unequivocal extensions of self-seeking. It is still less easy to argue away that Alexander was an intermediary of Asclepius for the good of mankind who attempted to further a healing initiative. On the other hand even the religious virtuosi who have received least systematic dismissal or discredit are not exempt from criticism in historical terms. If one is to be regarded as divine, one has a reasonable obligation to convince: threats of punishment or discomfiture against unbelievers at some unspecified future time can be construed as a contemptible form of religious blackmail, and few can be exempted either from it or from inability to stifle it in their followers. The more eschatologically reliant a holy man may be, the more the growth of his cult will be open to charges of spiritual or psychological coercion.

PERSPECTIVES

The variety and often piecemeal approach of ancient sources is matched by a corresponding variety in modern interpretation. The last half-century alone has seen a number of different perspectives of a type already emerging in the nineteenth century. Ludwig Bieler, in a doctoral thesis of the 1930s, had already given monograph status to the holy man in antiquity in general.[69] Few topics that can now be examined had not been touched upon there. But one has often the sense that this is a progress of 'Pythagoras to Plotinus' – with some ground beyond in either direction, but in which no holy man has time to emerge for quite long enough, even as a literary or subliterary stereotype. We are given an identikit outline, but no very clear idea of what it might really have been like to be a holy man in any given historical and social context. Moreover, some of the selection, at least for the early Empire, deserves to be broadened. There is plenty about Jesus Christ and Apollonius of Tyana, and Demonax the Cynic is in evidence; but the polemical traditions against Alexander of Abonouteichos and Peregrinus receive little more than a passing mention. And above all a great deal is concentrated on the literary picture: this is indeed 'Das *Bild* des göttlichen menschen' rather than the *theios anēr* himself.

It is a tribute to the success of Bieler's picture that it has held its place for so long; in a sense the brief English popular study by

Hadas and Smith has served to reinforce rather than revise the outlines.[70] A fresh and characteristically dynamic study by Peter Brown for Syrian holy men in late Antiquity marked a major shift from texts *qua* texts to the holy man in his social environment, as the popular outside mediator in a context of social tension;[71] but its later terms of reference have tended to cut it off from the period we are chiefly concerned with.

The same year as Brown's article saw also a bibliographical landmark by Morton Smith. But it was the latter's *Jesus the Magician* of 1978 that again showed how much the world has moved on.[72] Opposition to holy men had rated little more than random recognition by Bieler. Here however the hostile Jewish testimonia to Jesus Christ are coupled with a thorough acquaintance with the magical papyri and their thought-world. The result is that one superman is relegated to the horde of exorcists, medicine-men, and mountebanks who can be seen as *magoi* ('sages') or *goētes* ('tricksters') at will.

Since Smith's prolegomena no general study has been attempted, and for good reason: the available material has long mushroomed to unmanageable lengths: the scope of David Aune's monograph on prophecy alone[73] shows the sheer bulk of evidence that has to be absorbed on what is only a single facet of a holy man's operation. Such studies can only make the subject easier to survey in the future. What is perhaps less welcome is the tendency for broad surveys of the religious environment to allow holy men to drop out almost unnoticed. Such major syntheses as Ramsay Macmullen's *Paganism in the Roman Empire* or Liebeschuetz's *Continuity and Change in Roman Religion* find little room for holy men in their indexes;[74] and there has been a tendency in much recent scholarship on the religious and social life of the Empire to regard the Christian holy man in particular as a phenomenon of the age of Constantine onwards, a successor to the prestige of the martyr in the Great Persecution. Indeed the index to Lane Fox's broad survey of Christians and pagans over the second and third centuries does not notice pagan holy men at all, and Christian holy men only once in precisely this sense. Yet here we find a very perceptive treatment of Paul and Barnabas at Lystra.[75] Part of the trouble is the sheer effort of distinguishing divine manifestations. Gods can be seen in human form in the ancient world. Paul and his companion were so regarded, but declined the honour. They can hardly be denied the status of men who are felt by many to have supernatural powers, and supernatural status in the perception of some. Another part of the problem is that holiness in pagan antiquity may often be presented as a holiness of place rather than person. That is all very well until we are confronted with an available account of Alexander of Abonouteichos: shrines have to be founded on the initiative of someone, and operated thereafter.[76]

A recent and plausible tendency has been to advocate the setting of individual incidents in their social and cultural context.[77] One method is to sub-divide into clear-cut categories, and assume well-defined and different beliefs on healing for Graeco-Roman and Judaeo-Christian holy men, and further sub-divisions between conceptions of medicine, miracle and magic;[78] and to claim that this enables us to read the minds of those on the spot, and to call this history. So we could if it could be made to work. But what happens when, for example, Apollonius of Tyana performs a healing of a consular client's daughter in Rome,[79] in a manner very similar to the raising of Jairus' daughter or Asclepiades' raising of a supposed corpse? A Greek-speaking Asiatic of supposed Pythagorean persuasion operates in a climate in which Judaeo-Samaritan healers are also at work, as reported at second or third hand by a Greek sophist nearly two centuries after the supposed incident. For one thing cultural conditioning becomes progressively more meaningless in an international milieu.[80] The philosophers in Lucian's *Philopseudes* speak respectfully of a variety of miracle-workers of several exotic nationalities and belief-systems, but in terms of their results, because these were what mattered. It is not very helpful under such circumstances to quote Galen's theory of Humours, or insist that Jewish belief would attribute such actions to God and attach them to a moral code: we must conjecture a common identity in such reports: a figure with enough experience of medicine to know that death is not always to be presumed and that some supposed corpses can be brought round will do so regardless of explanations. Such a figure will be able to produce an occasional success; we need not have been told about the number of cases where a genuine corpse was correctly identified by him as precisely that, and no 'miracle' then resulted. Nor will any amount of conviction about announcing the coming of any supposed New Kingdom suffice to raise a corpse from the dead in any context that is historically meaningful.

One constant problem throughout our period is the sense of chronological progression. None of the figures we are dealing with had the means to generate reliable figures of attendance, and it is difficult to separate notions of growth from those of continuity. Clearly there is room for some sense of progression, but it is very difficult to measure; and the significant changes in Christianity and Judaism and in paganism itself are too slow to relate more than incidentally to the lives of individuals as reported to us. Some elements are so well established in our period as to call for no significant measure of change, as in the case of magic and demonology; they were there, and the extent to which they are noticed is at least in part a matter of chance survival of materials. It is fatuous to relate growth in irrationalism too closely to certain types of historical event: the relatively stable Antonine age produces irrationalism enough for those prepared to look for it without anything like the long mid-third-century crisis to activate it. On the whole it is well to assume that the society of Christian asceticism in the fourth and fifth centuries is much different from the climate of first-century Palestine: but ascetics are still ascetics whether they live on locusts by the Jordan or on top of pillars; and fifth-century monks had eschatological weapons at their beck and call as readily as John the Baptist had had.

I have rather taken the view that the basic necessities of a holy man's society – friends and enemies, clients and emperors, skills of communication and 'superhuman' performance – are matters which go with the world of later antiquity in general and have to be considered regardless of the shifting doctrines and ideological allegiances which help to generate them. What I am concerned to emphasise is that we are faced with a great diversity of holy men throughout our period, and a more or less consistent degree of ambiguity surrounding their motivation. That is necessary to counteract a sterile sequence of scholarship which sees an exclusively Jewish or Hellenistic holy man type influencing the other.[81] The nature of the Eastern Mediterranean and Near-eastern societies in the last centuries BC made it easy enough for any claims of holiness to be taken on their own terms by outsiders, and accepted or rejected on their real or supposed merits. It might well be argued that in a polytheistic society it is difficult to avoid being mistaken for divine if one has done any philanthropic act that is any way exceptional. But that is a limitation we have to accept.

So far, then, we have attempted to set the scene in which holy men will be able to operate: against diverse but sometimes overlapping religious backgrounds, with a variety of models and markets, and darkly visible through a variety of perspectives, ancient and modern. It is time to meet some representatives of the species with a view to focusing more clearly on their patterns of activity.

3

PATTERNS
Lives and lifestyles

One looks in vain for any single profile for the holy man, just as one does for a precise definition. But it is possible to find examples of those whose image and impact become clear enough in the course of a varied career; and to adduce some basic features of behaviour in which most will be seen to engage.

The case of Peregrinus Proteus in the mid-second century AD will serve as a suitable starting-point.[1] Lucian's detailed presentation in the *Peregrinus* (*de Morte Peregrini*) is avowedly polemical, but it presents much that is either factual or in context highly plausible. Peregrinus' father is a rich landowner in Parium, but after the latter's death in suspicious circumstances he leaves the city and becomes a Christian, rising to be the προφήτης καὶ θιασάρχης καὶ ξυναγωγεὺς ('prophet, cult-leader and convenor') of the new cult.[2] The Christians revere him, allegedly, as 'god, lawgiver and protector' next after the man crucified in Palestine. He is imprisoned and supported by the Christian communities as far afield as Asia, but freed by a governor of Syria fond of philosophy.[3] Returning to Parium, he cedes the remainder of his property to the city, with a great flourish; at first he lives off the Christians, but is disowned by them, perhaps over a difference of diet;[4] he then petitions the Emperor Antoninus Pius for the return of his property, but is turned down. Next he goes to practise asceticism in Egypt under an evidently Cynic teacher Agathoboulos; we then find him in Rome, abusing the Emperor, and expelled by the urban prefect;[5] he takes to abusing the people of Elis, encouraging a local uprising and libelling the locality's benefactor Herodes Atticus.[6] Amid so much controversial behaviour Peregrinus is most often cited for the exceptional feature of his life, his immolation just after the Olympic Games of AD 165. It might be misleading to describe the career of

34

Peregrinus as typical: self-immolation in particular proves to be a less than attractive option for Western ascetics.[7] But he does illustrate a range of the situations in which an eminent religious activist can expect to find himself and operate, and the kind of initiatives he will be expected to bring to bear. We might well choose to categorise Peregrinus as a Cynic philosopher who flirted from time to time with more exotic and more obviously religious activities, whether connected with Christians or Brahmans; but we shall soon come to recognise that ambiguity and elusiveness are themselves a recurrent feature of holy men.

It is useful to juxtapose such a biography with the brief *Life* Lucian has left us of one of his own teachers, the eclectic philosopher Demonax.[8] His subject comes from an aristocratic background in Cyprus. He studies philosophy with the Agathoboulos attended by Peregrinus, as well as with the Cynic Demetrius and the Stoic Epictetus. He is also a pupil of Timocrates of Heraclea, teacher of the Stoic Euphrates, the sometime associate of that ultimate holy man Apollonius of Tyana. Demonax combines personal hardihood with a taste for both eclectic philosophy and literary culture.[9] In a wholly secular vocabulary we are told that 'though he attacked moral lapses, he forgave those who committed them, and he used the analogy of doctors healing sicknesses but not being angry with the sick'.[10] We are moving here towards that characteristic association, forgiveness of sins and healing. Nor is the notion of the superman too far away: 'he considered that it is the mark of a man to err, that of a god or a superman (ἰσόθεος) to correct their lapses'.[11] His associates included the prosperous and poor alike, for whom he has predictably complementary advice. He has a social function which extends from reconciling family squabbles to calming civic strife.[12] This brings its share of controversy, and the accusation is on a religious issue: he is charged with never having sacrificed to the gods, and with being the only man not initiated in the Eleusinian Mysteries. He has succinct rejoinders to both charges, and offers himself as a sacrifical victim like Socrates.[13] We find him often enough on the fringes of religious activity, pretending to be able to raise a man's son from the dead (on an impossible condition), or challenging the foresight of a soothsayer.[14] Towards the end of his life, he accepts hospitality at random, and 'his hosts used to think it was some divine visitation (τινα θεοῦ ἐπιφανείαν), and that some good spirit (ἀγαθὸν δαίμονα) had entered their house'.[15] He commits suicide rather than face dependence on others.[16] In a sense Demonax is an 'un-holy' man, since most of his association with religious activity is no more than the plain man's challenge of the mystifying. But it is easy to see how near to the general picture his range of activities and lifestyle can take him none the less. He is held in awe, and is at least seriously concerned with religious affairs, characteristically as an outsider.

The best documented holy man in our period, and the most studied next to Jesus Christ, is Apollonius of Tyana, whose career would have spanned most of the first century AD.[17] In spite of the sheer bulk of surviving materials this paragon remains a bundle of contradictions. Apart from the gargantuan biography by the third-century sophist Philostratus,[18] we have attestation of a wide range of activities. These include simultaneous prophecy of Domitian's death,[19] an impressive range of talismanic prescriptions in the Near East,[20] an association with the teacher of the oracle-monger Alexander of Abonouteichos,[21] and a number of prestigious contacts in a supposed correspondence.[22] There is also his attraction – and repulsion – of a number of philosophers.[23] Controversy and shadiness colour the prevailing ethos. Philostratus' work adds to both. In what is obviously a ramshackle assemblage from a number of very different and at times ill-fitting sources, the biographer commissioned by Severus' consort Julia Domna does his best to make Apollonius into a phenomenon more orthodox than the orthodox, more Hellenic than the Hellenes, advising emperors and rebuking cities with impeccable Pythagorean panache.[24] As a sophistic writer Philostratus invokes prejudgement, and Christian late Antiquity was not slow to suggest that he was trying to make bricks with too little straw.[25] Yet the sheer bulk of material still contains a very large repository of information on the credible range of activities of the religious activist who accumulates prestige and controversy by going his own way.

From Neo-Pythagorean to Neo-Platonist: it is not too hard to see how such a figure as Plotinus in the third century can have his life as a philosopher recycled and recast in a religious mould. The anecdotal tradition recounted with an unusual profusion of chronological detail by Porphyry has his master recognised in a temple by a priest as having a god for his guardian spirit:[26] an enemy 'recognises' Plotinus' power over magic;[27] he expects (inferior) spirits to come to him;[28] his death takes place as a snake crawls from under his bed into a hole in the wall;[29] he practises asceticism and enjoys extremely influential clients;[30] he pays close attention to Christians and heretics, and to the casters of horoscopes (in order to refute them);[31] he travels with Gordian with a view to visiting the Persian and Indian sages; and he has a significant number of medical companions.[32] One senses here the formation of a penumbra of holiness which certain associations tend to impose, and which philosophers including Plotinus himself might do their best to discourage; but collectively they are part of the impact which moves Neo-Platonism in the direction of a mystical religion.

Not all practitioners of holiness could claim such repute. We have a hostile running commentary, again by Lucian, on the activities of Alexander of Abonouteichos, a figure with apparent Pythagorean colouring who operated an oracle on the north coast of Asia Minor with conspicuous success in the later second century AD.[33] Whatever his attacker Lucian may have thought or seen fit to infer, Alexander obviously performed a religious service to pious clients, and served far beyond his community with advice on any aspect of life;[34] accusations of murder and debauchery only reflect the tensions surrounding the holy man as such, and Peregrinus experienced no less.[35] He numbered at least one Roman general among his clients, and gave an oracle at the height of Marcus' Marcomannic Wars.[36] The cult of his deity, the snake-god Glycon, was a growth industry, and has much to suggest to us on how religious forces were able to enter the market-place.[37] Nor was Alexander alone in the drive to promote oracles. The career of Julianus the thaumaturge in the same century gives us a useful source of comparison. In this case his father, the elder Julianus, had been in the business, as a 'Chaldaean', and was recognised as such in Rome itself; he was the author of four books on demons.[38] The son was allegedly 'joined to all the gods and to the soul of Plato that abides with Apollo and Hermes'.[39] Small wonder that the pair should have been credited with the infamous Chaldaean oracles – supposedly dictated by Apollo and containing a large admixture of Platonism.[40] But a ragbag of oracles was not without result: we find the younger Julianus claimed as a companion of Marcus Aurelius on the Northern frontiers, and his name even associated with those who laid claim to the celebrated rain-making miracle there;[41] while in Rome itself his theurgic activities in due course became known to Porphyry himself.[42]

One figure in particular from our period illustrates the flexible parameters between sophists and holy man. Aelius Aristides is the rare example one could classify as a passive example of the species, an armchair – or rather sick-bed – holy man, or perhaps better still as a would-be holy man.[43] All his 'miracles', feeble as they are, he ascribes to Asclepius, but while he lies ailing in the sacred precinct at Pergamum or elsewhere he will quite happily claim to be stopping an earthquake by sacrifice, to be 'detecting' shipwreck, or to be able to 'correct' the décor of a temple, in the manner of Apollonius of Tyana.[44] As soon as he undertakes a reasonable number of such initiatives he is crossing the boundary between superstitious sophist and eloquent holy man.

So much, then, for a sample of pagan holy men in our period: each one is in some sense an individualist adventurer against a background of familiar religious and intellectual forces, and each is at least potentially capable of being seen in more than one way. We can expect an equally varied spectrum within the largely enclosed world of Judaism. At one pole we can point in the first century BC to Honi,[45] conveniently antedating both John the Baptist and Jesus Christ. Josephus mentions his famous exploit as a rain-maker, a tradition which would associate him with the famous exploit of Elijah in competition with the prophets of Baal. An attempt is made to force him to curse Aristobulus II and his followers who have taken refuge in the temple. On refusing, on the grounds that the besieged are priests of God, he himself is stoned to death.[46] A reputation for miracle, an entanglement with temple politics, a strongly-principled independence: Honi's career is a reminder that in some essential respects at least Jesus Christ is not altogether unique in the Palestine of his times. Indeed comparison can be extended by reference to the career of Hanina ben Dosa, as an example of a Galilean charismatic a little after Jesus Christ;[47] all the more so in view of his association with Arav, only some ten miles from Nazareth itself. There he is linked with the eminent Rabbi Yohanan ben Zakkai, as well as with (more probably the Elder) Rabbi Gamaliel claimed as a teacher by St Paul. His reputation is as a healer, and the superiority of his powers of prayer is acknowledged by Rabbi Johanan himself; he can perform distance healing, as for the son of Gamaliel.[48] He can also enjoy an immunity from natural perils, as when he is left unscathed by the bite of a poisonous snake (which does not survive the encounter), or when the queen of the demons spares him. Like Honi he too can control the rain by prayer, and he shares with Jesus Christ not only personal poverty but an unconcern with legal and ritual as opposed to moral issues.[49] In Hanina we have an example of a figure who has to be reconstructed entirely through later rabbinic and in many cases clearly secondary traditions. These do not include birth or death stories, and he is poor rather than ascetic; the most prestigious among the credible traditions is his healing by distance prayer of the son of Gamaliel. There is an apparently Galilean tradition of folkloristic stories; apart from snake-killing and almost literally switching a rain-storm on and off, he is credited with lengthening joists on a building by prayer. But he is also a son of God in a special relationship with the Father.

Both Honi and Hanina might be taken to show the progress of colourful individualists who set out at some stage of their career to break the mould of religious activity or belief. It is well to remind ourselves of the multitude of conformist religious activists that the Empire must have contained at any given moment. We can reconstruct an important career within established Jewish religious frameworks: the nature of rabbinical anecdote permits at least a connected series of vignettes of a Pharisaic leader in the first century, all the more important for his part in the events of the Fall of Jerusalem and the reconstruction of the sect thereafter. The career of Rabban Yohanan ben Zakkai is centred on the central activity of Phariseeism itself, the transmission and interpretation of Torah. Yohanan is alleged to have received his education as the last pupil of Rabbi Hillel, who had rationalised the tools and techniques of scriptural exegesis. We find him in Galilee, where he has the miracle-working Hanina as his pupil. Back in Jerusalem, he shows uncompromising wisdom and integrity in the interpretation of Torah, whose centrality is emphasised by his claim that its study is the condition for the existence of man. There is predictable conflict with high priests and Sadducees, and in the course of his exegesis he and his pupils appear to have mystical experiences as he solves the exegesis of the enigmatic 'chariot of Ezekiel'.[50] During the Jewish Revolt, when already old, he claims a clairvoyant interview with Vespasian, and is allowed to escape to Yavneh (Jamnia), where he sets up a school of scriptural exegesis before his final retirement. In some respects such a career might be seen as unspectacular. But Yohanan could claim a role at a crucial point in the Pharisaising of surviving Judaism, and by no means that of a purely establishment figure: there is no denying the virtuosity implied by the convergence of rabbinical traditions about him.[51]

By contrast Flavius Josephus is normally known to classicists as a historian and antiquarian, or as a political figure in his own right in the context of the Jewish Revolt (AD 66–73) which he himself describes. But the configurations of his own life bring him just as readily within the scope of our flexible definition of the virtuoso religious activist. His own accounts, whether in the first or third person, set him out as of noble background and education, and as a descendant of the Hasmonean priest-kings of the previous century.[52] He presents himself as sufficiently well-schooled around fourteen to be consulted by the chief priests and other notables on points of law: the Lucan story of Christ in the temple is not without parallel.[53] Not only does he sample the life of Pharisee, Sadducee and Essene, but he spends time in the wilderness with an ascetic Bannus for three years till his nineteenth year, before reverting to Pharisaism once more.[54] In the Jewish War he is part of a priestly embassy to ensure the proper distribution of armament; we find him as a prisoner before Titus and Vespasian; and he avoids being sent to Nero by prophesying Vespasian's future destiny.[55] When challenged he claims to have previously predicted to its inhabitants the fall of Iotapata after forty-seven days, together with his own captivity. Vespasian then gives him favourable treatment and privileges in Rome under the Flavians: and accusers find themselves executed, while Josephus goes on to enjoy the favour of Domitian.[56]

The Jewish examples, then, afford as wide a range of variations on a holy man's career and its presentation, from the radical individualist to the highly questionable conformist and collaborator, by way of the virtuoso rabbinical interpreter and politician. It should need no emphasis that our cross-section is not the only possible or indeed available one: an Essene, an eminent Sadducee and a Zealot leader would have provided a different but equally varied picture within the same parameters.

As within Judaism, so within the penumbra of emergent Christianity we can expect to find colourful and active individualists, all the more so in a context where there would have been fewer norms or controls at any rate in the critical first century. On the earliest fringe of Christianity we find Simon Magus evidently established with a great reputation as 'The Power of God' in Samaria,[57] a region with a mixed Jewish and Greek population, where he comes into contact with Philip, and more implausibly with Peter and John. He offers to buy the power the latter pair employ in the laying on of hands, and is duly rebuked.[58] So much for the canonical account in Acts: the apocryphal *Acts of Peter* adds much more, most of it credible in the context of a superstitious and receptive clientele.

Peter finds Simon also in Judea, where he enjoys the patronage of a rich lady Euboula, who regards him as a godly man; the apostle drives him out.[59] But he reappears in Italy at Aricia, where he divides the infant Christian community in Rome; he is received as God in Italy, as Saviour of the Romans; he is announced as about to appear out of a cloud, and duly does so.[60] By the time Peter has been warned in a divine vision to go from Palestine to Rome to deal with him, we find Simon staying with a senator Marcellus 'who was persuaded by his charms'.[61] A talking dog now acts as a messenger between Simon and Peter, and a demoniac in a crowd smashes a statue of Caesar, which the apostle promptly repairs; Simon is thrown out.[62] A series of conflicts follows, supervised by Marcellus and conducted in the forum, in which Peter proves the more proficient at revitalising corpses.[63] As a final throw Simon announces a repeat performance of his powers of levitation; in Peter's presence he meets with an accident and breaks his leg. He is taken to an exiled magician at Tarracina, in whose custody he dies. A further account attributes a false claim to be able to resurrect, which fails and results in his burial for good.[64]

The emerging church itself serves as a launching pad for no less difficult individuals. A close contemporary of Peregrinus, the heretic Marcion,[65] hailed from Sinope in Pontus; his father was already a Christian bishop.[66] Local scandal attributed him with the seduction of a virgin, and his father excommunicated him.[67] He journeyed to Rome in an attempt to have the matter set aside, or possibly to have a bishopric of his own restored; we have a tale of a spectacular dialogue with Roman presbyters.[68] There are allegations of his having been a substantial benefactor of the church in Rome, and having had his benefaction returned in view of his heresy. We find him associated with the Gnostic Cerdo,[69] and the subject of a colossal feat of polemic by Tertullian which reflects the very real danger of his standard of biblical criticism to the emerging canon of Christian scripture.[70] As often, too, the sheer hatred of the winning side in his controversies results in difficulty in assembling anything like a biography.

The result of the diversity of wisdoms offered, and the careers that embodied them is that dividing lines are often difficult to draw. The gradual emergence of a church and its hierarchy did nothing to stem the manifestations of individualism. Apart from the celebrated founders of Christian monasticism in the pre-Constantinian years one notes such a figure as Nepos, an Arsinoite bishop earlier in the third century.[71] The latter fathered an apocalyptic treatise, taking the Revelation literally, and offering a millenium on earth given over to 'indulgence of the body'. Infected apparently with Jewish influence, he claimed, according to his Christian opponent Dionysius of Alexandria, a special mystical status for his work, and rejected the allegorical for the literal.[72] His support in the local villages made him difficult to combat. Epiphanius identifies another ascetic package attributable to one Hieracas, who links strict asceticism with a paradise attainable only through effort, and stands against bodily resurrection as well as earthly marriage.[73] Nor is it difficult for the career pattern of a holy man to be consistent with even that of an early Christian bishop: we find Narcissus presented by Eusebius as performing many miracles, including changing water into oil to supply a Paschal lamp; some of the water was duly preserved as a relic. We find that enemies anticipating conviction for misconduct of their own brought accusations against him; Narcissus then left the community and spent years in contemplation 'in deserts and secluded regions', while his accusers began to be discomfited for their false oaths; the last of them made a public confession.[74] In the third episcopate after his own he appeared from some quarter as if come to life again. Two visions, one of his own, the other of the people of Jerusalem, brought Alexander from a bishopric in Cappadocia to Jerusalem on a pilgrimage; he assisted the restored Narcissus to complete his episcopate at an advanced age. [75]

PATTERNS OF HOLINESS

At this point we can attempt to impose some outlines on the diversity of patterns in our sample, and attempt to construct something appproaching a typical curriculum vitae for an early imperial holy man whatever his religious background. The holy man had a function in ancient society from villages in remoter Syria or Asia Minor to Rome itself. In some respects he was conditioned by his environment, but he had also to make himself master of it. He steered a course in and out of the civilised world; but his route was largely his own, and different in every case. We can chart the movement of Peregrinus sufficiently clearly to suggest where a holy man is likely to turn up. He had begun as heir to substantial estates in Parium. We find him in Palestine with the Christians, then in Egypt with Agathoboulos; but we also find him in Rome, or at the

Olympic Games, or even just outside Athens.[76] The career pattern is not difficult to recognise. It uses the grand tour accessible to any young man of wealth, and to philosophers and sophists. Once established like them he might enjoy the status of consultant in moral and religious matters. Peregrinus' example might lead us to reflect on how many of the holy men we have noted were men of comfortable means. That may be an acccident of survival, or it may be a self-fulfilling truism. Those who began with considerable advantage, even if they gave up their material wealth, did not give up their education. And they were well equipped to mix in urban aristocracies or pick up and obtain pupils and patrons.

There are some tentative geographical inferences to be advanced from our sample as well. We happen to know that the north and north-west of Asia Minor produced a fertile crop of religious individualists from the later first century onwards. Dio of Prusa, whose claims in this sphere are perhaps underestimated, came from Prusa in Bithynia;[77] Peregrinus Proteus was a Cynic and mystic from Parium on the Hellespont;[78] Alexander the prophet of Glycon from Abonouteichos in Pontus;[79] and Marcion the para-Christian heretic from Sinope.[80] With the exception of the next to inaccessible Abonouteichos, all these sites would have had good communications with Byzantium, and relatively easy access to the Mediterranean, the Black Sea and the interior of Asia Minor; they were natural enough receptacles for the mixture of cultures and the spread of cults. One could say the same for such teeming seaports as Corinth and Alexandria, which will figure no less prominently in due course.

The holy man's relations with his native community were also important. That was where he might expect the most dogged grass-roots support; and it was the environment that determined his own aspirations and outlook. While rejected in Nazareth itself, it is still in Galilee that Jesus Christ is able to establish his power-base.[81] Paul for his part notably reverts early in his missionary career to Syria and Cilicia, the province containing Tarsus.[82] When in Jerusalem, he evidently goes along with Peter; when the latter comes to Antioch, he opposes him;[83] we can reasonably suspect that territorialism had its part to play. Alexander of Abonouteichos starts his oracle among people whose superstitious disposition he understands, and in fact is able to bring to the attention of the world his obscure township on the Black Sea coast.[84]

But whatever his relationship with his home background, the

holy man can expect to have had a scintillating teacher, preferably somewhere which can be seen as both ancient and remote. Egypt is the most obvious place, but others were certainly possible. It was in a situation freed from family control for the first time, that a young man of means could take the first steps in rejecting the world and finding his own identity in a new and exciting environment; he could then return to impress the rest of the world with what he had learned. Peregrinus we find with Agathoboulos in Egypt 'where he practised that amazing training in asceticism, shaving half his head, plastering his face with mud, and no doubt demonstrating their notorious so-called indifference by having an erection among a huge crowd of bystanders, then practising flagellation on one another's backsides with a fennel-stalk, and playing the miracle-mongering game (θαυματοποιῶν) in many other even more adolescent experiments'.[85] Lucian wishes to present Agathoboulos' course in a way detrimental to Peregrinus; but elsewhere he had indicated that one of his own teachers, Demonax, had also been a pupil of Agathoboulos,[86] whose prestige is this time meant to stand unquestioned.

Jesus Christ would have been able to show a no less ascetic pedigree in association with the ascetic John the Baptist, and the temptation in the wilderness points to desert asceticism; the terms of the temptation narratives may well point to disapproval of those who claim to turn stones into bread.[87] Infancy and boyhood narratives may point to other associations again; with the learned teachers in the temple,[88] and more sinisterly with the magi,[89] who attend on Jesus at an apparently innocuous age. Apollonius of Tyana we find with a still more exalted range of companions; easily outpacing the local Pythagorean virtuoso in Aegeae, he finds even the Babylonian magi inadequate, the Egyptian gymnosophists still more so, and only the Indian Brahmans apparently on a par with his superlative self.[90] The eminently successful oracle-monger Alexander of Abonouteichos could claim a pedigree through a doctor who had taught him back to this byword for pre-eminence – in science or charlatanism according to one's point of view.

After such training regimes a holy man had to put some service at the disposal of mankind, based on some expertise, real or supposed. This might range from reading the horoscope of an individual to banishing a plague from a whole city or insuring a whole district against earthquake. At least a proportion of his skills have to have been seen to work within the recognised parameters of current belief: some very simple social skills as they might seem to us acquire a high prestige when placed in the context of belief in demonic possession. Instinctive and commonsense deductions can be greatly heightened by the language of prophecy. Professions real or so-called, such as oracle-mongery, provision of patent medicines, reading the faces of clients, or the proferring of aphoristic advice may be called upon, either as prime specialities or as adjuncts, separately or in combination, to a whole repertoire of skills. These may or may not be tied to some larger or supposedly overriding design: the proclamation of the present or imminent arrival of the Kingdom of God, the overthrow of the established order or the like. And such designs may entail a specific identity for the holy man himself: as a god, as a son of a god, or as a divine messenger.[91] On the other hand a holy man may simply be recognised as such by virtue of his unpretentious and unassuming life as a member of a philosophic school or religious sect, provided that he can display some distinctive element of individuality.

A holy man operates in something of a religious vacuum. He can expand into the spiritual space available as fast as his energies or delegation skills will allow: he can and must acquire a clientele of beneficiaries, with or without the aid of disciples. It is in the spread of a religious network that holy men of our period exhibit their most notable diversity. That spread is related to the forces that bound their spiritual space: the mere fact of a holy man's existence may stimulate opposition, whose action and nature may turn out decisive in the spread of any cult. It may nip the holy man and his activities in the bud by total annihilation; or by ineffective persecution may stimulate public opinion in his favour.

An important consideration throughout his career is how the holy man will be able to support himself. Indifference to bodily needs will be a concern, often ostentatiously enough expressed. But it must be backed up with a source of funds, a means of patronage, or some way of earning a living. The early part of Peregrinus' career in particular entailed a question mark over his very substantial inheritance; he leaves his estate and lives in a Christian community.[92] Well established, he cedes the inheritance to his city. Expelled by the Christians, he must claim it back. When he has lost it for good he finally turns to a Cynic regime.[93] But before his death we find him in the company of Theagenes of Patras, himself well off.[94] Jesus Christ could expect support in kind for disciples sent out on the Galilee mission; but residence at Bethany in a household where a jar of precious ointment can be used to anoint his feet will imply the availability of some means.[95] Paul for his part works among the Thessalonians, and urges corresponding efforts in their own community to ensure that others do likewise.[96] He protests to the Corinthians about his refusal to take fees for his preaching, and perhaps seems to protest too much.[97] Such fees were apparently allowed as of right to professional preachers, and the latter category may at least suggest the possibility of previous criticism in the matter of receiving fees.

It is often difficult to determine the reasons for the movements of holy men once they are fully fledged. In spite of his powers over the elements such a figure was well advised to winter in a single locality;[98] he might move on as a result of an invitation, or a move upwards;[99] he might simply have had enough, and decide to sample pastures new;[100] or he might be forcibly ejected from an area as the result of official ban or the intrigues of internal enemies.[101] It is interesting to trace the contrasting itineraries of Paul and Peregrinus, which both take in Athens and Rome, but reflect a strong difference of cultural focus. One does not expect the tent-maker from Tarsus and athlete for Christ to stage his last stand at the Olympic Games. But not all holy men were compulsive travellers, at least for any longer than they could help. Alexander of Abonouteichos had evidently been 'on the road' as a travelling oracle-operator, and had found his big break as a result of hospitality from a Macedonian lady, in whose company he had learned his trick handling of tame snakes. He could then reintroduce the novelty into an environment he knew well, and which could be relied upon to support him.[102] One notes too that his companion Coconnas favoured a site for an oracle at Chalcedon, because of its convenience for Thrace, Bithynia, Asia, Galatia, and the interior.

But against the attractions of spreading one's convictions or message to a wider world, there is an opposite pull. The desert, of whatever kind, emerges as a perpetual power-house from which the holy man's energy is generated.[103] One thinks of it as the training-ground for the solitary holy man's vocation; but it cannot escape attention how often the Palestinian deserts' solitude was violated by the exodoi of vast crowds in pursuit of a Messiah: John the Baptist attracts audiences to meet a colourful and reputable ascetic;[104] Jesus Christ has a crowd of thousands following him into the desert, perhaps more than once. But two other mass occasions emerge from Josephus: that of Theudas in the mid-forties of the first century AD, which was to entail a parting of the Jordan in the reverse direction from that of the original Exodus;[105] and again in the early sixties, when rebel leaders in the Jewish War also requested permission to withdraw to the desert.[106] Such crusades have an obvious relationship to the wilderness experience of the Jews; but such a mass phenomenon is not completely unknown in the larger Graeco-Roman *oikoumenē* either: one thinks of the mysterious Alexander-cum-Dionysus who travelled from Moesia to Asia Minor in AD 221.[107]

Various other geographical arrangements were possible: Alexander of Abonouteichos turned a relatively underdeveloped and inaccessible small town into a place of pilgrimage, while the Qumran Community, as well as the Therapeutae as described by Philo, had already combined a desert withdrawal with a coenobitic regime; the former at least were reacting against the temple priesthood, with an emphasis on purity and internal hierarchy, and at least some element of celibacy.[108]

Holy men had to show concern for the mass of mankind: as a matter of course we expect to find them operating in cities, or rather on them. Like sophists, they can gravitate to major centres where the major ills of mankind are to be found. We find both Paul of Tarsus and Apollonius of Tyana in Ephesus, Antioch, Corinth, and Rome;[109] Alexander of Abonouteichos' partner in crime wanted to make for Chalcedon. And indeed we find Apollonius' memory strongest in Byzantium itself.[110] Relationships with cities could take a number of forms. A holy man could mediate with Rome, or between internal factions within a city itself. Such relationships called for detachment, and the sage might choose to take his residence outside the city – receiving deputations and 'waiting to be asked' to intervene. Such tactics might preserve his air of detachment and remoteness and increase his standing: thus Lucian's mysterious Platonist Nigrinus pours his imprecations from a respectable distance against the city of Rome;[111] Apollonius waits at Cicero's villa before entering the capital;[112] while Peregrinus takes up residence outside Athens, where Aulus Gellius attends on him.[113]

A holy man might expect shelter in the city as a result of his religious associations: Apollonius taught in the temples and lived in their precincts;[114] Paul used local synagogues as his base;[115] and his appearance in the temple precinct at Jerusalem triggered off events, as it probably did in the case of Jesus Christ. Alternatively, a holy man might take up residence at a central religious shrine, or at a religious festival: Aristides seems to have been a resident in some sense of the temple at Pergamum.[116]

Sooner or later holy men find themselves in the big city, and not always on terms to their liking. Apollonius of Tyana criticises the Athenian conduct of the Anthesteria for its carnival atmosphere, and takes the city to task for gladiatorial shows;[117] Jesus Christ provokes the temple authorities in Jerusalem; Paul triggers riots in Ephesus and Jerusalem; Peregrinus succeeds in getting himself expelled from Rome under Antoninus Pius; the false 'Dionysalexandros' makes for Byzantium, apparently without incident. It is at this point that the holy man can enjoy maximum resonance and find the largest audience for controversy; not for nothing does the confrontation between Peter and Simon Magus work itself out in Rome.

As there is no inflexible career structure, so there is no standard way for ending the life of a holy man. Some either experienced or arranged a spectacular demise. Jesus Christ was crucified,[118] and an empty tomb claimed as proof of resurrection; Peregrinus immolated himself,[119] Apollonius simply disappeared;[120] in each case there were discrepant reporting of 'sightings' after the event. But many who are comparably regarded in their lifetime disappear with only some unusual feature to their tomb. Demonax refuses elaborate burial, saying that the stench will ensure it for him;[121] Antony the hermit asks for burial in the desert at the hands of his two faithful followers in an unmarked grave.[122] This may have been simply to avoid the local Egyptian practice of keeping an embalmed corpse in a house; but one cannot help thinking that the same distinction attended the death of Moses.

It is useful to apply the preceding formulae as a commentary to a case we have not used in constructing it. I choose a holy man who illustrates every aspect of our model and remains relatively inaccessible outside specialist patristic scholarship, Gregory Thaumaturgus.[123] Gregory comes from a wealthy pagan background in third-century Pontus, again within that happy hunting-ground of holy men in northern Asia Minor. He studies and is converted by Origen not in Egypt in this instance, but in Caesarea, then returns to Pontus.[124] The obligatory testing follows: Gregory remains aloof from Neocaesarea, and conquers the devils in a pagan temple there.[125] Triumphantly acclaimed on his arrival at Neocaesarea as bishop, he serves his community by such diverse services as controlling a river and drying up a lake, constructing a church that survives an earthquake, or stopping a plague at a festival of Zeus.[126] He encounters Jewish fraudsters, and his handling of routine opposition is enhanced by an exorcism.[127] Forced to flee during the Decian persecution, he returns to institute martyr festivals.[128] He mediates in the problems that surround the Gothic raids, and finally refuses a tomb for himself.

Gregory's memory survives in local folklore, so that the site of the lake, the boundary-marker of the river, and of course the church that survived the earthquake could still be pointed out; there is also a decisively enhanced Christian presence in the district. There are also substantial problems with the sources; the hagiographical *mémoire* by Gregory of Nyssa, over a century afterwards, belongs to the cultural milieu of the late fourth century, and the selection of worthwhile highlights skirts round such key events as the Gothic raid.[129] But no reader of such material is likely to dismiss Gregory as a Christian bishop, a missionary, or a mere hagiographical cipher. We have to see him performing in a way analogous to Alexander of Abonouteichos, close to the same area in the following century, fulfilling similar needs and making a similar psychological impact.

MOTIVATION

So much, then, for the outward manifestations of the holy man. But what of the individual himself? What can he expect to get out of it? The relief of suffering, the communication of divine wisdom, some recognition of merit, some satisfaction at a job well done, of doing what no one else is available to do. And above all, getting it right, and bridging the gap between human and divine in some significant way, however it might be expressed. Paul neatly embodies a quite general and genuine concern for human welfare (Gal. 6.9f.): 'So let us never become bored with doing good, for if we do not relax our efforts we shall at the right time reap the harvest. And so, as opportunity offers, let us labour for the good of everyone, especially the members of the household of the faith'. Foremost among the holy man's motivations if he is to acquire even reasonable plausibility is the good of the individual and the community, however the latter may be defined. This may sometimes be no more than a matter of ensuring an affordable price for corn or the avoidance of military exploitation. But the contents of the Sermon on the Mount are not entirely untypical of a preoccupation with alleviating the human condition: wrongs have to be righted in a larger context, and the holy man may choose to harmonise their being righted with some kind of divine plan. Claims may be made for a better life to come, as by Paul in Ephesians 4.22f.: 'leaving aside your old way of life, you must lay aside that old mortal nature which, deluded by desire, is being destroyed. You must be renewed in mind and spirit, and put on the new manhood vested by God in the just and devout life of truth'. But the thinking of the Marcan and Johannine traditions alike is towards an integration of healing miracles with the coming of the Kingdom, however that in itself is to be conceived either in a 'Kingdom of God within' or a full-blown apocalyptic tradition culminating in the Second Coming.

Detractors are always ready with a different answer, crediting to the successful delusions of personal grandeur. In particular Lucian is quick to attribute to the volatile Peregrinus motives of vainglory: 'After turning into everything for the sake of reputation, after countless changes of direction in this final instance he has even turned into fire'.[130] Not, as far as Lucian is concerned, until all other publicity-seeking devices have been exhausted: 'At last nobody paid any attention to him and he was no longer such a celebrity; for he had gone totally stale and he could not come up with any more novelty to dumbfound all comers and make them marvel and gaze at him – something he had a sharp craving for from the start'.[131] The same is clearly enough implied in the opposition to Jesus Christ, for whom insistence that this is the only way to the Father is seen as a matter of arrogance.

Lucian may be cynical. Paul could offer a similar accusation of 'being puffed up' or 'vaunting' against the Corinthians.[132] But the fact must remain that at certain levels of society holiness did carry a pre-eminence and an influence that might be difficult to attain in any other way. And by the time of the Decian persecution it might be claimed that the Christian episcopate carried such prestige.[133] The motif that the ranks of heresiarchs are swelled by those disappointed of preferment within the church adds to the chorus of *kenodoxia* ('vainglory'): James and John were themselves not without curiosity as to the seating arrangements in the Kingdom of heaven.[134]

We should note the not infrequent transition from drop-out to opt-out. A fair number of our subjects have some initial stigma in the path of traditional career expectation.[135] Peregrinus is an obvious example, with the suspicions over his father's death;[136] while Secundus 'the silent philosopher' had still more obvious cause for stigma over his mother's.[137] Nor can Paul lightly have escaped the shame of his part in the first murder of a 'Hellenist' Christian, and his preoccupation with a Gentile mission may have had guilt as an element,[138] to say nothing of the guilt that would have followed on Peter's direct denial of his master.[139]

In some contexts of revealed religion a notion of personal pre-selection and predestination is present: the recently discovered Cologne Mani-Codex leaves us in no doubt about its subject's calling:[140]

> In this way [my yokefellow, *syzygos*] called me and chose me and drew me and separated me from their midst. He drew [me to the divine] side . . . [and revealed to me] who I am and my body in what way I came and how my coming into this world happened, and who I have become among those who are most distinguished in pre-eminence, and how I was born into this fleshly body, or through what woman I was brought to birth and delivered according to this flesh, and from whom I was begotten.

Jesus Christ on baptism by John the Baptist is presented as having a supernatural sign that he is the Son of God.[141] Paul receives both a striking experience and a messenger; he is to be filled with the Holy Spirit and sent out at its prompting.[142] Even Alexander of Abonouteichos claims identity as of the line of Perseus and Podalirius.[143] Such self-discoveries amount to an inner compulsion, and again in the case of revelatory holy men this will be allied to missionary zeal. In the Christian case at least it is made especially urgent in the first century by eschatological factors: if the Second Coming is imminent the elect must be both prepared and extended. Paul threatens the destruction of those who do not open their minds to the love of truth so as to find salvation;[144] Jesus Christ and John the Baptist had already done likewise.[145] And Celsus makes his Palestinian holy man threaten that he is the only one who can save his audience from the wrath to come.[146]

At the opposite end of the spectrum is a total escapism: when Antony the hermit goes further into the desert, or a stylite saint has the height of his pillar raised, he is affirming a desire for remoteness and disengagement from human society which may enhance contact or closeness to the divine world:

> Then Antony, withdrawing by himself, as was his custom, to his cell, intensified his discipline and sighed daily, reflecting

on the dwellings in heaven, both longing for these and con-
templating the ephemeral life of human beings.[147]

The number of instances in which holy men would prefer not to
have the attention of clients bears witness to the media pressure
which may wish to make them something they do not wish to be:

> But when he saw that he was disturbed by many people and
> was not allowed to retire as he intended and wished, appre-
> hensive that, because of the things the Lord was doing
> through him, either he might become prideful or someone else
> might think more of him than was warranted, he considered
> carefully and struck out, departing into the Upper Thebaid.[148]

Perfectionism looms large in such motivations: Paul acknowledges
in Philippians that

> It is not to be thought that I have already achieved all this. I
> have not yet reached perfection, but I press on hoping to take
> hold of that for which Christ once took hold of me. My
> friends, I do not reckon myself to have got hold of it yet. All I
> can say is this. Forgetting what is behind me, and reaching out
> for that which lies ahead, I press towards the goal to win the
> prize which is God's call to the life above, Jesus Christ.[149]

In a fair proportion of cases an object, if not the object, of a
spiritual career is release from the body, temporary or otherwise, to
effect the return of the soul to its natural status of purity: if we
compare visions of Aristides and Zosimus of Panopolis we shall be
able to see how similar are the visions over quite different intellectual backgrounds. Zosimus has a vision of a priest who had descended the fifteen steps of darkness and the ascent of the steps of
light, perfected as spirit, by casting away the coarseness of the body
and undergoing unendurable torments; he later appears as a bronze
man in a place where preservation (embalming) of those who wish
to obtain spiritual *aretē* is taking place. And he himself, Zosimus
adds, will become a man of silver and even of gold. A subsequent
ascent with another guide, a venerable white-haired *agathos daimōn*, ends in the latter's being hurled into the cauldron; a third
similar vision completes the operation. Here the professional technical symbolism of alchemy is plain enough in operation; but
Zosimus is elsewhere conscious enough of its spiritual
dimension.[150]

After this [I was obliged to] go to the temple and perform a full sacrifice to Asclepius, and to set up sacred bowls, and distribute the sacred portions of the sacrifice to my fellow pilgrims. It was also necessary for me to cut off an actual part of my body to ensure the well-being of the whole. But this was a difficult business and so [Asclepius] actually allowed me a remission from it; and instead he ordered me to remove the finger-ring I wore and offer it to Telesphorus – for this had the same effect as sacrificing my finger would have had. After this you can imagine how I felt, and what kind of harmony the god restored to me again. For I engaged in all this almost is if it were an initiation ceremony, since my anxiety was balanced by great hope.[151]

For Aristides anything and everything is part of a move closer to Asclepius.

It is difficult to reconstruct the motives of individual holy men with any precision beyond the general headings suggested, but we should at least guess at the reasons for our difficulties. Clearly no source favourable to a holy man is likely to stress or even countenance such factors as personal ambition and prestige, and detractors are unlikely to countenance any other; though hagiography will allow initial acts of wickedness or dissolute lifestyle to stress the virtuosity of a holy man's reformation. One obvious difficulty remains the length of time that intervenes between a holy man's sense of purpose and the point at which perceptions of him become fixed either in an oral tradition or on papyrus; a further problem is that a genuine sense of discontent or misfitting may lead an individual through several different sects. Where there has been an accumulation of sampling and no surviving personal testimony, as in the case of Peregrinus, it may become practically impossible to disentangle all the threads. But we can hope to come at least a little closer to the inner motivation of our subjects by apprenticing ourselves to their various professions, real or imagined. That will give us some idea in due course of the impact they could make on their fellow men, to say nothing of the divine powers they might claim to influence or exert.

4

WISDOM
Crafts, cunning, credulity

In a letter that purports to come from the sage Apollonius of Tyana
to his sometime associate Euphrates, the following claims are made:

> If someone associates with a Pythagorean, I should tell you all
> the benefits he will derive from him: the arts of lawmaking,
> geometry, astronomy, arithmetic, harmonics, music, medi-
> cine, and every kind of divine prophecy. And there are the
> finer things: highmindedness, magnanimity, nobility, tran-
> quillity, piety, genuine understanding as opposed to mere
> opinion about the gods, knowledge about demons as opposed
> to belief in them, friendship with both gods and demons alike,
> self-sufficiency, eagerness, frugality, the limiting of one's
> needs, sharp perception, agility, proper breathing, a good
> complexion, health, courage and immortality.[1]

All such skills and benefits Apollonius himself is implied to be able
to impart. A substantial cross-section of them belong to the range of
disciplines or pseudo-disciplines open to amateur and professional
holy men alike; and some at least overlap with the interest of
established philosophical systems or professional skills which will
establish an air of respectability.

GOD, MEN AND NATURE

The holy man had to be able to recognise manifestations of the
divine, and of divine disposition towards the individual. Any discipline that helped was relevant, and anything that helped could hope
to become a discipline. One obvious and arresting way to proceed
is simply to announce a new deity as such: Alexander of
Abonouteichos arranges to 'discover' the snake-god Glycon, within

an egg in the foundations of a temple in the town. It is passed off as a rebirth of the healing god Asclepius, previously announced by an oracle from Chalcedon 'planted' by Alexander and a colleague, to the effect that Apollo and Asclepius would shortly be coming to stay at Abonouteichos. When the oracle proper is set up, it can announce itself as 'I am Glycon, the third blood (grandson) of Zeus, light unto men'.[2] One could also claim to be either a god or a son of a god in one's own right. Celsus ridicules the idea as typical of Palestine and Syria, where itinerant preachers will claim either honour, or pass themselves off as divine spirits.[3] Simon Magus makes such uncompromising claims for himself as 'The only power of God'.[4] But kinship claims are understandably much more common. Alexander of Abonouteichos claimed for his part to be a son of Podalirius, a son of Asclepius, while also being a descendant of the hero Perseus, patron of the old Achaemenid rulers of his native Pontus;[5] Jesus Christ is not only attributed with the title Son of God but is supplied with genealogies to make him son of Abraham, David and Adam as well;[6] Apollonius of Tyana is claimed as a reincarnation of Proteus, with his connotations as a founder of civilisation,[7] and Peregrinus appears to affect the name Proteus, perhaps suggesting identity with the same deity.[8]

As well as claiming to be or be related to a god, a holy man might wish to 'revise' or extend the worship of existing deities: St Paul finds an altar in Athens 'to an unknown god' – more probably to unknown gods in the plural[9] – and promptly proceeds to claim the god in question, in the singular, as Yahweh;[10] Simon Magus similarly uses an inscription in Rome to 'interpret' in favour of himself.[11] Both proto-Christian and Gnosticising holy men could revise the Old Testament God, by turning him towards the Gentiles or by separating him completely from the God of the Old Testement as therein presented; hence Marcion's view of the Old Testament god as unworthy and ignorant.[12] Or a holy man could restore neglected cults: Apollonius of Tyana is associated with interest in hero cults of Achilles and Palamedes – not without an element of threat if the Thessalians should fail to comply with the former's demands on them.[13]

The early Empire is well known for its archaising tendencies, particularly in the Greek world of the second century. There was opportunity here for holy men to concern themselves with what we might term religious archaeology; Apollonius of Tyana persuades the Amphictyonic Council at Pylaea to resume the rites at the tomb of Achilles.[14] He is also credited with a work on sacrifices (*peri thusiōn*): a possible extract includes directions on pouring libations over the handle of a cup, so as to use the part least used for drinking – not the last we shall see of the holy man doubling as hygienist.[15] We also find him explaining the attributes of a statue of the athlete Milo as priest of Hera, with its cap, pomegranate, and shield-base; but the detail of close-spaced fingers and feet the sage dismisses as no more than an archaic point of style.[16]

One notes a natural trend towards theological purism: Apollonius objects to the commercial sale of gods, or rather to the fact that a trafficker in mere images of gods would prefer the sage not to share the same ship as himself. Apollonius combines archaism with austerity: the gods accompanied the motley crew who sailed to defend Athens, and these gods were real ones; and ancient craftsmen are praised for (supposedly) not commercialising their wares;[17] Apollonius would prefer an image of ivory and gold in a small temple to a cheap earthenware image in a large one,[18] or a wholesome philosopher to the Colossus of Rhodes;[19] while Jesus Christ is accused of preferring a temple not built with hands, or himself condemns the Pharisees for cleansing the outside of a cup or dish.[20]

A significant contribution to the redefining of the divine was provided in our period by the proliferation of Gnostic theologies. By its very name Gnosis claims 'wisdom', and of a kind likely to produce holy men of a successful but contentious type. Gnostic systems offered a scheme of understanding of the universe and man's relationship to it which could make the perpetrator of the system a superhuman intermediary, able to rescue mankind from the baseness of the world and freeing the soul from material encumbrance, but in recognition of appropriate signs.[21] This made Gnostic systems particularly amenable to the paraphernalia otherwise associated with occult arts – pretentious jargon, bogus or evidently novel cosmology, and reliance on magical or near-magical apparatus. Moreover, its creation myths and their philosophic resonances gave it upper-class respectability. Valentinus and Basilides in the early second century were scarcely in the same league as the small-town medicine-man.

To compute the appeal of Gnosis we have to put ourselves in the position of someone encountering it for the first time. It is more convenient to illustrate from Valentinian material as the best documented: we have semi-allegorical cosmology and numerology.

Among much else of the kind we have Bythos (Primal Cause) bringing forth *Sīgē* (Silence) through *Nous* (Mind) and Truth; *Nous* brings forth *Logos* (Reason) and *Zōē* (Life) and they in turn Man and Church. The four pairs make up two tetrads, and the pairs of tetrads an ogdoad. Numerical progression now adds ten aeons born of *Logos* and Life and twelve of Man and Church.[22] Such a system, so similar to an Orphic-Pythagorean theogony, can then be suddenly juxtaposed to biblical numbers: the eight, ten and twelve add up to thirty, the number of Christ's years of silence before his ministry. Where all is hidden and assumed to be connected there is no limit to what may be about to be revealed.

The wisdom in Basilides' system is able to absorb a cross-section of culturally varied lore. If it is a surprise to have the Son of the Great Ruler of the Ogdoad compared with naphtha, or the use of 365 extended from the number of worlds to the parts of the body, it is less of a surprise to have the latter equated with the false horse in the Platonic myth of the soul's charioteer. It is no surprise either when likened to the enigmatic Old Testament text about Aaron's beard.[23] Gnostic wisdom is no respecter of the boundaries between Hellenistic and Hebraic tradition. We should not be tempted to infer from all this that Gnosis is all solemnity. The docetist Christ of Basilides – crucified only in appearance – would have been at home in the merry pranks of the *Homeric Hymn to Dionysus*. Having changed places with Simon of Cyrene, he joins in the fun, laughing at the crucifixion of his substitute.[24]

Nor is such a framework of beliefs always easily detectable. We are used to the perennial controversy on whether the *gnōsis* of which Paul complains in his opponents at Corinth is 'the real thing' in the sense of the full-blown second-century systems of Valentinus or Basilides, or whether it is simply an esoteric group of opinions within Jewish Christianity taken to constitute superior knowledge.[25] Either way Paul himself is not the only one to be vague about such matters. We find it alleged of Bassus of Corinth, associate and later enemy of Apollonius of Tyana, that he affected a false wisdom and there was no bridle on his tongue;[26] the latter part might correspond to *glōssolalia*, ecstatic utterance, which might well provide the framework for Gnostic revelation; or again it might be no more than mere talkativeness in the eyes of a sage so devoted to silence.

MAN AND NATURE

The most obviously professional skill available to the holy man was medicine: anyone with genuine expertise could easily give it an odour of sanctity.[27] Nor would it have occurred to secular doctors that Asclepius was not involved in their operations.[28] Given the nature of ancient misunderstandings of physiology, the practice of medicine was safest in the matter of tried herbal remedies, and here fringe practitioners were in their element. We can note Aristides' dream of even the philosopher Musonius' accredited healing powers, reported in a dream as urging a sick man to 'strike out the dead part of the soul and recognise god'.[29]

One incident will provide us with an idea of the interplay of medical practice and imagination so often involved. Apollonius of Tyana is alleged to cure the victim of the bite of a mad dog. He sends for the animal, which licks the wound and effects a cure. Whatever the principles behind the remedy, the cure itself was a tried one: the principle of 'the wounder will heal' was familiar to all students of Sophocles' *Philoctetes*. Either Philostratus or Apollonius colours the cure with a veneer of literature. The wounder is also the healer, and the boy has the soul of Telephus of Mysia.[30] Apollonius could have started from literary lore alone; but it seems more likely that he at least understood something of dogs as a source of infection; he also seems to identify a dog as (a manifestation of) this during the plague at Ephesus.[31]

A high proportion of the cures cited by the Elder Pliny in the repertoire of folk remedies turn out to rely at least partly on 'sympathetic' magic: the mole, with its obvious Chthonic significance, is prominent in such cures, to Pliny's annoyance;[32] toothache can be cured *inter alia* by scraping round the aching tooth with the left eye-tooth of a dog;[33] women can be forced to conceive by pulling hairs from the tail of the she-mule, pulled out while the animals copulate, then entwined as the humans do so.[34] Pliny also stigmatises cures administered and varied in relation to astrological signs, though he mentions magicians' remedies for quartan fever when he acknowledges that the orthodox treatments are ineffective.[35]

Only occasionally is it possible to discern both the real medical principle behind the cure and the reason for misconception inherent in the ancient application. 'And those puppies known as Melitaean relieve stomach-ache when laid frequently across the abdomen; the fact that the disease is transferred to the puppy is inferred from its sickening, in most cases even by its death.'[36] What will actually happen is that the body heat of the puppy will produce the alleviation to be expected from, for example, a hot-water bottle; but that in the case of infectious or contagious diseases of which the ache is a symptom, the puppy itself will be put at risk.

The holy man could try his hand at controlling the animal world as well as the world of men. Once more Apollonius is in the forefront. He could claim to communicate with animal transmigrations in accordance with Pythagorean theory of transmigration of souls; hence a tame lion hailed as the ancient Egyptian King Amasis (without much fear of contradiction).[37] But apocryphal gospels and acts have their fair share of counterparts: Peter and Simon Magus employ a talking dog, while Thomas discourses with a serpent and a colt.[38]

How easily such control can be contrived, or rather imagined, can perhaps best be seen from Aelius Aristides' account of an incident after his sacrificing to Isis and Serapis in the former's temple in Smyrna. Two sacred geese then precede him in his departure from the precinct:

> And I said to my friends and those who were escorting me, 'Look, even these are escorting me among my chorus of friends', and at the same time I spoke about the awesome majesty of the god . . . and [explained] that many times already my prayers had been answered. 'And now' said I, 'he has sent us these two to guide me on my journey' . . . . When we had gone some distance from the temple, by way of showing off to my friends, I joked about the geese and said 'you have sufficiently acquitted yourselves of your duty, gentlemen; be on your way!'. I had not got to the end of my sentence when they turned and were off.[39]

Even Aristides seems to have conducted this display in a tongue-in-cheek fashion; but he would not have been above taking it seriously.

One activity threatens to be lost sight of among so many other skills: an overall interest in natural history and natural philosophy, perhaps more conveniently labelled 'naturales quaestiones'. A glance at the kind of interest encompassed would include expertise in the properties of stones, plants,[40] and animals; and in earthquakes and weather phenomena, as well as in medicine as such. It is instructive to note how frequently such information seems to surface almost by chance in Philostratus in what we might be tempted to dismiss as mere paradoxography: on at least two occasions Apollonius' disciple Damis fails to recognise a kind of natural substance, and is presented as having recorded the fact. Substances extracted from animals for medicinal purposes might also carry a significance related to the 'virtues of animals': late antiquity sees the emergence of the *Physiologus*; Aelian had already written books *On the Nature of Animals*. One notes too Apollonius of Tyana's interest in the gold dust alleged to have been brought down by the river Pactolus in Croesus' time; this is consistent at least with an implied interest in metals as such. Or again Apollonius objects to the notion of trees older than the earth at Sardis, by mere common sense; interest in the earth is also a common denominator between many of the apparently isolated units about the sage: we find him interested also in the natural explanation for a volcano, which he prefers to attributions of volcanic activity to the giant Typho imprisoned under Etna.[41]

Among the most ambitious uses for such interest is the actual control of earthquakes. Apollonius claims to be able to prevent them by means of sacrifices; he has rivals with more expensive means of fulfilling the same claims by offerings to Earth and Poseidon.[42] And again in Antioch he can claim to link such a natural disaster to strife among mankind: a local earthquake is the occasion for a *peri homonoias* (discourse on political harmony) to the people of Antioch itself.[43] Indeed even Aristides could fancy that his sacrifices have stopped an earthquake.[44] Whatever could have lain behind such claims, Gregory Thaumaturgus had an even surer method, accordingly celebrated: to construct a building with earthquake-proof foundations, as he did a church in Neocaesarea.[45]

TRADITIONAL WISDOMS

The holy man and his disciples could claim expertise in god, man, and nature. But they could also master specific systems and the techniques based on them. The spectrum of skills is wide and varied, but we have to ask why certain specific disciplines would have appealed, and how they overlapped with the rest. Perhaps most commonplace and universal – as well as easiest to escape from – was the interpretation of dreams. Anyone could have them, and anyone could interpret them. The art was respectably ancient and sanctioned in Classical literature as in life. We are fortunate in possessing a manual of dream-interpretation from the middle of our period, all the more so because in purporting to offer a method based on a blend of theory and actual case histories it serves only to show the intellectual shortcomings of its author's system and the arbitrariness with which he applies it.[46]

One example will suffice to demonstrate: the significance for Artemidorus of a dream of marriage:

> Since marriage is analogous with death and is symbolised by it, I thought it would be good to make mention of it here. To marry a virgin signifies death for a sick man: for all the ceremonies which accompany marriage accompany funerals as well. On the other hand it is good for someone who wants to engage in a new enterprise – that signifies that he will succeed in his designs – and for some who hope for some advantage; for in every case the husband acquires some possessions, which the young bride brings him. For others, that signifies tumult and clamours, since there are not marriages without them. If one takes a woman already deflowered, one would have no regrets in engaging in enterprises not new but old . . . [and so on][47]

Such associative interpretations are not slow to indicate that any dream can be made to mean just about anything depending on the individual circumstances of the patient. But other things are also worrying about the probity of Artemidorus. There is a professional defensiveness in his instruction to his son:

> Remember that this book is dedicated to you alone, so that you may reserve it for your own use and not put it into general circulation. For if what I am about to write stays in your custody it will make you an interpreter of dreams superior to anyone else or at any rate second to none, but if you share it, it will make you appear no better skilled than others.[48]

And well might Artemidorus the Younger not distribute a book which gives him the following advice:

> And now (once more) I advise you to make use of anagram when in interpreting dreams for a client you want to appear to interpret more learnedly than someone else; but you must not use it at all when you are interpreting for yourself, or you will be completely deceived.[49]

From interpreting dreams it is not far to prophecy at large, and similar problems of flexible parameters will apply.[50] We have an example of prophecy at work when Apollonius interprets a three-headed child born in Syracuse, as portending the three Roman pretenders of the 'Year of the Four Emperors'. Some of the guess-work is intelligible: Damis is sent to check that the freak is both three-headed and male, and only after this investigation does Apollonius pronounce. There are rival interpretations: that this is a *peri homonoias* referring to the three corners of the island seems a considerably safer interpretation, which can always be 'fulfilled' by the slightest manifestation of disorder in Sicily; that it is a threat from the monster Typho imprisoned underground seems likewise a plausible attempt: there will always be subsequent volcanic activity: a three-headed hell-hound will fit the nature of volcanic eruption.[51]

Christian prophecy might range along the same lines. Antony the hermit is credited with clairvoyance of Arian violence which breaks out only two years later: he sees a vision in which the Lord's table is being defiled by the kicking of mules. But not only could so unspecific a vision be applied to a variety of other situations; it transpires quite incidentally that the Christian Bishop Serapion is actually present while the vision is taking place. He is of course reported by Athanasius as a reliable informant and first-hand witness. But are we to suppose that he has not been informing Antony on the development of tensions within the Egyptian church?[52]

In the case of astrology we have an art of prediction much more strictly tied to a fixed system. In the forms available by the beginning of our period it had a number of benefits to offer.[53] It was ancient, oriental and exotic, with roots in Babylon and a burgeoning branch in Egypt. It had a cosmic frame of reference, being concerned with the movements of stars in the heavens; and it had a scientific enough base by antique standards, claiming to interpret the influence of the unalterable course of the stars. Indeed it was far from being totally divorced from astronomy until as late as the eighteenth century. It had, moreover, acquired respectable philosophical connexions, in so far as Stoicism in particular would work hand in hand with a system which recognised the stars as divine helpers. Astrology was well placed to argue the possibility of stars influencing the destinies of men; and it could claim as readily as the Epicureans to free men from the influences of hopes and fears, this time through the acquisition of 'certain' knowledge of the future. Most important of all for its successful operation, it could argue that failures were the result of complexities in the operation of the science itself rather than the result of fundamental false premises in its conception. The famous potter's test of Nigidius Figulus was designed to demonstrate the difficulty of determining an exact point in the course of rapidly moving bodies.[54]

Moreover it was not divorced either from scientific prestige or from holiness. Ptolemy's *Tetrabiblos* in the second century AD attests to the enormous accumulation of serious astronomical labour that was yoked to the star of determinism: while Vettius Valens in the same century could easily elevate his commitment into a kind of cosmic consciousness:[55] the link between the astral regions and Gnostic and Neo-Platonic systems should not be difficult to understand.

A further specialised kind of prophecy was offered by apocalyptic or eschatological outpourings. These were endemic to Judaism and the Near East in general, where curses of the fate of cities had a long history. And they operated particularly effectively in a climate of tension on any thirst for revenge for injustice. All the evangelists and Paul from their respective viewpoints can find room for apocalyptic elements.[56] And discouragement against predicting the time of the Second Coming put no restriction on preparation for it, a factor which doubtless contributed to the speed of Christian missionary enterprise in the first century AD. The message was writ large in the Book of Revelation, which appears to employ *vaticinatio post eventum* to refer to persecution under Domitian as if prophesied under Vespasian. But the Christian examples belong to long-nurtured expectation: the Essene prophecies are already in the field, and throw light on the potent conjunction of Messianism and millenarianism, capable of being triggered by a sense of unrest or disaster and compounding it in turn.[57] It may well have been the oracle of Hystaspes, with its promise of a king arising out of the East, that contributed to the immediate causes of the Jewish War – and ironically produced the emergence of Vespasian, indeed a 'King from the East'.[58] The period of the Parthian and Marcomannic Wars and the plague produced more, including the Montanists' claim that the Second Coming was to take place in Phrygia.[59] So, predictably, did the increased instability of the mid-third century. The *Thirteenth Sibylline* is very specific about the political circumstances surrounding Uranius Antoninus and Odenathus of Palmyra: read with the *Twelfth* it gives the impression that all

Imperial history is ending with the emergence of a great man in Syria.[60]

But it is in the nature of things that eschatology, unlike astrology, could not be elevated into a continuing science. Each practitioner had only one chance to 'get it right', after which he stood to lose total credibility when the moment passed. The techniques of apocalyptic wisdom were easily accessible, and easily raised into a façade of fearful uncertainty. Reference to previous prophetic expectation, description of current unrest, prophetic language, interest in injustice and revenge, and a promise of salvation after repentance: such a combination will successfully launch an apocalyptic initiative. Techniques of numerology should, moreover, invest the other elements with an air of pseudo-scientific certainty.[61] Eschatology could of course be reversed by the notion of the return of a golden age: Virgil's *Fourth Eclogue* requires no further commentary. But Oenomaus of Gadara in the second century AD could complain of receiving an oracle with golden age elements from Clarian Apollo; while Diocletian was able to exploit a similar relationship with Saturn.[62] Indeed the emphasis of Jesus Christ on the coming of the Kingdom can be read as both: ever-present or already arrived in the easy converse of a god with men; or as some future coming to judge the quick and the dead.

A particular boom is noteworthy in the second century in the science of physiognomonics, and here again the subject was accessible from shrewd guesswork and literature. It was at least as old as a treatise by Antisthenes; two others were attributed to Aristotle;[63] the conviction that deductions about character and indeed events could be made from facial expression or gesture was as much a commonplace in antiquity as it quite properly remains. Of Catiline Sallust had observed: *colos ei exanguis, foedi oculi, citus modo, modo tardus incessus; prorsus in facie voltuque vecordia inerat* ('his colour was pale, his eyes horrible, his gait sometimes fast, sometimes slow: such madness was betrayed by his demeanour and expression').[64] The problem arises when intuitions or random observations made in specific contexts are reduced to a system or pseudo-system. The sophist Antonius Polemo is able to accept that racial characteristics will be capable of character deduction, as will resemblance to animals, quite apart from actual physical characteristics such as the shape of the chin or position of the eyes.[65] In subscribing to such principles, he unfortunately does not distinguish them from what we might call commonsense observation. While at a wedding he observes the odd behaviour of the bride in her collusion with a man other than the groom; he predicts an elopement which duly takes place. The important point is his facile ability to attribute his success to his art – a claim not far removed from the techniques of Calasiris in Heliodorus' novel when noting the behaviour of lovers.[66] While there is nothing specifically holy about the technique or its context, it was an obvious weapon in the armoury of a holy man; and anything that could be worked out by such means would be attributed to the supernatural skills and perceptions of the practitioner.

The same kind of virtuosity is in due course claimed by Porphyry for Plotinus; he is able to identify, merely by looking at him, the slave of his house-guest Chione, who had stolen her necklace; and his diagnosis is confirmed by subsequent confession. Or he could diagnose how a character would turn out: that his disciple, another Polemo, could be inclined to amours, and short-lived, as turned out to be the case. And Plotinus sent Porphyry himself away for a rest cure when a depressive illness was turning him to thoughts of suicide.[67]

By far the most all-embracing categories of skill attributed to the holy man by his detractors is magic.[68] The Elder Pliny offers an astute appreciation of its appeal:

Let no one be surprised that it has enjoyed such enormous influence, since it has been the only art to embrace three other arts that are themselves highly influential over the human mind and bring them under its own single control. None will doubt that it was first born out of medicine and that it insinuated itself under the pretext of offering health under the guise of a more exalted and holier system; hence by the gentlest promising of what everyone wants, it added to itself the powers of religion, over which even today the human race is completely in the dark; when it had also succeeded in this, it added astrology as well, since no one is not eager to hear what the future has in store for him and everyone believes that it is most reliably sought from the stars. Hence it has held human feelings in its threefold grip and grown to such a pitch that even today it prevails over a great part of the nations and in the East rules over the King of Kings.[69]

Pliny's following sketch of the 'evolution' of magic might well be fanciful invention;[70] but the astuteness of his analysis of the combination of forces is sound, like Lucian's perception of the source of

Alexander of Abonouteichos' success. Pliny next comments, with puzzlement rather than scepticism, on the alleged antiquity of the art and the uneven distribution of evidence (absence from the *Iliad*, frequency in the *Odyssey*). He notes the prestigious patronage it has enjoyed from Pythagoras, Empedocles, Democritus and Plato, all of whom travel overseas to learn it.[71]

We have a further useful *aperçu* of the interrelationship of magic and intellectual activity in the defence speech produced by Apuleius in the mid-second century, in response to an actual charge of magic. Again flexible parameters are the natural defence:

And so I should like to ask his most learned advocates what a magus is. For if what I read in most authors is true, magus is the Persian for our word priest: what crime is there in the end in being a priest and having proper acquaintance, knowledge and skill in ceremonial law, correct rules for sacrifice, or religious codes, at least if magic is as Plato presents it when describing the training with which the Persians imbue their young princes: I recall the very words of that divine man: 'A Persian prince is entrusted to four . . . and one of these teaches him the *mageia* of Zoroaster the son of Oromazes; and this magic consists of worship of the gods. And he also teaches him the arts of rulership'?

Do you hear, you rash accusers of the art, that it is an art accepted by the immortal gods, most expert in the materials of worship and of prayer, a pious art that understands divine manners, a noble art ever since the time when Zoroaster and Oromazes established it, and high priestess of the celestial powers? Of course it is one of the first matters for the instruction of princes, nor do they indiscriminately admit a person to be a magus, any more than to be a king.[72]

Then follows a similarly equivocal testimony: Plato quotes Zalmoxis to the effect that magical charms are merely beautiful words: 'If that is the case', Apuleius protests, 'Why should I not be allowed to learn the fine words of Zalmoxis or the priestly lore of Zoroaster?' (And if magicians are so powerful anyway, how could accusers possibly risk acccusing them?) Apuleius implies that the charge of magic is brought against natural philosophers (Anaxagoras, Leucippus, Democritus, Epicurus and others), who explore the origins and elements of material things. In addition there are accusations against those 'who investigate with greater precision the universal providence and employ more diligent devotion in the worship of the gods (as if they know how to enact everything they know to be performed). Such men were Epimenides, Orpheus, Pythagoras, and Ostanes in olden times, and then a similar suspicion fell on the "purifications" of Empedocles, Socrates' demon, and Plato's Good.[73]

Apuleius[74] comes round at great length to the accusation that he had commissioned the acquisition of a fish: he points out that it was for purposes of dissection: a rare fish not noticed by authorities on marine biology with twelve interlinked bones in its belly. But he retains the vital link that can act as the source of all such accusation: are augurs to be allowed to explore the livers of victims and may not a philosopher look at them too, a philosopher who knows that he can draw omens from every animal, that he is the high priest of every god? But for these investigations, together with the reading of Theophrastaus and Nicander on bites and stings, he claims Platonic authority for their amusement value; this is a dilettante pursuit proper to a second-century sophist.[75]

Apuleius was also accused of using a boy medium for purposes of divination (the boy himself having collapsed in his presence). He points out that the boy was already a recognised epileptic; but *en passant* he lets slip two other pieces of information:

> Why should I use a charm, when, as I read in writers on natural history, the burning of the *gagates*-stone surely and easily affords proof of the disease? The scent of this stone is commonly used to test the soundness or infirmity of slaves at the slave-market. Also, the spinning of the potter's wheel will readily infect a man in the same condition with a giddiness of its own, so does the sight of its rotations weaken his already infected mind; and the potter is far more potent than the magician for inducing convulsion in epileptics.[76]

If these facts were common knowledge, they were accessible to anyone who might wish to induce trance-states. Hence the magic wheel in the *Zauberapparat* of a magician.

The pursuit of magic entailed the use of a special category of the software of holiness, in the form of talismans: a substantial cross-section of our subjects resort to their use at some time or other. Accordingly we find Alexander of Abonouteichos prescribing a form of words to be used as a protection by his clients during the plague – with dire effect, perhaps because of the complacency the victims had built up: they consisted of a single line: Φοῖβος ἀκειροκόμης λοιμοῦ νεφέλην ἀπεϱύκει ('Unshorn Phoebus wardeth off the plague-cloud').[77] And Apollonius of Tyana appears in the non-Philostratean tradition as a consistent purveyor, particularly in Byzantium, against various classes of pestilence,[78] as well as being credited with a specific work on the subject of talismans.[79] Nor did Christianity in itself put an end to the practice: we find Gregory Thaumaturgus for one providing that rare thing, a ticket of admission for a demon to let him back into a temple.[80]

CHARLATANISM AND CREDULITY

Some charlatans were easily enough exposed. There was a prophet in AD 166 who delivered oracles from a wild fig-tree in the Campus Martius, to the effect that fire would fall down and the world would end when he should fall from the tree and change into a stork. In fact he fell out of the tree at the appointed time, and freed a stork from his clothing. He was simply pardoned.[81] Lucian for his part conjectured that Alexander's golden thigh was of gilded hide, gleaming in the light of torches.[82] But such exhibits are contemporary with the treatise γοήτων φώϱα, ('the exposure of charlatans') of Oenomaus of Gadara:[83] the time was right and the market was there. And much in the climate of belief could be readily sustained by simple methods, many of which were at least known to the more sophisticated sceptics.

Hippolytus' *Refutatio* from the succeeding century contains an impressive inventory of what we might call the hardware of γοητεία. Two motifs are prominent: the provision of quasi-miraculous distractions and atmospheric effects, such as the faking of thunder or even an earthquake, or the famous 'drawing down of the moon' by means of double reflection from a light source into a bowl of water and thence on to a reflecting surface;[84] the means whereby animals can be induced to kill themselves, presumably so that the 'operator' can claim to be killing them at a distance;[85] or of making a skull talk, doubtless a desirable adjunct to necromancy.[86] But no less important is the business of writing down material on a sheet so that it disappeared or appeared to be burnt, but could then be re-read, thus giving the operator prior knowledge of a client's request; by similar means answers could be made to reappear of their own accord.[87] Yet it should be emphasised that, even if exposed, some such tricks would have been regarded as defensible. To all intents writing that disappears is actually proof rather than disproof of miraculous operation, and constitutes a kind of proto-chemical 'wisdom'. Any deception will lie in the arbitrary association of such techniques with invocation of a deity in order to enhance the illusion.

Apuleius provides one of the most vivid accounts of a fluent deception in operation, together with the religious paraphernalia used to support it, all in full swing:

> After we had stayed there just a few days, burdened with their public munificence, and stuffed with the cash from our constant divination, those purest of priests [of Atargatis] invented a new source of gain; for by means of one single lot inscribed to fit every eventuality they made a mockery of a great many in the following manner. This lot went: 'to this end those oxen plough the earth, that in the rich crops it may germinate bounty for the future'. If one had perhaps demanded whether he should make a good match, they would claim the corresponding response: that they should be tied and joined in matrimony, and conceive a crop of children; if someone asked about the prospect of buying possessions, they said that it was appropriate for oxen, and that the yoke should announce a field flourishing from his sowing; if anyone should ask divine auguries when anxious about setting out on a journey, they said that these gentlest of beasts were already yoked and prepared and profit was promised from the sowing of the soil; if one were about to go into battle or hunt down a band of robbers and should ask whether it was profitable to proceed or not, they argued that victory was declared by powerful presage, since the necks of the enemy were about to submit to the yoke, and they would capture a rich and fruitful supply of booty from the thieves' ravages.[88]

Not only does the flexibility of so basic a metaphor as 'ploughing oxen' ensure success; the fact that the priests of Atargatis are itinerant protects them from the worst consequences of responses going wrong.[89]

Oenomaus of Gadara is reported as having tested the oracle of Apollo at Claros and received a similar experience. The same oracular response was delivered in answer to a number of different enquiries. What is particularly interesting is that the content of the oracle was itself similar to that of Apuleius' version: 'In the land of

Trachis lies the fair garden of Heracles containing all things in bloom to pluck every day, and yet they are not diminished, but with rains continually their weight is replenished'. This reply was not only given to an enquiry connected with commerce from Oenomaus himself, but was also given to Callistratus, a merchant in Pontus, and others in various walks of life.[90] It does not take too much ingenuity to see how cleverly the reply is balanced between raising the hopes of the enquirer and insuring the deliverer against some unforeseeable disaster.

VERSATILITY

It will be clear that the holy man equipped for every eventuality will have acquired a wide variety of the foregoing skills: not for nothing does Peregrinus evidently change his name to Proteus,[91] or local tradition credit Apollonius of Tyana with himself being the reincarnation of the same god.[92] Hippolytus gives us a portrait of Alcibiades of Apamea, who provides in Rome a combination of forgiveness of sins, circumcision, and metempsychosis (so that, for example, Christ could in theory be reborn in Alcibiades himself, though this is not itself stated); he offers other Pythagorean material such as incantation for the bite of a mad dog, exorcism, and the like; to these attractions were added millenniarist-style prophecy and astrological lore. The whole package was claimed as a revelation from a sacred book revealed from heaven by an angel of fantastic dimensions, the Son of God vouchsafed to a just man Elchasai: the book came from Serae in Parthia, and was passed on by him to one Sobiae.[93] Such resonant authority aside, Alcibiades evidently appreciated the advantages of 'something for everyone'.

The Elder Pliny notes similar versatility in his own early acquaintance Apion the grammarian:

> he revealed to me that the herb *cynocephalia* known as Osiritis in Egypt, was a divinatory plant and a prophylactic against all kinds of sorcery, but if it were totally uprooted the digger would die instantly; he confessed that he had called up ghosts to enquire from Homer the identity of his home country and the names of his parents; but that he did not dare to divulge the answers he said were given.[94]

We also have a particularly precise account from Lucian on the expertise of the oracle-monger Alexander of Abonouteichos. He had been, Lucian alleges, the lover of a follower of Apollonius of Tyana, 'One of those γόητες who promise enchantments, miracle-working incantations, charms for love-affairs, 'sendings' against enemies, disclosures of treasure-troves, and successions to estates'. To Lucian the very name Apollonius indicates enough said: but he does let slip that the man was also ostensibly a public physician, which at least implies a degree of recognition and accreditation:[95] medical oracles accordingly loom large in Alexander's own repertoire.[96]

Whatever disciplines a holy man chose to combine, he had to cultivate a versatility of a wider sort, the art of appearing all things to all men. Paul's protest about his balancing act between Jew and Gentile tells its own story:

> For I am a free man with no one as my master; and yet I have made myself a slave in the service of all men, to gain all the more converts. And I became as a Jew to the Jews, to win over Jews; to win those under the law of Moses, I put myself under that law, although I am not myself under it. To win those outside the law, I put myself outside the law, though I am not outside God's Law, but under the law of Christ. I become weak in the eyes of the weak in order to win over the weak. I have become all things to all men so that by all possible means I may save some.[97]

No less essential than versatility was a basic common sense and discretion: the holy man must often be prepared to make shrewd and skilful judgements from a slender array of available facts, and allow his inspired guesswork to be seen as inspiration. For example, Apollonius detects a rich Cilician who sacrifices extravagantly to Asclepius in proposed atonement for an inexpiable crime of incest.[98] Or so it seems, from Philostratus' telling. But in fact no supernatural communication is seen to be involved on Apollonius' part, though the priest who alerts him to the circumstances has a vision warning him of them. All Apollonius has to do is confirm the priest's suspicion that something is amiss, a matter already apparent from the fact that the sacrifice has not proceeded through the proper channels. The priest makes enquiries, then has the dream about the background of the culprit.

Or again, when Gregory Thaumaturgus is set up by demands for money from a prostitute, he resists the obvious trap – of dissociating himself from the woman, which would merely have ensured that he would remain under suspicion. Instead he insists on paying her – and she is duly punished with a seizure.[99] A silent and shrewd appeal to human nature is required and offered. Sometimes on the other hand a wider knowledge of the local situation will help. When Amoun of Nitria is confronted by the parents of a child bitten by a mad dog, his reply is 'Give back to the widow the ox which you have killed surreptitiously, and your child will be restored to you in good health'.[100] Even if the child does not recover, the saint can get himself off the hook: the father's misfortune will be put down to the crime the saint had on him, rather than the saint's shortcomings as a healer.

One final important component of the holy man's demeanour is authority itself. We are familiar with Jesus Christ's distinct mode of 'speaking with authority' in the synagogue, and arousing amazement.[101] Apollonius of Tyana is no less positive; when established he sees it as his business no longer to ask questions, but to teach what he has discovered: in answer to the question how should the sage converse, his answer is 'Like a lawgiver, for it is necessary for the lawgiver to make over to the many the instructions of whose worth he has persuaded himself'.[102] And the tradition surrounding Plotinus has the sage announcing that spirits ought to come to him, not he to them – a statement which is supposed to astound his biographer.[103]

So much, then, for the equipment in skills and techniques that the holy man could acquire in order to engage and satisfy his clients, or warn them of the wrath to come. But one overriding skill – and the ultimate instrument of authority – was at a premium throughout antiquity: the art of communication by means of the spoken word. Everyone from the most silent sage to the most slickly sophistic salesman of religion had to have it, and that is what we must now proceed to examine.

5

ACCLAMATION
The rhetoric of revelation

Holy men needed to 'get their message across' in a society where the normal mass medium was the spoken word. Few words could be more effective within the given space than the alleged dialogue of Apollonius of Tyana with the Spartans:

> When he arrived they asked him 'How are the gods to be worshipped?'. 'As masters'. And again they asked 'What about the heroes?'. 'As fathers'. Then they asked a third question, 'What about men?'. 'Not a Spartan question' . . . . And when they asked what advice he would offer about courage, 'Why, to display it of course'.[1]

Simple epigrammatic statements could go far towards affirming and enhancing a holy man's operations; and the simpler, the more memorable. We find Alexander of Abonouteichos' homespun rites including the traditional initial formulae of exclusion to mysteries: 'If any atheist or Christian or Epicurean has come to spy on the rites, let him be off, and let those who believe in the god perform the mysteries under the blessing of heaven'; it only takes such a formula to confirm the new god Glycon among legitimate deities, and to provide an element of exclusiveness. But traditional formulation soon becomes a more sinister instrument: Alexander says 'Christians out', while the crowd acts as a chorus to reply 'Epicureans out'.[2] There is more of the same to face when the Ephesians in the theatre maintain their chant 'Great is Diana of the Ephesians' for two hours on end in protest against the inroads of the Pauline mission.[3]

One kind of 'wisdom' was relatively easily come by, and might be said to require the least specialised skills. A holy man might make his mark by trafficking in a basic species of inherited folk-wisdom.

When Hadrian puts questions to the 'silent' Secundus such as 'What is man?' or 'What is death?' he receives gnomic, not to say enigmatic replies ('The mind encased in flesh', νοῦς σεσαρκωμένος; 'the desire of the afflicted', ταλαιπωρούντων ἐπιθυμία).[4] Such a style could also be taken up by more versatile practitioners; Philostratus tells us that Apollonius of Tyana had a manner that was close to oracular.[5]

Such equipment is ultimately oriental, in the sense that it embodies and could transmit some of the most ancient known attempts to come to terms with fundamental questions of existence. By our period *gnomae* of the Seven Sages would hardly constitute satisfactory philosophical explanations or answers. But they could still be elaborated by philosophical discussion, or they could be passed off as embodying authority rather than reason. Philostratus is well aware of the prestige conferred by simple 'authority';[6] Jesus Christ makes his initial mark on synagogue teaching in this way,[7] and Justin finds relief in Christian authority after his prolonged pilgrimage through more rational systems that turn out to be in conflict.[8]

The 'Q' source of the Synoptic Gospels contains a substantial stratum of sayings in which a popular type of wisdom is dispensed. For example, the saying 'Can the blind lead the blind? Won't both men fall into a pit?'[9] appears in a context of several similar sayings ('a pupil is not above his teacher . . . no good tree produces bad fruit, nor in turn does a bad tree produce good fruit').[10] What has to be noticed about wisdom of this kind is its versatility, as when a saying can be applied in a number of different contexts, to all of which it can add an air of moral certainty; and its instant applicability to the known world of the hearer, like Socratic similes of dye-working or cobbling. But such sayings can often contain an element of question-begging value judgement. If a sage says 'Can a blind man lead a blind man?', he might be felt to be saying no more than 'My opponents are blind; I am clearsighted; follow me!'. Even the claim about teacher and pupil is not strictly valid on its own terms: there are incompetent teachers and precocious pupils. More elaborate statements extended to the level of parables have a similar limitation: the gospel parables of the labourers in the vineyard and the three servants with their talents embody contrary principles which it would be more difficult to sustain at the level of logical argument.

We should note that much of the material known to us as parables of Jesus Christ will in many if not all cases have belonged to a common oriental stock of *exempla*: we are familiar with the tradition of the rich man's banquet, to which none of the invited guests turns up; accordingly the invitation is changed to include all and sundry from the highways and byways, the meaning being that the invitation of Jesus Christ is extended beyond the elite of Israel. A second banquet-story has the wise and foolish virgins awaiting the arrival of the bridegroom at some indefinite time. But we find the Pharisee Yohanan ben Zakkai using a similar tale of a bizarre banquet which is not identical with either parable but contains elements of both. This time the King invites his servants to a banquet and does not name the time: the wise come and sit at the palace door, while the foolish ignore the whole business, reasonably arguing that there is never a banquet without a set time. The King suddenly appears, and allows only those dressed for the banquet to share it.[11] We should suspect a common repertoire of teaching stories round basically familiar life-situations, capable of being redirected in accordance with the message of the moment.

Some paths to wisdom could be shrouded in a cloak of mystery. At first sight the Christian parable of the sower or the lighted lamp looks like the typical Socratic analogy drawn from daily life. But it is another matter when we are told

> And when his disciples kept asking the meaning of this parable, he replied, 'To you it has been granted to perceive the mysteries of the Kingdom of God; but to the rest they are in parables, so that even when they see they may not see, and when they hear they may not understand'.[12]

It is very difficult to see this as anything other than a distinction between secret teaching for an inner circle and so unintelligible to the rest, subsequently and incongruously 'explained' with a more detailed allegory, perhaps an extended gloss by the early church.

Out-and-out allegorical techniques by nature have a mystical appeal, and one notes a number of examples accessible to holy men during our period. The *Allegory of Prodicus* could always be used as an exhortation to virtue, and a versatile one: the two women between whom Heracles had to choose can be varied and decorated in any number of ways.[13] Rather more ominous is the version in which Paul asks the Galatians to interpret the offspring of Hagar as the Old Law and the child of a slave-girl and the New Christians as the offspring of Sarah in the New Law representing freedom from restraints of circumcision and the law. The arbitrariness of such use of allegory is patent, but its occurrence in the New Testament itself ensured a long and inglorious history as a handmaiden of any revelation its author might be pleased to purvey. But it is in Gnostic speculative theology that the notion of verbal keys to unlock the mysteries of the universe come into their own: the hours at which the labourers in the vineyard are sent (first, third, sixth, ninth, eleventh) add up to thirty, as do those Gnostic stand-bys the Ogdoad, Decad and Duodecad: thirty aeons can be established by one or other and confirmed by the second. Well might Irenaeus inveigh against such procedures – until he himself uses them to prove that there can only be four gospels as there are four chief winds.[14]

At the other end of the intellectual spectrum from perverted ingenuity, a holy man's wisdom might equally well consist in studiously anti-intellectual posturing. Paul quotes scripture to the effect

> I will destroy the wisdom of the wise, and set at nought the cleverness of the clever. Where is the wise man, where the man of letters, where the skilled investigator of this present age? Has not God made a fool of the wisdom of this world? For it is God's wisdom that the world has been unable to recognise Him through wisdom, but He deigned to save believers through the folly of the Gospel. And He chose to save those who have faith by the folly of the Gospel. Jews ask for miracles, Greeks search for wisdom, but we proclaim Christ.[15]

But it is difficult to sustain any argument at all consistent with such an attitude, and soon after Paul is no more consistent than Irenaeus was to be, when he claims 'I utter God's wisdom wreathed in mystery, his hidden purpose which he framed before the ages began to fulfil our glory'.[16] But both positions have two things in common: simplicity and sonority.

Verbal wisdom could attain to a still more mystical level when allied to the potency of the magical. When called on to exorcise a ghost at Corinth, Lucian's Arignotus the Pythagorean is made to say 'I spoke Egyptian, and employed my most frightful ruse, and drove him into a particular corner of a dark room'.[17] The magical papyri, both Greek and Egyptian demotic, give us some idea of the sort of flourish that might be entailed. A central preoccupation of these documents is the parade of deities and cult-titles that identify the force to be summoned. When Alexander of Abonouteichos wished to make an impact on his fellow citizens, 'by uttering some meaningless words like Hebrew or Phoenician he dumbfounded the simpletons, who did not know what he was saying except this one fact, that among it all he mixed in Apollo and Asclepius'.[18] The miracle of languages at Pentecost establishes 'speaking in tongues' (in some sense) at the very foundation of the early church, though the account of it in Acts conjures up rather the impression of a spontaneous translation service rather than the normal sense of possibly unintelligible ecstatic utterance.[19] The event might be taken as a symbolic story intended to convey the universal appeal of the new *kērugma* of Jesus Christ; but that in itself would not preclude some basis of fact behind the puzzling presentation. The words of the Lucan account deserve closer scrutiny, however: if one chants the vowels in random order it is not too long before one may hit on IAO, a 'sacred' configuration identified with Yahweh.[20] It may have been the very potency of spontaneity that turned the whole business of speaking in tongues so quickly from a post-resurrection novelty to an embarrassment to the emerging church establishment. For what was ideal for ecstatic apostles of an infant church might prove no less so for aspiring heresiarchs. A useful impression of the more conventional sense of speaking in tongues was afforded by a defensive passage of the early second-century *Didachē*:

> And as every prophet delivers his utterance inspired by the spirit, you are not to test him or pass judgement . . . but not everyone who is so inspired is a genuine prophet, only those who show the ways of the Lord. It is from their behaviour that you will be able to tell the false prophet from the real thing. And any prophet calling for a meal while possessed will not eat from it; if he does then he is a fraud. And every prophet who teaches the truth, if he does not do what he teaches, is a false prophet; and every prophet who is accredited and genuine, who reveals some cosmic mystery to the church, if he does not teach others to do as he does, you must not judge him: his judgement is in the hands of God . . . . And if anyone says while possessed in a trance, 'Give me money', or something else of the sort, do not listen to him. But if he tells you to give it to others who are in need, nobody is to criticise him.[21]

The implication of such a passage is clear; a trance state will sanctify quite mundane communication with divine or supernatural approval, and anything intelligible within a framework of unintelligibility will be enhanced and can be acted upon. The *Vision of Hermas* purports to have a similar frame of reference. In the midst of allegorical scenarios representing the state of the church we have injunctions of a different and more immediate sort, as that addressed to one Maximus promising affliction if he should 'deny a second time' (in the context of the persecution in Rome in the 90s?); and answers to specific questions (does a man sin if he continues to live with a Christian wife who is an adulteress? And what if he should remarry, or if a widowed Christian should marry for a second time?).[22] The mystical and the mundane are readily allied as instruments of control.

For just such a reason Paul cannot conceal his suspicion and denigration of ecstatic speech: in Gentile Corinth it poses a threat to any attempts at regulation of a growing Christian body. The apostle offers enough details to afford us some picture of what is on offer:

> To one man, through the Spirit, is given words of wisdom, to another through the same Spirit is given words of insight. To another, by the same Spirit, is given faith; another by that single Spirit is offered gifts of healing; another is given the power to work miracles; another is able to prophesy; another has the capacity to distinguish between different spirits; another again has the gift of tongues of different kinds, and another the ability to interpret them.[23]

But it is not long before this range of assorted expertise is modified into a hierarchy:

> Within the church God has appointed first apostles, then prophets, then teachers; next miracle-workers, then people with the gifts of helping others or guiding them, or the gifts of tongues of various kinds: you should aspire to the more important of these gifts.[24]

But the more such rankings are emphasised, the more we can infer the appeal and popularity of what they are meant to suppress. The ideal medium for effective prophecy is the combination of partial or likely fulfilment with an element of mystical sonority. Alexander of Abonouteichos advertises himself with typical vagueness: 'On the shores of the Euxine Sea in the neighbourhood of Sinope, there shall be born by a Tower, in the days of the Romans, a prophet'.[25] This is followed by a more esoteric enigma in which the name is spelled by a standard technique of *gematria*, by assigning standard numerical values to the letters $(1 + 30 + 5 + 60 = alex)$; and the solution is then more clearly hinted at in the final line of the oracle (the fourfold equivalent of a man who defends, i.e. *andros alex-ētēros* = Alexander). The conundrum is just mystical and just specific enough.[26]

But it is in the realms of magical spells that the sonority of rhetoric is most effectively coupled with mysticism: one might note not only the characteristically pretentious rhetoric but also the polyglot air of *PGM* 13.139–61: after a pretentious enough pre-amble in Greek 'I call on you who surround all things, I call in every language and in every dialect, as he first hymned you who was by you appointed and entrusted with all authorities, Helios ACHEBYKROM'; we have interjections in hieroglyphic, Hebrew, hieratic and 'bird-glyphic', with generous admixture of threefold groups of three-vowel sequences, and the Abrasax cryptogram.[27] The standard religio-magical principle of leaving nothing out creates a babble as impressive as it is unintelligible.

HOLY LETTERS

But holy men have tasks to perform, and obligations to communi-cate, which require plainer speaking. Letters are an indispensable part of any literate holy men's engagement in any but the most local activity. The surviving examples are too heterogeneous to allow easy generalisation: it is perhaps easier to say that they simply reflect the variety of levels of sacred utterance the holy man will require to produce in any case. One notes the relevance of letters, especially final letters, addressed to whole communities at a time: Peregrinus has his testamentary communications and last exhor-tations and regulations sent out by his 'messengers from the dead' and 'runners from the underworld'; the author of the Book of Revelation is no less dramatic in his responses to the Seven Churches of Asia.[28] But often again a cryptic arresting quality will convey an oracular tone and authority, especially in the case of sharp rebukes: at least a cross-section of the letters attributed to Apollonius of Tyana are of this order,[29] though we may be dealing in this case with extracts from larger units.[30] By contrast letters of Paul reflect the pressures of a missionary situation: broad theologi-cal issues jostle with immediate rivalries and self-justification,[31] day-to-day problems of the growing church communities with doctrines of a Cosmic Christ.[32] Eschatological expectation does not leave too much time for leisured literature. Others could be a good deal more direct, especially under the considerably greater pressures of the militarised state in the later Empire. Isidore of Pelusium writes to an Egyptian official:

> It is a custom among men, even if it is alien to divine laws, to take pride in many things – birth, wisdom, possessions, good looks or rank, and yet there is no benefit from pride for those who are of mortal clay and return again to it. The fact that you are completely lacking in all these qualities, not even you would deny. If then, you have nothing to be proud of, being a beggar of lowly birth, a deformed fool and a complete nonentity, why do you strut through the city as if you commanded more prestige than anyone else, the author of many a commotion? So either know yourself and adopt a manner that fits your own worthlessness, or prepare yourself for hard work and personal risk, in return for which the authorities will reward you.[33]

The technique of the rhetorical *psogos* – invective refined into a literary art-form – is available and was put to use. Its opposite, the encomium, was no less readily cultivated. 'Sacred rhetoric' encompassed the writing of hymns to deities as a literary genre.[34] The ceremonial occasions on which addresses to gods might be required such as religious festivals or the opening of temples would have been at their height in the prosperous decades of the first two centuries: it is not altogether surprising to find detailed prescriptions for the writing of prose hymns included in the Pseudo-Menander *peri Epideiktikōn*, most probably at the end of the third:[35]

> The scale of 'klētic' hymns is larger in poetry, because poets are allowed to mention many places, as we often find in Sappho and Alcman . . . poets are also allowed to describe the places themselves . . . . The poets' klētic hymns are therefore inevitably long. Prose-writers, on the other hand, must necessarily abridge the time spent on these topics. Rather they will follow Plato, who sets the pace in his use of the form: 'Come, ye clear-voiced Muses, whether it is for your song or for your musical Ligurian kin that you learned that name'.

Such conceptions might suggest a wholly perfunctory attitude towards religious experience: a series of religious 'pretexts' for self-indulgent sophistic rhetoric. Even the prose hymns of Aristides are patently conceived to score theatrical points, as when he assures us that 'The Sons of Asclepius alone are without rivals both in the number and excellence of their ancestors, since they are superior to those descended from Zeus and Apollo, as many of these as are heroes, of course by the addition of Asclepius to their ancestry'.[36]

But such techniques are not necessarily inconsistent with traditional piety. In his *Sacred Tales*, Aristides makes not infrequent reference to his own compositions in honour of Asclepius and other gods.[37] In that writer's own eyes they are clearly not display-pieces, but genuinely devotional exercises on the part of the deeply pious man who happens also to be a fully-fledged sophist. In some cases Aristides may actually dream his hymns first; or someone reports to Aristides as having dreamed that he performed one of the sophist's Paeans. On hearing this, Aristides promptly dedicates it to the appropriate gods.[38]

A sophisticated extension of this species of wisdom will take us into the familiar territory of philosophic rhetoric. We find Smyrna exhorting that 'it is more gratifying for the city to be crowned with men than with porticoes and paintings'.[39] Public edifices remain in one place, whereas good men are able to magnify the city wherever they go. The Zeus of Phidias is confined to the spot; that of Homer ranges freely. On the more immediate subject of faction he enjoins the paradox of 'a mixture of *homonoia* and *stasis*'; 'white and black could never be one and the same, nor could bitter form a healthy blend with sweet; but concord and party spirit can combine for the salvation of cities'.[40] The classical exponent in this vein is Dio of Prusa, a sophist turned philosopher, ready to turn his hand to a myth of the heavenly city in his discourse to an earthly one.[41]

Often a working holy man will find himself switching rhetorical registers in the course of his efforts to persuade. Paul uses a combination of popular parable-style excursuses combined with more sophisticated theological argument:

> You will say, 'Then why does God blame a man? For who can resist his will?'. Who are you, sir, to answer God back? Can the pot speak to the potter and say: why did you make me like this?'. Surely the potter can do what he likes with the clay. Is he not free to make out of the same lump two vessels, one to be treasured, the other for common use?[42]

Still more elaborate is the simile of the Gentiles as the wild olive grafted on after the dead Jewish branches have been lopped off.[43]

Elsewhere, however, the technique is that of standard Graeco-Roman rhetorical schools:

> 'We are weak, you are so powerful. We are in disgrace, You are honoured. To this day we go hungry and thirsty and are in rags; we are roughly handled; we wander from place to place; we wear ourselves out working with our hands. They curse us, and we bless; they persecute us, and we submit to it; they slander us, and we make appeal'.[44]

Antithesis, climax, tricolon and paradox are the servants of holiness, as readily as they were servants of the assemblies or the courts.

Finally, holy men could make their mark with full-blown theological orations. The most celebrated survival is the presentation in Acts of Paul's speech on or to the Areopagus.[45] There is little about either setting or content that has not been a matter of dispute, and it is almost always a forlorn hope to expect authentic verbatim reporting in anything which purports to be historical narrative in Antiquity. That is not to say that its contents are utterly implausible for a speech of Paul to the audience in question, but the most we can safely suppose is that it represents what the author of Acts writing much nearer the end of the first century would have expected Paul to have said to a sceptical and sophisticated Athenian public. What we have then is a near-contemporary version of 'the holy man delivers a *peri theōn* in Athens'. Paul notes Athenian piety in the worship of the gods by way of traditional courtesy and *captatio benevolentiae*, but has allegedly seen an altar inscribed to 'the/an unknown god'; this enables him to appeal to local piety and establish a knowledge of local antiquities.[46] He then describes the independence of God and his creation of the universe, with due quotation from Aratus. Worship of man-made images is unworthy; and judgement will come through a man raised from the dead.[47]

The message draws on what purports to be actual observation in Athens: a foreign visitor brings information about a local cult, and most of the content relates to a monotheist picture of creation that Stoics at least could feel as familiar: the Hellenistic ethos of the speech has long been noted, as has its well-chosen common ground with Judaeo-Christian assumptions.[48] Only in the last two verses, having secured the possibility of assent so far, does Paul add Christian apocalyptic and judgement: Christ is seen as a man raised from the dead, again a concept scarcely unfamiliar to an audience brought up on Heracles and Asclepius.

Whatever the precise relationship of his theology to both Old Testament and New, the skill of the operation should not be in doubt. Paul seizes on a matter on which Athenian theology has admitted defeat – the identity of a god (or gods?) yet unknown, and proceeds to a revelation, counting on Athenian 'love of novelty'.

It is noteworthy that not only Paul seems to draw almost a blank in Athens, but Apollonius of Tyana, much better equipped to tell a pagan audience about the best way to worship the gods, may have done little better. While Philostratus indicates the large amount of material on 'Apollonius at Athens', he chooses to reveal very little of it. This seems strange for a visit that should have been the centrepiece for so Philhellenic a philosopher; and we have the right to remain suspicious.[49]

But we do have important pagan speeches from the early Empire on the relationship of worship to images of the gods, addressed to a philosophically literate audience: Maximus of Tyre is useful for his treatment of a similar subject to that of Paul's Areopagus speech. But this time the kind of presentation would have been more likely to win the favour of the Areopagus itself. Maximus' sophistic showpiece Εἰ θεοῖς ἀγάλματα ἱδρυτέον ('Should one set up statues to the gods?') belongs to the mid-second century AD, but the materials themselves are a pastiche of well-worn commonplaces.

After an arresting first line, Ἀρωγοὶ ἀνθρώποις θεοί, πάντες μὲν πᾶσιν ('helpers to men are the gods, all unto all'), we are given *inter alia* different occupations and their gods, or the human need of images, not the divine: their variety ('The Greeks saw fit to honour the gods with the finest things: pure material, human shape, and precise workmanship; and not without reason do they think fit to set up statues in human likeness: for if the soul of man is nearest to God and most like him, is it not surely right to surround it with what is more like itself, the divine?').[50]   Then follows a rather less rapturous list of the practices of other nations: 'Should we not say to the Persians (as fire-worshippers): "Most foolish of men, ignoring so many such images, the gentle earth, the bright sun, the navigable sea, the teeming rivers, the nurturing air and heaven itself, why do you spend all your time on the wildest and fiercest of elements?" '. The barbarous customs of the Egyptians, Libyans and the rest follow (the Celts worship Zeus, but as an oak tree).[51] Maximus can then come in with his Platonist master-stroke:

'For God, the father and artificer of being, is older than the sun and heavens, greater than time and age and all moving nature, nameless to the lawgiver, unspeakable to the tongue, unseen by eyes; unable to apprehend his being we depend on voices and names, and living beings and impressions of gold and ivory and silver, and plants and rivers and mountains and streams'.[52]

And finally Maximus accepts their usefulness: 'Let all the nations know the divine, that it is one; and if the art of Phidias arouses the Greeks to the remembrance of god, the worship of animals the Egyptians and a river others, and fire others again, I do not find fault with their differences. Let them only know, let them only love, let them remember'.[53]

The author of this piece is not doing much more than going through the motions, and joining together conventional strands of received wisdom, as a glance at his performances on any other subject is likely to confirm. But sometimes sheer weight of rhetoric will do something to suggest the sincerity of its proponent. The language of compulsory panegyric and invective can scarcely be better illustrated than by the treatment of Gregory of Nyssa and Tertullian of a single topic, the *ecphrasis* (formal description) of the Black Sea:

> For who does not know the nickname applied to the Black Sea by all men of this race, a name which testifies to the virtue of those who have had the region as their home from the beginning? For alone of all land and sea this ocean is called the Kindly Ocean, whether the name testifies to the kindness shown to strangers by those who live on its coasts, or whether it is also because it lavishes the wherewithal for living not only to those who live in the region, both settlers and natives, but to those who come to it from every quarter.[54]

Hence, argues Gregory, it is a fitting environment for Gregory Thaumaturgus: the flamboyant expansiveness of this highly sophistic working gives a flourish to the triumph of Gregory's subject, his namesake's transformation of the region from pagan to Christian. But rhetoric is as neutral as ever: Tertullian had been able to present the same region as the no less fitting background to his arch-villain Marcion:

> The sea known as 'Euxinus' ('Hospitable'), has its name belied

by its nature. Its name is a joke . . . as if ashamed of its own barbarism it has retired from our kinder waters. The fiercest tribes inhabit it . . . their desires are promiscuous . . . . They carve up the corpses of their fathers along with the cattle and gorge on both at their banquets (*Parentum cadavera cum pecudibus caesa convivio convorunt*) . . . women have lost first the modesty, then the gentleness, of their sex . . . . Because of the ice rivers are rendered rivers no longer. There is nothing warm there except savagery – that infamous savagery I mean that has furnished the theatre with stories of Taurian sacrifices, love-affairs of Colchians, and crucifixions in the Caucasus. Yet nothing is so barbarous and ill-starred in Pontus as the fact that Marcion was born there, more horrific than a Scythian, more unsettled than a waggoner, crueller than a Massagete, more insolent than an Amazon, darker than fog, colder than winter, more brittle than ice, more treacherous than the Danube, more precipitous than the Caucasus.[55]

It is difficult to decide whether Tertullian's rhetorical over-indulgence is worse than his ignorance of geography: but there is again no disguising the flamboyance, or the sheer entertainment value, of his opening.

Holy men, then, can mobilise words as well as skills in the service of their impact on society. With so much sonority reverberating from market-places and missives alike, it is small wonder if some of them, like Paul at Corinth, might occasionally seem to fall short of their proclamation when they actually appeared. We must now at last bring our holy man face to face with his public in some real situations.

6

ACTION
Display and intervention

Equipped with his own particular brand of wisdom, and a suitable means of self-expression, the holy man could feel ready to reveal himself to his public.[1] He could choose to do so simply by speaking in the open on a sacred subject:

> It is almost three years since in my first days at Oea I gave a public address on the majesty of Asclepius, in which I made these same declarations and gave a tally of all the rites I knew. That discourse attracted a huge crowd, is read all over, and is in everyone's hands; it has found favour with the people of Oea not so much because of my eloquence as because it speaks of Asclepius.[2]

Only the place, Oea, would serve to betray that such an utterance comes from Apuleius and not from Aristides or Alexander of Abonouteichos: in Roman North Africa no less than in Asia Minor a religious topic will draw a crowd, particularly if a healing deity is in question. And it serves to underline the importance of propaganda and self-projection for any who aspire to a high religious profile. Others could go a good deal further, in some cases clearly over the line into charlatanism. Hippolytus mentions the story of Absethus, whom he presents as a Simonian-style Gnostic. After previous attempts to secure his own deification had failed, this enterprising operator is said to have collected a number of parrots, and taught them to say, 'Absethus is a god', letting them loose in different directions. A Greek then beat him at his own game by reprogramming some of the birds to say, 'Absethus, having caged us, compelled us to say "Absethus is a god" '. The impostor was then burned alive by the Libyans.[3]

If such a story has an air of *ben trovato* about it, the same cannot

be said for Lucian's vivid if unsympathetic account of the preliminary advertising and public relations of Alexander of
Abonouteichos in the inception of his oracle:

> Arriving in Chalcedon . . . they [Alexander and his com-
> panion Coconnas] buried in the temple of Apollo, the most
> ancient in Chalcedon, bronze tablets which declared that very
> soon Asclepius, together with his father Apollo, would be
> moving to Pontus to take up residence at Abonouteichos.
> Thanks to the opportune discovery of these tablets, this tale
> easily travelled to all Bithynia and Pontus, and far sooner than
> anywhere else it reached Abonouteichos. In fact these idiots
> voted right away to erect a temple and at once began to dig the
> foundations . . . . Alexander was sent in first; he now had his
> hair long, falling down in ringlets, and he was dressed in a
> two-coloured tunic of white and purple, over which he wore a
> white cloak; he carried a dagger in the manner of Perseus,
> from whom he claimed his descent on his mother's side.[4]

Meanwhile Alexander's accomplice Coconnas was left behind in
Chalcedon maintaining the supply of oracles:

> And so, by invading his native country with all this dramatic
> panache (μετὰ τοιαύτης τραγῳδίας) after a long time away, he
> was a figure of note and distinction; he pretended to have the
> odd fit of madness, filling his mouth with foam. This he easily
> contrived by chewing the root of the soapwort, the plant used
> for dying; but to his audience even the foam seemed divine
> and awe-inspiring.[5]

Having got ready in advance a goose-egg blown to contain a
serpent,

> Next morning [Alexander] leapt out into the market place in a
> state of undress, wearing only a loin-cloth (even this was
> gilded), carrying his now-familiar dagger, and tossing his
> loose head of hair the while as the devotees of the Great
> Mother do in their frenzy. He climbed up on a high altar and
> addressed the populace, congratulating the city for being so
> quick to receive the god's manifestation. As for the audience –
> for almost all the city, women, old men and boys and all, had
> come running – they stood agape, prayed and did their
> obeisance.[6]

Here the physical appearance of the holy man is an important part in the creation of his image: one notes the no less striking portrait of Mani in the polemical *Acta Archelai*:

> Now that same day Mani arrived, bringing with him chosen young men and women, to the number of twenty-two at one time; and first of all he looked for Turbo in front of Marcellus' doors. When he could not find him, he went in to greet Marcellus. When the latter saw him, he admired first of all his dress and clothing; for he had a kind of footware commonly called three-soled; and a multi-coloured cloak that looked like the heavens; in his hand too a very stout stick of ebony wood. A Babylonian book was under his left arm; he had covered his legs with breeches of different colours, one red, the other greenish; his face seemed like that of a Persian craftsman and general.[7]

A similar concern for staging may be discerned at a less elaborate level in the baptism of Jesus Christ by John the Baptist: one holy man formally advertises, then recognises, another,[8] as in the case of Coconnas and Alexander of Abonouteichos. The Mark-author's placing of the episode is particularly important. It is abruptly set at the beginning, with the credentials of John himself fulfilling a prophecy of Isaiah: the incident is clearly intended to guarantee Jesus' own position. And there is no less dramatic effect in the narrative, however it could have been realised in fact.

Apart from appearing on such dramatic occasions of their own choosing, holy men could enhance their image by appearance at (or even withdrawal from) the established public festivals. Philostratus makes Apollonius of Tyana appear at Olympia after his miraculous deliverance from Domitian.[9] And Lucian for his part gives a good account of the publicity organised for Peregrinus before his suicide at Olympia in AD 165. He has the event announced immediately after the previous Olympic Games of AD 161; and at the current festival his associate Theagenes further orchestrates the affair with a preliminary advertisement:

> Proteus, who was put in prison in Syria, who gave up five thousand talents (!) in favour of his native land, who was banished from the city of Rome, who is more radiant than the sun, who is able to rival even Olypian Zeus . . . but now this holy image is to take its departure from the world of men and

go to the gods, riding on the wings of fire and leaving us bereft.[10]

On the other hand Apollonius of Tyana can be made to make a calculated impact by turning down an invitation to the Olympic games: 'I would be present at the sight of bodies competing, if it did not entail my withdrawing from the greater competition of virtue'. The next letter appears to give a clue to the context: thanks to the games, it appears, the Peloponnesians are no longer enemies but are not yet friends. Apollonius also predictably objects to sacrifices at Olympia: the Pythagorean purist can always project himself as holier than even the most sacred of occasions.[11] Or a conspicuously successful holy man could of course go a step further and found festivals of his own. Alexander of Abonouteichos consolidated the dramatic spectacle at the foundation of his oracle by instituting a three-day festival of Glycon, patterned on the more august and familiar mysteries of Eleusis.[12]

But we also have instances of conspicuous sanctity displayed and acknowledged in private:

Even from the time of his birth Plotinus had some extra quality. An Egyptian priest came to Rome and made his acquaintance through some friend. This priest was anxious to give Plotinus a display of his 'wisdom' and asked for him to be present at the manifestation of his own familiar spirit. Plotinus willingly complied. The summoning took place in the temple of Isis, for the Egyptian maintained that that was the only pure place he could find in Rome. But when the spirit was summoned to manifest itself, it was a god who appeared, and not a mere daimōn. At this the Egyptian exclaimed 'You are blessed indeed to have a god as your guardian spirit and not a familiar of the lower ranks!'. But there was no opportunity to put any question to the manifestation or even to look at it any further, because the friend who was participating with them in the 'viewing' strangled the birds that he held as a precaution, either out of envy or out of some sort of panic. And so Plotinus, having a more divine being as his guardian, continued to direct his divine eye up towards that being.[13]

The anecdote is inherently interesting for its selection of (puzzling) detail, and as the cornerstone in the case that Plotinus himself favoured theurgy.[14] But it may have a different light to throw. It illustrates two familiar themes of religio-magical practice: things go wrong just before anything can happen that will make or break the operator's reputation, as happens in Lucian's sorcerer's apprentice story.[15] Commentators do not perhaps sufficiently countenance a totally fraudulent performance by the priest and the 'friend' working in collusion: Plotinus could have been shown some luminous phenomenon (traced on the wall in luminous paint or the like, and activated by a shift in the light), then cut off at this impressive point by the 'accident' – since Plotinus was presumably a shrewd and sophisticated observer. The incident might then have gone unquestioned because it so obviously flattered the enquirer.

Recognition at a shrine features also in the annunciation story of John the Baptist: his father Zechariah is struck dumb on entering the sanctuary to burn incense, and recovers only after insistence on the name John for the child. Whatever the explanation of the incident, such as a stroke and recovery, the matter is taken to be momentous: ('and in all the upland region of Judaea all this news was the topic of conversation; it made an impact on those who heard it, who asked "So what will this child be?" '). Such an incident can hardly have originated as propaganda as such; but retrospective interpretation could easily have allowed it to redound to the prestige of John.[16] The simple clairvoyance given by Jesus Christ to the woman of Samaria has a similar effect: the fact that he knows the number of her husbands – an obvious matter of common gossip – spreads the word for him:

> So the woman left her water-pot and went off into the city, and said to the people, 'Come here and see the man who told me all I ever did' . . . many Samaritans were convinced by him of the strength of the woman's report.[17]

In neither of these two cases was there intentional propaganda instigated by the holy man himself. Yet it is worth noting that a number of prescriptions of holy men for apparently other reasons could be turned into a form of self-advertisement. When Apollo at Claros demands a statue of himself to be set up in a community as an apotropaic for a plague (especially if it is to be at the city's entrance),[18] his oracle is storing up prestige for the future and reminding the community whom to trust in any subsequent emergency.[19] Moreover, the *prophētēs* of an oracle could use it to advertise himself: it is not too surprising that the 'god' Glycon at Abonouteichos was quick to extol his 'controller' Alexander:

Honour I bid you bestow on my servant the prophet,
No great care do I have of possessions, but much for the
prophet.[20]

Of the same order is the kind of self-advertisement at Didyma for
the *prophētēs* Titus Flavius Ulpius, who uses his office to extol
himself and his ancestry, or Ulpius Athenagoras, who actually
claimed the highly unusual distinction of a spontaneous oracle,
otherwise unknown for shrines of Apollo in historical times. Nor
was Apollo's offspring Asclepius lacking in the reflexes of self-
publicity: he prescribes as part of his healing instruction that his
client Apellas should write down the procedure for his healing.
Given the intellectual framework, there was mutual benefit to both
enquirer and shrine. The cure would redound to the prestige of the
god; but it was also a special mark of divine favour to the recipient.
Both accordingly stood to benefit from its wider advertisement.[21]

Moreover, oracles could lend support to individuals or less established oracles. Alexander of Abonouteichos did not enjoy a monopoly of their patronage. When Apollonius returns from India
Philostratus gives him the support of oracles: 'Those from the
oracle at Colophon enthusiastically declared that he shared its own
brand of wisdom and was consummately wise'. Similarly he has
patients referred from Didyma and Pergamum; one notes the oracles that were to support Alexander of Abonouteichos two generations later.[22]

Any change in matters divine can be commemorated in inscriptions as well as announcement. We have one such in which a third-
century priestess of Demeter, one Alexandra, asked the god why,
ever since she had taken up her office, the gods had been appearing
in visitations as never before to girls and women, but also to
children and boys. She may be conjectured as making genuine
enquiry;[23] but it is still difficult to dissociate her gesture from a
propaganda coup for the priestess herself. Now that she is priestess,
the gods are really on the move.

MIRACLES, POWERS, PROPHECIES

But whatever his powers of self-advertisement and self-publicity, or
his activation of other advertisers, a holy man had to stand or fall by
his public performance. There was no point in employing one who
could do nothing about famine, earthquake or pestilence in practice.

The most obvious way for an operator to achieve success was in medicine and its fringes, to which divine power could be readily allied. Isis, Asclepius or Yahweh could be invoked, and demonic control was common to both cultures, as we have seen. And any bona fide physician would easily be invested with an aura of divinity: Pliny's sarcastic aside against Asclepiades has much to tell: *universum prope humanum genus circumegit in se non alio modo quam si caelo demissus advenisset* ('He surrounded himself with almost the whole human race as if he had dropped down from the sky', *NH* 26.12–20). Exorcism was a dramatic business, yet its prospects of success were at least promising in the short term. All one has to do is to have had a sharp encounter with a mentally unstable person who has subsequently calmed down, and one has cast out a devil. Thereafter the operation could be embellished in a variety of ways, and we have promising cases for comparison across a wide spectrum of our materials.[24]

Philostratus provides a detailed and plausible account of an exorcism. A young wag pokes fun at the pedantry of Apollonius' regulations for sacrifice. He is proclaimed to be possessed. As he is exorcised he throws down a statue; the young man is calm, and becomes an enthusiastic supporter.[25] Of course we can say with hindsight that such an account is self-fulfilling: a fit of pique and a calming down is interpreted and explained by a standard belief in the existence and operation of malevolent demons. But even Philostratus admits that not everyone took the same view of such an event; some merely thought that the victim's behaviour was a result of youthful high spirits.

New Testament accounts of exorcism do not differ substantially from the pagan accounts of Philostratus or even Lucian. The shared belief in disease-causing demons common to Jews and pagans ensured that they should not. The spirit 'recognises' Jesus Christ; it is then rebuked and reduced to silence. It comes out 'throwing him into convulsions and shouting with a loud voice'.[26] Again it is clear that the parameters used to establish authority and recognition are comfortably wide. The holy man brings off an impressive performance; someone in the audience exclaims 'You must be the Son of God!' Either the acclamation can be allowed to stand, in which case it 'confirms' the fact that the holy man is recognised; or the holy man, anxious to dissociate himself from such exaggerated claims, takes them to be the words of a devil, and accidentally as it were exorcises his own admirer – thus confirming his perception of evil and ability to silence it – and so 'confirms' the authority he is properly trying to deny. Or he turns on a cynical heckler and turns the crowd against the latter by identifying the heckler as possessed by a devil – and his own reputation is once more enhanced accordingly. There were further refinements. Jesus Christ, it is claimed, 'would not allow the demons to speak, because they knew him'.[27] If his clients acknowledge him, they are demons and their ceasing to speak is construed as 'being cast out'; if they do not speak, they are not allowed to speak. Either way the belief in a non-existent category of beings allows them to be interpreted in a manner favourable to the holy man.

Sometimes we can recognise another type of problem behind what a source will routinely present as an exorcism. Philostratus presents Apollonius as driving out a demon in India.[28] The spirit in question claims to be a man whose wife married another soon after his death, and will bring a woman's child blessings if not reported. The possessed victim, a boy of sixteen, speaks with a man's voice and goes out into the desert. It may be that all Apollonius is addressing is a teenager in revolt; the 'devil's voice' is the normal voice break at puberty; the boy's claim to have a devil may not have been more than a cock-and-bull story manipulating parental belief; as a demonically possessed victim he can get away from his mother's apron-strings and be himself. He threatens suicide (the devil threatens to put the son into a pit or over a precipice). But another explanation is possible within the limits of the elliptical narrative provided by Philostratus. We are told that the devil is in love with the boy; is the latter then in some homosexual relationship with a second party who has concocted the story about being a devil who hates women to enlist sympathy, with supernatural promises to placate and silence the distraught mother? Apollonius for his part is ready with an epistle presumed to contain threats against the ghost. There is no follow-up study for such a case: the threats may have been designed to scare either the boy or any 'demonic' lover. It may be that the kind of threats had the desired effect for circumstantial reasons. A mysterious stranger produces a spell in partly unintelligible language. The boy calms down; the demon is deemed to have left him; or the homosexual partner is warned off by an ominous alien presence. We simply do not know enough about the case.

It is exceptionally rare to have the opponent or victim's view of such an exercise. Yet we know that Lucian visits Alexander of Abonouteichos and insults him, secure in the knowledge of having brought a military escort. But he notes the level of local fanaticism. Alexander holds his henchmen in check and promises to transform enemy into friend. In a private interview with Lucian, he promises to do a deal: he can advance Lucian's prospects in the eyes of his own powerful patron Rutilianus. In any case Lucian sees the safer course, and emerges as his friend. 'And it seemed no small miracle to the beholders that I had changed my mind so readily.'[29] If nothing else this passage shows how, in the eyes of a sceptic, a combination of religious and political patronage and/or pressure could be applied. Subtle intimidation (only Alexander can avail to hold his followers back) produces an all too necessary change in Lucian's behaviour for the moment; but Alexander 'scores' another miracle in the process.

More impressive than routine exorcism is the raising of those thought to be dead, sometimes by remote control. The classic account is the healing of Jairus' daughter by Jesus Christ. The patient is reported first as ill, then as actually deceased. The healer himself asks for faith without having seen her – only later are we assured that she is not dead but sleeping. She is then taken by the hand, addressed, and revived.[30] Philostratus presents a closely similar incident from the repertoire of Apollonius: the latter asks the name of the 'dead' girl (in this case from a consular family). He touches her, whispers something – the name, one might assume; and makes over the reward as a dowry to the girl. But Philostratus' rationalisation is of the utmost importance, as it at least suggests a clue as to how such 'resurrections' could have been rendered possible in the first place. 'And as to whether he discovered a spark of life in her, which had escaped those who were caring for her – for it is said that as it was raining at the time, the vapour was visible as it rose from her face – or whether he had restored her life which had actually been extinct by applying warmth – the solution cannot be determined, and puzzled the bystanders as well as the narrator' (*VA* 4.45). This manner of reporting clearly implies that the possibility was raised at the time, and that the debate and the event may have been transmitted together. It also suggests of course that Apollonius did not see fit to make the company any the wiser.

Nor are Christ and Apollonius the sole practitioners of this kind of operation. Apuleius is the not surprising purveyor of an account of a 'medical resurrection' (so to speak) from the first century BC; the Epicurean philosopher-physician Asclepiades comes upon a funeral at which the deceased has been already embalmed and prepared for cremation: he raises a hue and cry when he detects symptoms of life. The sequel is important for such 'resurrections'. Not all the crowd either trust Asclepiades or share his concern, and there is even the suggestion that *captatores* do not wish the man to return alive. Apuleius glosses the matter as 'reclaim from the underworld'. But any will to bury the apparently dead as quickly as possible with no questions asked must have increased the total of possible 'resurrections'.[31]

Only in the case of a Jewish example do we have any suggestion of how the holy man actually felt his own instinct to be operating:

> Once the son of Rabbi Gamaliel fell ill. He sent two scholars to Rabbi Hanina ben Dosa to ask him to pray for him. When he saw them he went to an upper chamber and prayed for them. When he came down he said to them: 'Go, the fever has left him'. They said to him: 'Are you a prophet?'. He replied 'I am neither a prophet nor the son of a prophet, but I learnt this from experience. If my prayer is fluent in my mouth, I know that he is accepted; but if not, I know that he is rejected'. They sat down and made a note of the exact moment. When they came to Rabbi Gamaliel, he said to them: 'By the temple service! You have not been a moment too soon or too late', but so it happened; at that very moment the fever left him and he asked for water to drink.[32]

One must respectfully presume that when confronted with a terminal cancer or appendectomy Hanina would have found his prayer a good deal less fluent in his mouth, and hence with a means of backing off from a less surmountable challenge.

There is just a hint of distance healing in a pagan text of the period. When one of Demonax's friends suggests that the pair of them go to the temple of Asclepius to pray for the friend's son, Demonax gibes: 'You think Asclepius is totally deaf, if he can't hear our prayers from here'. There is not the element of confident prediction here, but if the boy recovers the effect will be the same: the sage does not need to move to effect results.[33]

In some cases we may suspect that there is some significance in the timing of cures by remote control. We are told in the case of Jesus Christ's healing of the official's son 'that the fever had gone from him the previous day at the seventh hour'. But since it was common belief that the seventh hour was the critical time for any fever, all the potential healer has to know is when the fever began;

'foreknowledge' and medically informed prediction will then be enabled to coincide.[34]

'Raisings from the dead'[35] need not in any case have been confined to resurrections as such: they might also encompass the consultations of the dead for specific purposes. It is worthwhile to note that necromantic technique was available to a second-century pagan or a fourth-century Christian alike. In Lucian's *Philopseudes* we find a Hyperborean magus who brings up a boy's father to grant his permission for a love-affair;[36] in Apuleius the Egyptian Zatchlas is on hand to elicit a dead man's account of his murderer;[37] he proves his case fully by disclosing information only he could have known. Heliodorus provides a chilling consultation of a dead son by his mother, an Egyptian witch.[38] On the other hand in a story in Rufinus' version of the *Historia Monachorum* we find that Macarius, faced with an innocent murder suspect demanding sanctuary, arranges for the corpse to be consulted: it exonerates the victim.[39] But the holy man in this case does not ask who the real murderer is: his standing seems to require a delicate equilibrium, or he is insufficiently informed, and will not risk a suspicion of his own; or he deems it wiser to let sleeping dogs lie.

Other operations claimed for holy men are no easier to explain on available evidence. One cannot help noticing the prominence in Near Eastern materials in general of a kind of display for which no single satisfactory explanation exists, but which is prominent in the repertoire of holiness. This is the phenomenon of the miraculous meal.[40] The gospel miracles – with their respective doublets[41] – consist in the number of baskets of waste, inferred from, but not explicitly tied to, the small number of loaves and fishes available for distribution to a crowd of thousands. The explanation of a symbolic Messianic banquet is a plausible one.[42] But it is particularly necessary to note how readily such a gesture may have multiplied into a miracle. In Luke's account there is no allowance made for the possibility that some of the crowd took and shared out supplies of their own, not necessarily with the knowledge of the disciples.[43]

But it may not be necessary to attempt to explain the phenomenon away; the pagan world clearly knew of similar feats. Celsus describes the ability of holy men to produce the illusion of miraculous meals, and the Lamia at Corinth encountered by Apollonius of Tyana had a similar facility.[44] A knowledge of ancient pharmaceuticals seems the obvious starting-point for some kind of answer, conceivably a hallucinogenic plant; but a satisfactory specific solution continues to escape us.

A different kind of sustenance miracle is described in detail by Irenaeus to the discredit of a Gnostic enemy: he names one Marcus, 'a most experienced operator of magical deceit', who has won over disciples 'as one possessed of the greatest wisdom (*gnostikōtatos*), and possessing the greatest power from the unseen and ineffable regions'. He performs a pretended sacrament in which the blood of Grace seems to drop into a cup through his invocation, and enables 'Grace' to flow from a smaller into a larger vessel. This makes him appear a *thaumatopoios* to the deranged women participating in the rite.[45] Such a feat seems to demand either a concealed reservoir, or a concentrated preparation which is able to dilate inside the larger vessel. But the important contribution of Irenaeus' description, vague as it is, is the emphasis on the theatrical presentation of Marcus' sacrament. Again it should be emphasised that the feat would have been no less miraculous for having a physical or chemical explanation known in advance: chemical or physical wisdom could have been claimed as *gnōsis* in its own right.

Scarcely less opaque is the kind of experience represented by the transfiguration accounts in the Synoptic tradition. Jesus Christ goes up with Peter and John to a mountain. As he is praying his face seems to change and his raiment becomes dazzling white: Moses and Elijah appear in glory and speak of his imminent departure at Jerusalem. Peter and John are just awakening and enveloped in mist, and a voice is heard from the cloud; nothing is disclosed at the time.[46] The Synoptic tradition precedes this episode with discussion and prefiguration of Christ's suffering; here such material seems to have been transferred to a visionary context around a week later. Jewish Merkavah mysticism provides a framework of belief, but does not rule out the physical explanations which would reinforce it. The acknowledgement that Peter is drowsy, coupled with the suggestions implanted in the disciples by the previous week's discussion, actually lends some air of authenticity to the proceedings. Think of Moses, Elijah, and a Christ who promises departure. Go to the place where oxygen is thinnest, and you will be amazed at the effect. The context in which Christ is commended from within a cloud is here open to manipulation. A religious leader may suggest whatever he pleases in the middle of a mist to exhausted and preconditioned followers. The possibility of a Brocken Spectre can scarcely be ruled out either. But the admission that the experience was not reported at the time can only enhance the degree of suspicion that such an incident must in any case attract.

One further conjunction of activities calls for consideration: the use of miraculous displays to reinforce the authority of doctrinal statements. One notes Jesus Christ's reluctance to provide signs on demand to the Pharisees.[47] That at least suggests that spectacular displays of religious power are called for before new doctrines can be felt to have been authenticated. In the apocryphal tradition the disciples have no such inhibitions: Simon Magus produces displays, and so must Peter, able to take a dead fish and revitalise it in water.[48] Such a conjuring trick is at least as old as the Egyptian adventures of Djedi;[49] while Hippolytus does not hesitate to attribute to Simon the conjunction of magician's tricks with philosophic exposition of a Gnostic system.[50] In the case of the miracle tradition surrounding Jesus Christ, it is not always easy to separate elements of display from 'non-display'. The narratives of the temptation are highly suspect, in the sense that the subject would be credited with supernatural powers whatever he does: he will be seen as a divine man or the like if he changes stones into bread, survives a death-leap, and is the servant of the prince of demons; and he is divine if he refuses, or fails, to do either of the first two operations.[51] Dissociation with some desert-dwellers who might have claimed to be able to do either (John the Baptist or some associates?) can be claimed as a victory over temptation.

PRIVATE SOURCES

But a holy man's reputation need not rest on spectacular *tours de force*; indeed these alone might invite a charge of showmanship or personal ambition, if not one of magic as such. Their effect could be enhanced by instances of helping the community at large in rather more down-to-earth matters, such as finding lost property. Apuleius cites a case from the late Republic in which one Fabius had consulted Nigidius Figulus over the loss of 100 denarii – traced partly to a hoard and partly to individual circulation – evidently by means of boys inspired by incantations. Were these the thieves-turned-snouts, terrified by the threats of the magician into revealing the whole affair?[52] We are not surprised to find Apollonius of Tyana involved in the discovery of treasure, though he may not have known of its existence in advance. A financially embarrassed client is persuaded by the sage to buy land, and it yields a profitable crop – and a buried treasure. Local tradition, not least the testimony of the grateful beneficiary, would have credited the sage with foreknowledge of both. But the story does illustrate the use of a holy man as a guide to investment.[53]

Alexander of Abonouteichos offered a service of detecting buried treasure or runaway slaves. Such operations could be all the more readily undertaken where so little would have been available by way of what we should call 'community policing'; the local holy man might well be the man best placed to detect crime; he will also have been the best placed to hear local gossip and anxieties. One oracle purports to reveal to a husband a conspiracy between his wife and his slave-lover to poison him, with names named and even the hiding place of the poison.[54] Or Paul's Epistle to Philemon could be devoted to a personal appeal over a single runaway slave. Perhaps our clearest testimony on how such a service worked can be gained from a much later incident in the Byzantine *Life of St Theodore of Sykeon*. A man came to the saint to report that his son had run off with funds belonging to the church. Theodore's role is really confined to being told about the theft and exacting from the father a promise not to punish the son: that way the latter can at least be persuaded to come home. As to detection, the son behaves in a suspicious manner – running around in circles while lost in an unfamiliar community; these gyrations are noticed and he is turned in, but this behaviour is put down to the prayer of the saint. On such a flimsy basis it would have been easy enough for Alexander to have claimed similar success.[55]

A further function of 'community policing' will be the holy man's interest in cases of murder. An Epicurean challenges Alexander for having wrongly brought about an accusation for a murder that had not in fact taken place, with the supposed victim turning up only after the supposed perpetrators' execution. The matter reflects not only on the type of query that Alexander felt competent to answer: a young man has disappeared on a foreign tour: who is guilty? In fact Alexander does not necessarily condemn the man's servants, but brings about their trial before the governor of Galatia.[56] The real failure to allow for reasonable doubt may have been the court's, with Alexander merely pointing to the most obvious possibility to be explored. On the other hand the verdict could have been swayed by the local powers of the oracle in suggesting the accusation in the first place.

Less explicable mishaps are naturally also a matter for oracles and their operators. In the case of one enquiry to an oracle of Apollo, it has proved difficult to reconstruct a scenario. The god is asked about nine men who have died in a field. But Philostratus can give us a clue: he notes in passing a case in Lemnos where eight reapers had been struck by lightning, though here the marks of burning were clear enough.[57] Apollo in the present case attributes the mischief to Pan. Perhaps this is mere literary archaising, but more likely it was dictated by the fact that fellow-rustics from the field had initiated the enquiry. It may well be that Apollo has drawn a blank and is content to refer the matter to a more local divinity.

In a day-to-day context any of life's upsets could qualify for the attentions of a practitioner in esoteric skills. The eminent sophist Polemo gives a lively account of a case he witnessed at Perga in Pamphylia:

> Outside the city there was a temple known as the Artemisium, of great size and beauty and impressive construction, which men are wont to frequent for worship from far-distant regions. The dress in this country is for women such that each clothes herself in a great robe that covers everything and allows nothing to appear but the eyes and the nose. There among the women I saw one entering that temple, marked with the sign of the great ill about to befall her. And there was great amazement on the part of those I informed as to how I had made a judgement by observing her eyes and the type of her nose, when I exclaimed 'What a great ill will befall that woman!'. But there was a sign, that her nostrils and nose had become dark and her eyes troubled and excessively open and yellowing, and her head was moving a great deal and her feet were running about as if they were distracted by grief. You will not see these signs except in the insane, or rather you will be sure that ill will befall them. Already as I was looking there suddenly appeared to me another woman who had scarcely reached her, lamenting when she told her that her dearly-loved only daughter had fallen into a well at home and drowned [the woman is distraught and strips, compounding her misfortune with humiliation].[58]

One notes the presence of the diviner in the vicinity of a temple, though in fact nothing specifically sacred is involved. The deduction is merely a matter of common sense: the woman looks distraught. And although the case is claimed as a victory for physiognomonics, it is not that alone that should be given the credit, as Polemo claims. Although the women wear something like a shadur, he is not dealing with eyes and nose alone; it is the whole behaviour of the woman that gives her away, and one would hardly have needed the specialist skills of the physiognomist to guess that something was wrong; Polemo has in fact done little more than keep his eyes and ears open.

Many such skills would have been used in the context of private consultations reported only incidentally in surviving material. We have a good glimpse in an anecdote which the Younger Pliny tells against his contemptible rival Regulus:

> Verania, Piso's widow, was lying in a bad way . . . he [Regulus] actually sat down by her bed and asked the day and hour of her birth; when he heard he put on a solemn expression, fixed his eyes in a stare, moved his lips, worked his fingers, and did the sums. Not a sound. After keeping the unhappy woman in suspense for a long while, he announced: 'You are going through a period of crisis, but you will survive it. However, in order to make matters clearer to you, I will consult a soothsayer (haruspex) with whom I have had frequent dealings'. Without delay he performed a sacrifice and declared that the entrails were in accord with the stars. Feeling herself in danger, Verania believed him; she asked for a codicil to her will, and put Regulus down for a legacy. Soon she grew worse and died, exclaiming with her dying breath against the treacherous criminal, worse than a perjurer, for swearing her a false oath on the life of his son. Regulus performs this unscrupulous trick regularly: he calls down the wrath of the gods (which he himself evades day in day out) on the head of his unhappy son.[59]

The anecdote can tell us a good deal. The sharp practitioner is a well-connected all-rounder in high society; Pliny knows him as a disreputable advocate. Here he is practising not only astrology but haruspicy as well, on a 'client' still more elevated; her late husband had been adopted as an imperial heir, in which capacity he himself would have had every motive for consulting astrologers. What is interesting is the back-up: if Verania does not believe the stars, there are always the entrails; and both in turn are guaranteed by a particularly dangerous oath. The client is vulnerable, female and ill; and practice on Regulus' part habitual.[60]

But a holy man could not expect to spend too long in a community without gaining insight into its more general ills and preoccupations. As a matter of course he might be expected to take a strong moral initiative in the direction of social justice. The outpourings of Graeco-Roman moralists against the burdens and inequalities of riches or conspicuous consumption would have gained a more pressing perspective in a small and politically sensitive province such as Judaea. John the Baptist threatens the multitudes who come for baptism, using the analogy of fruit-trees to be burned for failing to produce good fruit: the haves are to share their food and clothing with the have-nots; tax-collectors are to collect only their due, soldiers are to be content with their wages rather than resort to robbery 'with recourse to violence or false accusation'.[61] And Peregrinus for his part stands accused of supporting a little-known case of social unrest in mid-second-century Achaea;[62] while Apollonius of Tyana is attributed with both social concerns and the capacity to take Roman power to task: 'Some of you have responsibility for harbours, buildings, walls and walks. But, as regards children in the cities, or young people or women, neither you nor the laws have any thought for them. Otherwise, it would be a fine thing to be governed by you'.[63]

But the holy man's position may not always be revolutionary or even consistent. Apollonius is just as likely to preach acquiescence: 'Poverty should be endured like a man, wealth like a human being',[64] a sentiment one might have heard as glibly from the morally ambiguous Seneca. Jesus Christ will recommend conspicuous acts of charity, by suggesting that the rich ruler should give his substance to the poor; or in another context will condone what the reasonably outraged Judas regards as frivolous waste.[65] Such contrasts are easy enough to extrapolate out of our meagre evidence; but in both cases we might suspect that the shrewd holy man must be allowed to judge the context for himself: it may prove more advantageous in the long run to indulge the whims of the very rich in the cause of more sustained long-term support.

THE HOLY MAN AND THE COMMUNITY

Over and above his action on behalf of individuals, the holy man can have dealings with whole cities at a time. That is where the great mass of mankind and their ills were concentrated, then as now; and where the assembling of crowds and the whole business of communications would have been fastest. The *Letters of Apollonius* at least wax eloquent on the prestige of Caesarea in the eyes of a travelling sage:

> In the first place men need the gods, for everything and above everything else, and next they need cities. These should be honoured second only to the gods, and every sensible man should put his city's interests before his own. But if we are talking not just about any city, but the greatest city of Palestine and the most outstanding of the cities of that region for its size, its laws, its customs, the bravery in war of its past generations, and even more, their behaviour in peacetime – as your city is – then it is the duty of both myself and every other man of good sense to hold it in awe and honour it above all other cities.[66]

Apollonius himself receives deputations 'from the cities, inviting him to be their guest, and asking him for advice about life as well as on the dedication of altars and statues, and he gave directions about various affairs, sometimes by letter but in other cases by promising to visit them'. Such visits might entail nothing more than curiosity: Smyrna evidently invites the sage 'to see and be seen'.[67] But the holy man has been able to establish himself as a civic consultant.

This function reflects the self-consciousness and limited independence of the cities themselves. It would have been as natural for a city in the early Empire to address enquiries to a holy man as it was and had long been to consult an oracle. It was proper to keep one's channels of commmunication with the gods and the supernatural in the best possible working order. If one's rites were open to inspection (and correction) then any divine favour to be had would be more accessible, and with it the city's increased status and prosperity.

Even Ephesus finds itself rebuked by Apollonius for its dancers, pantomimes, noise, and effeminacy;[68] the Spartans are not exempt from this last charge either, and Tarsus is in disfavour with him for its languid indifference and sensual indolence.[69] One thinks of Dio's rebukes to the Alexandrians, Tarsians, or Rhodians;[70] while Smyrna can be taken to task for the un-Hellenic use of Latin names.[71] And both Apollonius and Demonax protest at the practice of gladiatorial games in Athens, doubtless from a combination of humanitarian and cultural motives.[72]

The so-called *Letters of Apollonius* reveal what purports to be a cross-section of the likely activities of a single holy man in relation to cities. At one end of the spectrum there are the routine diplomatic courtesies: we are shown the sage accepting an honour of some sort from Caesarea Maritima, apparently hinting at its conduct in the context of the Jewish War; Apollonius does not seem to have visited the city personally.[73] His contact is one Apollonides son of Aphrodisius, who seems to have been entrusted to the sage as a pupil.[74] And we find, as we might expect, the sage received by his own community of Tyana; having won fame and glory, and the goodwill and friendship of outstanding cities and men, he now seems to be recalled (from an embassy?).[75] Other letters deal in various ways with the predictable topic of rivalry within cities: we have a *peri homonoias*, an exhortation to concord, addressed to the inhabitants of Sardis, who fall into factions tantalisingly named *Koddaroi* and *Xuresitauroi*.[76] In the case of Antioch the incidence of a local earthquake is used as an occasion for another such appeal.[77] In a mysterious world where all things are potentially sympathetic, a city torn apart literally will mirror a city torn apart politically.

The role of Apollonius as 'guarantor' of local antiquities also emerges incidentally in the *Letters*: the Sardians are rebuked for their local tradition about trees older than the earth, while Apollonius accepts their claim that the Pactolus could wash down gold.[78] In Smyrna Apollonius is shown the Panionian cup. He pours an appropriate libation over it and prays *inter alia* for protection against earthquakes.

But such relationships might turn out to be volatile, as Paul and Barnabas find at Lystra. Paul heals a man crippled from birth:

> When the crowds saw what Paul had done, they exclaimed, in their native Lycaonian, 'The gods have descended to us in human guise'. They called Barnabas Jupiter, and Paul Mercury, because he acted as their spokesman. And the priest of Jupiter whose temple stood just outside the city brought oxen and garlands to the gates, and wanted to offer sacrifice (to them) along with the crowds.

Paul and Barnabas frantically dissociate themselves from the proceedings, with an affirmation of the living God; the moment Jews arrive from Antioch and Iconium the crowds can be won over to stoning their lately-hailed divine visitors.[79]

But in general holy men could have the upper hand over cities. They are not disinclined to curse those who reject them. The gospels contain anathemas against those who do not receive the agents of Jesus Christ (though he himself rejects a 'fire and brimstone' response to a Samaritan village which has rejected him).[80] It has been suggested that Alexander banned oracles to people from his enemy Lepidus' city of Amastris out of inter-city rivalry as such.[81] But a simpler and more likely explanation is to put pressure on Lepidus not to attack him, thus barring his fellow-Amastrians from the privilege of consulting the oracle.

On the other hand what a holy man can do for a particular locality is well shown by Montanus no less than by Alexander of Abonouteichos. A Christian named Apollonius accuses Montanus of renaming Pepuza and Tymion, insignificant towns in Phrygia, as Jerusalem, in the hope of persuading people to gather there.[82] And the citizens of Neocaesarea were under no illusion about the prestige they could accrue from Gregory Thaumaturgus' association with their city; he accordingly declines in the first place to return.[83]

But it was in situations of natural disaster that holy men were most likely to be able to advise panic-stricken communities. Alexander of Abonouteichos was able to provide a hexameter talisman about Apollo for the great plague – only to risk inducing in Lucian's view a degree of complacency which had the opposite effect: the recipients of the oracle failed to take precautions and so fell victim to the outbreak.[84] The oracle at Claros furnishes a not dissimilar response to an unspecified plague, more than likely the same, to the settlement of Caesarea Troketta in Lydia, counselling water purification, the 'sprinkling of houses with nymphs who have become pleasant', and the provision of an apotropaic statue of Apollo.[85] The whole representation is a much more elaborate, polymetric performance, but was in response to an embassy; Alexander's was an autophone 'to all nations'. Similar responses from Claros to the great plague vary the prescriptions, but tend to insist on the statue.[86]

Against the background of a plague at Ephesus the episode of Apollonius and the beggar in the city represents a spectacular coup. Apollonius has been summoned to take charge during an epidemic. He assembles the citizens in the theatre where a shrine of Heracles *alexikakos* has been set up. He invites the (commendably reluctant) Ephesians to stone a beggar, who turns out on subsequent post-mortem inspection to be a devil in the guise of a huge hound. A statue of Heracles is set up on the site, and the plague is considered to have been purged.[87]

This bizarre episode serves to illustrate the exhibitionist nature of a holy man's activities; but also the sinister corollary that a mob can be manipulated, and a hagiographer conditioned, to believe in a self-confirming type of witch-hunt. In one respect Apollonius' actions represent sound ancient (and modern) doctrine on disease control: one has to isolate the source of infection in order to remove the problem; it does not much matter whether we call the source a devil or a virus. But the two 'proofs' that the beggar is a devil are actually induced by the actions of the crowd itself. The look of incredulous panic on the part of the innocent victim is read as the gleam in the devil's eye; and the mutilated remains by their very nature can be interpreted as anything the beholder pleases. One notes in the midst of horrific butchery Apollonius' customary etiquette to the gods; the affair takes place at the site of a shrine of Heracles, duly marked by a subsequent statue.

In some cases it might be suggested that the holy man achieves a result inversely proportional to his exertions. Philostratus notes several appearances of Apollonius in which the sage had only to maintain his Pythagorean silence and wait for the deadlock to break. This is implied to be an easy matter as regards normal faction over public entertainments: a look or a gesture from the holy man is enough to induce a sense of shame in the opposing parties. But Philostratus records in more detail Apollonius' impact during a bread riot: his silent presence both secures a hearing for the archon currently under pressure, and lets the profiteers off with no more than admonition: his rebuke is delivered in writing. The incident is perfectly credible as it stands; but it presupposes an already established reputation on the part of Apollonius. A less dramatic version of the same situation is known, of a bread riot facing Lollianus of Ephesus in Athens, only saved from the mob by a Cynic of few more words than Apollonius ('Lollianus sells words, not bread').[88]

We have an even more effortless feat, as well as an illuminating insight into the psychology of 'earthquake control', from the private meditations of Aelius Aristides:[89]

People dashed back and forward in a panic. The continual, fearful earthquakes were amazing. And on the one hand, they sent observers to Clarus and vied with one another to consult the oracle; on the other hand they held their supplicatory olive-branches and processed round the altars, the market-places and the perimeter of the cities; no one dared to stay at home. And in the end they gave up on their supplicating. In this situation the god commanded me – I was living in Smyrna, or rather in the suburbs, at the time – to perform in public the sacrifice of an ox to Zeus the Saviour. While I held back, since I was both suspicious and apprehensive of that previous prophecy, some notion occurred to me to this effect, that I was not to sacrifice a cow, and that I did not even need to taste it. But then I had the following vision, clear as day, and it gave me courage to perform the sacrifice. For I dreamt that while I stood at the very altar of Zeus in the market-place and was asking him to grant me a sign if it were better to sacrifice, a shining star zoomed through the market-place and sanctioned it. So I took charge and sacrificed. As to what happened next, the man who wishes to believe must believe; I have no time for those who do not. For all those earthquakes stopped, thanks to the service I was compelled to perform, and after that day there was no further trouble.

Aristides in effect credits himself with the cessation of the earth-quakes – with the implication that his gesture was efficacious where that of the normal oracles and supplications were not.

Perhaps the most elaborate and detailed glimpse of a holy man in any urban crisis is offered by the Byzantine tradition of Apollonius at Antioch on the Orontes. The sage appears in the city, where the local establishment persuade him to supply a collection of talismans, including those against the north wind, against scorpions, and against gnats. He invited the populace on the seventh of the month Daisios at the horseraces to brandish small wands surmounted by small leaden images of Ares, complete with shield and dagger, and cry as they went 'May the city be without gnats!', and to take the objects home with them afterwards – and never again did a gnat appear in Antioch.[90] Such a testimony is of considerable import-ance. It is the work of a chronicler who knows his native Antioch well, and is not dependent on Philostratus. He gives us just enough detail to enable us to broaden our picture of Apollonius' *modus operandi*. The sage is 'called in' by local aristocracy or officials, but Apollonius takes advantage of a local festival which will secure him the maximum publicity. He organises his *telesmata* on a large scale: the whole population are involved in the driving out of the gnats. If that is all, then indeed Apollonius would in a sense be practising magic, by organising a protective talisman. He is dabbling in theurgy, in the sense that the magician and his agents are trying to make the image of the god drive out the gnats, but is there something more to it? What instructions were there to follow up? Was there something in the composition of the talisman that was unattractive to gnats, and was that something brought into play by the continued uses of the apparatus domestically (to frighten the gnats with the noise, or simply swat them with a fly-swatter)? We should note that if the talisman as such is not the sole or real cause of the practitioner's success, it none the less serves as a visible piece of propaganda on his behalf.

But Apollonius does not push his luck. He is also faced with a request to restore a talisman set up by a philosopher Debborias under Gaius (a statue with an apotropaic inscription set up on top of a column); he turns down a request to produce a more permanent means of protection for the city. Approached a second time, he inscribes a tablet: 'Your lot, Antioch, is to mourn and this time you will suffer. A time will come when you will be laid low beneath great upheavals. Twice if not more, you will burn on the banks of the Orontes'. The tablet is given to the elders.[91]

This passage gives something like a context to an Apollonian 'visit' to a city. Here it appears that he is deterred by the failure of a previous talisman; he does not presume to repair or replace it. It may be that he has forewarning of further earthquakes in the future, and gains credit for predicting something already obviously about to happen. It also gives credence to the idea of 'letters' of Apollonius, in a prophetic context, of which there is further Byzantine evidence: Apollonius in effect gives an oracle on this occasion to the Antiochenes. And of course his prediction can never really be discredited; for all its starkness, the oracle does not specify the number of times, the scale of the conflagration, or the time-scale: two lightning-bolts starting small fires will be enough to fulfil it.

GOING OUT IN STYLE: THE HOLY MAN'S DEMISE

From the holy man's displays and actions we come to the ultimate convergence of both. Such an occasion undoubtedly provided opportunity for display. It was of course up to individual holy men how and to what extent the opportunity was used. But it should be stressed that for any practitioner with sufficient reputation in life, modesty in death was very difficult to secure – the more he might seek to avoid publicity, the more those around him might be tempted to impose it upon him. Antony the hermit retreats further into the desert with only two fellow-monks to attend his deathbed; Athanasius asserts that this is to avoid the Egyptian practice of venerating the bodies of holy men preserved rather than buried; these two are instructed to bury the body in an undisclosed tomb. But Athanasius still has to enhance the death (implausibly) with a deathbed homily to the two attendants;[92] while in the burial itself one infers comparison with the burial of Moses in an undiscovered tomb.[93]

The death of Apollonius of Tyana is scarcely devoid of the suspicion of having been 'orchestrated'. Philostratus quotes three local claims about the sage's death.[94] The first puts his demise in Ephesus as a prelude to the prosperity of one of his surviving handmaidens. There is no supporting evidence one way or the other, though it is conceivable that a source of Philostratus infers the sage's death in the city from the handmaid's connexions there. The other two incidents are interconnected; in both cases the sage is claimed to have disappeared within a temple, either of Athene at Lindus (without further detail) or of Dictynna in Crete.[95] In the latter case we already have a local tradition of Apollonius, quoted in VA 4.34. One can only draw attention to the tendency of rival cities to vie with one another in claiming prestigious connexions with prestigious figures: one thinks of the various sites claimed for the burial place of Antonius Polemo. In Apollonius' case it would have been perfectly conceivable for the sage to have died of natural causes during the course of a sojourn at the shrine, where he customarily took up residence. What goes without saying is that local priests would then have had a strong vested interest in claiming that so evidently prestigious a sage had departed this life from their own place of worship. By quietly disposing of the mortal remains they could have claimed a local 'miracle'. In the case of Apollonius and Dictynna there might well be more than meets the eye: the sage's last appearance is his departure into the temple after having been arrested as a suspected thief: one might well suppose that under such circumstances a holy man would storm back into the shrine – and run the risk of dying of a stress-related disease. To counter the embarrassment of having arrested him, the authorities would produce an 'ascension' narrative, complete with self-opening doors which swing back into place, and a women's chorus. That too has to be interpreted: one does not know what might have happened. Apollonius could have burst in at a late devotional rite, so that some part of the ritual was taken as a *klēdon*-type oracle[96] – or there might have been a sarcastic rebuke, sending Apollonius about his business.[97]

The death of Peregrinus remains an exceptional phenomenon in the annals of Imperial holy men. Of course his enemy the sceptical Lucian set out to impute the basest possible publicity-seeking as a motive, but religious explanations are harder to prove.[98] Why should a holy man of whatever complexion have chosen to set fire to himself in public at the end of the Olympic Games of AD 165? It must be noted that there was nothing against suicide, more particularly for a philosopher of either Stoic or Cynic allegiance, and Peregrinus had the latter. And a suicide might be the occasion for much edification of survivors, as it was at the (enforced) suicide of Seneca a century before.[99] Peregrinus claims to be about to join the Cynic hero Heracles, immolated on Oeta[100] – but as a result of wearing a poisoned robe – to end a life of incurable misery. Brahmanic models were also known and are suggested by Lucian;[101] given the prestige of the sect with Apollonius of Tyana, these too are a conceivable role-model, but we hear of no previous interest on Peregrinus' part. We are told of his design to 'commingle with the ether', a possibly Stoically or even Gnostically coloured ambition;[102] and Peregrinus had had links with some form of Christianity. But no one else took this particular path: attainment of some sort of immortality through purification seems a conceivable motive in itself; but all suggestions seem to underline that there may be some factor of which we know nothing, such as some fatal debilitation which Peregrinus sets out to anticipate. But if so it would have required early diagnosis, since he is already announcing the immolation at the previous Games.[103] What his detractor Lucian preserves is the sense of occasion and spectacle:

> Proteus himself came forward with a huge entourage, after the contest of the heralds, and had something to say about himself: he recounted the life he had led and the dangers he had braved, and all the troubles that he had undergone for the sake of philosophy. Now what he had to say was lengthy, but I only heard a little of it, thanks to the crowd of bystanders. At length I was afraid of being crushed by such a throng (for I saw this happening to many others) so I went away, with a

long farewell to the sophist who longed for death and was rehearsing his own funeral speech before he actually died.

But this much at least I did overhear: he said he wanted to put a golden tip on a golden bow; for a man who had lived like Heracles had to die like Heracles and be mingled with the heavens. 'And I wish', he went on, 'to be of service to mankind by showing them the way to despise death; and so all mankind ought to serve in the role of Philoctetes to me.' The less intelligent among the crowd started to weep and call out: 'Save yourself for the sake of the Greeks!'; but the more determined among them roared 'Carry out your resolution!'. At this the old man was really quite put out, because he was expecting that everyone would hold on to him and not give him over to the flames, but hold him back in this life – reluctantly of course![104]

A holy man can as a matter of course be credited with 'action' beyond the grave. Philostratus is able to give Apollonius of Tyana a domestic 'success': he claims that the sage advised that a handmaid should not be freed from slavery; she was subsequently sold into what turned out to be a good marriage.[105] Philostratus wishes his readers to believe that the sage foresaw the consequences of his action, when any number of other factors might have brought about his decision. But retrospective interpretation redounds to the sage's credit. A more typical phenomenon occurs when a sceptic at Tyana is 'converted' to belief in Apollonius through becoming the medium of an oracle. We are told that he has already prayed persistently for nine months to Apollonius to reveal to him the *logos* of the soul; when he is at last possessed he claims that Apollonius visits him alone.[106]

Peregrinus Proteus would appear to have been more enterprising in arranging the future. Apart from the beginnings of a cult we hear that he 'sent out letters to almost all the cities of repute, by way of testaments and exhortations and regulations; and to attend to this he appointed certain ambassadors from among his companions, with the titles of messengers of the dead and underworld couriers'.[107] Given Peregrinus' own background in Christianity, he may well have known letters of Ignatius carried by *theopresbeutai* and *theodromoi* ('divine ambassadors' and 'divine couriers').[108] We also hear of a testament of Apollonius of Tyana.[109]

The question of post-resurrection appearances[110] of Jesus Christ belongs to the same order. These are variously recounted and witnessed, but the difficulties outweigh the claims: the collective interviews with the twelve are difficult to see as more than collective hysterical experience – or an embellished account. It is not much 'proof' of resurrection if a body has wounds that can be felt, then proceeds to melt though a wall. The appearance to two disciples on the road to Emmaus demonstrates the real difficulty in its sharpest focus: Jesus is seen as different, and only recognised over a meal.[111] One might argue that speed of recognition depends on expectation. But the real obstacle to credibility is the ancient belief that gods can go about in different earthly bodies.[112] Athene can assume any number of disguises in the *Odyssey*, confronting Odysseus in the guise of Nausicaa's playmate or a shepherd on Ithaca.[113] Against the same framework of assumptions Christ can be thought of as manifesting himself in the body of a total stranger: such a reflex is not foreign to Jewish thinking, or not foreign enough to prevent Jesus himself from being hailed as the returned Elijah or John the Baptist. The knowledge of the fact of the empty tomb will then do the rest.

We have been able to review, then, the channels of action through which the holy man could apply his variety of skills of both word and deed. It is difficult to know what to make of many of them: much of any given holy man's record is related to the framework of assumptions his public would have been already conditioned to accept; and it is not hard to see that for every one who seems to have an inkling of how the impression of miracle might be produced there is someone else who is predisposed to hail it as just that. Two themes run through the course of activities: in case after case display and action are intertwined one way or another, not always simply; accounts themselves are almost consistently just lacunose enough to suggest that a key factor or component of explanation is missing, though random details can often point us in the direction of respectable guesswork.

But holy men have to be seen in their social context, in many cases still inseparable from their work itself. We must look now at how the holy man can relate to his supporters, and in doing so enhance his impact once more.

7

ALLIANCE
Disciples, clients, patrons

A holy man may well be no more than a voice crying in the wilderness if he does not have disciples, colleagues, helpers, or some other kind of contact and support. Despite the occasional miracle of bilocation, he cannot normally expect to be in two places at once, and the more eyes and ears he has in society at large, the better equipped he will be to respond to its needs. And only the most extremely introverted will deny benefits for his fellow-men as he accrues a spiritual treasure-trove for himself. It is time to extend the holy man's actions to his personal relations.

FAMILY, HELPERS

In at least a proportion of cases known to us our holy man would have found support in his family background. A holy man or religious virtuoso might belong to a family which had held hereditary priesthoods, as in the case of both Josephus and the Emperor Elagabalus; and at least some other sacred virtuosi also had a father-to-son occupation.[1] The Younger Julianus continues the theurgy inherited from his father;[2] the dream-collector Artemidorus reserves hints on tricks of the trade for his son, with the proviso that the latter is to keep them for his own use and not pass them on to the customers; and Titus Flavius Ulpianus was able to boast of a father, grandfather, and three uncles as prophetic predecessors.[3] More reputable figures such as Marcion and Mani had fathers already installed in a religious establishment: Marcion's father was allegedly a Christian bishop, Mani's an influential figure among the Babylonian Elchasaites.[4] Holiness could always become a hereditary business.

In the matter of rapid expansion of the Christian organisation the element of family connexion receives less prominence than it might. The Synoptic tradition tends to stress the alienation of Jesus Christ from his family after the start of his ministry; but that is only a small part of the picture. John the Baptist is presented in Luke as a relative of Jesus, a detail which might immediately alter our perspective on the initial recognition at the Jordan.[5] Moreover James, the head of the infant church in Jerusalem, is presented as his brother;[6] and Simeon, Jesus' cousin, takes over as its head after James' martyrdom.[7] All but the first of these connexions is open to several avenues of interpretation; after the alienation of family from Jesus,[8] the prominence of James may have been due to guilt on the latter's part over previous estrangement, or to baser motives such as the closeness of family to a successful cult in the making; both or neither such motive is obviously feasible. As the church grew the *auctoritas* of figures inevitably close to the master would have grown – or at least the pressure from others for them to assume it.

Whether or not family encouragement was available, most prominent holy men could expect to flourish with the help of some sort of partner, and we can name a number of obvious associations: Alexander and Coconnas, Peregrinus and Theagenes, John the Baptist and Jesus Christ, Paul and Barnabas, Apollonius of Tyana and 'Damis'. Such pairings flourish or purport to flourish through some part of a holy man's ministry, more especially in its more vulnerable early stages. In the case of Alexander of Abonouteichos we have a detailed if hostile description of such an arrangement:

> He formed an association with some Byzantine chorus-writer, one of those who go in for competitions, whose character was far more vile than his own – I think his nickname was Coconnas; and they went around as quacks and sorcerers, 'trimming the fatheads'.[9]

Lucian has his two villains conceiving their project in the same vein, turning over between themselves the fears and vulnerabilities of mankind and keeping the matter going until they conceived the project of founding a prophetic shrine and an oracle,[10] an enterprise which by its nature might require more than one person to operate.

Alexander's choice of Coconnas may well have been shrewd. His own expertise was in medical 'remedies'; he may well have felt the need for a more literary public relations man. Aside from some sensible advice on the site for their activities, Coconnas is then needed to stay behind composing oracles about the coming prophet

Alexander; the latter takes his home town of Abonouteichos by storm.[11] It is this role of supporting announcer that we note recurring for a number of holy men. We find Theagenes of Patras making prior announcement at the Olympic Games of AD 165 that his fellow-Cynic Peregrinus is to immolate himself;[12] apart from hyperbolical comparisons with both Zeus and the Brahmans, he is credited with citing a Sibylline oracle on the subject,[13] and finally with holding a torch at the burning itself, as no bad second (οὐ φαῦλος δευτεραγωνιστής).[14] John the Baptist performs the function of announcer for Jesus Christ, or rather he is presented as so doing: his looking forward to a baptism with fire [15] need not necessarily be seen as reference to Jesus Christ himself, but obviously implies some apocalyptic figure. In John's own case a prophetic element is invoked by someone: the Matthew-author sees John himself as foretold by Isaiah.[16] In general the role of a right-hand man is perhaps best illustrated by our incidental glimpses of Paul's helper Timothy. As co-addresser of the Epistle to the Philippians he may be Paul's amanuensis: it is hoped that he will be sent to Philippi soon, from Paul; he is acknowledged to be the only one who sees things as the apostle himself does, and is already known to them ('You know that he has been with me, as a servant of the gospel like a son with his father').[17] And since he is a Jew whom Paul himself has personally circumcised[18] he might be seen by the latter as closer in background than for example the uncircumcised Gentile Titus.

The relationship of the elusive 'Damis' to Apollonius of Tyana has presented an ongoing puzzle. Philostratus makes him the factotum of the sage Apollonius as well as the author of a suspect set of memoirs of his companion.[19] But the data are at least valid in showing the sort of qualities a close associate of a sage might be conceived as likely to possess. He evidently has the complementary skills of language invaluable for an Eastern trip;[20] he can be sent to investigate details of portents that it is apparently beneath the sage's own dignity to do; and above all it is his function to recognise the sage's divine quality when he is able to slip his chain while imprisoned in Rome.[21]

In some instances a holy man's assistants will have amounted to a staff, and in the case of Alexander of Abonouteichos we can actually trace its growth. First Coconnas, who acts single-handed as the oracle's first 'advertising manager'; then after the initial success, Alexander had 'by now many men round about him as associates, assistants, investigators, oracle-writers, security staff, clerks, sealers and expounders' and he 'shared out [his profits] among all of them, giving each one a sum in proportion to his worth'. Alexander soon has his private civil service to operate his oracular sorting-office.[22] Nor is this all: 'by this time he was was even sending people abroad to create rumours among the different nations about the oracle and to declare that he made predictions'. He will also have needed a staff to run his three-day festival.[23] Lucian makes a fool of the rusticity of the participants in his mystery spectacles, but we can infer something that he does not say: that the oracle would have been a source of local employment and local pride. It is not surprising to note an increase in staff at Apollo's own oracle at Claros in the same century.

But the normal entourage for a holy man is disciples rather than a staff. The gospel directives for Jesus Christ's Galilean mission give an insight into their organisation: the disciples are sent out in pairs, travelling light and relying on short periods of local hospitality, practising healing, including exorcisms, and calling for repentance. Luke adds an expansion to seventy-two disciples towards the end of the missionary activity.[24] In spite of the flavour of some sort of doublet, the expansion is plausible enough as the movement gathers momentum. Moreover, the picture of Christ calling the disciples from their trades recognises an ever-present economic reality. One can always go back to fishing, and Christ is never lost for a boat: subsistence professions provide subsistence, and can be reasonably combined with freelance attachment to a charismatic leader.

The disciples of Apollonius of Tyana offer a sharp contrast. We seem here – in Philostratus' eyes at any rate – to be dealing with the well-to-do young philosophy students who can afford a grand tour of the East, so that ten of them could be preparing to visit the master in Asia just as he himself arrives in Athens.[25] But disciples could desert as well when the going came to be rough: Apollonius' followers melt away (though less dramatically than those of Jesus Christ) when the threat of a violent regime has to be faced; or they can desert for intellectual reasons, as Origen argues that philosophers did when unconvinced by Apollonius.[26]

CLIENTS

Beyond actual disciples an active holy man can expect to have clients, and his social and particularly religious contacts may range throughout the social spectrum. In the case of Jesus Christ the parable of the Good Samaritan is addressed to a lawyer who wishes a definition of his neighbour. Nicodemus the Pharisee comes to Jesus by night and acknowledges him as from God, and may be identical with the rich young ruler of Markan tradition;[27] while Christ has a Pharisee as his host on more than one occasion in Luke.[28] The centurion whose servant is healed has actually been able to provide a local synagogue at Capernaum, and communicates with Jesus through 'Elders of the Jews'.[29] Paul's associates include the more socially or professionally elevated: the epistle to Titus mentions a lawyer Zenas active as a missionary; while Luke himself is a physician.[30] The usefulness of the latter to anyone who might be expected to perform miracles should not be underestimated: like Vespasian's doctors, he could always be expected to advise in areas where the master should at least be tempted to try his hand. A further conspicuous addition at a very early stage is one Erastus, 'treasurer of the city' itself.[31]

A recurrent figure in such a clientele is the often well-to-do woman patron, as much a part of the scene as she is likely to be a source of scandal or hostile criticism. We note that Simon Magus in the apocryphal tradition has an association in Samaria with a rich lady Euboula, whose religious effects he and his two associates are minded to purloin;[32] while Alexander of Abonouteichos had taken his 'big break' from a rich Macedonian lady (who may have kept tame snakes).[33] Alexander's own practice enables him to continue such fruitful associations: women are attracted to him, and they and their husbands regard his sexual exploitation of them as good fortune.[34] And the same kind of relationship is well suggested by Lucian's remarks on the private (philosophy) tutor in rich households ('many have promised predictions, cures, love-charms and curses against enemies').[35] The cult associations of the salon-lady are familiar enough from the connexions of Jerome with his Aventine ladies in the fourth century.[36] And there was no lack of other cases: Paul's Procla,[37] Montanus' female charismatics,[38] and even the attraction of the rich widow Pudentilla to the eloquent and magically well-informed Apuleius. The women disciples of Christ cited in Luke 8 had all been healed by Jesus himself: 'Mary, known as Magdalene, from whom he had cast out seven demons, and Joanna, the wife of Chuza, Herod's steward, and Suzanna'. The mention of Joanna indicates also a potential source of court information, if not the possibility of an actual friend at court. The catalogue continues:

'and many others, who rendered them services from their private means'.[39]

In several cases we can look more closely at the services that could be supplied to women clients. In the course of Apuleius' *Apology* we hear of his observing a woman at the behest of a doctor. Apuleius would of course have claimed to be a philosopher, but he had strong religious interests and was actually accused of magic as such. In this instance he does not deny the allegations; he has been called in for a second opinion in a case of tinnitus of the ears.[40] He now produces an extended disquisition on the Platonic theory of humours and the consequent physiology of epilepsy. This leads to authorities on why infection of the right side is an indication of the difficulties of cure. He can then trump his accusers:

> I have deliberately quoted the discussions of prestigious philosophers, and carefully mentioned their books, and have avoided touching upon any reference from doctors or poets, so that my opponents may no longer wonder that philosophers should have learned the causes of diseases and their remedies in the course of their own research. And so, when an ailing woman was brought to be examined by me to obtain a cure, and since it is clear from the evidence of the doctor who brought her and from the reasoning I have just offered that this was the right course, my opponents must lay down that it is characteristic of an evil magician to heal disease.[41]

The service thus provided by Apuleius might arguably be detached from his strong religious interests, in so far as religious and philosophical proclivities could be separated in this period; but an explicitly religious relationship with a female client is provided for the second century in the letter of the Gnostic Ptolemaeus to his disciple Flora. This Gnostic theogony is not presented as an exposition for its own sake, but as an appendage to an interpretation of Valentinian ruling over marriage. The other commandments are to be taken at face value: certain other Old Testament teaching is to be rejected as man-made or interpreted symbolically. The situation was ordained by god – not *the* God but the *dēmiourgos* middle between perfect God and devil; but Flora is not to worry about these for the moment.[42] Such teaching is important as an indication that Gnostic systems did not exist in a vacuum, for the personal gratification of their mythologising inventors: they are linked, however absurdly, to quite practical problems of early Christian behaviour, and painstakingly interact with scriptural pastiche, by means of an allegorical decoding which quite happily makes all things possible:

> What is laid down about offerings, circumcision, Sabbath, fasting, Passover, unleavened bread, and things of the kind: all these, being images and symbols, were changed once the truth appeared. As far as their outward appearance and physical fulfilment is concerned, they were destroyed; but in respect of their spiritual meaning, they were restored: their names remained the same, but their content was changed. For our Saviour enjoined us to make offerings, but not those offered by means of irrational beasts or in the form of incense, but those made through spiritual praises and glorifications and thanksgivings, and through fellowship and doing good to our neighbours.[43]

In fact towards the end of our period we become increasingly aware of seriously intellectual female participants: Julia Domna, the wife of Septimius Severus, is not only a friend of Philostratus, but the commissioner from him of a biography of Apollonius of Tyana. And we know of the relationship between the alchemist and syncretist Zosimus of Panopolis and a fellow-alchemist Theosebeia, the addressee of the treatise *On the Final Quittance*, and twenty-eight books *On Alchemical Matter*. Moreover, she is offered the following advice of an apparently spiritual nature:

> Do not roam about searching for God, but sit calmly at home, and God who is everywhere, and confined to the smallest space like the demons, will come to you. And, being calm in body, calm also your passions, desire and pleasure and anger and the twelve portions of death . . . . When you realise that you have been perfected (by destructive sacrifice to demons) and have found the natural tinctures, spit on matter and hastening towards 'Poemandres', and receiving baptism in the mixing-bowl, hasten up towards your own race.[44]

One might well begin to guess what Julia Domna might have gleaned from a circle of astrologers and philosophers at the beginning of the next century.

PATRONS

Some of the clients will themselves have doubled as patrons of their
holy men, in return for spiritual services rendered. Lucian provides
a lively, if doubtless biased, picture of Alexander of Abonouteichos'
supporter Rutilianus:

> First and preeminent among these [foreign dupes] was
> Rutilianus: in other respects he was a fine upstanding figure,
> who had emerged with distinction from many Roman
> appointments, but in religious matters he was very unsound
> and held outlandish beliefs about the gods. He had only to see
> anywhere a stone anointed with oil or bearing a wreath, and
> he would at once fall on his face, offer obeisance, and stand at
> it for a long time praying and asking blessings from it. And so
> when this man heard all about the oracle, he just about
> dropped his current appointment to fly off to Abonouteichos.
> Well anyway he sent one wave of messengers after another,
> and those he sent, only ordinary household servants, would be
> easily taken in, and when they returned, they recounted not
> only what they had seen, but also what they had heard as if
> they had seen it as well; and they threw in still more for good
> measure, so as to go further in their master's good books. So
> they inflamed the old wretch and drove him really crazy. And
> Rutilianus himself, who had many powerful friends, went
> around not only telling what he had heard from his envoys,
> but adding more again on his own account. So this man
> flooded and swamped the city, and plunged most of the court
> into excitement, for they themselves immediately were
> anxious to go and hear something about their own affairs.[45]

Lucian is perceptive on the possibilities of second- and third-hand
reporting; where there is belief or a predisposition to believe, any
information can be subject to exaggeration. He recognises, though
he ridicules, the propensity for a man of education and standing to
find satisfaction in an operation of this sort. But he does not perhaps
do full justice to the advantages accruing to Rutilianus himself. And
apart from this (rather Theophrastan) portrait Lucian gives us three
vignettes of Rutilianus' relationship with Alexander. In the first he
simply consults the oracle about a son by a previous marriage to ask
who should be his tutor. Alexander's reply specifies Pythagoras and
Homer; the son dies very shortly afterwards. Lucian takes the

oracle to have been caught out, and credits Rutilianus himself with foolishly trying to 'rescue' Alexander by interpreting the response to mean that the son is now receiving his lessons from these reputable masters in Hades itself. But the response may just as easily have been concocted through professional competence. Alexander may already have known any problems attached to the son's health; or he may have kept his prophecy vague enough to cover such a contingency in a way that specifying some living teacher could not have done. In any case he did not lose an opportunity to advertise Pythagoras himself.[46]

In a second enquiry Rutilianus asks about his own previous incarnation: he is told that he had been Achilles, then Menander, doubtless two answers tailored to suit his patron's own personal vanities; he is to become a sunbeam, and his age is extravagantly predicted as 170. But only the last of these revelations is actually vulnerable or subject to any sort of verification; and the actual wording of the oracle is just vague enough to allow the figure to refer to the duration of the transmigration into the sunbeam, or to include the ages of previous incarnations as required; whatever age Rutilianus lives to, the oracle will be reasonably covered. Alexander may have been even less of a fool than Lucian supposed.[47]

The third response is less conventional and more revealing. Rutilianus marries Alexander's daughter in response to a further command from the oracle. Lucian presents his own subjective view of the matter. Rutilianus made a fool of himself as a sexagenarian bridegroom; Alexander may well have conceived the connexion in terms of cynical and self-interested social climbing.[48] But Rutilianus would also have had interests of his own in such a union. This was not an eccentric liaison with a backstreet oracle-monger. Alexander's own social standing would have been highly respectable. Rutilianus could have used the connexion for political prestige, given what Lucian tells us about the political blackmail against others among Alexander's clients.[49] There is a worthwhile analogy with the case of Septimius Severus a generation later: his second marriage was to the daughter of a priest-king of Emesa, to the profit of his political destiny.[50] And from Rutilianus' side things may have looked different; he was marrying the daughter of a respected philosopher and doctor, a consultant who might give advice to emperors. The relationship certainly worked for Alexander's protection. Lucian, attempting to prosecute, found himself faced with a governor Lollianus Avitus who said he did not wish to offend

Rutilianus. Lucian's own suspicions fell now on Avitus: what was the point of proceeding in the face of an official who confessed to being inhibited by his relationship to Rutilianus? In fact Avitus may indeed have been in Alexander's pocket: he was a friend of Apuleius while serving as proconsul of Africa.[51]

Rutilianus' part went beyond the passive protection of Alexander's shrine. When the latter died it fell to him to arbitrate on a successor.[52] Not only did Alexander himself acquire the backing of Rutilianus: his successor, had he actually been nominated, would have enjoyed such backing in advance. As it was, the appointment was not made, but reserved for Alexander even after his death; we can at least be assured of the personal loyalty the prophet had at his command.[53] One of the would-be successors, actually specified by Lucian, was himself a doctor: the shrine had indeed acquired respectability.

We can usefully piece together a number of other clients of Alexander: not only the Roman general Severianus, whom we shall meet under military clients, but the wealthy Sacerdos of Tius, who inscribes a dialogue about his transmigrations on an expensive inscription in his home; if the details themselves have an air of the suspect about them, the practice itself is perfectly credible: one thinks of the private indulgence of the inscription set up this time in praise of Epicurus by Diogenes of Oenoanda; or the flattering murals which Trimalchio has on the subject of his own life and destiny and relationship with Mercury in the *Satyrica*.[54] Alexander knew how to appeal.

Nor would Rutilianus have been alone in his patronage of a favourite oracle. We have a very strong case for identifying as a client of the oracle at Didyma one Aelianus Poplas to whom are assigned oracle responses by the so-called *Tübingen Theosophy*: in response to a question as to whether he should 'send concerning money to the Emperor for his advancement', he is advised to send a mission to Rome, as well as praying to 'the immortal eye of all-seeing Zeus'; a second oracle advises 'appeasement of the glorious eye of Zeus' in the context of illness, loss of property, and general misfortune. Now we know of an Aelianus Poplas who held office under Elagabalus (eight offices are recorded altogether);[55] and a later kinsman Titus Flavius Ulpianus who administered self-congratulatory oracles on his own account.[56] There were plenty more where Alexander's clients came from.

We should not discount the possibility of similar relationships for

Apollonius of Tyana: *Ep.* 58 purports to be addressed to a Valerius, governor of fifty cities, whom Cichorius plausibly identified as the Valerius Festus who was consul in AD 71. The tone of the letter is such as to make it highly implausible as a forgery to suit a collection: that would only have required a single utterance in gnomic manner on the futility of mourning or the like. It is highly specific in its details, and seems to presuppose that Alexander has already met the proconsul's wife Fabulla. There is just the chance that this is by a successor of Apollonius, writing as in his person after his death, but that is not really the natural meaning of the final sentence: Ἀπολλώνιος εἰ παρῆν, Φαβούλλαν ἂν μὴ πενθεῖν ἔπεισεν ('If Apollonius were present, he would have persuaded Fabulla not to mourn'). Holy men are allowed to set themselves apart in the third person.[57]

A similar relationship can be reconstructed in the case of Apollonius' association with the Neronian consular Telesinus; Philostratus insists on this, and is not likely to have forged it: the case of Rutilianus itself shows that there was nothing absurd about such an alliance. Philostratus' reconstruction can at least be seen as the scenario within which a *pepaideumenos*, a 'man of culture and sensibility', conceived the relationship between holy man and friendly official. We are told that Telesinus encounters Apollonius on a visit to Rome by the latter in the reign of Nero: he has already heard of the sage by repute, and is ὑποθεραπεύων τὸ θεῖον ('inclined to a pious disposition').[58] The prayer Apollonius offers him contains a clear political overtone in very guarded language 'that the laws may not be overturned, that wise men may be poor, but that others may be honestly rich'; Telesinus for his part offers him permission to stay in shrines in Rome, and becomes a pupil.[59] He turns up again in the context of Apollonius' further Roman visit under Domitian as part of the sage's supposed alibi: both were attending the bedside of Apollonius' fellow-pupils Philiscus of Melos; and Telesinus himself has a vision of the survival of Apollonius in a sea of fire.[60]

No less interesting is the relationship between Simon Magus and the Roman senator Marcellus, also in the reign of Nero. When the *Actus Petri* present Peter arriving in Rome to combat the alleged heresies of this Samaritan Gnostic, we find the latter at Marcellus' house; he has foresworn his previous charitable acts. Simon is unable to face Peter when summoned by a talking dog; Marcellus has him thrown out.[61] As it happens we do have a senator Marcellus from Nero's reign: he is none other than the notorious *delator* Eprius Marcellus, whose reputation in Tacitus ill accords with any notion of charity as described in the *Actus*.[62] But it would certainly make sound sense for a senator on the make to have Christian connexions, given those of the Imperial family itself. And contact with Simon Magus might mean no more than contact with a resourceful gossip-mongering soothsayer who might well act as an informant. A curious piece of banter between Marcellus and Nero is also presented: the former is jokingly accused of being likely to plunder the provinces to relieve the poverty of the Christians.[63] It is indeed the case that Marcellus was suspected of 'plundering the provinces', since the Lycians brought a charge of extortion.[64] The notion that such plunder would have been directed at Christian charity may transcend the strangeness of fiction.

A consistent feature in the literature of holy men is the presence of military clients. John the Baptist is asked by soldiers what is required of them, and enjoins that there should be no bullying or blackmail: they are to make do with their pay.[65] In the case of Jesus Christ we have a less predictable transaction. When he is asked to heal the centurion's servant, we are given the detail that the centurion has Jewish elders to vouch for the fact that 'he is well disposed to our nation, and he is the person who built our synagogue'.[66] Another element is the centurion's evident rapport with the holy man as a source of authority: 'Say the word and my servant will be cured. For I too am under orders, and have soldiers under me. I say to one man "March" and he marches, to another "Come" and he comes'.[67] The client of Peter, Cornelius, is again liberal in his support of the Jews and a Jewish sympathiser.[68] The pattern of contact here is still more revealing. His military orderly is also described as a religious man, sent to contact Peter on the centurion's behalf.[69] Cornelius himself evidently speaks in tongues of ecstasy to the amazement of Peter's Jewish companions from Joppa.[70] We are not surprised to find military personnel looming large in the more thoroughly militarised Empire of the third and fourth centuries: a military officer Martinianus makes a nuisance of himself soliciting a cure from Antony for his daughter's demonic possession.[71] If these clients had no specifically military significance, some of Alexander's did. A holy man could make a crucial contribution to a military situation, as when Severianus consults the oracle of Abonouteichos[72] before his hoped-for victory at Elegeia in AD 162;

and all Vespasian's holy associates in Egypt may be said to have cultivated military friends.[73]

One operator we seem able to detect in relation to more than one such client. We meet bar-Jesus, otherwise Elymas, as a Jewish *magos* in Cyprus in the retinue of the governor Sergius Paulus; he is worsted by Paul in a vituperative display, and for the Acts-author he sinks without trace.[74] But there is an interesting postscript. We find a Cypriot Jew turning up eight years later in the service of Felix, procurator of Judaea. In order to marry Drusilla, the wife of Azizus, 'He sent to her one of his friends, a Cyprian Jew named Atomos or Simon, who pretended to be a magician, in an effort to persuade her to leave her husband and to marry Felix . . . . She was persuaded to transgress the ancestral laws and to marry Felix'.[75] Now Atomos is unattested as an actual Greek name; the only other Cyprian magician we know is Elymas, in some manuscripts presented as 'hetoimos' or the like.[76] It is a plausible conjecture that hetoimos and Atomos represent the same man; the name itself would be a nickname ('Presto'). Whatever the truth behind the polyonymous figure in our two notices, it seems entirely plausible that an anti-Pauline Jewish consultant of one governor would turn up in the retinue of another, performing one of the time-honoured tasks of *magoi*, as go-between in love-affairs. One notes the ambiguity of the identity: like Pliny's Regulus, he could put on the mantle of an operator when it suited him.

The function of consulting an oracle that provides 'the answers' may be otherwise served by consulting a reputable philosopher. The Younger Pliny consulted the Stoic Euphrates, and gives a revealing account of the matter:

> And yet why say more about a man whose company I am never able to enjoy, except to make me feel all the more frustrated that I can't? For my time is occupied with official chores as boring as they are important. I sit on the bench, put my name to petitions, prepare accounts, and write a host of very routine letters. I often complain about these chores to Euphrates – I do sometimes get the chance – and he consoles me: he maintains that to engage in public duties or judicial enquiries and pass judgement, to give legal opinions and to apply what the professionals teach – these occupations are a part of philosophy, and indeed the most admirable part. But over this one thing he cannot convince me – that it is better to

do all such things than spend whole days with him just listening and learning.[77]

No less than a shrewd oracle-monger, Euphrates is able to listen to Pliny, and having listened, to tell him what we ourselves can work out and what Pliny himself would most have wanted to hear. Pliny is a somewhat naively conceited individual bent on hearing his own praises sung: what better ploy than to tell this philosopher *manqué* that his lifestyle makes him the best type of philosopher there is? The counselling role of a philosopher could scarcely be clearer – consistent with his dispensing sound Stoic doctrine, that Stoicism itself is compatible with a life of active sevice.[78]

A second of Pliny's 'consultations' is relevant, this time with his correspondent Licinius Sura on the subject of ghosts. But even in Pliny's case the subject and enquiry may not be as simple as they sound. The second of the three cases he cites is a straightforward ghost story, but the other two call for closer examination. The first concerns one Curtius Rufus, hailed in a visionary experience by 'Africa', who tells him of his future career, including the fact that he would be entrusted with 'her' province, and die there, to be met with the same figure on disembarkation at Carthage. Pliny notes that Rufus 'interpreted his future from the past and misfortune on the strength of his previous success', thus giving up hope.[79] But Pliny himself has more interest than that of a carefully sceptical raconteur: he has a powerful career motivation of his own, on the same level of ambition as that of Rufus. He would doubtless wish to know how to take any future encounter of his own – with any lady who might introduce herself to him as 'Bithynia-and-Pontus'!

Pliny's final story concerns two of his own slaves. On two occasions slaves in his household had their hair cut in the middle of the night. Pliny is not content to see the matter as a mere dormitory prank (in which, one presumes, the first boy at least thinks he is dreaming what is actually taking place). It is Pliny's envoie that is revealing. 'Nothing to speak of followed', he confides, 'unless perhaps the fact that I was not put on trial, as I was destined to be had Domitian (under whom these events happened) lived longer. For in his desk was found a file on me from Carus; from this, since it is usual for accused persons to allow their hair to grow long, it can be conjectured that the cutting of my slaves' hair was a sign that my impending danger was averted'.[80] The whole matter seems rather pointless: even Pliny seems aware that he is forcing the interpretation of two trivial incidents that happened to other people to apply to something that might never happen to him. But he would have been anxious to put about any suggestion of political danger under Domitian, in view of how conspicuously well he seemed to have done even in the most dangerous years under a tyrant.

Pliny's various enquiries mark him out as something of a dilettante in intellectual and religious matters: others could be more single minded. Thessalus of Tralles, of well-off background, developed his occult interests in Alexandria, where he was studying literature after his grammatical education in Asia. This had come about through 'burning excessive desire' for medical theory. Having discovered a treatise by Nechepso on astrological medicine, he had become an object of ridicule to his fellow-students when he had failed to produce effective cures, and having also announced his newly acquired skills by letter home, he had now to find something more convincing. He had premonitions of converse with the gods, to whom he had prayed for 'some dream-vision or divine inspiration, some favour' that would enable him to regain his self-confidence and send him back in triumph to Alexandria and home. An aged priest of Thebes obliged him by arranging a vision, by request, of Asclepius, obtained after a three-day fast; body and soul were fainting at the sight. Asclepius assured him that in time as his achievements became known Thessalus would be worshipped as a god. Asked what he wished to know, he made enquiries about the Book of Nechepso. The book, he was told, did not lack wisdom, but divine communication; and Asclepius duly reveals the curative powers of plants in accordance with their astral affinity.[81]

Such an account is very properly suspect: we have here at least the syndrome of the sorcerer's apprentice, the naive young man who wishes to run before he has learned to walk. In Thessalus the priest has a readymade dupe, in the sense that having disgraced himself once he has to be seen to be vindicated in the same area. Rational procedures have failed, or at any rate procedures in rational circles; he must trump them with revealed irrationalism. His case and reputation might either have been known beforehand in Thebes, or divulged in confidence to the priest: whatever the case, he would have had a predisposition to submit to anyone who could offer any prospect of restoring his credibility.

It is worthwhile to compare and contrast the impact of the holy man on enthusiastic outsiders. The first extract is worth quoting in full as probably the best preserved and most direct enounter with pagan holy men in our period, all the more remarkable because it has so frequently gone unnoticed. Philostratus reports a letter of the second-century Athenian magnate Herodes Atticus to his friend (Antonius) Julianus:[82]

> This was a youth on the threshold of manhood, as tall as a towering Celt (he was actually about eight feet high) . . . his hair grew long on both sides, he had bushy eyebrows that met as if into one, and his eyes gave forth a bright flash which gave a hint of his impulsive nature; he had a hooked nose and a sturdy neck, the result of hard work rather than diet. His chest, too, was well-shaped and youthfully slim, and his legs bent slightly outwards, which made for a firm stance. He was draped in a garment sewn out of wolf-skins, and he used to take on wild boars, jackals, wolves and bulls in heat, and would display the scars from these contests. Some say that this Heracles was a 'son of the soil, sprung from among the people of Boeotia', but Herodes says that he heard him say that his mother was a woman of such strength that she served as a cowherd, while his father was the farmer-hero Marathon whose statue stands at Marathon itself. Herodes asked this Heracles whether he was immortal as well. But he replied 'I only live longer than a mortal'. He asked him also what he lived on and 'Heracles' said 'I live on milk most of the time, and am fed by goats and herds of cows and breeding mares, and the she-ass too offers a good light milk. But when I come across barley meal, I consume ten quarts, and farmers in Marathon and Boeotia supply me with this banquet; and they give me the nickname Agathion ['little goodfellow'] because they think that I actually bring them good luck'.

Agathion attacks three varieties of urban phenomena: barbarised speech, tragic performances, and gymnastics:

> So Herodes was much impressed with him, and was anxious for Agathion to dine with him. 'Tomorrow', the latter replied, 'I will meet you at midday at the temple of Canopus, and you must have there the largest bowl in the temple full of milk not milked by a woman'. But when he had raised the bowl to his nose, he said 'The milk is not pure, for the smell of a woman's hand assails me'. And with these words he went away without tasting the milk. So Herodes paid attention to what he had

said about the woman, and sent people to the cowsheds to find out the truth; and on hearing that this was indeed the case, he recognised that the man had a superhuman nature.

It is instructive to review what Herodes had actually come across: an impressive, apparently well-educated wild rustic, living a partly self-sufficient, partly mendicant life in country districts, taken for a Robin Goodfellow by the locals, seen as the son of a local spirit, and using a temple as his venue in Athens. A cultural purist and moralist of Cynic tendency, with a good nose for the bouquet of milk as the only 'miraculous' qualification. If he is not a holy man, he is actually claimed as a cut above.[83]

The brief episode of Agathion raises the role of the ἀγαθὸς δαίμων, the 'beneficient spirit' in general: the good spirit so often associated with those on the fringe of magic and holiness. There is a useful catalogue of the social services such a spirit can be expected to provide in the magical papyri:

> If you give him a command, straightway he performs the task: he sends dreams, brings women or men without the use of magic material, he kills, he destroys, he stirs up winds from the earth, he carries gold, silver, bronze, and he gives them to you whenever the need arises; and he frees from bonds a person chained in prison, he opens doors, he causes invisibility so that no one can see you at will . . . and he will tell you about the illness of a man, whether he will live or die, even on what day and at what hour of night. And he will also give you both wild herbs and the power to cure, and you will be worshipped as a god since you have a god as a friend.[84]

The catalogue of the attributes of divine assistant comes quite close to the less reputable tasks of the holy man himself. For the spell to have any real application or to work, it presumably has to represent the planting of an assistant on the client. The first holy man has only to release a falcon which will be attracted to the incense burned by the client. After the latter's purifications his powers of perception will be reduced, and he can be set up to take into his household a second assistant and an intermediary, who can then liaise with the first operator. He is certain to be given hospitality: a pair of professional scroungers would be able to perform the act very well. The whole business has to be kept quiet, with the possibility of only a child witness, and only passed on to a legitimate son. If this is a spell by which the client Kerux the God-fearer could acquire a divine servant, it was also the means for a divine servant to find a master good for a meal, with absolute discretion assured.

It remains to examine briefly the matter of the sexual attachments of holy men. That this can and should be done briefly is due to the attitude of the sources on the subject. Sources favourable to a sage will either insist on the perfect probity of the holy man, or imply as much *ex silentio*; there will be no shortage of allegations in the hostile press of sexual scandals on a considerable scale. And among Gnostic texts one can anticipate a division along the lines of puritanical versus libertine sects.[85] Hence Philostratus insists on the continence of Apollonius of Tyana, not without allusion to a hostile tradition of sexual licence in Scythia, or to an alleged affair with the mother of Alexander Peloplaton;[86] the gospels generally avoid the sexual life of Jesus Christ, apart from the tantalising allusion to the 'disciple whom Jesus loved'; but it is left to the Pauline tradition to offer an overt condemnation of homosexual behaviour.[87] As a general rule it is worth noting that some holy men do marry, but that on the whole we are dealing with unmarried masters who may choose to withdraw with numbers of young men; the traditional allegations that attach to such situations are duly brought.[88]

So much, then, for those disposed to the holy man in a friendly way: family, assistant, disciples, patrons male and female, clients military and civilian, and even divine assistants and possible lovers. It is difficult to generalise among so much evidence, often so randomly distributed. As the holy man has to be all things to all men, so all men can be something to the holy man in turn. Whether fraudulently or otherwise, someone always stood to be helped by him and help him in turn, whatever the quality, or indeed the probity, of the benefits. And these mutually beneficial relationships, for good or ill, were necessary to protect the holy man from the opposition, which we must now encounter in turn.

8

OPPOSITION
False prophets, cheats and charlatans

The quarrels of sophists and philosophers in the early Empire are a familiar phenomenon. Those of holy men are considerably more dramatic, and yet have received less attention in their own right. And they could reach more violent conclusions more quickly. Apollonius of Tyana commanded the crowd to stone a beggar; while Saul of Tarsus lent his approval to the stoning of the Hellenist Christian Stephen.[1] Holy men were not inclined to tolerate rivalry, nor always to conceal their differences amicably.

AUTHORITY

Often the holy man has to face the problems of coming to terms with a religious establishment. Apollonius of Tyana has a dispute with the Epidaurian festival: he appears as a freelance antiquarian, scoring a point over the not-so-authoritative authorities. The current hierophant refuses to initiate the sage, on the grounds that he is a mere γόης ('magician'), and hence impure in spiritual matters. Apollonius counters that he himself knows more about the initiation rite than the priest himself, refuses a climbdown, and names a successor from whom he will receive initiation in due course.[2] He encounters similar obstruction when attempting to consult the oracle of Trophonius: one might suspect that someone was expecting to be 'found out', so that this religious 'inspector' *par excellence* has to be turned away.[3] By contrast we find the Cynic philosopher Demonax criticising the mysteries for excluding foreigners, though themselves founded by the Thracian Eumolpus;[4] while he himself refused initiation because of the element of secrecy: if the mysteries are evil he will divulge them; likewise if they turn out to be good.[5] It is the privilege of the freelance to assert his independence with the

131

maximum of embarrassment to those unaccustomed to be questioned. The holy man will be the outsider, working to a self-proclaimedly higher standard in all mattters of contention.

Such confrontations also occur in a Judaeo-Christian context: apart from Jesus Christ's cleansing the temple, a less well-publicised incident is attributed to Gregory Thaumaturgus. The temple this time was a famous one in Neocaesarea in Pontus: the demons were accustomed to approach the priests and provide divination and oracles. Gregory and his companions occupy the temple and cleanse it with the sign of the cross, terrifying the demons with the name of Christ. They stay all night with hymns and prayers, turning it into a 'house of prayer'. The demons are unable to obtain access, until the priest capitulates by asking Gregory to let them in again, which he does by means of the operation of a talisman (a fragment of a book on which he writes 'Gregory to Satan: come in').[6] But we should be in no doubt that one side's cleansing will have been the other's violent occupation.

Few founders of revealed religions fail to discover to their cost that no one has a monopoly on revelation. Prophets must issue warnings to beware of false prophets, with all the monotony of a government health warning. If Jesus Christ himself warns against them – or if gospel writers make him do so to meet the conditions of later generations – Paul wastes little time in cutting the Holy Spirit down to size once it has produced the initial *élan*, and he himself has had his own revelation experience:[7] the Holy Spirit orders me to talk and you to listen. Hence when Alexander of Abonouteichos sets up his revelation of the new incarnation of Asclepius he has to protect himself against the reactions of Epicureans and Sceptics, and attempt to discredit them in turn. And there is a striking similarity between the tone of the polemic we have against Alexander and the material Eusebius quotes from Christian sources against Montanus, who presents with the help of female charismatic prophetesses a revelation that the Second Coming is going to come in Phrygia. Alexander and Montanus were not far apart in either time or place (Pepuza was close to the border of Mysia). Alexander had begun with ecstatic prophecy, and Montanus maintained the practice. Both attract the accusation of financial impropriety, and elicit the parallel gibes that a co-worker in the cult sustained a miserable death (Coconnas of snakebite, Theodotus of a trance). More orthodox attempts at opposition (from Lepidus and Zoticus respectively) are shouted down or threatened by local feeling.[8] Every new revelation represents a voice that some established revelation will wish to silence by any means at its disposal.

PURISM

Much of the cause of tension can be subsumed within questions of purism,[9] in any number of forms: Apollonius of Tyana rejects a disciple with Trojan blood in response to a seance by Achilles;[10] or chastises a community which allows the adoption of Latin names as opposed to Greek.[11] And even Jesus Christ seems to have his doubts about healing a Syrophoenician woman when his mission is to Israel.[12] But one of the most persistent causes of disruption is over the question of the purity of food. In ancient societies where the concept of public health is inseparable from religious practice there will be a constant dissonance between members of different sects: to ask someone to eat polluted food is to invite them to poison themselves, or consign them to damnation; to pollute one-self in front of them is still the worst of bad taste. Hence Paul has such difficulty in Antioch even over the issue of commensality with those who keep strict Jewish dietary laws; he accuses Peter of dining with Gentile Christians until the arrival of a deputation from James, then siding with the Judaisers, when others including Barnabas side with him.[13] We are not surprised to find the second-century Palestinian Christians breaking with Peregrinus over the eating of some forbidden food: there may be a reference here to the notorious Cynic 'indifference' to food, and hence the eating of a dinner of Hecate (interpreted by Christians as meat offered to idols) at a cross-roads, in a part of the world where Jewish Christianity would still have been strongest;[14] while in the next century Mani for his part owed his break with the Elchasaites in large measure to his argument that purity in the preparation of food was null and void when bodily excrement was as impure from eating pure foods as from impure.[15]

Competition in the matter of ritual cleanliness was an inevitable element in the life of sectarian Judaism. To the protagonist in his struggle for or against modification of written Torah this might all too easily become an end in itself; but a social reality was also involved, with the middle and lower orders whose livelihood might depend on temple service having to bear the brunt of maintaining themselves in a state of perpetual purity.[16] Two instances out of many will suffice to illustrate the complications in practice.

Yohanan ben Zakkai sends his pupil Joshua to interview a local figure in Bet Ramah with a reputation for holiness. The man claims to eat a pure preparation made with pure utensils on a range: the pair differ as to whether Torah anywhere lays down the purification of the range itself: Joshua proves that it does, and that the conceited local celebrity has never eaten a clean meal in his life.[17] On a more general level, there was disagreement between Pharisees and Sadducees even about whether lustration was called for after handling temple scriptures.[18] Nor is this a mere esoteric pedantry confined to the most internalised aspects of Judaism: one confrontation is to be found in a unique papyrus source between Jesus Christ and a Pharisaic high priest over a question of purity. Jesus is taken to task for walking in the place of purification in the temple court, when his opponent accuses him of not having performed the necessary ablutions beforehand. He himself is then accused of having bathed in the pool of David, but with water contaminated by dogs and swine, and of chafing his skin like that of prostitutes; Jesus and his disciples by contrast claim immersion in living water.[19] The arguments against rejection of this non-canonical episode have been disposed of. At its face value it underlines once more the antipathy between contrasting interpretations of cleanliness. The Manichaeans for their part will be able to take similar stances on the conception of 'clean foods'.[20]

ASCETICISM AND INTEGRITY

Sometimes the issue of purity will extend into a matter of lifestyle, and the extent to which it can be freed from material needs. Men who turn their backs on the world have to decide how far they must come to terms with it again in order to stay alive. In spiritual terms there are 'degrees of asceticism'. The differences between Jesus and his immediate disciples over the anointing at Bethany offers an obvious illustration: should the three hundred pence for a jar of precious ointment have been used to feed the poor, rather than anoint the feet of one holy man, whether or not as an anticipation of his funeral rites?[21] The pagan world had its equivalent in the divisions between Stoic and Cynic, or indeed in the stock accusation against the venality of philosophers.[22] The problem emerges most clearly in the *Life of Apollonius of Tyana*: Euphrates asks Vespasian for money, and from then on the two holy men are rivals. We can follow this up, for in material terms Euphrates went on to 'do well for himself', integrating into Roman society with a prestigious marriage, while Apollonius eked out a modest existence as an itinerant guest in any temple-precincts that would have him.[23] And Apollonius of Tyana mocks Euphrates with a repertoire of possible charges his rival might make against himself:

> 'Apollonius flatly refuses to take a bath.' 'No one ever sees him moving any part of his body.' 'He grows his hair long.' 'He wears a linen garment.' 'He practises divination . . . but that sort of thing is not fitting for a philosopher.' 'He relieves men of physical pain and puts an end to their sufferings.' 'He has his meals alone.' 'He talks little and speaks briefly.' 'He abstains from all kinds of meat and from the flesh of all animals.'[24]

It is clear enough what Apollonius is presented as implying: these are the range of characteristics of the impressive ascetic holy man that Euphrates for his part sees fit to reject.

EXPERTISE AND INTEGRITY

Nor was lifestyle the only potential cause for quarrel. Much of the energies of freelance holy men could be devoted to clearing themselves of competitors in their own or rival disciplines, with a variety of arguments intellectual or anti-intellectual as the opportunity arose. The guiding principle is often no more than the fact that I practise my profession with probity, while you are a charlatan and a mercenary.[25] Specific disciplines had their specialist critics. One notes that Lucian's friend Celsus is credited with a work κατὰ μάγων ('against magicians'),[26] while Favorinus delivers a telling intellectual argument against astrologers (though his reporter Aulus Gellius seems not totally sure of the sincerity of the indictment).[27] Astrology, the sophist maintains, is not as old as it is claimed to be, and its originators were con-men and not its supposed founders. Favorinus correctly breaks the correlation between all earthly functions and heavenly bodies: just because the moon and tides correspond, it does not follow that we should think 'that a suit at law which someone just happens to have about a water-channel with his opponents, or with his next-door neighbour about a party wall, is controlled as if bound by a kind of rein from the sky'; an astrologer might expect to be invoked on either issue.[28] Moreover, human intellect could not encompass foreknowledge except in the vaguest way, and the findings of the original Chaldaeans do not apply to regions where a different set of stars is observed; if they cause different weather in different regions, why do they not have different effects on destinies in different places? (And in any case human knowledge of the courses of the stars he reckons imperfect.) Many similar arguments are accumulated, including the uselessness even of correct knowledge it if could ever be obtained. Favorinus also inveighs against the honesty of practitioners themselves, who can chance on correct predictions, or can find out truths by other means.[29]

One obvious external threat to holy men is from any outsider who can match the holy man's own communication skills. Hence we find Apollonius of Tyana opposed to forensic orators; sycophants and clever lawyers are worse even than the tyrant Domitian himself, and the sage 'drove off his sheep whenever he found forensic orators approaching, lest the wolves should fall on the flock'.[30] Even Dio Chrysostom, claimed as an associate of Apollonius, is criticised for his rhetorical affectations.[31] We may be dealing here with the traditional antipathy between philosophy and rhetoric; and it is maintained that the sage is responsible for emptying rhetoricians' schools by making philosophy so fashionable. But there is also a hint of hostility at the social ills of profiteering *delatores*, experienced by Apollonius in prison.[32]

Philostratus provides another case of rivalry within a single discipline, reported without apparent embellishment. Egyptians and Chaldaeans offered to perform apotropaic rites against earthquakes on the Thracian Chersonnese for a sum of ten talents on deposit. Apollonius performs the required rites cheaply and effectively, having first driven out the others for making money out of human misery.[33] The implication is that Apollonius' rivals would have secured the sum and performed the sacrifice at a substantial profit. It seems tempting to assume that this was the occasion when Apollonius asked for sacrifices not to Earth and Poseidon, but to Achilles; this would indeed have been much cheaper, one might assume. And it would account for Philostratus' statement 'when he had realised the causes of the wrath'. It would also have ensured additional rivals for the sage in the future. We also have here an insight into the financing of a holy man's operation: Chaldaei and Egyptians can actually demand their fee to be deposited in banks: the cities were to have raised it by a mixture of public and private contribution.

We find a similar contretemps between Peter and Simon Magus at Berytus. Since an earthquake takes place on Peter's arrival in the city, a group headed by Simon Magus is able to accuse him of practising as a *magos* and causing both earthquake and diseases. Peter threatens to practise the powers credited to him and the crowd expels his rivals with cudgels.[34] Similar tensions surface in the *Life of Demonax*. He challenges a soothsayer who makes public predictions for money: he is asking too little, if he can change destiny; if he cannot, then what is the point of his soothsaying anyway?[35]

A further tension interwoven with the question of professional integrity is the conflict between reason and unreason,[36] or between rational and mystical.[37] There is an obvious conflict between the medical and paramedical: Lucian's Tychiades objects to the use of quack remedies and incantations (when medical principles can do the job); but the context in which he does so shows how fine the distinction might actually appear even in intellectual circles.[38] We have at least some indications of a quarrel between Favorinus and Polemo in this field:

> (Favorinus) was a very cunning enchanter and would lay claim to conjuring tricks, proclaiming that he made even the dead alive; and by this means he used so to entice people that huge crowds of men and women would come to him. Besides he would persuade the men that he could persuade women to come to them, as well as men to women . . . he was the finest doctor in procuring harm, and used to collect species of poisons.[39]

On the other hand Aulus Gellius offers an extended account of Favorinus in action which shows that he gave what was regarded as bona fide medical advice on the subject of breastfeeding.[40] It may be that Polemo's comments are no more than routine abuse; we know that he had a spectacular quarrel with Favorinus, of which this may have been a part;[41] but Polemo himself claimed to be an expert in a rival discipline, that of physiognomonics, of which Favorinus for his part may well have disapproved,[42] as we have already found him condemning astrologers.[43]

One strand in the quarrel between Euphrates and Apollonius of Tyana was perhaps of this order. From the point of view of reason, the Stoic might well have stood at the centre, the Pythagorean at the fringe: the one might have chosen to preach the good life while the other dabbled in cosmic powers and herbal remedies. At any rate we find Euphrates condemned by Apollonius for association with 'sophists or *grammatistae* (schoolmasters) or any other such sort of wretches'.[44] And it would have been in this area too that some at least of the Gnostic problems in the early Empire belong: Gnosis implied an esoteric system and a more refined perception,[45] and its enemies condemned it accordingly.[46]

We have a number of encounters between the holy man and a sceptical opposition which regards itself as more sophisticated, but which will not necessarily retire from a contrived encounter unscathed. Antony the hermit's reply to philosophers epitomises the situation: 'If you come to a foolish man, your toil is superfluous; but if you consider me wise, become as I am, for you must imitate what is good'.[47] Those who accuse Antony of illiteracy fare much worse: 'Which is first, mind or letters, or the letters of the mind?'.[48] With these routed, a third group arrives, from 'those of the Greeks considered wise'; these are courted by a more sophisticated apologetic speech ('Which is better – to confess a cross, or to attribute acts of adultery and pederasty to those whom you call gods?').[49] And Apollonius for his part encounters a literary fop who falls foul of the sage in two fields of the latter's interest. The fop boasts of an encomium of Zeus, when he does not feel qualified to write an encomium on his own father; and he is ready to praise diseases in paradoxical encomia (while Apollonius is naturally predisposed to healing them).[50] In the first place one might interpret the scenario as a fairly typical sort of encounter between the two cultural interest-groups of rhetoric and philosophy. But the real spark of Apollonius' rebuke is in the fact that the fool can only praise diseases, a matter which Apollonius can be made to rebuke with the maximum of irony. On the other hand, behind Apollonius' encounter with the rich bird-trainer, it may be possible to detect another sort of tension: not just a conflict of ignorance and education, as Apollonius himself makes out, but a different interest in the language of birds: Apollonius is attributed with having learned the natural language of birds in Mesopotamia, presumably for purposes of divination; the fop merely teaches them to speak literal human languages as a novelty entertainment.[51]

PERSONALITY

Most elusive to the historian is the question of any given holy man's personality differences with his rivals. We seldom have enough resources to study its contribution; and when we do, that study is inclined to be overshadowed by other considerations. It can at least be strongly suspected that Paul's correspondence reveals – and conceals – the strongest potential for personality clash. One notes in particular that the Corinthian Christians are seen as divided along the basis of individual loyalties: 'Each of you is saying "I am Paul's man", or "I am for Apollos"; "I follow Cephas", or "I am Christ's" '. It later transpires, from Paul's point of view, that 'I planted the seed and Apollos watered it'.[52] And always the other is in the wrong:

> There are certain persons who are filled with self-importance because they think I am not coming to Corinth; I shall come very soon, if the Lord will; and then I shall take the measure of these self-important people, not by what they say, but by what power is in them. The Kingdom of God is not a matter of talk, but of powers. Choose, then; am I to come to you with a sword in my hand, or in love and a gentle spirit?[53]

For Paul has the air of one who knows he is right not only now, but has always been so, and is more than surprised to find himself under fire. He has always been reasonable; the present crisis, whatever it might be, is attributable to the malice of others. There is often an air of protesting too much.[54] We can at least look for some of the factors behind this defensiveness. One at least will have been the view others might take of his past as a persecutor, and his status as an 'upstart' apostle. One has a sense that Paul has a strong sense of possessiveness towards his spiritual master:

> Now some proclaim Christ for jealous and quarrelsome motives; others proclaim him out of genuine goodwill; and the latter group act out of goodwill (towards me) knowing as they do that I am lying here in defence of the gospel. But the former, moved by ill-feeling, present Christ for unwholesome reasons, wanting to stir up fresh trouble for me here in prison.[55]

Other tensions might also be attributable to questions of personality itself. The stresses and strains of continual companionship need no elaboration, particularly when the master may enjoy, or wish to enjoy, a monopoly of prestige. Apollonius and Euphrates seem to quarrel over Bassus of Corinth;[56] one notes that Paul and Barnabas undertake one journey together, but not a second, 'because of John Mark',[57] who has apparently failed to complete the first mission. And the charge of hypocrisy against Peter may all too readily reflect the fact that different degrees of compromise by uncompromising natures do not easily co-exist.[58]

In some cases, however, it can be difficult to distinguish potential competitors from friends. We find Jesus Christ demonstrating his achievements to John the Baptist's two envoys, and after their departure giving an encomium of John to his own disciples.[59] But the actual message, and the enquiry itself, might be deemed cautious, even reserved: John has to ask Jesus whether he is 'the one who is to come'; Jesus, after reciting his activities, adds only 'blessed is he who does not take offence at me'. The encomium is similarly equivocal: 'I tell you, among men born of women there is none greater than John; yet the least among the Kingdom of God is greater than he is'.[59] On the other hand an account in John has enquiries addressed to the Baptist: people are now going to Christ for baptism instead of to him. He is made to utter a somewhat Gnostically-coloured encomium of Jesus; but the potential for conflict would plainly have been there.[60]

The most consistent opponents of Jesus Christ are presented as the Pharisees, a small but influential Jewish sect devoted to strict observance of the Law, and the safeguarding of its limits by a penumbra of oral tradition. Christ himself is represented in the many reported exchanges as able to join in the game of bandying scripture with scripture. Through such encounters two contrasting views of religious contamination and forgiveness occur: there is conflict over who has power to forgive sins,[61] or over Jesus' association with tax-gatherers,[62] banned from the synagogue and treated as collaborators, or over disciples eating corn on the Sabbath.[63] But apart from the suspicions of anachronism about this hostility, the gospels do not present a relationship of total antipathy: Luke cites at length an incident closely resembling the anointing at Bethany, locating it at the house of Simon the Pharisee, who withholds the small courtesies from Jesus provided by a dubious woman.[64]

There are other sources of opposition, however: Christ is shown the door from the country of the Gerasenes, for an implausible reason: they are allegedly overawed and hence frightened by Jesus' mastery of the demons accompanying a madman.[65] But they are just as likely to have counted the cost of an exorcist who is prepared to sacrifice the lives of a whole herd of swine to secure the sedation of a single madman. Or he is effectively discouraged from a Samaritan community opposed to pilgrimage to Jerusalem in view of their own rival shrine.[66]

Whatever other factors might be involved, the fact remains that some figures seem to emerge as natural controversialists: the career of Dositheus,[67] pieced together from a patchwork of hostile sources, is not much different from that of Peregrinus. He went over to the Samaritans to avoid a charge of adultery among the Jews, and contrived a similar charge against a Samaritan sage. He failed to make a scholarly impression on the Jews with his emendations in the Pentateuch. He left writings in the custody of a widow: those who bathe in a certain pool emerge imbued with them; while he himself hid in a cave and starved to death. He was also alleged to have had an association with Simon Magus, with whom he shared Messianic claims.[68] The counterpoint between individualist and adventurer is characteristic.

URBAN TENSIONS

Time and again we find the quarrels of holy men intertwining with the pressures and problems of urban aristocracies.[69] Peregrinus had an elaborate quarrel with his native Parium over an inheritance. He left with a charge of patricide hanging over him and joined the Christians in Palestine.[70] Returning to find the affair unabated, he ceded his property to the city; he then attempted succesfully to regain it.[71] Thus far Lucian, of course with a malicious gloss. Various milder possibilities suggest themselves. Parium was in an area where we might suspect an already sizeable Christian presence:[72] was the charge of patricide levelled at Peregrinus because he was already a Christian, or was he driven to the Christians as the last refuge for a reputed patricide? The fact that the charge of murder was dropped on his ceding his property[73] might also conceal that the motive for the accusation was greed for Peregrinus' land.

We have ample testimony to the tension that will arise when holy men wish to operate on divided communities of Jew and Greek. Where Paul and Barnabas are in the business of giving and withholding eternal life – giving it to the outside world and withholding it from the Jews – the latter are 'jealous of the crowds'.[74] Their operations are revealing. The Acts-author accuses them of 'stirring up feelings among the women of standing who were worshippers, and among the leading men of the city'.[75] The best defence against a holy man is to mobilise the local aristocracy, including the influential women, against him.[76]

Paul's second letter to the Corinthians gives an important indication of how tensions can develop between the holy man and the community over which he wishes to exercise care or control. The rebukes of a previous letter have been received with dismay, and communicated not to Paul himself, who has failed to fulfil a previous plan to visit, but to Titus. The composite letter that is now presented as going to Corinth is replete with defensive nuances, and we can at least begin to see some of the problems that have arisen. One objection is quoted directly: Paul does not fulfil in his actual presence the personality implied in his letters;[77] there may also have been some notion of financial irregularity.[78] But there is also a somewhat clearer notion of 'the opposition' seen through Paul's eyes: as so often the true holy man sees himself as set in opposition to pretentious and outlandish mercenary charlatans.

But what might still have been perceived as private Jewish or Judaeo-Christian infighting was only one dimension in the diversity of the religious squabbles of the cities. One case in second-century Athens[79] is well known to us thanks to a long inscription in the Roman Market-Place.[80] The dispute was heard by Marcus Aurelius, and entailed an accusation brought by one Sentius Attalus and others that the office of sacred herald was being held by a member of the Eumolpid clan, Valerius Mamertinus, neither of whose parents comes from the Kerykes as traditionally required.[81] The matter was 'important' in the sense that the archaising tastes of the Greek Renaissance would themselves have demanded 'correctness' in such a detail;[82] secondly, who held what priesthood was an intensely political matter: we have no lack of other hints that the year of this affair marked the culmination of bad relations between the Athenian populace and individuals among the urban aristocracy against the millionaire magnate Herodes Atticus,[83] and a series of manoeuvres to 'take over' symbols of power and influence through irregular distribution of priesthoods is only one of a number of 'moves' in an infighting we still have to view from the outside.[84] But we cannot assume that its religious dimension was isolated: we shall shortly note the dispute which the Syrian Goharieni brought to Caracalla, in which their religious opponent obviously enjoys enviable political exemptions (from taxation and liturgies); we can suspect that religious sensibilities may be all too readily coupled with personal enmities.

Much more immediately dangerous was the disorder caused by Paul's stay in Ephesus. In this case Demetrius the silversmith not only makes out Paul to be a threat to the livelihood of his fellow craftsmen: he correctly sees the possibility that Paul's activities are a threat to the cult of Diana as such, and hence by implication to the position of Ephesus itself in Asia.[85] The town clerk raises the issue of public order, for which the Ephesians may be called to account; but insists on the harm Paul and his associates have done to the sacrifices to the goddess herself. The incident at least serves to show the scale of opposition; a full theatre chanting 'Great is Diana of the Ephesians' for two hours on end, so that Paul himself has to be restrained from appearing.[86] By contrast we find Apollonius of Tyana dealing with the temple-suppliers' profession in a characteristically different way, when he is made to rebuke the exporter of gods: the livelihood of artisans means little to the purist Pythagorean.[87]

A CASE STUDY: CALLISTUS

Time and again the various contributory elements in the quarrels of holy men seem to intertwine. The nature of the subject makes it impossible to be sure of ever getting to the bottom of any such disputes: we must be content to illustrate the varied facets of only a few. The career of Callistus, designated as heretical by Hippolytus,[88] usefully reflects the interacting pressures of the late second century of a figure who 'stayed with' the church in conditions where Peregrinus did not. Callistus begins auspiciously as a kind of Christian Epictetus, a slave of a Christian member of Commodus' household. He is entrusted as a fellow-Christian by one Carpophorus with banking deposits and accumulates holdings from widows and brethren. Suspected of embezzlement by the latter, he tries unsuccessfully to escape by sea; eventually released under surveillance, he begins in business again, and this time his business irregularities are mixed up with disturbances involving a Jewish congregation who bring him before the prefect for disturbing their assembly; the prefect has him sent to mines in Sardinia, where be obtains a pardon by the intercession of a presbyter Hyacinthus, allegedly acting on behalf of Marcia, concubine of Commodus; Victor, head of the church in Rome, has him live away from the city. Hippolytus does not state how Callistus came to be ordained: we simply find that under the patronage of one

Zephyrinus, 'an unlettered simpleton', he is able to play both sides against the middle, bribing Zephyrinus and 'inducing him to create continual faction among the brethren', to whom he himself could then play all things to all men. As bishop, he stands accused of perverting Sabellius and admitting heresy with patripassionist overtones;[89] as a social anarchist, he stands accused of forgiving sins on his own account and allowing women of rank to have slaves and freedmen recognised as husbands.[90]

One can scarcely begin to disentangle any sort of objective account of such a career from Hippolytus' narrative, which is content to see Callistus as the incarnation of villainy, leading on any simpleton he is able to delude. He appears as a rather more exclusively Christian version of the Peregrinus so consistently disparaged by Lucian. But two factors at least can be interpreted differently. The episcopal policies of Callistus can be seen as obvious enough cases of pragmatism: Callistus has to allow 'classless' Christian marriage to avoid the danger of lapses through mixed marriage, and he has to reconcile sinners to prevent lapse into paganism.

Some of the complex polemic levelled at Montanus by his opponent, a Christian Apollonius, has a similar ring. According to an informant Alexander the prophet lived with him for years: 'his robberies, and the other outrages for which he has been punished, there is no need for me to retail: the record office has the file. Who pardons whose sins? Does the prophet forgive the martyr's robberies, or the martyr the prophet's greed?'. A trial for robbery is mentioned before the proconsul Frontinus at Ephesus, as well as previous convictions. 'Then by a fraudulent appeal to the name of the Lord he brought about his release, having hoodwinked the faithful there; but the diocese he came from would not receive him, because he was a robber.'[91] Financial and theological accusation have again been allowed to coalesce, and again a unilateral account will not allow us to disentangle them.

The quarrel between Euphrates and Apollonius of Tyana is also notable for the diversity of accusations. A recurrent theme of contention in the purported correspondence of Apollonius is once more the theme of wealth: Euphrates appears to teach for pay and is even urged to distribute his possessions; wealth brings misery to the rich, and Euphrates is a *nouveau riche*.[92] He has twice accepted a sum of money from Vespasian, and has received gifts of money and citizenship,[93] possibly on the pretext of accepting it on behalf of his native land. But money seems to be far from the only problem:

Apollonius is made to express distaste for Euphrates' lifestyle in Italy,[94] and it may be something of a sore point that he himself has not had such an invitation;[95] his lifestyle as a whole seems divergent, and Euphrates is alleged to regard Pythagoreans as *magoi*.[96] There is also a more specific contention over Bassus of Corinth, the allegedly dissolute youth who has fled from Corinth in bad company and is evidently accepted by Euphrates but not by Apollonius.[97] Two letters of the latter deal with the subject. The youth and the sage had first had a happy association;[98] but two likely causes of friction can be deduced from the given material. As ἀγωνοθετής of the Isthmian Games, Bassus would have been vulnerable to correction or criticism from Apollonius;[99] while the sage's medical opinions might have been available in the case of the alleged poisoning of Bassus' father.[100] One notes also the unnamed Corinthian who had sarcastically asked if the Spartans intend to celebrate a theophany of Apollonius;[101] but there is currently no way of proving that this is Bassus or one of his associates.

THE COURSE AND CONDUCT OF DISPUTES

The variety of rivalries between holy men is such that we cannot lay down any rules of engagement for the conduct of disputes. But some observations can be attempted. The routines of exorcism themselves[102] could become a matter for competition. The Book of Acts offers a narrative in which seven sons of the Jewish priest Scaeva attempt to practise exorcism using the name of Christ ('by the Jesus proclaimed by Paul').[103] The spirit to be exorcised then answers back 'Jesus I recognise, and Paul I know, but who are you?'.[104] The unclean spirit-possessor then beats them up. Is this to be construed as violence by a militant supporter of Paul against his enemies, simply stating that he 'refuses to recognise them', but because of his violent behaviour is construed or declared to be out of his mind? The incident is certainly presented as good Christian propaganda: Jews and pagans alike are awestruck, and the prestige of Jesus Christ is enhanced; there is then a burning of magical books used by the new adherents to Christianity.[105] A similar scenario of competition invests the story of Paul's encounter with a Jewish rival in Cyprus:

> When [Saul and Barnabas] had gone through the whole of [Cyprus] as far as Paphos, they encountered some Jewish

sorcerer and false prophet by the name of Bar-Jesus. He was an *amicus* of the proconsul, Sergius Paulus, an astute man, who had invited Barnabas and Saul to join him and was eager to hear the word of God. But this Elymas the sorcerer (as his name is translated) opposed them and attempted to turn the proconsul away from the faith. But Saul (or Paul), was filled with the Holy Spirit, stared at him intently, and said, 'you low-down smooth-operating impostor! You son of the devil, you enemy of all righteousness, will you never stop twisting the straight paths of the Lord? And now look, the hand of the · Lord is on you: you shall be blind, and you shall not see the sunlight until it it time'. Instantly mist and darkness came upon him and he groped around at once for someone to take him by the hand. Then the governor, who had seen what had happened, became a believer, dumbfounded by Paul's teaching about the Lord.[106]

This incident might have been equally at home in the succeeding chapter. Here it preserves two details: that a Roman governor had a Jewish prophet on his staff, and that he was also prepared to show an interest in Saul and Barnabas; and further that he is prepared to take their abusive disconcerting of an opponent as a sign of superiiority. A religious consultant is a perfectly natural adjunct to a provincial governor; but he is judged on results, and failure may result in replacement.[107]

But what really could have happened in this case to bring about the discomfiture of Elymas? A historian's or theologian's perspective might be to dismiss the story, but it may be more instructive to look at it through the eyes of a jury. When the hand of the Lord struck Elymas, what was the hand of Paul doing? Was it pointing up to heaven, as the Acts-author may wish to imply (and may have believed); or was it planted between the eyes of the unsuspecting and therefore improvident Elymas – the first knockout in the history of muscular Christianity? We should hardly hesitate to believe that the cloakroom attendant for the stoners of Stephen was incapable of a little well-publicised violence on his own account; or that Paul would have interpreted such an assault during a private audience as a threat to public order. A reasonable guess at interpreting the sequence of events is that the apostle lost his temper and rendered Elymas insensible with a hand that he claimed was the hand of the Lord.

146

Plotinus emerges from such contests no less resilient. We hear that his magician rival Olympius of Alexandria's scheming went so far that he attempted to direct, through magical operations, the evil influences of stars at Plotinus. But he realised that his attempts fell back on himself, and he said to his friends that the psychic powers of Plotinus were so strong that the attacks of those who wished to hurt him rebounded on themselves. Plotinus did sense the attempts of Olympius to undermine him and said that his body had felt, at the time, like a purse whose strings had been pulled together; his limbs had been squeezed just like that. Olympius, however, ran the risk of hurting himself rather than Plotinus, and so he gave up.[108] Again we may well be dealing with a much less pretentious business than Porphyry's language would wish to imply. Does Plotinus in our parlance simply shame Olympius out of his malevolence?

In the case of Alexander of Abonouteichos we have an opportunity to see an actual campaign in progress between two rival forces:

> But when at last many sensible men recovered as if from a severe bout of intoxication, and got together against him, especially all those who were Epicureans, and when in the cities all his con-artistry and showmanship began bit by bit to be found out, he issued a terror manifesto, saying that Pontus was full of atheists and Christians who had dared to cast the vilest blasphemy against him; these he ordered them to expel with stones if they wanted the god to be propitious towards them. And on the subject of Epicurus he uttered an oracle which went something like this: for when someone asked him how Epicurus was managing in Hades, he replied 'with leaden fetter on his feet in filthy mire he sitteth' (Harmon). And his war against Epicurus was absolutely without truce or parley, as well it might have been . . . . Now disciples of Plato, Chrysippus and Pythagoras were his friends, and there was unalloyed peace towards them; but 'the untouchable Epicurus' – for that is the title he gave him, was rightly his bitterest enemy, since he took all that sort of thing as a big joke. Hence Alexander hated Amastris most of all the cities in Pontus, knowing that Lepidus and his followers and others like them were in the city in large numbers; and he refused to deliver any oracle to an Amastrian.[109]

Alexander has a readymade resource: the oracle on which his

reputation depends is his principal weapon against the opposition. The response on the fate of Epicurus is a reply to a loaded question which could easily have been planted by a supporter or a dupe of Alexander's own. Lepidus himself has been identified with the honorand of an inscription from Amastris itself ('Tiberius Claudius Lepidus, Chief Priest of Pontus and President of the Metropolis of Pontus'), as priest of Augustus.[110] It is not wholly clear, though strongly implied, that Lepidus himself is an Epicurean, a fact which would not necessarily preclude his agreeing to undertake a priesthood. But the principal cause of antipathy might well have been the diminution in status that the oracle might well have caused for the holder of such an office: the establishment has to close ranks against so suddenly successful an outsider.

The doctrines of Mani excited a similarly comprehensive backlash, like Lucian's pamphlets on Peregrinus or Alexander, or the account of Jesus Christ presented in Celsus from hostile tradition to discredit the Christians. This is embodied in the attack on Mani in the *Acta Archelai*.[111] This document purports to narrate the routing of Mani by the bishop of Carchar (Carrhae?) in a debate before Marcellus, a wealthy local Christian. According to this account Mani was the slave of a widow who had inherited the books of Terebinthus, disciple of one Scythianus, a man learned in the lore of the Egyptians, who had died in a 'flying accident' from the roof of the widow's house. Mani revises the books, and aged sixty disseminates his teaching, in the meantime having gone to Persia and changed his name. Having failed to cure the son of the King of Persia, he was imprisoned; in prison he sets to adapting Christian works he has bought. He escapes impending death, warned in a dream, by bribing the gaoler. Over the border in the Roman Empire he stages an unsucceessful confrontation with the local bishop of Carchar, before being rearrested and put to death by the King of Persia.

Such disputes and confrontations could be in danger of escalation to considerable levels of violence. The case of Apollonius' stoning the beggar in Ephesus is not an isolated instance of the potential violence of holy men.[112] The case of the deaths of Ananias and Sapphira are often cited as a pointer to how soon the Christian church had been perverted from the spirit of tolerance advocated by its founder.[113] But we find that very example cited with approval by Gregory of Nyssa: he defends the punishment of a rogue who, abetted by his partner, pretends to be dead on the road in order to defraud Gregory Thaumaturgus. When the latter puts a cloak over him the rogue is punished with genuine death; the narrator wastes no time in emphasising that he had got his deserts.[114]

One theme of the Book of Acts is the capacity of Jewish opposition to react often violently against Paul: at Antioch in Pisidia they mobilise the aristocracy, male and female;[115] the same thing happens at Iconium, where there is a plot to kill Paul with the connivance of the city authorities.[116] At Lystra the population which had taken Paul and Barnabas for pagan gods is won over by Jews from Iconium and Antioch;[117] while in Jerusalen itself it is Jews from Antioch who identify Paul and create a violent disturbance while he is deliberately engaged in dictinctively Jewish observances.[118]

We should, however, note that not all the confrontations of holy men are the result of spontaneous eruption of spontaneous opposition. One becomes aware also of a small and ill-assorted series of critics who might be described as trouble-shooters against charlatans. Oenomaus of Gadara is an example nearly contemporary with Apollonius of Tyana: he is a Cynic from Menippus' own native city and survives into the reign of Hadrian. He enjoys good relations with Jews at Tiberias and protests after three consultations of the oracle of Apollo at Claros have produced nonsense reponses and one oracle given indiscriminately to more than one recipient. The title of his work, quoted with relish by Eusebius, was γοήτων φώρα, the 'exposure of charlatans'.[119] The same label might justly be attached to much work of Lucian, especially in respect of his treatment of Alexander of Abonouteichos;[120] nor would he have been totally isolated since his addressee is one Celsus, the author of a *kata magōn* ('against magicians').[121] Lucian's record against Alexander amounts to an active role. Some such label must attach no less to Irenaeus, Hippolytus and Epiphanius in a Christian context: the rooting out of charlatans could readily concentrate on heresy-hunting.[122]

The study of antagonisms among holy men might be extended indefinitely. Enough illustrations have been offered, however, to suggest that almost anything can be drawn into a contest likely to degenerate into self-righteous fanaticism and ultimately violence, both of which may serve to obscure their origins still further. Too often we are left with a situation in which we seem to have only one side of the story, or where some important factor or wider context seems to be missing. One common factor or context seems present:

the holy man is an individualist who does not easily tolerate opposition, all the more so from those close to him; we can also expect volatile reactions from large populations in the hands of individuals offering the hope of revelations. And the holy man has his own way of coping with opposition: perhaps the last word should go to the epistolary tradition surrounding Apollonius of Tyana (*Ep.* 48.2):

> If two different accounts of me are given at present, and will be in the future also, what is surprising about that? For it is inevitable that conflicting stories are told about everyone who appears eminent in any field; . . . but good men accept the truth, as if they share some affinity with it; while the worthless do the opposite.

The manipulation is not subtle: do not believe my critics or you too are worthless. We must now attempt to view such defences from another point of view, as we see the holy man through the perspective of political authority.

9

AUTHORITY
Caesars, principalities and powers

We have seen the kind of situations in which a holy man will acquire friends and enemies: it is worthwhile to review how civil authorities, in particular Roman emperors themselves, could interact with mysterious strangers who claimed to have information in their interests – or to have powers beyond their own.

VESPASIAN AND THREE HOLY MEN

It is tempting to start by noting the part holy men of a variety of descriptions either played or are claimed to have played in events surrounding the revolt which brought Vespasian to power, and included his proclamation in Alexandria on 1 July AD 69. Josephus provides a characteristically inflated account of how he himself, when captured by Titus in the Jewish War two years before Vespasian's accession, had prophesied the latter's rise even when Nero was still emperor. One can readily appreciate the advantage of such a prophecy to both parties: it would have ensured that Josephus could not be handed over to Nero, since the prophecy would have endangered both its beneficiaries, Vespasian and Titus; and it would have been opportune for the Flavians to have on hand an important religiously connected Jewish leader to make such a prophecy independently, as it would have appeared. And after the event Josephus himself had no inhibitions about using it to magnify his own reputation.[1]

It is no surprise to find such a proclamation attributed also to Apollonius of Tyana. On hearing that Vespasian rises long before dawn to be at his correspondence, Philostratus has his sage claiming ὁ ἀνὴρ ἄρξει ('the man will rule').[2] But such a prophecy is contrived with caution: in context it might just as readily be taken to mean that Vespasian will exercise authority or has the makings of a competent administrator, without any real reference to imperial claims at all, a convenient and necessary fall-back should any coup fail.[3] We have similar accounts, this time from Jewish rabbinical sources, about an interview between Yohanan ben Zakkai and Vespasian. In spite of considerable variation, the three agree that Yohanan escaped from Jerusalem during the Jewish War and received the general's permission to go to Yavneh (Jamnia), there to reconstitute the survival of rabbinical Judaism. He foretells Vespasian's impending accession through a tradition that the temple will not be surrendered to a commoner, but to a king. According to one of the two principal versions he heals Vespasian of an attack of dropsy, and earns the right to save the life of his fellow Rabbi Zadok; in the other main version he is already known to the general, and is accordingly able to ask for retirement in Yavneh before he predicts the accession.[4] Whatever the religious complexion of a holy man, the foundation of a new dynasty was too momentous for him not to claim to have predicted.

Such predictions were not the end of the matter of Vespasian's accession. He himself also came to be cast in the role of a sacred healer. While still in Egypt he is presented in the historiographical tradition as beset by two requests from the blind and maimed for a cure, which persisted against his initial scepticism.[5] Tacitus offers an account of how an aspiring emperor can fulfil aspirations more properly associated with oriental expectations of divine kingship:

> One moment [Vespasian] was afraid of earning a reputation for vanity [if he failed]. The next, the entreaties of the afflicted men themselves and the words of his flatterers encouraged him. Finally he asked the doctors to estimate whether these particular conditions of blindness and atrophy could be cured by human means. The doctors discoursed on the various outcomes. As for the blind man, his vision was not totally impaired, and would return if the impediments were removed. The maimed man's limbs had been dislocated, but could be restored by correct manipulation. Perhaps this was the will of the gods, and the emperor had been chosen as their minister. In the last resort, the credit of effecting a cure could go to Caesar; the ridicule of a failure would fall on the victims. Accordingly Vespasian supposed that the way forward lay open to his destiny, and that no further step was beyond

belief. So with a smile on his face and the surrounding crowd
agog he carried out their request. At once the maimed man
had the use of his hand restored and the daylight dawned once
more for the blind man. Even to this day eye-witnesses recall
both acts after there has ceased to be any advantage in making
false claims.

Here we have an interestingly explicit commentary on the fact that
even a total amateur had nothing to lose by the 'staging' of a
miracle, provided he had the proper advice. But here the important
role is that of the entourage, either of the Serapeum at Alexandria or
of Vespasian himself; he requires a professional in the field before
he can assess the risk. It should of course be emphasised that the
healing took place in the Serapeum, and could therefore have been
properly attributed to Serapis himself. But there can scarcely be any
doubt as to the propaganda point that Vespasian or his advisers
were attempting to make.

A related event is still more characteristic of the likely methods of
holy men, though none such is actually named. Vespasian decided
to visit the Serapeum at Alexandria. Although the building had been
cleared, he claimed to have seen one Basilides in the building, whom
he knew to be both elsewhere and indisposed. The sighting was
taken as a portent of Vespasian's impending rule, thanks to the
element *basileus* ('king') underlying the supposedly divine appar-
ition.[6] Holy men had their uses, even if holiness might consist in the
opportune possession of a 'royal' name; and Vespasian might have
had occasion to reflect on the similar success of Alexander the Great
on his visit to the oracle of Zeus-Ammon at Siwa.

HOLY MEN AND IMPERIAL CRISIS

Not only at his accession but at any crisis in his reign an emperor
could come to rely, or be presented as relying, on a holy man. The
problem of the so-called 'thundering legion' in the reign of Marcus
Aurelius provides an example no less controversial than the role of
holy men in Vespasian's accession. In AD 174 a Roman detachment
had been surrounded by the Quadi, and were under pressure from
both heat and thirst, only to escape thanks to a dramatic rainstorm.
Dio's own comment is as follows: 'And in fact the story goes that a
man called Harnuphos, an Egyptian magician, who was in Marcus'
entourage, had summoned by means of some enchantments a

number of deities, including in particular Hermes, the god of the air, and by this means had brought about the rain'.[7] At this point however Dio's epitomator Xiphilinus intervenes on his own account and accuses Dio himself of suppressing the true cause of the miracle. He assures us that Marcus is not reported to have taken pleasure in 'consorting with magicians and acts of charlatanism' (μάγων συνουσίαις καὶ γοητείαις), and tells the story of a legion of Christians who, at the behest of Marcus, prayed to their own god, whose help Marcus duly acknowledged in a letter; the enemy was struck with a thunderbolt and the legion was accordingly nick-named κεραυνοβόλος ('bolt-hurler').[8]

It is difficult even to begin to make sense of such an incident: there was indeed a 'thundering legion', which had been so entitled ('fulminata') since Augustus. It seems totally improbable that a whole legion could have been Christian as early as the later second century. What for our purposes is important is the double attribution of the miracle – and its nature – to staff soothsayer and Christian presence alike. Marcus would have been an uncharacteristic tactician if he had not encouraged the maximum divine interest in the army's plight; a hedging of bets would have resulted in contradictory claims. The mere fact of a thunderstorm more advantageous to one side than the other is a perfectly credible basis for the claims. The Romans had more to gain from a break in the weather, and their military psychology was more likely to have profited from it.[9]

We have testimony of similar activity when Alexander of Abonouteichos issued an oracle during a previous campaign of Marcus against the Quadi and Marcomanni, directing that two lions be thrown into the Danube as part of a sacrifice to ensure victory. When disaster this time ensued, Alexander correctly defended the oracle, in that Glycon had not indicated which side would gain the victory.[10] Lucian takes the episode to indicate the barefaced fraudulence of Alexander; but once again it might just as readily be taken to indicate the latter's professionalism. The oracle has not over-committed itself in a very uncertain military situation, and presumably its author knew better than to try.

Amid the general propensity of holy men to dabble in Imperial matters, one phenomenon in particular impresses itself: the susceptibilities of emperors throughout our period to the professional astrologer.[11] The monotonous frequency of such patronage is related to the political situation itself. A man will be brought to court because he has information concerning the Emperor. If lucky and astute enough to be successful, he becomes indispensable to his master, and indeed cannot be allowed to fall into the wrong hands. For example we have no fewer than four accounts of a story about the future Emperor Tiberius. He would consult astrologers, then have the suspects thrown to their deaths to prevent their revealing the consultations – until one Thrasyllus foresaw his own likely fate and so proved his powers of foresight.[12] The historicity of such a tale is justly suspected; but it serves as a suitable paradigm of the ambiguous relationships which anyone claiming supernatural skills could expect from emperors and authorities. Thrasyllus undoubtedly survived to do well. Already a friend and astrological consultant of Tiberius during his period in Rhodes, he received Roman citizenship, taking his patron's name, and was able to contract a prestigious marriage with the daughter of Antiochus of Commagene. His son, Tiberius Claudius Balbillus, was consulted in turn by Agrippina the Younger, Nero and Vespasian; his grandson-in-law Macro had an important part as linkman in the fall of Sejanus. Astrology had served Thrasyllus and his family well.[13]

Nero's consuming interest in magic, and its motive, are ruefully noted by the Elder Pliny, for whom the Emperor's already exalted fortune only fired him with the ambition to issue commands to the gods as well; but he still abandoned the pursuit of the art, the supreme proof according to Pliny of its falsehood.[14] The same source gives us an insight into Nero's first-hand encounter with a magus of the most genuine variety, in the person of the client-king Tiridates: the latter had refused to travel by sea, because of the taboo held by the magi against polluting the sea with spittle or bodily functions. He had brought fellow-magi with him, and initiated Nero into their banquets; yet as Pliny wryly observes, the man giving him a kingdom was unable to acquire from him the magic art.[15]

Tiridates at least has an air of respectability: but the boundary between μαγεία and γοητεία was thinnest in the context of Imperial politics. Dio provides chilling testimony, and at first hand, to the effect of such operators when strategically placed as court favourites:

A eunuch took control over us. He was a Spaniard by the name of Sempronius Rufus, and his line was that of healer (φαρμακεύς) and juggler (γόης); for on this charge in fact he had been confined by Severus on an island.

His qualification had been that 'Caracalla devoted the best part of his leisure to indulging his curiosity above all his other diversions. For people brought him word of everything from every quarter, even the most trivial matters'.[16] Dio's purpose in reporting such a matter is of course to complain of senatorial indignity at the hands of a eunuch informer. But his report supplies a valuable insight into that most elusive of imperial interests: it is in the convergence of leisure, curiosity and security that an emperor is most exposed to the advice of holy men, soothsayers, or the like. Herod's much more familiar consultation of the magi in Matthew's Gospel had already provided just such a combination.[17]

A 'physiognomist royal' would have been equally well placed as the eyes of an emperor at court. Under Hadrian the sophist Antonius Polemo[18] recounts a case in his *Physiognomonica* of an encounter with a Corinthian with sunken eyes: the latter had joined the Emperor's entourage on a journey into Asia, where Polemo had turned his attention to him. The subject and his entourage had surrounded Hadrian under arms, in a menacing fashion; Hadrian was preparing for a hunt and so incommunicado, while Polemo and his companions were discussing the Emperor's predicament, and made specific mention of the intending offender, who had overheard them from the cover of a thicket. Confronted with their suspicions he confesses 'indeed, it is the work and dreadful design of a demon in my mind; alas, I am lost!'.[19] Here we have a good opportunity to notice the parameters around which perceptions can operate. Polemo attributes all his suspicions of a potential conspirator to physiognomonics, although both in the story and beforehand others factors are mentioned, including the man's drunkenness. The conspirator unmasked blames his behaviour on a demon. What we have, then, is an 'equal of the gods', as Polemo regarded himself, travelling with an emperor, exposing a demon, and confounding its supposed victim; from a different perspective, he might have been presented as an opportunist quack taking advantage of a series of intuitions and a lucky accident.

Even the many-sided Apollonius could appear to cast himself as a court informer. When the citizen body at Tarsus present a petition to Titus which he is about to refer to Vespasian, Apollonius urges that the former be as quick to confer a boon as he would be in punishing treason. But we should note the introduction to Apollonius' remarks: 'If I were to convict some of these men here of being enemies of yourself and your father, and of having sent representatives to Jerusalem to excite an uprising, and of being the secret allies of your most open enemies . . .'.[20] Here there is an implied hint that Apollonius had or might well in the future expect to have such information, and that his co-operation in divulging such confidences at the appropriate time might be prejudiced by delay in granting privileges. Apollonius' relationship may be more subtle than mere philosophical *politesse*.

A holy man's career might be considerably enhanced, at least in the eyes of a sympathetic biographer, by some spectacular act of defiance against an emperor; or an emperor might choose to turn a blind eye to abuse not directly associated with a threat to the state. Peregrinus had petitioned the mild Antoninus Pius for the return of his property, and was successfully counterpetitioned by his community of Parium. He accordingly attacked the Emperor, but suffered no more than expulsion from Rome.[21] As an unsuccessful petitioner of Cynic disposition, he could have been expected to be seen as little more than an exhibitionist nuisance, and treated accordingly.

But a holy man could also intervene against intemperate official action: Apollonius is attributed with a letter against Roman quaestors: 'First you hold office. So if you know how to hold office, why is it that during your term of office the condition of our cities has deteriorated? But if you do not know how to hold office, you ought first to have learned how to, and only then should you have done so'.[22] It is difficult to envisage any specific target or occasion: but the rebuke is carefully balanced between criticism and the prospect of constructive reconciliation. But more specific intervention was possible. When a Cynic philosopher accuses a local proconsul of depilation, Demonax suggests that the penalty for his insolence be commuted from the stocks or exile to – depilation for any future offence. The important point is that Demonax's opinion should have been asked at all.[23]

SOME DIVERSIONS

The witty rejoinder offered by a passing savant in this case offers a transition to another function of the holy man. Someone of such wide and often esoteric interests and experience is likely to be a source of curiosity and diversion to an emperor. The evidence is necessarily more miscellaneous than under other heads. We find Hadrian's witnessing a demonstration by the Egyptian Pachrates, duly proclaimed by a magical papyrus.[24] This boasts that 'Pachrates, the prophet of Heliopolis, revealed [the spell] to the Emperor, revealing the power of his own divine magic. For it attracted in one hour; it made someone sick in two hours; it destroyed in seven hours, it sent the Emperor himself dreams as he thoroughly tested the whole truth of the magic within his power. And marvelling at the prophet he ordered double fees to be given to him'. This Pachrates seems to have a fictional counterpart Pancrates ('All-powerful'), an Egyptian priest and holy man who figures in Lucian's version of the 'Sorcerer's Apprentice' tale, and may indeed have been something of a celebrated figure in the early second century.[25] But we are still left wondering about the nature of what Hadrian could actually have been shown: presumably the Emperor did indeed attend the rite as well as the preparation (on a high roof at moonrise); but does he actually sanction what would have purported to be an act of murder? And if so, of whom or what?

But the situation itself is familiar: we find Vespasian able to take time off from his political adventures to witness the exorcism performance by Eleazar 'the Essene': a ring containing a Solomonic prescription is applied to the patient's nostrils, and the demon is drawn out, while the patient falls down.[26] Any new advance in demon control is legitimate Imperial business, whatever its cultural context.

Some encounters with royalty are still more exotic: we find Apollonius of Tyana, for example, credited with encounters at Parthian and Indian courts,[27] or apostles converting the courts of Ethiopia or India. Even Jesus Christ is credited – by no less than Eusebius – with a consultation by letter from Abgar of Edessa,[28] the first transaction in that city's proud and prolonged Christian involvement. In most such cases there is a strong reflex to discredit material out of hand: it can rarely if ever be checked against the traditional triad of classical historians, and much oriental anecdote has an air of *ben trovato* about it. But it is worthwhile to look at several more exotic encounters in their own right.

One of the oddest phenomena that the religious diversity of the second century could produce was the account of the interview between Hadrian and Secundus.[29] The latter is a philosopher studying away from home; on the death of his father he decides to test the maxim that 'every woman can be bought' by testing his own mother's chastity. Posing as a visiting Cynic philosopher he arranges to seduce her; when she agrees he reveals his true identity;

she commits suicide, while he imposes a vow of silence on himself and becomes a Pythagorean on that account. His silence attracts the attention of Hadrian on a visit to Athens, presumably as a virtuous curiosity. The Emperor orders Secundus to break his vow, the sage refuses, and our philosopher is sent off for execution. But the excutioner is told to execute Secundus only if he *breaks* his silence; when he still refuses, he is brought back, and agrees to answer twenty questions in writing.

It is much easier to regard the whole account as an apocryphal tale, possibly with some foundation in fact, than as anything resembling an authentic account. Would Hadrian of all people have behaved in this way? Yet not only were this emperor's relationships with intellectuals uneasy and unpredictable;[30] the supposedly irrational condemnation order could have been justified on much the same grounds as Pliny's procedure against the Christians.[31] Secundus has committed an act of *contumacia* by refusing to answer the Emperor; by speaking subsequently to a mere executioner, he would have confirmed that this was indeed an act of defiance against the emperor, rather than a conscientious principle applied against all mankind.

But we are still left asking whether such a Secundus really existed. His Pythagoreanism has rightly been questioned: a lifelong silence may be a misunderstanding of the five-year novitiate; the questions-and-answers, while arguably Pythagorean in manner, are not distinctively so in matter.[32] It is possible that he is identical with the Athenian teacher of Herodes Atticus,[33] yet such a figure would ill accord with Secundus' reputation for silence. But there is another Secundus who may fit. We know a Valentinian Gnostic of that name,[34] and the *floruit* of the school would fit an early second-century date. The Valentinians were particularly interested in numerology, with which their whole creation theology was intertwined. Moreover, they held in high regard one *Sīgē* (Silence), whom they regarded as a fountainhead of wisdom. The curious tale might then have been the working out of an allegory ('I tried woman, and found her wanting; I consorted with *Sīgē* and it was the beginnings of wisdom'). The question remains unsolved, but the story would be less surprising in the light of such an identification.

Less silent but no less provocative is an encounter of Mani in the next century: the prophet is presented as disturbing the Persian Bahram I at an awkward moment, arriving for an audience when the King is in the middle of a meal and before he is to go hunting: he is already in the presence of Kerder, his personal enemy, and the King tells him he is unwelcome.[35]

> 'What wrong have I done?'. The King said: 'I have sworn not to let you come to this country'. And in his anger he spoke thus to the Lord [Mani]: 'Eh, what are you good for since you go neither fighting nor hunting? But perhaps you are needed for this doctoring and this physicking? And you don't even do that!'. The Lord replied thus: 'I have not done you any wrong. Always I have done good to you and your family. Many and numerous were your servants whom I have freed of demons and witches. Many were those from whom I have averted the numerous kinds of ague. Many were those who were at the point of death, and I have revived them'.[36]

The nature of Mani's services here are at any rate clear enough: like Jesus Christ, he claims to have been an exorcist and a healer.

One particular confrontation continues to puzzle, between the Roman Emperor Caracalla and the Syrian Gnosticiser Bardesanes of Edessa:

> He [Bardesanes] made a stand against Apollonius, the comrade of Antoninus, when he was requested to deny his Christianity. He almost joined the ranks of the 'confessors' and gave cleverly-contrived answers, in his courageous defence of the faith, saying that he did not fear death, which would inevitably be his lot even if he did not oppose the emperor. And so this man was highly endowed in every field until he fell into the error of his own heresy.[37]

Bardesanes is seen making a show of defiance against Caracalla, no doubt when the latter subjugated Edessa in AD 216 and took Abgar IX as a prisoner to Rome.[38] But who is this Apollonius? No such personage appears to be known in the entourage of Caracalla. But the name has a different kind of resonance under the Severi: it may not be a friend of Caracalla in the normal sense who emerges as the opponent of Bardesanes, but the long-dead Apollonius of Tyana, of whom Caracalla's mother commissioned the biography by Philostratus.[39] That he had views on fate might reasonably be surmised from the attribution of four books on astrology (though the whole business is hedged by Philostratus).[40]

The involvement Philostratus assigns to this same Apollonius of Tyana entails a strong association with Roman emperors and their retinue from Nero to Nerva. Not all of the material can be allowed to stand in precisely the form in which Philostratus presents it, though at least a proportion of his slips may stem from attempts to harmonise treacherously incompatible sources. For the reign of Nero, Philostratus presents in effect a syncrisis between two encounters of Apollonius: with Telesinus, one of the consuls for AD 66, favourable to the sage; and with the hostile praetorian prefect Tigellinus.[41] Apollonius is never made to confront Nero directly, and the hiatus is difficult to interpret. It is generally felt that Philostratus has clumsily obtruded an involvement with Rome in the reign of Nero to make up for the fact that his role at this time was either non-existent or next to it. But there is an element of plausibility in the 'warning-off' of a distinguished religious expert in a hearing *intra cubiculum* by the praetorian prefect: Tigellinus wants 'no trouble' and acts as *agent provocateur*, by asking what Apollonius thinks of Nero: he receives a skilful answer worthy of a *chreia*: 'Better than you do . . . for you think it is a fitting act for him to sing, while I think it is fitting for him to keep silent'. The criticism is patent enough; but it can be read as a carefully contrived compliment – from a Pythagorean.

Under Vespasian Apollonius is again somewhat equivocal: the early 'proclamation' and advice to the prospective emperor is balanced by explicit criticism of the withdrawal of freedom from the Greek cities;[42] Apollonius emerges in a manner which appeals to the sophistic and Philhellene Philostratus, but no less plausibly on that account. The relationship to Titus is rather more bland: commendations for not shedding blood or for obedience to his father; diplomatic intercession on the subject of the Cynic Demetrius,[43] or polite intervention on behalf of Tarsus;[44] but more ominously a prophecy to guard against Domitian, and a cryptic indication of prospective poisoning.[45] With regard to relations with Domitian himself, the sources seem to point Apollonius in two different directions. The *Life of Apollonius* has its share of sniping at rulers. Apollonius will be held to defy the tyrant – from a safe enough distance. The sage demonstrates at the theatre against a governor of Asia when a play of Euripides is being performed with reference to tyrants;[46] or he reminds governors that there are hymns in honour of (the proverbial tyrannicides) Harmodius and Aristogeiton at the Panathenaic Festival.[47] He remonstrates with the sun against the impunity of Domitian's execution of vestal virgins – and his other murders, by implication;[48] or pours scorn on the highly unpopular vine-edict.[49] All such situations are presented in ways that connect them with Apollonius' religious interest in some way; so is his intervention in the rites at Ephesus in honour of Domitian's marriage with Julia, whose husband the emperor had murdered.[50]

By contrast, the two alleged letters of Apollonius to Domitian are exceedingly mild, and it is not too difficult to envisage how this sage would have been able to survive the reign on the strength of them: 'If you have power, as you do, you should also have to acquire wisdom. And again if you had wisdom but had no power, then you would need power. For each of these requires the other, just as vision needs light and light needs vision; you must shun the barbarians and not rule over them. For since they are barbarians, it is not right that they should do well'.[51] But there may be a sting in the tale: the phrase οὐ γὰρ θέμις αὐτοῖς βαρβάρους ὄντας εὖ πάσχειν could just be taken to mean 'it is not right that being barbarians they should suffer you lightly'. If anything should go wrong with Domitian's frontier policy, then Apollonius would still have been on record as having opposed it.

THE MECHANICS OF AUTHORITY: THE HEARINGS OF PAUL AND JESUS

The best documented encounters we have of prominent holy men being processed by Roman authority are the cases of Paul and Jesus Christ. The Luke-author who supplies them in the greatest detail is far from objective; his aim is the partly apologetic one of setting the new covenant community of his Judaeo-Christian God in harmony with the Graeco-Roman environment, through a variety of sometimes symbolic encounters.[52] But this wider theological motive does not obscure a consistent framework of Roman legal procedure either;[53] to anyone familiar with Pliny's subsequent treatment of Christians there will be few real surprises.

Paul's first serious encounter with authority is in Corinth before Lucius Junius Gallio, the brother of the philosopher Seneca, in his capacity as proconsular governor of Achaea. The latter takes the strict line that criminal activity must be distinguished from 'raising questions about words and names and your Jewish law'; and he leaves the matter with the Jewish community, in this case embodied in the local synagogue, even to the extent of turning a blind eye when Sosthenes, the chief officer of the synagogue, is beaten up in full view of the bench.[54] But a more serious and complex adventure with authority arises in Jerusalem: 'Jews from Asia' assert that Paul, seen in company with Trophimus of Ephesus, has let the latter, a Gentile Greek, into the exclusively Jewish precinct of the temple. A riot situation threatens to develop over the lynching of Paul, who is promptly arrested; but the tribune is unable to ascertain any facts from the mob.[55] Paul speaks Greek to the local tribune, Claudius Lysias, and establishes that he is not a recently infamous Egyptian rabble-rouser, a confusion which would have prompted Paul's rescue in the first place; he is a Jew from Tarsus, and is given permission to address the crowd (in Aramaic, strategically). The spectacle is not easy to envisage as it stands – not least thanks to the detail that Paul, so recently manhandled by the crowd, is able to make a speech at all.[56] In his subsequent performance, moreover, he does not mention the accusation, but rather makes a general apology for his life; the crowd still call for his death, and when he is to be interrogated under the lash he appeals to his Roman citizenship.[57] He is now brought before the chief priests and Sanhedrin, and reveals himself now also as a Pharisee, in common with many others present, and divides them against the Sadducees.[58] He is now transported to Caesarea by the tribune to forestall a reported plot by Jews to kill him, and sent to the Roman governor Felix.[59] In view of his Roman citizenship this step would have had to have taken place in any case. The hearing before Felix eventually results in adjournment, and several further interviews. Two years later Porcius Festus succeeds Felix and imprisons Paul to gratify the Jews.[60] When the chief priests and leaders of the Jews secure a hearing in order to lay an ambush, he appeals to Caesar to forestall Festus' favouring the Jews.[61]

At this point procedures are complicated by the interest shown in the case by the client-king Herod Agrippa, who would have had no competence to deal with the case given the pending appeal to Caesar. The presumed point is that Agrippa, though not governor of Judaea itself, is none the less an expert in Jewish affairs (he has custody of the priests' vestments and could depose the high priest); Festus announces at a large hearing before Agrippa that he wishes the King to cross-examine so that he can put it in his report to Caesar.[62] This is the cue for another apologetic speech by Paul,[63] with Agrippa likewise unable to find any fault, but rather able to indulge in some good-humoured banter with the accused.[64]

Such a sequence of proceedings bristles with difficulties not to say improbabilities, and one notes certain tendencies which naturally impose themselves on the narrative: consistent throughout is the theme that Rome has no quarrel with Paul nor Paul with Rome; that he has broken no law, and that only a Jewish inability to compromise or rather tolerate is to blame; while exposure to the highest echelons of Roman authority has repeatedly cleared him. A subtheme of the proceedings is the tendency of Roman officials to wish to placate the Jewish authorities when possible in religious matters in which they themselves have no interest or competence.[65] A third trait might be suspected as a characteristic Pauline tendency, of only revealing a small part of his identity at a time, to maximum climactic effect: that he is from Tarsus, a Roman citizen, and a Pharisee.[66]

Otherwise it is difficult to distinguish a kernel of facts from literary reconstruction: in particular Luke could have had no first-hand eyewitness information of the private conversation between Festus and Agrippa.[67] But one tendency once more may account perfectly plausibly for at least a proportion of the improbabilities: the generally improvisatory nature of the proceedings. If Pliny had no experience of hearings about Christians before his encounter with them in Bithynia,[68] then Felix and Festus would have had still less opportunity to familiarise themselves with the 'New Way'. They would simply have had to play the affair by ear in the light of the local situation, convening such hearings as they could. If Festus chose to let Agrippa have a go, that was fair enough, so long as Paul duly arrived before 'Caesar' in due course.

The trial of Jesus Christ entails related problems, all the more closely since one of the four evangelists will also have been the source for the hearings undergone by Paul. The overall impression in all four gospels is similar enough: that Jesus was condemned under pressure from the Jews, to whom Pilate, himself sympathetic to Jesus, reluctantly gave in. How much such a state of affairs fits the total pattern of evidence may emerge; the problem is that it fits so neatly the political climate of the period when the gospels themselves would have been written, from the mid-sixties onwards, when close association with Judaism in the eyes of Rome would have been awkward. Christians were not at war with the Roman Empire; the Palestinian Jews were, and immediately after the Jewish War they were dominated by Pharisaism: why not dissociate Christ from 'anti-Romanness' and blame the Pharisees for his death?

The evidence for the trial proceedings, as in the case of Paul, leaves plenty of scope for doubt and misgiving. There is an extraordinary meeting of the Sanhedrin after the arrest, designed to catch

Pilate at an opportune moment; Jesus Christ is then accused before Pilate, who proposes the unheard-of alternative of releasing a robber Barabbas instead.[69] Jews assert that they have no power to impose the death penalty; one evangelist, Luke, mentions yet a third stratum, a hearing before Herod Antipas.[70] Jesus gives reticent answers, to say the least, and he is handed over to be crucified, despite Pilate's acknowledgement that he can find no fault with him.[71] The penalty of crucifixion was a Roman one; from the Jews one would have expected stoning.

A bold attempt was made over two decades ago to make historical sense out of all this from the side of New Testament scholarship. S. G. F. Brandon[72] took Palestinian politics for the basis of a charge that the evangelists systematically and almost totally cover up the embarrassment that Jesus was crucified by Roman authorities on a charge of sedition. Occasionally in the evangelists' accounts it is let slip that Jesus claims to be the King of the Jews; he has only just been at the head of a triumphal entry into Jerusalem, immediately after which he has 'cleansed the temple'. Brandon sees this as a complement to the Zealot rising, in which Barabbas was probably involved; and points out the potential political overtones of names like Boanerges ('sons of thunder'), to say nothing of the associations of Simon Zelotes. In other words Christ would have had the ambition of overthrowing the temple, and whatever disturbance took place there, he had clearly gone too far for the temple authorities; but Roman authorities were also likely to look with more than dispassionate interest on someone who attracted vast crowds into the wilderness and there had been offered some kind of Messianic kingship.

This line of argument has the merit of trying to see how Jesus Christ would have appeared to Roman authorities, though in the handling of the temple-cleansing and its background it tends to rely on over-extended hypothesis. The central improbability it sets out to explain is that Pilate would not have acquitted Jesus and then connived at his execution. But we do have just such an instance, from a Christian context, as soon afterwards as the early second century. Pliny gives Christians a hearing, puts them in an awkward position *vis-à-vis* the Imperial cult, then executes them; but not without conducting an investigation of their doctrines and practices and finding them harmless.[73] One suspects (economic) pressure by local informers;[74] but whatever the reason or complex of reasons, the fact remains that a Roman provincial administrator was perfectly capable of executing people he believed to be relatively harmless on the strength of nothing more than local ill-feeling and the vague premiss of setting an example of the rewards of *pertinacia*. One might suspect that Christ would have fared no better under the humane and well-meaning Pliny than under Pontius Pilate. Ironically there is the same familiar twist: it is sacrificial meat for sale once more that gladdens the heart of Pliny;[75] as it would doubtless have gratified the temple authorities after the removal of their outspoken critic.

However unique such hearings might appear in the eyes of Christians, it is important to note that they were certainly not the last of their kind. The problem of the religious disputant with substantial claims of spiritual power could come in the pagan world as well. The case of the false 'Dionysalexander' did not result in any imperial hearing. But a not entirely dissimilar matter had been heard by Caracalla only a few years earlier in AD 216: the proceedings were recorded on a temple column a short distance east of Damascus. The local villagers, the Goharieni, protest to the Emperor by the unusual device of direct petition: a usurper who enjoys tax immunity and exemption from liturgies has taken to wearing a gold crown and exercising a right of precedence, and duly equipped with a sceptre has now proclaimed himself the priest of Zeus.[76] In the eyes of a Roman emperor such claims would not have been so very different from those of the man accused of calling himself King of the Jews in the context of a disturbance involving the temple authorities; but nothing resembling the possibility of a Jewish Revolt was at stake here, and Caracalla presumably found in favour of the petitioners, if we are to account for the setting up of the inscription at all.

Holy men, then, could expect a mixed reception from authority. Support of a dynasty might well produce alliance and reward; opposition could expect at best tolerant indifference, and any holy man perceived to be a threat to public order could expect much worse; but Roman authority was not primarily directed against vaguely other-worldly figures as such. And between the extremes we find practitioners whose aims might be to interest, divert, or persuade a curious official or emperor, or enlist or be claimed to enlist hard-pressed and bemused officials to vindicate their own personal probity against public or private opposition.

10

TRAVEL
Holy men on the move

We have now seen something of the holy man's relationship with his fellow men; but for some at least a good deal of their time must have been spent in actually reaching their eventual clients. For some holy men the nature of their vocation either meant or entailed a substantial amount of travel, and it has been and remains the task of modern scholars to recreate their likely *modus operandi* in the field.[1] In some of the most conspicuous cases we have little more than inference to go on. The dramatic spread of Marcionism in the mid-second century implies relentless missionary activities on the part of Marcion or his most immediate followers, as far as Italy, Egypt, Arabia, Syria, Palestine, Cyprus and Persia. A useful clue as to the means of accomplishing much of this is offered by the orthodox Christian gibes against Marcion himself, as *nautēs* or *nauklēros* ('sailor, sea-captain'): equipped with his own vessel a holy man could be assured of accomplishing a great deal more than on foot, as Jesus Christ himself would not have been slow to realise: not for nothing are the first disciples fishermen. If called from their nets, none the less they subsequently ensured that their master had the use of a boat. Faced with the prospect of getting Thomas to India, the author of the *Acts of Thomas* has Jesus Christ fraudulently arranging for his apostle to be passed off as a slave who can be sold to a sea-going merchant about to sail for the sub-continent.[2] Distance in the ancient world was most readily traversed by water-transport, given the nature of terrain and roads alike.

It is in this context that the movements of St Paul are by far the best documented – though never well enough – and provide a starting-point for the whole subject, by apprising us of the travel requirements of one missioner over a relatively restricted area. The Book of Acts appears to distinguish three 'missionary journeys'. In

167

spite of more or less constant query over individual details, not least in regard to text and redaction, the outlines of such journeys make fairly sound and self-consistent sense as they stand. Paul's first journey takes him with Barnabas to Cyprus, hence to Pisidia, Lycaonia and Pamphylia in southern Asia Minor.[3] As Barnabas was a Cypriot, and Paul a native of Tarsus in Cilicia, each was in an area where he might have the greatest hope of previous contacts. Lystra in particular was far enough into the interior to offer a supposedly barbarous attitude to strangers with spiritual revelations to offer; apart from consolidating the Galatian mission itself, Paul does not appear to try his luck up country again. The so-called Second Journey begins as a consolidation of this area, but with first a change of partner, Silas (Silvanus), allegedly because of a quarrel with Barnabas over the presence of John Mark. The consolidation does not evidently allow further proselytisation 'in the province of Asia' which is 'prevented by the holy spirit'.[4] We have already surmised a reason; but there may well have been others still outside our knowledge, not least in respect of the distribution of Diaspora Jewish communities that might act as a base, or the capacity of Paul's Jewish-Christian opponents to reach them too fast. Only when Paul reaches Troas, and experiences a vision of an invitation to Macedonia, does the mission proceed by sea to Philippi, and landwards along the coast.[5] The criterion may well have been the stated presence of substantial Greek-speaking Jewish congregations in the towns, though this seems not to have been the case in Philippi itself; it is explicitly so at the following, Thessalonica and Beroia, the latter more receptive than the former.[6] Paul then presumably sails to Athens, and finally arrives in Corinth, where he stays for at least eighteen months. Again one can surmise the benefits of persevering in an international commercial centre with excellent sea communications; any disadvantages of a partly transient congregation would have been offset by their ability to take the Gospel of Paul to the largest number of other maritime centres. He returns to Syria by sea via Ephesus to Caesarea, before again consolidating his work in Galatia and Phrygia.[7] The itinerary evokes a variety of different responses to Paul's missionary activities; and a variety of different opportunites for support and hospitality.

A third journey consolidates the work of the second, and again, despite the elliptical nature of the Acts-account, enables us to make inferences about the practicalities of travel. The narrative from Acts 19.21 proceeds as if Paul simply decides to revisit Macedonia and

Achaea, and proceed to Jerusalem. But it seems clear enough from the concluding events in Ephesus, in particular the riot of silversmiths, that Paul is either a liability there or at the very least that his own life is in danger.[8] He travels to Macedonia, presumably by sea, and subsequently encounters a further threat to his life (in Achaea) as he is about to embark for Syria: this would have given rise at least to the suspicion that the plot was to be carried out on board ship, hence the decision to retrace his steps and go via Macedonia. The sea journey is catalogued step by step from there onwards: Philippi to Troas (five days); Paul is picked up at Assos (hence to Mitylene, past Chios and Samos to Miletus). Here he elects to meet representatives from Ephesus: 'For Paul had decided to pass by Ephesus and so avoid having to spend time in the province of Asia'.[9] Once more Paul's evident unpopularity in Ephesus itself is simply glossed over. The voyage then continues via Cos, Rhodes, Patara, and possibly Myra. There the transfer is made to a (cargo)-ship bound for Phoenicia: they round Cyprus and sail to Tyre, thence by means unspecified to Ptolemais, Caesarea, and finally Jerusalem.[10]

We are conscious throughout this part of the narrative of careful preparation on the part of Paul's party: Timothy and Erastus are sent to Macedonia ahead of Paul, while there is a seven-man team (again including Timothy) to act as an advance party from Macedonia to Troas (Paul had evidently stayed behind to celebrate the Passover in Macedonia). The actual purpose of the mission to Jerusalem is not stated (the carrying of monies as poor-relief); Paul seems to protest over money in his conversation with representatives from Ephesus.[11]

The movements of Jesus Christ are far more difficult to determine or account for than those of his most well-documented apostle. Much of his missionary enterprise would seem to have been confined within Galilee itself,[12] though fame of it is claimed well beyond: the geography of the region entails close interaction between parallel valleys and high hill-country,[13] so that a holy man can withdraw and reappear in and out of the community as he pleases. The Sea of Galilee could act as a rapid transport to and from the attention of crowds. In general individual gospel accounts are not only vague but given over to schematising the movements of their subjects for editorial reasons, as when the Egyptian journey in the infancy narrative in Matthew is invoked to correspond to the prophecy 'Out of Egypt have I called my son'. It may also be the case that our itineraries are incomplete, as when Jesus curses

Chorazin and Bethsaida;[14] there is otherwise no mention, but a clear enough implication, of his having visited the former. Capernaum on the other hand may have served as a convenient base because of Simon Peter's associations there.[15] But again there is no record of activity in the far more populous Sepphoris or Tiberias, for no obvious reason. Yet the facts of social geography in the first century AD may be able to tell us more than this. It is useful to reflect on the pattern pointed out by Freyne that Galilean unrest throughout the period tends to erupt in Jerusalem: its inhabitants have a strong provincial independence whose loyalites are expressed by pilgrimage to Jerusalem, and trouble there is a safety-valve rather than Zelotic revolution at home.[16] This would make good sense of Jesus Christ's own pattern of action, in which actual violence in the course of the Passion week contrasts with a generally placid pattern of activity in the north.[17] But activities are by no means confined to Galilee or Jerusalem: Jesus visits Caesarea Philippi, the Decapolis, Tyre and Sidon, and Samaria; and whatever the reservations of the evangelists, serves a non-Jewish as well as a Jewish population.

But the most dramatic impact of a holy man in his lifetime during our period would have been Mani.[18] His point of departure was from the Syriac-speaking area which included his homeland in southern Mesopotamia. At twenty-four he had broken with his father's sect of Elchasaites, to travel through north-western Iran and subsequently India; he arranged his own missionaries to evangelise the West with what he conceived as a world religion and successor to the local religions of Buddha, Jesus and Zoroaster, and himself converts the brother of the Persian Shapur.[19] Given the ambitions of his design, the most significant 'holy men on the move' in the mid-third century would have been the Manichees. Their founder had the advantage of an upbringing among the Elchasates whose activities would have stretched aross the none-too-well-defined boundaries between the Roman and revitalised Sassanid Empires. It seems clear enough that Mani set out with an even wider and more ambitious vision of a world religion than even his acknowledged model Paul had done. He is aware that messengers of God have brought their messages to local areas in the past – Buddha to India, Zarathustra to Persia, Jesus to the West:[20]

> But my hope, mine will go toward the West, and she will go also towards the East. And they shall hear the voice of her

message in all languages and shall proclaim her in all cities. My church is superior in this first point to previous churches, for these previous churches were chosen in particular countries and in particular cities.[21]

Moreover, to a religious man with a mission who would have been an Aramaic speaker in Iran, the world would have looked very different to the perspective of Christ or Paul, with a much stronger awareness of India and China and Ethiopia. Furthermore, like Paul and unlike Jesus Christ, Mani was a literary communicator. Not only did he himself travel extensively within the Sassanid Empire, but he commissioned disciples who were sent to the Western Empire (Adda, Patik, Gabyab, Pappos, Thomas, Akouas). We know that the first two of these were equipped with a scribe, and that Adda was subsequently sent three more.[22]

Beside the basic missionary enterprises, one exceptional pilgrimage can be noted: the progress of Ignatius, Bishop of Antioch, to martyrdom in Rome. Condemned around AD 107 under Trajan, Ignatius was able to communicate with churches or their representatives *en route*. Representatives of the churches at Tralles, Magnesias and Ephesus met him at Smyrna; at Troas he wrote letters to the Philadelphians, to the congregation back at Smyrna, and to its bishop Polycarp.[23] The issues at a crucial point in the history of the church would have benefited immeasurably from such a journey to martyrdom: the martyr had here an opportunity to use the enormous potential prestige of his forthcoming status both to enjoin others in his example and to insist on the status of an orthodox ordained clergy at a time when standardisation by creed and canon was still very far from being attained.

CURIOSITY: VIEWING WONDERS AND ANTIQUITIES

But holy men did not always travel to spread a message: they might wish to enlarge their intellectual as well as their spiritual horizons, to act as pilgrims or sacred tourists,[24] or so to plan their itineraries that these motivations could converge. Lucian well recreates the intellectual horizons of the wealthy young Eucrates, the 'Sorcerer's Apprentice', travelling from second-century Athens to the Nile:

When I was staying in Egypt while I was still a young man (I had been sent on my travels by my father to finish my education), I had the urge to sail up to Koptos and go from there to Memnon in order to hear the statue sound its miraculous greeting to the rising sun. Well then, I heard from it no meaningless voice, as ordinary people tend to do, but in my case Memnon himself actually opened his mouth and gave me an oracle in seven verses; . . . but on the voyage up-river it so happened that we shared our voyage with a man from Memphis, one of the temple scribes, amazingly learned, and knowledgeable in all the lore of the Egyptians . . . I realised that he was some holy man, and gradually, thanks to my friendly disposition, I became his unofficial companion and associate, so that he shared all his secret knowledge with me . . . and I want to tell you what I heard from Amphilochus in Mallus, when the hero spoke with me in my waking state and gave me advice about my affairs, and what I saw with my own eyes, and then in proper order what I saw at Pergamum and what I heard at Patara; for when I was returning home from Egypt I heard that the shrine in Mallus was very eminent and very reliable, and that it gave a clear response, answering to the letter whatever a person wrote in his tablet and handed over to the prophet. So I thought that it would be a good idea to give the oracle a try when I was sailing past and consult the god for some advice about my future.[25]

Eucrates' 'round' of oracles is little different from what one might expect of Aristides; and his naive garrulity is not too far removed from that of Egeria. He had met Pancrates ('All-powerful'), whose name must at least allude to the Pachrates who demonstrated before Hadrian.[26] And like Aristides he is prepared to interpret each and every religious phenomenon as a mark of personal favour to himself.

Not too far removed from such motivation are the journeys attributed to Apollonius of Tyana. Here we have no *kērugma* and no Second Coming to impart a sense of urgency, and no very precise itinerary available to us; but that must not be taken to mean that Apollonius' journeys would have been any less purposeful: if anything they would have been typical enough for the first century. Apollonius first gains a reputation with the shrines of Asclepius at Aegeae, Aspendus and Antioch; then follows a visit to Parthia and India; a round of Mediterranean visits including Antioch, Cyprus, Ephesus, and Smyrna, with a return to Ephesus for the plague; a visit to Rome, with an excursion westwards as far as Cadiz; a visit to Egypt and Ethiopia, and a further visit to Rome. And throughout Philostratus presents his subject as 'nowhere failing to exhibit his constancy . . . for the sage will never reform bad character unless he has schooled himself beforehand never to change his own attitudes'.[27] Most of Philostratus' outline has been questioned: the sages he himself respects are the most remote from Mediterranean civilisation, while the visit to the Ethiopian gymnosophists seems to reflect a very suspect geographical location;[28] but there is no denying the existence of a strong local tradition at least on the eastern seaboard of the Mediterranean for Apollonius' visits.

Two instances of Apollonius' less exotic travels may have received less attention than the overall ensemble. In Phlegon's collection of miracle-stories we have a report of a jar of stone ('as Apollonius says') at Messena in Sicily which was shattered by the force of the storms and torrential rain; a threefold human head fell out of it, each with two rows of teeth. People enquired whose head it was, for it bore the inscription 'of Idas'. The Messenians accordingly made another, so Phlegon tells us, at public expense and worshipped the hero, seeing he was the one of whom Homer says 'And of Idas, who was the strongest of mortal men of that time: indeed he shot an arrow against Apollo for the sake of a beautiful nymph'. Now Phlegon's treatise does not tell us who this Apollonius was: but his next entry but one has an Apollonius 'grammaticus' cited as a source for earthquake in the reign of Nero. One conjecture should strike us right away: the likely consultant would have been not either of the available early Imperial grammarians for which such matters would have been right at the edge of their natural range, but Apollonius of Tyana, in his capacity as a religious conservationist and restorer; we know from Philostratus that he did indeed visit Sicily, by implication in the reign of Nero.[29]

Again, Apollonius restores Palamedes' shrine opposite Lesbos. Philostratus, himself a native of nearby Lemnos, had seen it, so that here we seem to be dealing with local tradition.[30] The actual details are duly elaborated with considerable dramatic panache by the biographer, but the reasons for Apollonius' emphatic affinity with this particular hero are not stated. From the same author's *Heroicus* however they emerge more clearly: Palamedes is responsible for the standard discoveries of a culture-hero;[31] in espousing a hero so conspicuously unmentioned by Homer, Apollonius can show himself once again superior to the tribe of grammarians and littérateurs.

We are in the world of sacred periegesis dear to Aristides[32] and Pausanias[33] in their very different ways.

SAVING THE SACRED SHIP

One motif naturally arises out of the constant traffic of religious messengers along the trade-routes of the Roman Empire and well beyond: the idea that religion itself is a portable material commodity. A Manichaean view saw the apostle's route as that of a merchant who sails back with a double load of merchandise.[34] Christian polemic was not slow to see Manichaeans as the merchants many of them may well have been. For Epiphanius, 'This Scythian . . . acquired skill in the foolish tenets of the world. He was always making visits to the land of India for business trips and did a great deal of trade. As a result he acquired a great load of earthly goods, and would travel by way of the Thebaid';[35] and it has been plausibly, though not conclusively, argued that the merchant Julianus of Laodicea, commemorated at Lyons, would have been a carrier of Christian spiritual merchandise rather than conventional cargo.[36]

Apollonius of Tyana's former associate Euphrates does not escape such an accusation at the hands of the master:

Once you had an ordinary cloak and a long white beard and nothing more. How is it, then, that you now slink back to sea with a ship full of silver, gold, goods of every sort, multi-coloured clothing, and every other kind of adornment, besides conceit, pretention and wretchedness? What is your cargo? What manner of peculiar merchandise is this? Zeno was a trader only in dried fruits.

And again: 'If you reach Aegeae and empty your ship there, you must return to Italy at the double and flatter all alike, the sick, the aged, orphans, the rich, the dissolute, and every Midas and Getas'.[37] As so often, the ultimate situation in the genre is provided by Philostratus. Apollonius of Tyana is intending to travel on a ship whose owner is planning to export statues of gods from Athens to Asia Minor (luxury statues of gold and stone, and of gold and ivory). The image-maker wishes to decline to take passengers in company with his gods, thereby inviting a harangue from Apollonius about the sanctity of his own person, and the impiety of anyone who had made the gods a trade.[38] Or when passing into

Mesopotamia Apollonius himself is asked by the customs-officer what he is taking out: 'Sophrosyne, Dikaiosyne, Arete, Encrateia, Andreia, Askesis, and a host of similar female names'. He is mistaken for a trafficker in slaves, whose names he is obliged to record. He replies that this is impossible, 'for I do not leave them off as slaves but as mistresses'.[39]

When at sea holy men are perhaps the more inclined to feel the elements at their beck and call. When a voyage ends safely the holy man will take, or at least be given, the credit for safe arrival: any holy man lost aboard ship with his faithful biographer and all hands will not of course be represented in any statistics.

In the course of Mark's account of the stilling of the storm[40] Christ is made to give orders to the wind and the waves; but the 'miracle' could have been reported in exactly the same way if he had merely cursed the wind (ἐπετίμησεν) and told any of the disciples who had wakened him to be quiet and calm (σιώπα, πεφίμωσο). The most that can be credited is that a practised seafarer on the sea of Galilee has some idea when a storm is at its height and times a dramatic outburst accordingly.

No more remarkable is the report that Apollonius of Tyana disembarks from a Syracusan ship at Leucas, and continues on a Leucadian vessel to Lechaeum: the Syracusan vessel sinks. (Apollonius has already claimed reincarnation from being a pilot: he may simply have known enough to suspect the unseaworthiness of a vessel for less favourable weather).[41]

Or in crossing from Clazomenae to Phocaea, Aristides' ship is beset by a storm: all he needs to exclaim is 'O Asclepius!' and the ship is saved. But it is still fated to him to suffer shipwreck, as Asclepius reveals to him the following night: he has accordingly now to 'arrange' a fake shipwreck, in order to comply: 'And the contrivance of the shipwreck seemed wonderful to all: wherein we also knew that it was even he who saved us from the sea. An additional benefaction was the purgation'.[42]

Our fullest account of a holy man's reaction to a storm is in that which befalls Paul's ship when he is travelling to Rome and stormbound at Malta:

> Since a good deal of time had gone by and the sea-voyage was already risky, because it was already after the fast, Paul gave them this warning: 'Men, I see that the voyage is going to involve injury, and heavy loss not only of the cargo and the

ship but also of our lives',[43] [an easy enough warning to give, after the end of the sailing season] . . . . 'And as of now take my advice and keep your spirits up. For you will not experience any loss of life – only the ship. For an angel of the God I belong to and serve stood by me this night and told me 'Do not be afraid, Paul, you have to stand before Caesar, and look, God has granted you the lives of all those sailing with you'.[44]

No real prognostication need have been involved: the remark makes sense as an observation of the escorting officer – interpreted *post eventum* as a guarantee of safe conduct.

It is difficult to be sure about details of Luke's account. Paul probably misconstrued the chances that the crew was about to defect, and may even himself have been responsible for the shipwreck – only to be presented by Luke as the man of the hour and the saviour of the ship. But it is not inconceivable, as Dibelius and Haenchen assumed, that a person of fanatical persuasion will make improbable speeches in the middle of a howling gale. When the ship has been riding out the storm for fourteen days, it is anchored off a lee shore, but the crew wish to lower the boat in order to secure bow-anchors. Paul prevents them, having convinced his military guard that they are trying to escape. The jolly-boat is then cast adrift, making it ultimately necessary to beach the large ship itself. In fact the apostle's divine intuitions failed to tell him that no self-respecting sailor would prefer to strike for the shore in a small boat at the height of a storm when he can ride it out in a large vessel securely anchored.

From the would-be seafarers we can pass to those convicted of the same cowardice as the rest of their fellow-men: Lucian retails with relish how Peregrinus disgraced himself by wailing along with the female passengers during a storm in the Aegean – 'this wonderful phenomenon supposedly superior to death'.[45] But he is scarcely the worst offender. Aulus Gellius also repeats a first-hand account of how he had shared a voyage with a Stoic philosopher who behaved no better at the moment of crisis. Gellius is right not to accept the fellow's defence that he was entitled to lament the loss of a life as egregious as his own, while lesser men's lives were scarcely worth their laments; but the naive Gellius is satisfied with a cock-and-bull lecture on how even the Stoic sage's reactions are altered in some extreme circumstances.[46] The sea brings out the worst pretentions and the greatest credulity in those who are not professional mariners.

Lastly, an exotic journey that has received much less attention than those of Apollonius. During the course of his exile Dio of Prusa had visited Borysthenes (Olbia), a Greek Black Sea centre off the coast of Thracian Pontus near the mouth of the Hypanis. Although his purpose was periegesis rather than pilgrimage (he had intended to visit the Getae),[47] he nevertheless took the opportunity for a religiously coloured *epideixis* to the inhabitants of the town, if only as a distraction from barbarian raids:

> It is contrary to divine law for gods to strive to be defeated by one another, for they are friends, or by other superior beings; but they carry out their respective actions without hindrance, and all of them enjoy complete friendship always. The most illustrious of them take their own independent courses, not wandering aimlessly without thought, but dancing a dance of happiness in their wisdom and profound intellect; the rest of the host are led along by the general motion, with the whole of heaven of one mind and impulse. For we must acknowledge that that is the one truly happy constitution, the partnership of gods with one another.[48]

Dio's Stoicising cosmology culminates in a Platonically coloured myth attributed to the Persian magi:[49] He is the dispenser of revelation indeed, and not for nothing is he hailed as one who appears 'to have been sent to us from his island by Achilles'.[50]

Here, then, we have a reminder of the variety of the holy man's exertions and diversions, coupled as so often with calculations which make sense in terms of local knowledge and careful planning. We also have a reminder of how little claims and exertions could sometimes correspond, nowhere more so than when a land-based holy man sets foot on board ship. But we have a sense that while Peregrinus was being seasick Marcion was organising serious seaborne expansion.

It is on exotic voyages that the holy man comes nearest to the realms of fiction and fantasy: it is now time to look at the kind of appearances he could make in such media as an established character in his own right.

11

REPRESENTATION
The holy man in fiction

The holy man is a familiar character in fiction[1] no less than in life, and the testimony for our period is particularly rich. In the first instance the presence of so much material indicates the hold of the subject on the popular imagination. Moreover, some of our fictional instances have a plausibility and sense of realism which offers genuine documentary value, in the sense that they aim to present what is obviously credible and probably typical. Sometimes a fictional recreation fills in a missing part of our factual mosaic quite convincingly; more often it is in matters of ethos or psychological motivation that fictional texts are able to enrich our appreciation of more strictly historical evidence.

The very nature of his calling places the holy man on the borderline between fact and fiction: it is difficult to know how much to trust the account of Plutarch of an exotic figure who lives as a hermit by the shores of the Red Sea, and holds Pythagorean or Platonic doctrines. He meets men once a year, but otherwise deals only with nymphs and demons. He is handsome and free from illness, thanks to eating a bitter medicinal herb once a month. He also knows many languages, but speaks Doric for the most part, in a poetic manner, and as he speaks the place is invested with fragrance. He devotes himself to various sciences, but once a year he is inspired as a prophet. Such a figure may remind us of the sort of anchorites the pilgrim Egeria met on one of their two days in the year for public appearances; or just as readily of the much more doubtful figures known to Lucian, who has them prophesying once a year after drinking from a magic well in India.[2]

In the case of Apuleius' *Metamorphoses* we have clearly crossed the borderline into fiction, but not without a strong measure of social observation and authenticity. The journey of the hero Lucius

from Hypata to Corinth dwells on a substratum of ancient society –
the day-to-day life of relatively small communities avoided in conventional polite literature, and observed at uncomfortably close
quarters by Lucius-turned ass. Here we have a unique characterisation of how a team of *galli* – castrated priests of the Syrian goddess
Atargatis – moves from village to village collecting alms for (itself
and) the goddess:

> The next day they all went out, decked in their different
> colours and looking garish, with their faces daubed with a
> filthy colour and their eyes painted with makeup; they wore
> little caps, yellow robes, and garments of linen and silk. Some
> of them had white tunics with purple stripes running this way
> and that, with girdles round them, and yellow shoes. With
> their arms bared to the shoulder, they wrapped the goddess in
> a little silk cloak and put her on me [the ass] to carry; they
> carried huge swords and axes, and with their cries they leapt
> about like madmen as the sound of the flute excited them. And
> after passing through a number of small settlements they
> arrived at a villa with a rich owner; and the moment they
> rushed in they broke into raucous chanting, dashed about
> madly and for a long time with bowed heads they twisted their
> supple necks and swirled their long hanging hair, and fre-
> quently biting their flesh they finally slashed their arms with
> the double-bladed knives they carried. Amid all this one of
> them excited himself more than the rest and drawing frequent
> heavy sighs from the depths of his lungs, he put on a show of
> abject madness, as if filled with a divine spirit . . . . He began
> with a lying declaration of guilt declaimed in prophetic tone to
> run himself down and incriminate himself as if he had some-
> how offended against the holy law of his sacred cult, and
> besides to demand the just punishment for his heinous crime
> from his own hands. Finally he seized a whip that these half-
> men carry, with tugs of woolen yarn knotted with sheeps'
> knucklebones, and showered himself with blow after blow
> from the knots.[3]

The passage abounds in revealing details. In the first place the venue
– the doors of a local patron, in the hope of a large donation, one
suspects; the pilgrims are associated with a local centre of power.
Secondly, the sense of spectacle: a procession in honour of the
Syrian goddess, with orchestrated ecstasy, and – to the bystanders,

no doubt – miraculous feats of endurance. Appropriate advertising for a mobile advice centre peddling infallible advice. Apuleius gives details of the group's support: their display receives a collection, some of it in silver, and substantial donations in kind; in due course a local patron affords them hospitality.[4]

The duping of potentially powerful patrons affords a theme for satirical fiction in its own right. In Lucian's *Philopseudes*[5] both the principal guest and the host turn out to have had experience of the same Egyptian holy man,[6] and the guest Arignotus comes close to having the credentials of sanctity in his own person:

> At this point Arignotus the Pythagorean came in, the long-haired one with the impressive face – you know the one renowned for his wisdom, the one they call holy. And I for my part breathed a sigh of relief when I saw him, for I thought, 'Aha! an axe has arrived for me to use against their lies', for I said 'The wise man will put a stopper in their mouths when they reel off such amazing nonsense'. And I thought that Fortune had brought this man for my benefit, like the proverbial *deus ex machina*.

Arignotus' first concern is Eucrates' illness, then the subject of the existence of δαιμόνάς τινας καὶ φάσματα, spirits and apparitions already under debate. At first his opponent 'Tychiades', representing Lucian himself, is modest in the august presence of Arignotus; the latter tries to give him an escape-route by suggesting that only the violently killed still walk abroad; assured that this is not the case, he takes refuge in the claim that everybody sees them, and in his own personal exorcism of a ghost.

It is not surprising to find the next point of reference in Lucian's fictitious conversation as Pancrates, Arignotus' own teacher: 'a holy man, clean-shaven, in white linen, always deep in thought, not speaking proper Greek, tall, flat-nosed, with protruding lips and thinnish legs' (reading Harmon's text). 'That very same Pancrates', he said, 'and at first I didn't know who he was, but when I saw him performing all manner of wonders whenever we anchored the boat, especially riding on crocodiles and swimming along in company with the creatures, as they fawned and wagged their tales, I realised that he must be some holy man.'[7]

An earlier story in the same dialogue (14f.) offers a number of insights into how a holy man might be able to rely on teamwork. A young man who has just inherited property is infatuated with a married woman in the same locality, and the matter is of some concern to his philosophy tutor. The latter accordingly engages a Hyperborean magician to perform a 'summoning' of the beloved, which duly happens after a considerable display of necromancy and other magical exhibitions. Nothing in the story, however, is actually impossible to arrange, given the one fact that Lucian's mouthpiece Tychiades volunteers towards the tale: that the lady in question is in fact the local whore. All the Hyperborean would have had to do is arrange for her to arrive at a stated time; and provide stand-ins for the lad's father, for Hecate, and for Cerberus. A three-headed dog would scarcely be a difficulty in a society which accepted unquestioningly the *trompe-l'oeil* of Glycon, the human-headed snake; the dead father would be smothered in grave-clothes and could plausibly be made to sound different. But the theatricals and stage-management of such an affair are of secondary importance beside the social relationships embodied in the tale. An impressionable youth has money to spend; his teacher will arrange a sexual initiation or escapade; an exotic holy man (Hyperborean and so an outsider) doubles as the local pimp; and everyone is satisfied with the outcome except Lucian.

The highest degree of social realism in any ancient work of fiction is attained in Petronius' *Satyrica*, and in this case the casual 'stream of consciousness' aimed at in conversation is able to throw similar light on a scam at the expense of the freedman host Trimalchio. He has gone through a number of facets of religious experience already, from the introduction of a bizarre trio of household gods to his own nomination *in absentia* for the post of *sevir augustalis*.[8] His friends have run through the business of the *laudator temporis acti* – things are bad because nobody worships the gods any longer – and have already discussed the sort of ghost stories which the audience may believe only too well.[9] Trimalchio himself naturally has Mercury as his patron, now commemorated on his wall;[10] but there is always room for more:

> I was quite fed up with doing my own trading, but it was an astrologer (*mathematicus*) who encouraged me. He had just happened to come to our colony, a Greekish sort of chap called Serapa, a consultant to the gods. This fellow even told me things I had forgotten. He spelled it all out for me from A to Z. He knew my inside – the only thing he hadn't told me

was what I'd eaten for dinner the day before. You'd have thought he'd been with me the whole time.

Tell me, Habinnas – I think you were there: [he told me] 'You got your good lady from "you-know-what". You're unlucky in your friendships. Nobody ever gives you the thanks you deserve. You've got large estates. You're nursing a viper in your bosom'. And he told me – though I shouldn't pass it on – even at my age I still have thirty years, four months, two days to live. What's more, I'll soon receive a legacy. It's fate that's telling me this. But if I'm allowed to join my estates to Apulia, I'll have gone on long enough. Meanwhile, while Mercury was my Guardian spirit, I built this house.[11]

In spite of Trimalchio's financial astuteness, he is blind to the fact that Serapa's information is drawn from the area where two types of information readily converge: what can easily be gleaned from local gossip (which Petronius has already illustrated brilliantly in the freedmen's conversations), and what Trimalchio simply wants to hear. He has an openly turbulent relationship with his wife; and has so many slaves as to receive legacies as a matter of course from their *peculium*. The prediction of his lifespan is not likely to be proven or disproven till after Serapa is well on his way, fortified no doubt with a more precious *apophorēton* than Trimalchio gives to less valuable guests.

At the other end of the repertoire from realistic fiction is the kind of popular storytelling which borders on folktale. The bizarre biography of 'Secundus the Silent Philosopher'[12] has its hero begin as a Cynic philosopher, educated away from home, and on his return choosing to test the allegation that all women can be seduced, with his own mother as the test. She prepares to accede, and hangs herself when she discovers her future lover's identity. Secundus now goes off on his wanderings, with a Pythagorean regime of silence. This attracts the attention of the Emperor Hadrian, whom he refuses to answer. The Emperor gives instructions that if he breaks silence to save his life he is to die. He does not, and instead is allowed to write down the answers to twenty 'wisdom'-style questions.

Here again it is difficult to begin to distinguish fiction from fact in such an ensemble, or to conjecture how far popular transmission may have conspired to reshape any facts about any given individual

round typical elements of folktale. But the alternation of philos-
ophies is a familiar theme at all levels of the holy man's activities; so
is the role of acute domestic scandal; and one expects an emperor,
particularly Hadrian, to be a natural audience for curiosities of this
kind. His reputation for brutality to intellectuals may also have
played its part. But behind the whole business may lurk a much
older tale, perhaps ultimately oriental; the need for silence is a key
motif in tales connected with the frame-tale of the *Book of Sinbad*
and its analogues, an oriental cycle whose roots and ramifications
have yet to be fully traced.

Holy men can travel still further in the same direction by participating in pure fairytale. The notion of 'laying up treasure in heaven'
known to the New Testament provides the basis for visionary
accounts in both Gnostic Christian and Manichaean contexts. In the
former the Apostle Thomas undertakes to build a palace for King
Gundophorus, and does so by building a heavenly dwelling with his
builder's fees in place of the earthly one commissioned by the King.
Only when Gundophorus' brother actually reaches heaven can he
testify that the apostle has indeed built a heavenly palace, awaiting
Gundophorus on his death: he duly communicates the good news
to the King in a vision.[13] In Mani's case, the sage asks the King's
brother whether his earthly gardener can compare with the garden
the prophet can offer him in heaven, and duly leads him away to
more worthwhile pursuits.[14] Lane Fox misses the point when he
implies that no owners of very good gardens could be so persuaded;[15] the whole point of the story is that the gardener is
attracted by the prospect of an even better one in a better place.

The status of such a work as the *Acts of Thomas* is no less difficult
to situate between fact and fiction.[16] Its uncanonical status is more
than explained by its blatant displays of Gnosticism. But if nothing
else it can be used as a reasonable picture of how an author of
Gnostic sympathies of the third century would have conceived the
activities of his apostle. In the first place Thomas goes to India as a
carpenter and stonemason: the missionary effort of the holy man is
conceived of very plausibly as supported by a trade. He has a
medical activity, curing a man of a poisonous snakebite; and reviv-
ing a girl after a *crime passionnel* and a eucharistic clairvoyance. He
is able to offer counselling after a double rape, thereby acquiring a
powerful friend at court (Misdaeus, captain of the guard).[17] None of
Thomas' miracles falls outside the normal parameters except those
that concern talking animals:[18] if these represent actual occurrences,

then they would be explicable enough by ventriloquism: moreover Thomas is able to offer the perfect interpretation and justification of such a technique: it would be the Lord or the Holy Spirit who would be causing the beasts to appear to speak. Since we have already heard of the Lord impersonating Thomas himself, the circle of deception or self-deception in a good cause would be complete.

A different insight again is afforded into the holy man's operations by the texture of apocryphal acts. The lack of literary sophistication in such works, and their destination for a devotional readership, serves to emphasise the qualities in holy men that are likely to appeal to an undemanding and uncritical audience. The focus is on the holy man's power to control a situation with prophecy or miracle, on his impact on individuals or the whole community, and on his often high-handed superiority to enemies or authority. The tortuous plot of the *Pseudo-Clementines* focuses on Peter as the reconciler who unites the family of Clement, whose mother has departed with two sons at the pretended behest of an oracle when in fact temptation has taken her away on an extramarital adventure. He conquers Clement's father's claims for the power of astrology, identifies the missing persons by listening to both halves of the story, and reunites the family.[19] What he has done in effect is perform the normal social function of the holy man: he has kept his ears open, used his common sense, done his 'good turn', and taken the opportunity to use it to refute astrology and preach Jesus Christ. The texture of the *Recognitiones* serves as a container for elaborate homilies of a type which seem most obviously to require the palliative of an entertaining story.

At the other end of the cultural spectrum stand two complementary mid-second-century works by the satirist Lucian, poking fun at the philosophic investigator and his journeys to the world of the supernatural. Lucian has his Hellenistic philosopher-satirist Menippus ascend to heaven to probe the fantasies of philosophers about Zeus – stopping in the vicinity of the moon to adjust his vision with the aid of a quack remedy suggested by the moon-spirit Empedocles, before going on to dine with Zeus, inspect the workings of Providence, and return to earth with an apocalyptic warning for philosophers. There is little here that could not be explained in terms of traditional bookishness, but Menippus' place of origin may be significant. Gadara in Syria was not an unlikely origin for a man who tried his hand at learning to fly: Simon Magus from Samaria kept up the tradition. The current reality coincides neatly with the traditional caricature: a little theosophic hocus-pocus in the region of the moon would not have been out of place for a contemporary philosopher with theological interests. Menippus' other journey takes him to the underworld itself – characteristically through the offices of a (mercenary) Mesopotamian *magus*.[20] However respectable philosophers are or appear to be in themselves, they have rapid access to more dubious company.

Much of the most effective fiction exploits the holy man's potential for amiable roguery. In the *Acts of Thomas* Jesus Christ himself tricks the reluctant Thomas into going to India by posing as a slave-master in a slave-market, so that the moment Thomas acknowledges him as his master he can be mistaken for a slave and sold – a kind of prank quite foreign to the Christ of the canonic gospels. But for sustained cunning he has nothing on the figure of the Egyptian priest Calasiris ('Linen-cloth')[21] who constitutes the true hero of Heliodorus' massive novel the *Aethiopica*.[22] If the whole frame of reference is a vaguely remote past, none the less almost the entire curriculum vitae of this figure offers a commentary on the practice of sagecraft, and from a unique angle: not extreme rationalising scepticism, nor hysterical apologetic, but a sympathetic and highly detailed portrait which gives full attention to the psychological interplay of characters and enables the holy man to cope with almost any situation with only the occasional use of some benign sleight of hand.

Calasiris begins his career as an Egyptian priest from Memphis, but is forced to leave by foreknowledge of a quarrel between his two sons for the succession, and by a scandal over his own infatuation with the foreign voluptuary Rhodopis. In the course of his wanderings he is (allegedly) commissioned by the Ethiopian Queen Persinna to find her exposed daughter. On arrival for a scholarly sojourn at Delphi he receives an oracular message, and finding the girl by accident secures proof of her identity. Under pretext of curing her of the evil eye, he secures her elopement with her husband-to-be Theagenes. After duping a pirate chief he conducts the pair safely back to Egyptian soil, arranges a further liaison for their companion Cnemon to a Phoenician merchant's daughter, witnesses a bizarre necromantic rite, and arrives back at Memphis with Chariclea just in time to prevent bloodshed between his sons, and to secure the legitimate succession to his priesthood.[23] His charges go on to succeed to the Ethiopian throne.

The more picaresque aspect of a holy man's operations can be seen in some detail in the trickery of Calasiris. When he is trying to prise his Ethiopian princess Charicleia away from her stepfather Charicles, and conceal her love-affair with the hero Theagenes, he does so by using the language of demonic possession as a cover. Even Charicles has guessed that the patients 'illness' stems from the fact that she is in love; Calasiris advises that she should be cured by being placed in contact with the object of her affections – knowing that Charicles will bring the wrong man. The language of demonology takes over (4.7.12f.):

'Charicles, you were not wrong in saying that the young girl is possessed. She is under pressure from celestial powers I myself brought down on her, of course mighty enough to compel her to act against her nature and will. But there seems to be some opposing spirit who is countering my action and struggling against the demons who are supporting me. Now or never is the time to show me the girdle you said was exposed with your daughter, and which you were given with the other recognition-tokens. I am very much afraid that this band may be full of sorcery and inscribed with curses which are making her rude and savage, because some enemy conspired to make her a rebel to love all her life and deprived of posterity.'

Perhaps the most frequently quoted episode from a novel for religious history is the episode of the initiation of Lucius in the mysteries of Isis in Apuleius' *Metamorphoses*.[24] There can be no doubt of the propaganda value to the goddess and her priest of the presumed transformation of an assman Lucius back to human form. The episode can be seen as a fictionalised version of a healing miracle, in which the goddess is seen to act at a point of maximum publicity, in the context of her own spring festival, the Ploiaphesia; while her priest administers rebuke for the past life of Lucius himself. Nor is the life-history of Lucius as a dabbler in magic, down on his luck and restored by an Egyptian priest, so very different from the real life-history we have already noted for Thessalus of Tralles.[25] And the vision in which Lucius in the course of his initiations views a maimed priest of Osiris who turns out to be one Asinius ('Assman') Marcellus,[26] has the air of the sort of 'sacred coincidence' of which Aristides was able to make so much. However opposed their temperaments, the *Hieroi logoi* of Aristides and Apuleius' 'sacred ending' are convergent.

From such a sample of the fictional roles and treatments of holy men we can draw several inferences. Writers such as Lucian and Apuleius could present their picaresque characters with reference to observable figures such as Peregrinus or Alexander, and so produce a convincingly authentic control of detail; or in Apuleius' case draw on what must obviously have been a genuinely informed curiosity about the occult in general. Heliodorus' creation embodies a genuine preoccupation with religious detail, quite often spiced with humour and genuine interest in religious manipulation and mystification. But it is difficult to point to many fictional texts that do not employ the activities of a colourful holy man of some sort: the type is firmly embodied in eastern Mediterranean and Near-eastern experience, and in fiction as in fact he will be the miraculous enabler. Fact is none too easy to separate from fiction at the best of times in the study of holy men: it is now time to study how the latter comes to overlay the former in the biographies of even the best documented of our subjects.

12

PRESTIGE
The enhancement of holiness

A holy man's reputation did not need to end with his death. His departure created a vacuum which others might feel obliged to fill. How and why should he become a saint, a hero, or a cult-figure? Lucian had no doubts about one case: he 'foresaw' in the case of Peregrinus an oracular shrine at the site of the pyre, with Peregrinus himself as a *daimōn* and a healer, and priests and their accoutrements, with a nocturnal mystery and dadouchia.[1] Of course he selects details which bring in references to fire; but he was not so far wrong. Peregrinus' native Parium did in due course boast a statue of him which gave oracles;[2] the holy man's status had been enhanced, and quite predictably so.

Lucian's testimony well parodies the tendency for stories about holy men to grow in the telling:

> For the fools agape for the story, I would dramatize a bit on my own account, and say that when the pyre was kindled and Proteus went and threw himself in, first there was a great earthquake, and the earth groaned, then a vulture flew up out of the midst of the flames and went aloft to Heaven, saying in a booming voice, 'I abandoned the earth, to Olympus I go'. Now these folk of course were open-mouthed with wonder, and had a little tremble as they performed their devotion; they asked me whether the vulture was borne east or west; I just gave them the first answer that came into my head.
>
> When I got back to the festival, I came across some grey-haired man with a venerable countenance, I can tell you, on top of his beard, and his whole air of solemnity, telling all the rest of the stuff about Proteus, but especially how, after his cremation, he had beheld him in a white robe not long before,

188

and had only just left him walking about in the portico of the Seven Voices, and complete with halo, wearing his garland of wild olive; then on top of everything else he added the vulture, swearing would you believe it that he himself had seen it flying up out of the pyre.[3]

A fourth-century example may help to throw some light on the matter of witnessing bodily ascensions. In the *Life of Antony* the saint claims to have seen the soul of Amoun borne up to heaven.[4] It is, moreover, implied that the ascending monk has been perceived despite the thirteeen-day journey from Antony's vantage-point to Nitria. But the *Historia Monachorum* offers a rather different perspective: Antony has invited Amoun to visit him: he tells his friend to leave a certain spot only when he has died. The fact that he has left the spot will presumably trigger off the notion of an ascent.[5]

Nor was this the first account of its kind in a Christian context. Apart from the ascension tradition itself, the second-century gospel fragment of a *Gospel of Peter* offers a peculiar account of the resurrection which for the first time reconstructs it as taking place before Jesus' enemies: two youths come down from the sky; the stone moves of its own accord; they bring out Jesus and assume gigantic proportions. The soldiers tell Pilate, who is not presented as hostile. It has long been recognised that such a confection appears to be an accretion to the canonical gospel tradition, of which it incorporates a cross-section, and that what is new is not just some Gnostic-type features, but a whole new apologetic angle, which would *inter alia* reconcile Roman and Christian.[6] But there is more to it than even this: this is a vulgarly triumphalist resurrection, a first staging-post to medieval harrowings of hell. If Hollywood religious epic is still some way away, the taste and emotional need for it are already securely in place.

But not all adjustments and corrections of tradition are of this order or magnitude. Often the image of a holy man will not be so much magnified as modified to accommodate a more subtle change in viewpoint. We have several versions of the story in which Hanina ben Dosa acknowledges that he cannot perform successful healings 'unless his prayer is fluent in his mouth'. But in one case the context is different. It is used in a case where it seems to illustrate that an error in a fixed prayer will then turn out badly: the redactor seems to have rabbinicised a situation which refers to the improvised prayer of a charismatic to serve the purposes of the opposite camp.[7]

Similarly the story of Hanina and the snake is constantly reshuffled to serve a variety of different purposes and appears to be developed round a saying devoted to the invulnerability of the holy man, while the rain-miracle under Marcus Aurelius can be ascribed to the absent Emperor, Jupiter, the Christian God equated with him, the Egyptian Harnouphis, or the Chaldaean Julianus the Younger, according to the needs of the source or the time.[8]

Some miracle-stories can only make sense as secondary accretions. Hanina lengthens joists in a house so that they knit together – by prayer.[9] And it has been recently shown that the succession of accounts of Honi the rain-maker, a Jewish miracle-worker of the first century BC, have been revised in the Mishnaic and Talmudic accounts by the process of progressive 'Rabbinisation': prayer has failed to produce rain, and Honi in effect does so only by a magical ceremony; but the Mishnah then contradicts itself by glossing the procedures as an act of prayer, and adds a curious pericope about excommunication in the name of Simeon ben Chetah, one of the early figureheads of Rabbinism. Honi is now made liable to sectarian punishment; a further element makes him fulfil a teaching of scripture. Since rain-making was felt to have been localised in the temple, the takeoever entails the remaking of a rain-maker as a good rabbi.[10]

In some cases the process of divergence among traditions will begin in an unobtrusive way. Some of the variations between Mark and the expanded versions of Matthew and Luke in the Synoptic tradition can show us at least the beginning of distortion, often at first in trivial or barely perceptible details. In the Lucan account we find that the paralytic's house has a tiled roof, and a central opening is implied. This arrangement would have been more intelligible to a Gentile audience, but appears to contradict the style of Palestinian house implied in Mark, where a turf roof would have been natural, and so easily broken to allow the patient to be lowered into the house.[11] By a similar process we find a difference in perception between Mark and Matthew on the story of the wise and foolish builders: Matthew strengthens the local colour in his source by placing the foolish man's house specifically in a wadi.[12]

Some of the divergences are more fundamental, however. Where Luke has a beatitude promising blessedness to the literally poor and hungry, Matthew changes the meaning entirely to refer to the spiritually poor and hungry;[13] while Luke is guilty of allegorising with a superimposed interpretation in his own right by taking the bridegroom analogy to refer to Jesus Christ's own death.[14] And not only the substance but the context of sayings can be altered. In Matthew the blind can lead the blind, in a specific attack on the Pharisees,[15] while the bad tree is cut down in apocalyptic discourse;[16] both are collected in Luke in reflections on character and action.[17]

An important aspect of the growth of early Christian tradition is the variation in material attributed to Jesus Christ, itself a reminder of the original oral nature of the content. Apart from the individual viewpoint of the gospel redactors themselves, the enormous advances in the publication of papyri and other sources of 'alternative' tradition increase our view of the fluidity of the tradition as a whole. Christian readers will be familiar with the aphorism ascribed to Jesus in the Synoptics 'a prophet does not find acceptance in his own country'; but two witnesses outside the canonic gospel tradition add a parallel analogy ('nor does a doctor cure people who know him'). One of the contexts in which this occurs is the Gnosticising *Gospel of Thomas*;[18] but the other is a mere collection of sayings of Jesus in an Oxyrynchus papyrus.[19] There is nothing to prevent the second saying from being authentic, and no special motive for its importation by a redactor. The same Oxyrynchus text has a cry of despair from Jesus over the stubbornness of mankind which in some respects seems to share features with both Synoptic and Johannine traditions ('I stood in the middle of the world; I appeared to them in the flesh, and found all of them drunk, and none among them found I thirsty').[20]

Sometimes a differently aimed gospel will contain a nugget of information that seems to throw a genuine new light on this or that individual incident: Jerome was aware that in the Nazarene and Ebionite gospel versions, the man who had a withered hand was a mason: hence 'I was a mason and earned my living with my hands; I pray thee, Jesus, to restore me my health that I may not have to beg for my bread with ignominy'.[21] The additional detail need not have been added out of any desire to make sense of a cryptic or unintelligible story. Rather does it seem probable that it heightens the point of the narrative. This client had more to lose than most from his condition. But the detail would also add another implication to this particular story, namely that the man in question could not have been suffering from any congenital abnormality. Again, Origen knew a version of the rich ruler story (Matt. 19.16–24) in which there were two rich men involved.[22] The version also adds a specific addressee to the saying about the rich man and the eye of the needle, in this case addressed to Simon son of Jonah.[23]

One notes that the risk of embellishment is particularly great when we are dealing with anecdotal matters on the fringe of Roman official history. Two of the accounts of Yohanan ben Zakkai's prediction of the rise of Vespasian make the mistake of fulfilling the prediction with the announcement of the death of Nero, thus in effect cutting a whole year out of the Jewish War. But one names Nero, the other does not; we may be looking at an error in the making.[24] An account not naming the previous emperor will still be historically correct. But a careless compiler who knows simply that the war began under Nero and ended under Vespasian, and whose interest is in the rabbinical subject-matter, will produce a major howler without necessarily undermining the probability of the interview with Vespasian himself. One notes also the degree of alteration which single tales can undergo. The story of the centurion's servant may well be a divergent version of the story of the official's son in John; not only is the relationship already different (son as opposed to servant), but there are now also several versions of how the official got in touch: by coming in person to Jesus (John);[25] by sending elders from the Jews to make the request (Luke); or by meeting Jews as he came to Capernaum (Matthew).[26]

RELICS

Apart from actual alterations and divergences in reports of holy men, there could be a corresponding alteration in the status of anything connected with him: places and objects will acquire a sanctity of their own by association. An incidental digression in Eusebius' *Ecclesiastical History* offers an insight into the sub-culture of Christianity long before the golden age of pilgrimage at the end of the fourth century. At Caesarea Philippi the woman who had an issue of blood is commemorated: her house is now pointed out, as are memorials of the event.

> For it is said that there stood on a high plinth at the gates of her house a bronze relief of a woman, bending down on one knee and with outstretched hands in the manner of a suppliant, whilst opposite to this statue there was another of the same material, a likeness of a man standing upright, dressed in an impressive double cloak and stretching out his hand to the

woman at his feet. On the actual monument there was some strange species of herb growing, which stretched up to the border of the double cloak of bronze, and served as an anti-dote to all manner of diseases . . . and there is nothing surpris-ing in the fact that those heathen, who long ago had good works done for them by our Saviour, should have made these objects; for we found the likenesses of the Apostles also, of Peter and Paul, and in fact of Christ himself, preserved in painted pictures. And this is what we should expect, for the ancients were in the habit, according to their heathen custom, of honouring them as Saviours in this way without inhibition.[27]

Eusebius' testimony is doubly revealing: Christ has acquired a healing statue in Caesarea, at some quite early stage; but Eusebius somewhat condescendingly seems to put the whole business down to a superstition extending indiscriminately to the disciples. We should not be surprised to find Athanasius and Serapion receiving a bequest of Antony's sheepskin, with his hair garment left to two ascetic companions; and, Athanasius adds, each of the recipients 'keeps it safe like some great treasure. For even seeing these is like beholding Antony, and wearing them is like bearing his admoni-tions with joy'.[28] One can well understand the instruction for the anonymous burial of Pachomius[29] in order to avoid such a cult.[30]

The subsequent reputation of Apollonius of Tyana affords a large but tantalisingly incomplete picture of the ramifications of a holy man's reputation over a long period. Not only does he attract the interest of Hadrian, who makes a collection of letters,[31] but also of Julia Domna, who commissions a large-scale biography of sorts from the sophist Philostratus;[32] but we find him the subject of a favourable pamphlet by one Hierocles, a provincial governor under Diocletian, already drawing parallels with Jesus Christ, and refuted in turn by Eusebius of Caesarea.[33] Since the latter's work survives and presents substantial indication of Hierocles' treatise, we can discern something of the significance of the holy man in the struggle between Christian and pagan. Thereafter a totally different *Nachleben* emerges in Byzantium and the East, and it is from there that the more popular and decidely shadier side of Apollonius appears to have been preserved. If we cannot get a clearer picture of Apollonius from the growth of tradition, we can at least hope to view the growth of the tradition for its own sake.

Much of the case for and against Apollonius is made to rest on the accumulation of prestige already accruing to the sage in comparison with Jesus Christ: for Hierocles it weighs heavily against the latter 'that an allegedly divine nature should shed its light on men, but end its career in obscurity so soon, rather than display its virtue for ever after' (in contrast to the works of carpenters and builders).[34] There is also an attempt on the part of Eusebius to accuse Apollonius of inconsistent treatment of Euphrates.[35] An important point in the argument revolves round the reputation of Apollonius as a magician: the ghost of Achilles is suggested as a mean *daimōn*,[36] and there is no lack of sophistry on the theme 'if you are x you are a wizard; if you are not x but y, then you are still a wizard'.[37]

The casual reader of Philostratus might be surprised to find a persistent thread of tradition running well into Byzantine literature, reporting the prestige of Apollonius of Tyana in Byzantium itself, and stressing that talismans he set up in the city against a number of different plagues are still *in situ* (and effective). This might seem all the more remarkable when we consider the refounding of the city as Constantine's Christian capital; but in fact we even have a testimony which seems to imply that Constantine himself encouraged the whole business by importing statuary from Tyana itself (though Apollonius himself is not directly mentioned). One thinks, however, of Constantine's ambiguous policy towards magical practices. If such tradition is well founded, why did Philostratus fail to mention it? The nearest he gets is to mention the sage's activities in the Troad, in which he carries on apotropaic rites of some sort. It may well be that Philostratus did not wish to pursue any mention of Byzantium, the thorn in the flesh of the rising Severus, or that he simply did not know of it; or it may be due to his aversion to material which might reasonably have been considered on the borderline of magic. But it usefully corroborates the background of Alexander's oracle: his mentor may well have learned his craft from Apollonius' sojourn in the area; and the area which was so accommodating to Apollonius' reputation may have been the ideal place for Alexander.[38]

A tantalising problem in the growth of their respective traditions is the anecdote about the competition of three such figures in Anastasius Sinaita:[39] Domitian consults our trio in order to rid Rome of a plague. Apuleius will take fifteen days to rid a third of the city, Apollonius ten days to do his sector; Julianus, pointing out that by fifteen days there will be no one left, does his sector at once, then the other two, and so wins the contest. It is easy enough to dismiss the anecdote as such, but another matter to explain either its formation or its chaotic distortion of historical fact. The chief problem is that Apollonius belongs to the first century AD, Apuleius and Julianus to the second, if the latter is the thaumaturge credited with the rain-miracle under Marcus Aurelius. No plague of significance is known under Domitian. The vital clue may lie in our choice of starting-point. The obvious one is that the anecdote arises from, or is transmitted by, a tradition favourable to Julianus; at some stage the transmitter of the anecdote confuses the Juliani, father and son, and peoples the anecdote with rivals who can only be contemporary with one of the two. Since 'the' plague was under Marcus Aurelius, not Domitian, the correct personnel for the story would be the Younger Julianus, Apuleius in his 'iatrosophistic' role, and possibly some such figure as Alexander of Abonouteichos, who did produce an apotropaic oracle for the plague, and was himself a second-generation pupil of Apollonius; an earlier quarrel between Julianus the Elder and Apollonius might obviously have contributed to the anecdote's formation. The tale-type itself is a traditional one in the Near East, and perhaps not unrelated to the tale of the three fastidious men at the King's court; as in the case of the tale of Secundus we may not yet have reached the root of the tradition.

The century which saw the Christianising of the Roman Empire saw a marked increase in the prestige and proliferation of holy men, or at any rate in those we are able to trace; no less did it see an inflation of the reputations of holy men from the preceding centuries on both sides of the Christian–pagan divide. Eunapius is particularly illuminating as a guide to the sort of decoration that is going on in a thought-world where Neoplatonism was influential in the upper echelons of Christianity and paganism alike. In the early third century Philostratus is fulsome enough on the reputation of Apollonius of Tyana; by the end of the fourth century we find Eunapius calling the same sage 'not just a philosopher but some being midway between the gods and mankind'. And to the title of Philostratus' work he feels obliged to add the reservation 'though he should have called it "The visitation of god to the human race" '.[40] The hyperbole has begun to accelerate.

Similar inflation attends the doyen of late antique philosophy, the Neo-Platonist Porphyry. Eunapius makes him a well-educated student of rhetoric with philosophical inclination, from Tyre; he is fully converted to Plotinus in Rome, but we find him in some kind of ascetic experience in Sicily (a nuance which however seems to garble the facts as given by Porphyry himself). We are told that he claims to have an oracle (and indeed was the author of a treatise on *Philosophy from Oracles*). He claims to have expelled from a certain bath some sort of local demon known as Kausatha. We find him credited with excellence in all departments, significantly ending with natural philosophy and theurgy: ('let those be consigned to the province of holy rites and mysteries').[41]

There is nothing in this or the rest of Eunapius' brief account that would surprise too much: the facts themselves could easily have fitted a *pepaideumenos* of even the second century: but there is just a hint in the florid enthusiasm of Eunapius' style that the balance has shifted significantly: philosophy has become imbued with a mystical aura of divine ecstasy.

With his treatment of Iamblichus matters are in still sharper focus: we are assured that he had so many brilliant pupils from all over 'that it seemed amazing that he could satisfy them all; and indeed he was lavish in his devotion to them all. A few rites, however, he did perform alone, apart from his friends and disciples, when he devoted himself to the Divine'. His pupils are curious and their spokesman asks his divinest of masters (ὦ διδάσκαλε θειότατε) through his slaves whether they have heard that when he prays to the gods he is seen to practise levitation to a height of over ten cubits; Iamblichus discounts this as a prank. But he manifests 'mighty manifestations of his divine nature' by detecting that a corpse had been carried along the road and still more amazingly – in the writer's view – by calling forth two boy bathers from two springs, by a summons, as if they are water-spirits (though even Eunapius is constrained to admit that this is due to a third-hand account).[42] We have a sense of the most trivial actions (where they are actually intelligible) distorted by a pseudo-intellectual journalism: we have come down a more ominous path than that represented by the dramatised resurrection fireworks of the *Acts of Peter*. There is a determination to spare no kind of superlative in enhancing one's holy man.

In tracing the history of holy men in the first three centuries it is important to resist any over-schematic approach. It might be tempting to note A. D. Nock's detection of 'a clear rise in the tension of piety' in the third century, and to apply such a model to the history of holy men – proliferating at the end of the third century onwards with the impact of Christian monasticism, and wresting philosophy from the hand of rational men. But we have no guarantee that a work conceived like the *Historia Monachorum* would not have been possible for the pagan holy men of the first two centuries, however we might care to define them. For every Peregrinus or Alexander we know we can suspect any number whose activities must continue to elude us: the activities of Gnostic missionaries would have been conspicuous enough for a start to elicit the refutations in Justin and Irenaeus. The moment false prophets are mentioned in the sources in the plural we have yet another group of unknowns. Only a chance encounter with Paul brings no fewer than seven sons of Scaeva to our attention: how many others did the Acts-author just happen to miss?

13

PROGRESS
Continuities and comparisons

The traditions of the kind of holy men we have reviewed can be followed in two directions: forward into the fourth century and the great proliferation of Christian monasticism; and forward towards the holy men arising in other cultures and as a result of more recent developments, wherever similarities are seen to occur. In both cases comparison is instructive. We can find in the burgeoning of holy men at the end of Antiquity a proliferation and consolidation of the kind of figures we have witnessed; and we can note persistent similarities with more recent and less directly related examples of the type. We are constantly forced to ask why this or that similarity should be there at all. In attempting to answer all such questions we can hope to move gradually nearer to attempting to identify the essence and appeal of the holy man as such. The most obvious difficulty with both classes of comparative material is its sheer bulk; we shall be forced to be increasingly eclectic.

A useful starting-point is the author we have just left. In dealing with the philosophers of his own time Eunapius gives a revealing *aperçu* into the relationship between holiness[1] and intellectual life in the fourth century, in so far as one markedly inferior sophist was capable of seeing it.[2] His narrative is largely built round religio-magical anecdotes about his sophists[3] and philosophers, cemented together by meagre notices and extravagantly Platonising hyper-bole. What is striking is how hard he seems to strive to superimpose a sanctity which on the evidence of his own anecdotes is not really there. We are told, for example, how Aedesius[4] receives an oracle on the back of his left hand, offering him a choice of lives, between immortal renown as a sophist and true immortality as a shepherd. He opts for the latter, only to be pressurised into the former by prospective pupils.[5] He has plainly failed the test of the solitary, divinely directed way; yet he is celebrated as if he had not. One is also tempted to ask how the oracle itself was actually produced: some such mechanism as those so copiously described by Hippolytus[6] seems the obvious explanation, where the victim's hand is pressed over a reverse tatoo of the oracular message. But the details of the consultation are too vague: we are told that it was a dream-oracle of the kind he preferred. The subject-matter itself is characteristic enough: one might compare Pliny's choice between town and country, and of course it is as an estate-owner rather than shepherd that Aedesius would have retired to the countryside. Eunapius allows him to fulfil the terms of the oracle with characteristic hyperbole ('his reputation touched the stars').

One is left with the same suspicions about a story of the sophist Eustathius' embassy to Sapor, which culminates in the familiar topos of a battle of magicians: we are first told that the charm that sat on his tongue and lips seems nothing less than witchcraft: he placated the brusque monarch

> and by his discourse gained such influence over him that the King of Persia all but put off his upright tiara, his purple attire and his bejewelled splendour, exchanging them for Eustathius' philosopher's cloak; for so convincingly did the latter condemn the life of luxury and the vain accoutrement of the body, and to such misery did he reduce those in love with physical things. But certain magi who just happened to be at court prevented this, alleging that he was an out-and-out charlatan.[7]

Eustathius actually lost; and the intellectual level of the biographer characteristically leads to a magical explanation. The demons are still abroad.

A second anecdote on Eustathius shows the extent to which rejection of superstition could be construed by the superstitious as further proof of divinity. Omens were given that Eustathius would visit Greece. When he failed to do so, an embassy was sent to him to establish the reason for the omens' failure. He asks a description of the omens, and points out that it was not his own visit that the omens foretold: 'he gave out an utterance that in my judgement was beyond a mere mortal, for he replied that the omens were too trivial and too slow to manifest themselves to accord with such virtues as his own'.[8] A typical flourish of sophistic arrogance is now construed as superhuman utterance.

But the classic case of sage, saint and sophist in the fourth century is without doubt Maximus of Ephesus: contact with the young Julian, not yet the last pagan Emperor, is first made on the strength of an attack on theurgy by Maximus' associate Eusebius, a fellow-pupil of Aedesius. Eusebius describes to Julian how Maximus had caused the statue of a goddess to smile and even laugh, and her torches burst into flame. Even Eunapius for once gives us enough information for a reasonable deduction of 'how it was done': the incense burns, distorting the light in front of the image of the goddess; this distortion is construed as the smile; the incense crackles and by so doing can be interpreted as a laugh; the heat eventually ignites the torches. And even Eunapius can only see such a display as that of τὸν θεατρικὸν ἐκεῖνον θαυματοποιόν ('the old familiar theatrical wonder-worker').[9] What is worrying is Julian's immediate aknowledgement that this is the man he is looking for: Maximus finds a niche in the boy's entourage for his like-minded friend Chrysanthius. Now Maximus does not in fact take part in the overthrow of Constantius (an unnamed hierophant of Eleusis was his coadjutor on that occasion); they take omens before setting out for Julian, and Chrysanthius is deterred by the omens. Maximus sees it as his obligation 'to struggle with the divine nature till you force it to incline to the man who cultivates it'; he persists till the omens change. His prestige enhanced by mob hysteria, he goes off to meet the Emperor.[10]

Even the sympathetic Eunapius is dismayed at the corruption of Maximus at court. After surviving Julian's fatal expedition, he persists in favour under Jovian; Valentinian and Valens have him fined for extortion; under torture his wife procures poison, but he does not carry out his own part in an apparent suicide pact. He is now restored to favour by Valens' favourite Clearchus, proconsul of Asia (by supernatural agency according to Eunapius). Maximus tries an abortive attempt as a performing sophist, but returns to philosophy and recovers much of his prosperity, and risks a test of his innocence in the matter of theurgy, acquitting himself with enhanced reputation. The result is a court intrigue against him: he demonstrates his amazing perception (as Eunapius sees it) by applying to himself an oracle framed against him: he prophesies Valens' unusual death and failure to attain burial; but is taken off to execution in Asia nevertheless and despatched by the disreputable Festus – whose own death is brought about after a revenge dream in which Maximus lassoes him and drags him down to Hades before Plato![11] The age is long gone in which a Polemo[12] or Apuleius[13] can leave the suspicion of only dabbling in darker matters; or when a Lucian or Oenomaus is on hand to deal with *goēteia* in the accustomed manner.

The other end of the cultural spectrum is still better documented in late Antiquity. The biographies of Antony the hermit by Athanasius[14] and of Martin of Tours by Sulpicius Severus go far towards characterising and publicising the late antique Christian holy man. It is a matter of continuing fascination to look for continuity between the lives of such paragons and those of their possible predecessors. Why did Christian asceticism take so long before burgeoning so successfully? Was there a direct continuity with the holy men of the past? And if so what explains the dramatic suddenness of Antony's or Pachomius' entry on the scene?

One consideration must be the element of propaganda. Antony might well have enjoyed the fate of such a figure as Dositheus had the matter been left to himself; his war with demons, in spite of the sheer intensity involved, was spectacularly different from that practised by Lucian's Jewish exorcist in the *Philopseudes*; and it is pure accident that the Essene phenomenon is so well documented by Philo. But besides Athanasius' biography the sudden political ascendancy of Christianity cannot be overlooked, nor the moral ascendancy of the survivors of the persecutions (though Antony's own position in regard to the latter may have called for some circumspection in Athanasius' presentation).

In Antony one is conscious of that quality of social service so well characterised by Brown's treatment of Syrian holy men; but one is conscious none the less of an opposite current: of a crusty old man much happier getting rid of imaginary devils than spending time with real people. It takes little by way of illustration from these classic lives to appreciate the continuity with holy men of the preceding centuries. The fourth-century version can effortlessly acquire the wisdom of the fool: Antony can argue that writing is unnecessary for his purposes with the same assurance by which Socrates rejected the natural sciences (though one must suspect Athanasius' hand in the shaping of Antony's sermon after twenty-five years in the desert).[15] Yet if pressed he might well have claimed his expertise in the recognition and exorcism of demons.

The element of display is also present: after twenty years in the desert Antony makes an all the more resounding impact, and he will engage in the customary activities - he can throw his weight into doctrinal condemnation of the Arians;[16] he can heal or channel requests for healing, and even advise judges.[17] Moreover, the familiar balance between friendships and enmities is also recognisable. The phenomenon of Antony practising Christian asceticism on his 'inner mountain' near the Red Sea evokes on the one hand the image of the solitary religious virtuoso in the desert; but on the other, something again akin to the phenomenon of Alexander of Abonouteichos. This is no longer the *prostatēs*, the champion on the edge of the village, but a kind of Christian oracular service serving a much wider area, and with its own staff. Antony seems to have a protective screen of middlemen who 'vet' potential visitors; and he can call on interpreters. He deals with requests and communications from all levels of society: medical cases, the mentally disturbed, curious philosophers, judges, and even Constantine and his sons;[18] the perspective of Alexander of Abonouteichos in turn can be sharpened by comparison: the new guru in an out-of-the-way, insignificant and relatively inaccessible part of Paphlagonia, who can send messages that the stolen property is under so-and-so's bed, or can issue directives acted upon by a hard-pressed Roman army on the Danube, could not have been too different from his Christian counterpart.

By the end of the fourth century little has changed. The holy man is still in command, or so it will be claimed, in an urban crisis. Macedonius is ready to intercede with the Emperor Theodosius after the Antiochenes had rioted in the affair of the statues in AD 387: he joins his voice to that of Libanius, and to that of the Christian bishop Flavian. Macedonius comes down from his mountain to mediate with the Imperial envoys: the Emperor is to remember that he too is a mere man, and not for the sake of images to destroy men made in the image of God; he is respected by the envoys and contributes to their reprieve.[19]

Furthermore, for the fourth and fifth centuries we have a wider spectrum of holy men at work: the *Historia Monachorum in Aegypto* affords a number of facets of individual ascetic personalities, at a single time and place, something we conspicuously lack for the centuries that preceded. The *Historia*'s author unguardedly betrays much about the environment: it is taken for a point much in favour of such men that they are cut off from the outside world and in some cases are totally unaware of it: indeed John of Lycopolis spends forty years in isolation in the desert, not seeing a woman during that time.[20] The result is that prestige can be nurtured in a vacuum: his own interview includes John's revelation that one of the visitor's companions is a deacon, something he modestly denies (it is not clear whether the detection is due to psychology or prior information).[21] The same John foretells the rebellions of 'tyrants' against Theodosius, their destruction, and the annihilation of barbarian incursions.[22] A general consults him on the Ethiopian occupation of Syene, and is advised to march against him, successfully.[23] His reputation for clairvoyance is understated by the neighbouring fathers; he sends a dream to the over-persistent wife of a tribune; and he tells another senior officer that his wife has delivered a son but is at risk of her own life.[24] John does not perform cures, but will dispense an oil; a senator's wife asks for a prayer from him, receives the oil, and is cured on the third day, while one of the author's own brethren is cured of a stomach-ache.[25] We are still in a familiar world, but the body of consultants has proliferated.

The *Life of Martin* had comparable consequences for the prestige of holy men in the West.[26] Once more we can recognise the typically recurrent situations which Sulpicius Severus is able to write about from a combination of personal interview and local testimonial. It is Martin's very monastic detachment which brings about his episcopal election, and after it he still practises *askēsis* in a suitably remote cell.[27] What looms large here is the extent to which the saint is given credit in evidently exaggerated terms for the control of people. He stops a pagan funeral cortège on suspicion that sacrifice is about to take place; the predictable confusion he induces in the mourners is accordingly interpreted as a triumph over powers and authority.[28] More of a risk is his challenge to pagans to stand in the path of a sacred tree if they will cut it down.[29] But then even the poet Horace had been able to claim divine favour for an escape from a falling tree.[30]

Patterns of continuity in pagan asceticism are direct and discernible. The world of Christian asceticism presents a necessarily different picture, but the differences are readily accountable, and not as marked as they might have been. Immediately after the generation of Antony and Pachomius, the Christian holy man could operate in the conditions of relative security that his pagan counterpart had always been able to take for granted. Much of the impact of St Martin or St Jerome can be readily related to the world of Jesus Christ, Apollonius of Tyana, or the Peregrinus Proteus who had a foot in both camps. We still find the Christian holy man as an outsider to the religious establishment, in Martin's case as a monk among bishops (despite his being forced to accept a bishopric himself). And we can still see the family tension and retreat to solitude (even as a bishop), as well as the same range of miraculous or quasi-miraculous activities (Sulpicius Severus insists on Martin's self-effacing publicity-shunning character, but in the monks of Marmoutier he had the familiar means of publicity). There are still the enemies, not least Martin's more worldly successor Brice; the statutory defiance of Imperial authority; and the same difficulty in constructing a biography out of essentially hagiographic tradition.

More secure is the enormous amount of data that can be assembled for the East Roman continuation of our subject, the Byzantine saint. In this case there is direct continuity through the thought-world of later Antiquity. One might suggest that there is no special reason why there should not have been stylite saints in the third century rather than the fifth, had it not been for the fact that Decian and subsequent persecutions provided a more urgent and immediate test for religious endurance. Society itself and the range of social situations are relatively unchanged, at least from the holy man's point of view. The ideology of demonic possession remains, as does the holy man's obligation to do battle with demons: society still polarizes into allies and opponents, and the range of services provided to it continues.

Accordingly we find St Daniel the later stylite dispossessing a church of its demons: two nights he spends in the buildings, disregarding their imprecations. One is reminded of the incident which secured the fame of Gregory Thaumaturgus in the third century, the occupation and incubation in a temple from which the demons are expelled; or for that matter Lucian's account of Arignotus the Pythagorean wrestling with the ghost which possesses a house in Corinth.[31]

One notes too that when Daniel does aspire to stylite status he sets up his pillar in relation to Constantinople, in that golden vicinity of early Imperial holy men, whence he can remain in easy contact with the city itself; and the Emperor Leo duly consults the holy man at Anaplus when about to send Zeno as general against the Thracians: one thinks once more of the advice sought from Alexander of Abonouteichos on the Parthian War.[32]

The root cause of the similarities between Byzantine hagiography and the holy men of the Empire is not just a matter of continuity of tradition; the social needs and conditions had not changed radically at grass roots level. Without any changes in the popular outlook on the physiology of disease, or the phenomenology of weather, it will still be attributed to demons and the saint will be credited with the removal of toxicity;[33] without any increased understanding of the physical world he will be credited with ending droughts and earth-quakes or the confinement of rivers. Daniel the Stylite can continue the feats of Gregory Thaumaturgus in several departments,[34] while Apollonius of Tyana is still useful centuries afterwards in Byzantime times.[35] Nor were holy men any less inclined to use techniques that are really magical in concept: Theodore of Sykeon could let three locusts die in his hand, as a sympathetic gesture towards the death of all the rest.[36]

Nor is their well-publicised level of religious virtuosity foreign to the early Empire: neither Christian nor pagan could lay claim to stylite saints or iron-caged anchorites, yet the latter phenomenon can only be said to mark a difference of degree. The Cynics and solitary prophets had long-established models of minimum self-sufficiency and contempt for the outside world, and pagan solitaries had been claimed to live for decades underground, or simply to disappear for long periods.[37] It was still in imitation of John the Baptist that Theodore of Sykeon had shut himself off in the wilder-ness,[38] with no apparent ambition for human awareness of his feat, or for the religious orders preferred him even under age when he was discovered.

Peter Brown characterises the early Byzantine holy men with conviction and panache: his presentation of the function of these figures is beyond argument. But one is less clear about the business of their 'rise': Brown seems to opt for a clear distinction between the *theios anēr* of classical Antiquity for whom he postulates an intellectual elitist characterisation, and the man who makes his practice as the outsider and patron of the Byzantine village cul-ture.[39] But it is not too long before such a distinction begins to break down: Brown himself cites the case of Apollonius of Tyana; but it is by no means clear from our survey that he can be used as a symbol of all the kinds or levels of activity that were possible in the early Empire, especially in the Jewish sphere.[40] Brown also seems to characterise Lucian's analysis of Hope and Fear in the holy man's clientele as superficial and insignificant; but this is to downgrade the particular at the expense of the general too far.[41]

We can look for examples of the Byzantine type so characteristic in at least a cross-section of the classical examples: Jesus Christ and Gregory Thaumaturgus provide suitable paradigms from first-century Palestine and third-century Asia Minor respectively.

Certain factors must of course have acted upon the holy men during the transition from the early Empire to late Antiquity. Yet we do not hear for example of Antony's clients escaping liturgies, any more than we hear of Jesus Christ's sympathising with nationalist aspirations: a holy man continued to be the proponent of compromise and the status quo.

COMPARISONS

A number of motifs are persistent in the repertoire of miracle-working, and it is illuminating to use instances from more recent religious practice to authenticate them and provide further commentary. In a pagan fictional text of the third or fourth centuries we have seen extended reference to the precautions a holy man might take to protect his client from the evil eye. The passage of Heliodorus already studied shows Calasiris, the Egyptian holy man *par excellence*, going through the motions of rescuing his charge Charicleia from the envy that attaches to great beauty: she has supposedly been enchanted by a look from the Thessalian noble Theagenes. As a precaution Calasiris burns incense and recites various formulae: the whole business is a charade to enable him to inspect her recognition-tokens, which include jewellery and a coloured belt.[42]

A recent survey of the evil eye in the Muslim Near East[43] confirms Heliodorus' depiction almost down to the last detail. The suspected offender, Theagenes, is characteristically an outsider; beauty is especially at risk, given the base of envy for the eye-superstition. Modern Egyptian precautions are to recite verses of the Koran when one burns alum, which pops like the bursting of an eye;[44] Calasiris uses libanotos and some nonsense prayers. In one detail there is perhaps greater difference: Calasiris suspects that Charicleia is being jinxed by the belt, so he tells her father;[45] in practice it would have been of bright colours as an apotropaic against the eye: Heliodorus is not likely to have slipped up; this may be one of the frequent pretences and manipulations of current superstitious belief.[46]

In the foregoing instance one might argue for direct cultural continuity: a practice plausibly attributed to the apotropaic techniques of pagan Antiquity can be transmitted to perform the same need in the same general geographical area in a modern Islamic context. We can now attempt a comparison where the time-span is shorter but the geography more diffuse. The credibility of Philostratus' *Life of Apollonius* is nowhere more obviously at breaking-point than when he claims that the disciple Damis had described Apollonius and the Brahmans as floating in mid-air: 'I saw Indian Brahmans living upon the earth and yet not upon it; after they anointed themselves and bathed, then the earth arched itself like a billow of the sea and sent them two cubits high into the air'.[47] But comparative evidence can warn us not to reject the affair entirely: we do have a medieval Western specific for a witches' flying ointment administered externally, as the witch administers the ointment in *The Golden Ass*.[48] Apollonius and his associates are likewise anointed. Actual chemical testing establishes that the medieval recipe gives the subject a delusion of location:[49] one *feels* as if one is flying. A report of a group use of such an agent can be easily misrepresented as a general vision of collective flight seen from the outside.

Lastly, a still less likely source of support for an ancient account: *The Life of Hajji Baba of Ispahan* is an uproarious comic-picaresque account of life in rural eighteenth-century Persia, where the author James Morier himself was born. The tale includes a carefully observed account of a holy man's procedure for the detection of a thief, in this case commissioned to recover a sum of money which a young student had buried at home but lost. Despite the lapse of time and the purportedly fictional context, the account can be given next to documentary status in an era before the advent of the anthropologist. The holy man recovers the empty vessel from the floor and summons the family. He gives them a test; all who can break down a ball of rice with their teeth will be exempt from suspicion. That turns out to be everyone except the son's mother and tutor, one of whom protests that they cannot break down the rice without teeth. This leaves them partly under suspicion, and the technique itself is open to doubt. But the holy man then makes a mound in the corner: he expects to discover the money in the mound the next morning, then does so.[50] How is it done?

There can be no doubt that the holy man can legitimately claim a success: he has done exactly what he had been commissioned to do. But the crux of the matter is not in his test for culprits, but in the reasons why he should have chosen that particular one. We can suspect that he had already formed his own unprovable suspicions as to who was most likely to have found and removed the money – the closest personal acquaintances with access to the house. He needed then to select a way of putting suspicion on the culprit which will frighten him into supposing the holy man is on his track and using infallible resources against him. Once that is established, it is only a matter of recovering the stolen property without further ado – and without pointing a finger of guilt at any one too precisely. The property is returned, but the culprit is allowed to remain undetected on a 'no questions asked' basis. We should have no difficulty in reconstructing how closely oracles of Alexander could avail themselves of the psychological weapons shown here.[51]

Some comparisons can be advanced on a broader front. A large area of promising convergence between ancient and modern holy men is in the employment of the techniques of the shaman, which have long played a part in the historical study of ancient religion.

> It was here that the new religious pattern made its fateful contribution: by crediting man with an occult self of divine origin, and then setting soul and body at odds, it introduced into European culture a new interpretation of human exist-ence, the interpretation we call puritanical.[52]

E. R. Dodds looks for this not in the Near East but rather by finding the occult self in the shamanic cultures still extant in Siberia: he is right to take the wide extent of diffusion of the phenomenon as evidence to fit Antiquity. By his definition

> a Shaman may be described as a psychically unstable person who has received a call to the religious life; as a result of his call he undergoes a period of rigorous training, which com-monly involves solitude and fasting and may involve a psychological change of sex. From this religious 'retreat' he emerges with the power, real or assumed, of passing at will into a state of mental dissociation. In that condition he is not thought . . . to be possessed by an alien spirit; but his own soul is thought to leave its body and travel to distant parts, most often to the spirit world. From these experiences, nar-rated by him in extempore song, he derives the skill in divina-tion, religious poetry and magical medicine which makes him socially important. He becomes the repository of a super-natural wisdom.[53]

The term 'shaman'[54] is technically concentrated on the practices of operators still observable in central Asia, particularly Siberia, and analogous cultures in primitive societies over parts of the Third World. The shaman's claim to holiness is through variously induced trance states involving claims of supernatural journeys, as well as healing miracles and other lesser 'holy' attributes. The most obvious parallels to such claims lie in the legend of Abaris the Thracian[55] and Aristeas of Proconnesus,[56] and ultimately in the former's contact Pythagoras. The grounds of plausibility adduced are the northern connexions of the first two and their association with Greek awareness for the first time of the culture-area of the Black Sea. One must therefore ask whether shamanic elements will 'explain' anything about Neopythagoreans, such as Apollonius of Tyana or possibly Alexander of Abonouteichos.

Initial examination carries a certain promise: Abonouteichos is itself on the southern Black Sea coast,[57] Tyana in deepest Anatolia;[58] both could claim to be close enough to the 'fringe' of the Graeco-Roman *oikoumenē* to offer an outlet for a primitive type to make a renewed penetration of the thin veneer of Greek civilisation. Of special interest in relation to Apollonius is the fact that he is alleged to have spent a year in Scythia, traditionally the home in Greek perception of shamanic practices. The fact that this is emphatically denied by 'Damis' proves nothing.[59]

How well does such a blueprint fit the subjects of our investigation? It helps with Apollonius of Tyana or Peregrinus or even Jesus Christ: bilocation may be implied[60] in the transfiguration narrative,[61] and all three would have claimed to have an element of divinity in their own right rather than possession. At the same time, the emphasis of what we know of each of these figures tends to play down the trance state and the magical element, for obvious enough reasons; though the Gnostic Christs have a closer claim than their canonical counterparts.[62]

One might note for Alexander the initial 'trance' exhibition on his return to Abonouteichos, induced by the chewing of a specified substance (soapwort-root).[63] But all in all, a shamanistic element is all one might be tempted to allow to Alexander, among a highly complex and eclectic religious vocabulary; if anything it is as easy to explain his activities as a commentary on the life and background of oracle personnel as such.

For Apollonius we have more evidence, characteristically difficult to interpret. For a start we have a description, attributed to Damis, of what appears to be some sort of 'trip', possibly hallucinogenically induced, for the sage in India.[64] Nor does an Indian rather than a 'Scythian' sphere of operations serve to disqualify Apollonius: in point of fact the word shaman can be related to Strabo's term Sarmanes[65] for a sect of Indian sages (though

Philostratus himself does not use the term itself). As usual we are
left wondering.

A PERIOD COMPARISON: ELIZABETHAN
ENGLAND

A still wider field of cross-cultural comparison is to be sought in
situations where traditional beliefs and practices familiar to the
Roman Empire still survived almost intact, at least at a popular
level. Such, for example, was the situation in the England of the
sixteenth and seventeenth centuries in which astrology, magic and
prophecy enjoyed a well-documented vogue sometimes in well-
nigh unaltered form. It is the merit of the major study by Keith
Thomas[66] to be able to supply an overall rationale, sometimes
intellectual and sometimes sub-intellectual,[67] for the satisfaction
such practices were able to provide. In the absence of scientific
certainty astrology, for example, could provide an explanation and a
means of coming to terms with misery and affliction, and the
witchcraft craze could furnish *inter alia* a means of identifying
scapegoats.[68] The parameters for astrology in the seventeeth century were no better than for Ptolemy and Vettius Valens in the
second; in the words of George Herbert 'Astrology was true but the
astrologers could not find it'[69] – they could hope to do so less and
less as the discovery of more heavenly bodies, and more about their
natures, complicated the detection of planetary influence to an
impossible degree, while the abolition of supra- and sub-lunary
regions served to undermine the traditional cosmology as dear to
Plutarch as to the astrologer.[70]

One notes some familiar unchanging aspects: the continued
unease of secular authorities in the face of the casting of royal
horoscopes.[71] On the other hand we do have much evidence from
the Roman Empire on the balance of fear so evidently typical of
African societies and not unknown in the Renaissance, as in the
paranoia over witchcraft as a means of coping with inexplicable or
unbearable misfortune, and the corresponding search for the scapegoats responsible. We can of course supply a great deal by reasonable inference; when a figure who prophesies earthquake is in turn
accused of causing it, since he was previously 'in the know', then we
have the right framework of belief for this particular sociological
safety-valve. One thinks of the Christians bearing the blame for the
silence of the oracle of Apollo which sparked off the Great

Persecution[72] (a process Christians would have been eager to boast of on the principle of 'he would not suffer the demons to speak'). Again, where magic was suspected in summoning the services of a lover, it is a reasonable guess that the supposed magician would have been the potential victim of local reprisal on behalf of any injured party. Yet continual legal restraints on noxious magic should serve to confirm the existence of a general fear; and opponents of Jesus Christ were held to attribute his successes in exorcism to the work of the devil.[73]

Not least important where comparative methods are in question is the greatly increased prospect of finding out 'how it was done'. Thomas has assembled a wide-ranging dossier on cunning men in the sixteenth and seventeenth centuries: part of the time at least such operations can be used to show retrospective light on the divination practice of older cultures (as they themselves can sometimes be illumined from modern primitive ones). It is particularly interesting to see physiognomics as a living art in the popular repertoire, certainly not obtained from Polemo's treatise which survived only in Arabic;[74] while a form of coscinomancy, mentioned in Lucian's treatise on Alexander, is well attested, this time calling for shears as well as sieve.[75] The importance of comparison lies in the difference as well as in the similarities. We hear nothing in Alexander's or Apollonius' techniques of what use was made of suggestive lists of suspects in the process of divination of theft; but the sixteenth-century evidence is strong enough to raise at least the possibility that such techniques may well have been part of the game in Antiquity as well.

The forms of magical operations themselves can be illuminated by cross-cultural comparison. The late antique magical papyri are characterised by their impressive displays of apparent gibberish that can be at least partly broken down into Semitic and other formulae.[76] In the sixteenth century we find that the unintelligibility of Latin at a popular level gives it the same esoteric place: five Paternosters, five Aves and Creed, followed by three more Paternosters, three Aves and three Creeds, all for nine consecutive nights, offers an attested curative spell; as Thomas points out, 'The pronunciation of Catholic prayers in Latin long remained a common ingredient of the magic treatment of illness'.[77] And Hebrew and other forms still served the same purpose as in the papyri.[78] Indeed the thin dividing line between ritualised healing and treatment by prayer can be seen to be as thin as it is in the New Testament accounts themselves; the practice of writing prayers and hanging the writing round the parties' necks is orthodox amulet technique by another name,[79] and no less ancient is the practice of spells by diminution of letters. The same parameters would have applied in the event of the failure of such formulae: the more complex and esoteric the operation, the more difficult it would have been to 'get it right' on any given occasion. Hence the formula itself would not have been impugned in cases of failure: the next case of success would have been used to guarantee or confirm its efficacy.[80] The test of the fluency of prayers is known in sixteenth-century England, just as surely as it was to Hanina ben Dosa in the first century.[81] And the cure by royal touch for the King's evil scrofula and related disorders follows the same assumptions as Vespasian could have counted on at Alexandria (sometimes, as in the case of James I, with the same degree of misgiving);[82] the English use of this technique is as old as Edward the Confessor.[83] The basic assumption in both cases is that which underlies the legend of the 'King of the Waste Land', that there is a direct correlation between the health of the sovereign and that of his people,[84] and that only the legitimate claimant could expect his touch to be efficacious.[85]

It is hardly surprising that one of the seventeenth-century healers, Valentine Greatrakes, should have had a career reminiscent of those of the Imperial practitioners; his touch could cure the King's evil, so it was felt. He had an astronomer as a client, as well as the support of Cambridge Platonists and serious scientists: if he failed both with a female member of the aristocracy and with a royal demonstration before Charles II, he still suggests the high success rate possible for someone who was a healer by conviction (his ambitions were neither social nor financial, and he seems to have believed in his initial divine injunction). He certainly experienced the divisiveness of such operations, and he may have had some sectarian impulse; a country squire who could cure the King's evil would have devalued the prestige of the King himself in this department. An earlier predecessor felt the power go out of his body every time he performed his stroking. Such a claim may be a comment on the physiology of charismatic cure; but it might also be felt as imitation of a gospel report; or as a reflection on the fact that constant crowd pressure, like royal handshaking, can be imagined as an exhausting business.

In Antiquity and the Renaissance the underlying market forces remain the same: they are related to the state and availability of medical services, and their inability under the most ideal conditions to provide total satisfaction, let alone the kind of drama and simplified causation associated with divine or magical healings and their counterparts.

The English examples also attest to the versatility of 'cunning persons' of both sexes; and to the role of patronage in their protection, as well as the grudging acknowledgement of their supposed successes by the opposition establishment of orthodox religion. It is worth stressing that at least some ancient rationalistic responses were as sophisticated as those of Elizabethan and subsequent rationalists, or as modern interest in 'placebo effect' or psychosomatic symptoms and cures. Lucian could claim that Asclepius and his sons performed their healings by administering drugs, not by sticking on lion- and weasel-skins. He could also comment intelligently on the phenomenon that those who used Alexander's prophylactic against the plague were the very ones who actually stood to catch it, through chance or complacency.[86]

SOME ISLAMIC COMPARISONS

It can be no less useful to note a Near-Eastern inheritance from late antique holy men with a quite different series of parallels. Perhaps the most valuable insight into the causes of conflict among holy men comes from a group of medieval Sufist exempla, sensitive to the diversity of response of individuals to the behaviour of holy men. Jesus the Son of Mary is fashioning birds out of clay: the other boys complain to the elders who rule that this cannot happen on the Sabbath: the elders react in a variety of different ways (the feat is impossible, and so cannot be Sabbath-breaking; a second elder wants to learn the art for himself; a third dismisses it as deception).[87] In fact the beginning of the story is already known to infancy gospel tradition: the rest represents the essence of religious controversy, fundamental to *magos-goēs* disputes as well as to the problem of oral interpretation of the Torah. Still more perceptive for the dissensions between holy men is a late Sufist story of three men in search of 'Deep Truth'. Each misidentifies the same unknown stranger who leads him to the truth: one is told he will find it in the country of fools, the second in the Magic Mirror, a third with the aid of the Jinn in a whirlpool. Each finds the truth as promised for himself; but the result is that their disciples know of only one route to the truth for the future.[88] It is small wonder that eminent Sufists could in fact count on Christian disciples,[89] or that Muslims were scandalised at the variety of religions represented at the funeral of the Muslim Sufist Jelal:[90] some at least had come to recognise a common ground all too often lacking in the fanatical sectarianism of at least the Judaeo-Christian tradition in the Empire.

One episode in particular has specific relevance to the Christian account of the transfiguration. Jelal has been preaching on the subject of the Old Testament prophets Moses and Elias.[91] A student takes a stranger to be Elias: the stranger refers him back to Jelal, who acknowledges all the prophets including Moses and Elias as his friends.[92] The story itself may be an Islamicisation of the transfiguration narrative,[93] transferred from Christ to Jelal. But it also prompts us to ask whether it is not a reflex of the holy man's disciples to associate their master with these two prophets *par excellence*. The association in this case may have been all the more readily occasioned by suggestion in the first place.

The literature relating to Muslim devouts in the medieval period does contain a distinctive element normally foreign to Western Christian hagiography: a flourishing picaresque literature which acknowledges rogues, cheats and charlatans among the practitioners of holiness. In particular a cluster of stories has occurred round the proverbial al-Hallaj,[94] who appears to emulate some of the more dubious operations of Alexander of Abonouteichos. The ruses stretch to a miracle of producing fish in a waterless region – with the help of a concealed reservoir stocked for that specific purpose;[95] on discovery of the source the informant similarly fears for his life, and is duly threatened with the loss of it.

Al-Hallaj is also attributed with the coating of the inside of vessels with a sugar preparation reduced to a paste. 'Those who drank it were unaware of all this; they thought the water had been transformed into rose syrup and they believed whatever he wanted them to.'[96] It is not too difficult to surmise how a trick of turning water into wine might be organised without the narrator's knowledge. The same sharper could enhance the effects of his presence by expanding his body to fill a room, relying on a ventilator shaft passing below his seat to inflate a voluminous silk tunic: 'People said that he appeared in glory in the House of Majesty'. From such a figure we are entitled to expect an optical illusion of the sun rising in the West (by means of the reflection of a candle on a bronze bowl), or a speaking tube which produced a voice from heaven. And resurrection of the dead can be produced by means of a classic

Scheintod trick, requiring a prepared tomb with a concealed exit, after which he could stage an exhibition with prophetic 'authority'. Yet the perpetrator, Bahayarbad al-Majousi, is still 'a devout among the magi'.[97]

AN OUTSIDE COMPARISON: MODERN AFRICAN CHARISMATICS

The sociology of religion has made available the possibility of comparison with primitive modern societies, and we are at least able to face the difficulties of comparing observed data on holy men in a primitive society with non-observed data in a complex and sophisticated one. Evans-Pritchard's classic study allows us to look at a brief camera-glimpse of an un-Europeanised indigenous central African culture's use of the supernatural over a short period of continuous observation in the 1920s:[98] it is first and foremost a reminder of what the historian can never do for an ancient society, and what the anthropologist has not in this case done for a modern one. There is no single technique for constructing a 'day in the life of' Jesus Christ or Alexander of Abonouteichos, as through the eyes of an objective outside observer: an Herodotus could for this purpose have been worth more than any pair of the three Synoptic evangelists to the historian. Nor is there any way of taking a longer historical perspective of the Azande to take account of the development of a complex of beliefs that go to make up the thought-world recreated by Evans-Pritchard. That thought-world includes the constant consultation of a poison oracle for even quite routine matters of daily life, and no less constant preoccupation with protection against witchcraft and sorcery.

But two broad points of comparison do emerge as worthwhile between the Azande and the sub-culture of the ancient Near East. First, the preoccupation with protection from an evil felt to be physically inside the person: casting out demons and protection against witchcraft have that much in common. And second, the ubiquitous acceptability of oracle-operation as a means of regulating society. Lucian clearly regards such a state of affairs as irrational and aberrant;[99] to the Azande there is no other way; and the people of Abonouteichos may well have felt likewise, though the degree of dependence is clearly different.

A comparative perspective can also be adduced from the study of thaumaturgic techniques relative to millenarianism in modern

215

Third-world societies. Bryan Wilson[100] has found the former more common than the latter over a wide cross-section of developing cultures, and for good reason: 'thaumaturgy does affect mental attitudes, reassures men, confirms their diagnoses (in witch-finding), utilizes trickery and self-confirming devices (in ordeals), and normally escapes objective test; only millenarianism stakes all on a prophesied external event to occur cataclysmically, suddenly, and soon, and proceeding from the action of external agency'.

Such a state of affairs is not less true of the Roman Empire. Millenniarist prophecies are generally localised to the special social and political conditions of a Jewish context; and emerging Christianity is able to fall back on belief in resurrection past to offset any delay of the apocalypse to come about. 'The many little failures of magic are less disturbing to believers than the big periodic failure of the millennium, and are more easily explained away.'

Observations of charismatic thaumaturgic movements in the Third World are not only useful as a resource for comparison to antique holy men in general: one can see in some at least a potential for a closer understanding of such a phenomenon as Montanism, for example. The career of the charismatic visionary Isaiah Shembe in the foundation of the Nazareth Baptist Church in 1911 could restore the tribal dignities and hierarchical pride of its local community;[101] but it also owned land in the form of an ancient tribal territory: in connexion with Shembe's village at Ekuphakameni, one thinks of the special significance for the Montanists of Pepuza as the New Jersualem in Phrygia. All the more completely comparable is the Zion City Moria Church of Edward Lekganyene, where 'there is a prediction . . . of a future time when Christ will descend to Zion City, which God has chosen as his holy place'.[102]

Wilson writes of magic and millennium as increasingly marginalised and *passé*: 'magic does not work; the millennium will not come'.[103] He was writing before the tide of Islamic Fundamentalism could demonstrate the power of forces outside the comprehension of Western political analysts, but embracing well-recognised sociological forces in the face of injustice and discontent. Such generalisation as the following now have a hollow ring:

Existent Messiahs are not revolutionist; the response to the world which they canvass cannot be as direct as that of even the typical revolutionist sect, for whom the overturning of the world will be a possibility only when the messiah arrives or decides. A living Messiah cannot make claims that are post-poned in this way. There is no leeway of latency. His world-transforming potential cannot be stressed. It must be muted. In consequence it is his therapeutic and thaumaturgic powers that are extolled.

We have not seen the last of the holy man, millennial or otherwise. And there is nothing to suggest that he will be any less versatile in the twenty-first century than in the first.

14

EPILOGUE
Varieties of ambiguity

'Difficult concept, charisma', says Henry Beamish in *The History Man*, about a book he is never going to bring himself to finish. We are left in the same quandary. Whatever charisma may be, it has manifested itself in no uncertain fashion even during the course of the writing of this book: it was begun before an Iranian Holy Man had toppled the Shah, and imposed a *fatwah* on Salman Rushdie; and finished before the end of the siege in Texas of the Branch Davidian Sect with heavy loss of life. What are we to make of holy men in the Roman Empire and the charisma that surrounds them?

In the first place virtuoso religious activists were widely perceived to exist in both Graeco-Roman and Judaeo-Christian traditions, and in the increasingly substantial overlap between them. They could function within an establishment, but were more likely to appear in opposition to it. They had substantial and prestigious precedent, a fact which frequently prejudices current and subsequent perception of them. That perception is prejudiced further by the difficulties ancient and modern of distinguishing medicine, miracle and magic, which in this context function more as categories of perception than as objectively definable realities; and by the natural tendency of sources to polarise their subjects into saints and charlatans; the differences in the character and distribution of sources that cover, for example, Jesus Christ and Apollonius of Tyana militate against objective attempts at a historical consensus on the nature of either, let alone the chance of comparing them.

That said, there are certain basic requirements a holy man has to have: virtuosity need not be based on any one skill of the many available; but all were capable of achieving results, and the figure who combined results, vision, common sense and conviction was likely to make an impact. That impact had social consequences: on

218

individual clients, on cities, on some still larger notion of community as the case might be; though any given holy man has a choice between continuity and radical change or renewal.

A holy man may of course choose to exist in total detachment; such figures are necessarily unreportable. The vast majority have social contacts, ranging though the whole spectrum of co-workers, disciples, clients, and patrons; the more varied their constituency the more effective they are likely to be in widening their impact on society as a whole; and the more likely they are to stimulate opposition, whether based on purely religious motives, or on self-interest, jealousy, distrust, ignorance or competition. One's opponents are automatically more self-seeking and less pure, and ambition and purity will be defined in such a way as to confirm the point.

Official interest in holy men may take the form of opposition if a holy man is perceived as politically subversive; but just as often official patronage of such figures is likely to be a matter of political opportunism or sheer curiosity. The holy man must move among mankind or find an effective means of communication: in the context of the Roman world the Mediterranean itself is likely to be the ultimate medium. The holy man may be commemorated in fiction, satirical or romantic, as a familiar type; and he is inevitably open to the distortions of transmission and to comparisons with his successors and social analogues.

But I suspect that the real value of our materials lies less in broad generalisations than in our renewed perception of individual situations. Something in society is going awry; a holy man appears – something of a mysterious outsider, and somehow or other the situation is put to rights: the price of corn goes down, the thief is found, the epileptic is calmed, and that is all part of the way society works. If the holy man goes beyond such intervention, particularly in the direction of eschatological fervour, the results may be less predictable: his followers killed in a show-down, a regime toppled, or a world religion founded. What is most consistently missing is the holy man himself: we are still left asking how he sees himself. And there I suspect lies the key; it is the holy man's ability to serve his society and yet keep us guessing in a way which mystifies and fascinates that is more likely to preserve the notion that he knows something that we do not. This may be a simple matter of modesty or manipulation on his part. The point is that we never know quite enough to know which.

My own approach is perhaps best summed up by the fourth of Lucian's *Dialogi Marini*: the Homeric hero Menelaus is in conversation with Proteus, the old man of the sea, who has just given a demonstration of his powers of changing shape; having witnessed them, Menelaus is still not quite convinced. How is it done? In the manner of a *polypous*, says the glibly reassuring Proteus, but Menelaus is still left wondering how the same person can turn from water into fire. There is always something missing, something that does not fit, and one's task is all too often to try to account for what it might be. I have tried to maintain an initial scepticism, a kind of Celsus-eye view of much of our evidence; but against it has to be balanced a consciousness that holy men are sustained by competence as well as conviction; and that those who equate faith with credulity must none the less summon the historical imagination to realise that holy men were a source of communal continuity as well as change.

In looking at holy men I have emphasised the practical dimension as far as possible. Holy men with a specialist skill, be it prophecy, healing, or some other, emerge as prestigious, powerful and self-assertive figures, often uncomfortable or controversial in their relationships with one another and any religious establishment with which they may come in contact. The interlocking cultures of Judaism and Graeco-Roman paganism created a cultural *koinē* in which they could easily flourish, and Rome used their services as often as it opposed them. In the end they give the world at least one new world religion, with a still deservedly controversial founder. What emerges is that virtuoso holy men were in some sense impressive and effective, deservedly or otherwise, and that controversy is a corollary of their effectiveness. It may generally be easier to explain such holy men away than it is to explain them at all. In the end it was not necessarily their lives that brings this situation about; but the deaths of martyrs for the faiths they founded, holy and unholy alike, for which the professional holy men themselves can only take limited credit.

I have set out to emphasise the diversity and versatility of these still often enigmatic figures, their conditions of operation, and how they might have been able to see themselves. I have sometimes none the less emphasised the practical at the expense of the theoretical: blind men wish to see, regardless of the credentials of the healer; and they may be left seeing the world as it is, rather than the community of a new age. And the nature of revealed religion tends to prejudice objective analysis: when two figures enter such a territory simultaneously with contradictory or incompatible claims, then it is tempting to tarnish both with the caricature of the self-seeking charlatan. That in itself is of course a caricature: there were for the most part easier channels of self-advancement in ancient societies than that of the professional holy man, and we must resist the assumption that our subjects were a systematic succession of albeit amiable villains or self-deluding individuals competing for the minds and material rewards of their clients. At the same time we must be alive to the element of pious cliché in certain aspects of a holy man's activity: renewal of a community for a new age may be no more than a disingenuous way of saying 'I stand for my idea of progress, and anyone who dares to oppose me is an enemy of it'. The problem is highlighted by a familiar passage of the *Didachē*: members of a Christian community are blithely assumed to be able to tell the difference between the purveyors of true and false revelations. This is no more within the competence of a second-century Christian congregation than it was for those faced with Jesus Christ or Alexander of Abonouteichos.

What we can say is that holy men for the most part were doers: to stay in operation they needed satisfied clients, whether or not that need entailed some in fooling at least some of the people some of the time. The holy man has to be in some sense at least an explorer of the holy, and any disagreement with established explorations may bring personal risk to himself and his followers. For self-perpetuation into memory and into cult a chain of succession is necessary, or a missionary base, and a certain equilibrium of cultural conditions; beyond that it is up to the individual.

Much of our survey depends not just on interpretation, but on interpretation of interpretation. One man's theurgy is another's magic; one man's community of the new age is another's deluded victims of apocalyptic scare-mongering; one man's faith is another's belief without proof. And those holy men who are presented as concealing or obfuscating their identity for whatever reason can scarcely be surprised if they are misunderstood. We can also say that holy men were, and are, a force for good or ill: they have all the moral ambiguity of fanatical conviction. The West may have been recently horrified by the death-sentence passed by an Islamic religious leader on an author thought to have blasphemed against Islam; but Western Christianity is founded on the cult of a leader presented in the New Testament as counselling mutual love and respect on the one hand, while on the other threatening judgement against his opponents, to say nothing of cursing a fig-tree.

APPENDIX: JESUS THE JEW;
JESUS THE MAGICIAN

No account of holy men in the early Empire can avoid the fact that one of their number – at least as he would have appeared to contemporaries – was the founder, knowingly or unknowingly, of what subsequently became a world religion. For our purposes it is neither practical nor proper to devote substantial space even to a history of the problem of the historical Jesus.[1] It seems more appropriate to illustrate the kinds of problems that result when the biographical traditions are subjected by those claiming a historical approach to some larger context. This I attempt by looking at two recent and deservedly controversial treatments which in different ways treat Jesus Christ as a holy man: Geza Vermes' *Jesus the Jew*[2] and Morton Smith's *Jesus the Magician*.

The main thrust of Vermes' argument is that Jesus should be seen as one of a number of *hasidim* – of wandering 'Devouts' within Judaism, who functions as a preacher, exorcist and healer, and who can fairly claim a familiar role as a Jewish prophet.[3] But the distinctively Christian dimension to Jesus, that he claims to be and was 'the Messiah' and that titles such as 'Son of God' and 'Son of Man' embodied a distinctive claim to divinity are then denied either as misunderstanding or secondary accretion, in the light of claims of the resurrection, itself dependent on nothing more than an empty tomb.[4] Jesus is accordingly seen as narrowly Galilean and Jewish in focus; not as the architect of a designer world religion for export.[5]

The foremost advantage of such a picture is that it is so thoroughly disengaged from the presuppositions of Christian belief. It serves as a reminder to all historians of early Christianity that in this human dimension, Christ was not the first Christian – in the sense that one cannot be said to follow oneself; and it stresses how Christ would have been seen throughout his life, as a Jew by fellow-Jews for the most part. Such an emphasis has a correcting and diluting effect. One is left asking whether Christ is any more of a martyr for mankind than Honi, the Jewish rain-maker killed for refusing to use his powers to curse to order;[6] or whether Jesus' banter with the Pharisees was very much different from the normal rivalry over the law between any other pair of Jewish interested parties.[7]

The most important impact is the cumulative argument over the titles of Jesus. For Vermes the fact that Jesus is non-committal over claims of Messiahship, and that these are understood in a different sense, is a corrective to the Christian argument that Jewish expectations of a Messiah were misconceived. For Vermes one has only to say that if Jesus so differently understood the word he was not claiming to be the Jewish Messiah in any meaningful sense.[8] As to the titles 'Son of Man' and 'Son of God', the latter is applicable to any number of claimants within Judaism, and is therefore meaningless as any sort of indication of a special relationship with God; the former is a distinctively Galilean Aramaism apparently indicating reference to 'oneself'.[9] Only the incidence of an empty tomb will be necessary to convert the claim of 'Son of God' into something more distinctive.

The general presentation of Vermes' argument is consonant with the views developed so far in this study from a quite different perspective: that Jesus Christ falls very comfortably within the parameters of the wandering holy man in general. But there are also dangers, or at any rate lost opportunities for rather different interpretations of the same small group of facts. Indeed the picture Vermes produces works essentially by reliance on the simplest parts of the Synoptic tradition, a middle distance view of Jesus, and the discounting of the theologising images of the much more immediate Pauline letters and the more exotic image in the Gospel of John. This is in a sense a standard procedure, but it perhaps too easily produces an obviously desired effect in this case. The problem is whether Mark's image of Jesus is in some sense *the* authoritative one, and John so far removed from it as to be an implausibly distorting image, or whether it may have something genuine to contribute as a separate historical tradition in its own right. Vermes does not even recognise such a possibility. There is also a somewhat different way of looking at the question of titles: the general practice of other holy men would suggest that the accumulation of a number of titles round a religious figure tends to add a resonance and mystique that transcends any precise connotation. It confers the kind of prestige that may invite but will just as easily refute scepticism.

Moreover, in pointing to post-crucifixion elaboration over Jesus, Vermes seems unwilling to acknowledge the possibility of religious sharp practice. The general idea that the disciples were either too naive, too honest, or too shell-shocked to do anything about the body begs a crucial historical question. Peter had three times lied about Jesus in his master's own presence:[10] was he incapable of a little body-snatching on his own account? We still cannot seriously afford to rule out an element of pious fraud at the foundations of any given cult when it was so commonplace in others (and in Christian accusations against them), and in the forgery of Christian relics ever since.

JESUS THE MAGICIAN

A further image of Jesus, not necessarily exclusive to that of Vermes, concerns his relationship to the world of magic: did he owe his impact to any factors that might be construed as magical practices? The debate should be seen in the context of a long history of attempts to see Jesus Christ in any larger context which can throw light on the basic sources, such as their affinity with the literature of 'aretalogy', or the insistence on the Jewish background we have just seem. But 'Jesus the magician', as propounded by Morton Smith,[11] has a provocative sharpness lacking in the 'Jesus the Jew' of Vermes five years before. Its treatment here is not occasioned by any wish to treat Jesus as a special case, but rather as a typical one of the stalemate involved in evaluating vociferous polemic where the evidence is so incomplete.

Smith's case is to draw attention to the open accusations of demonic alliance in the gospels with accusation in later rabbinical tradition that Jesus was trained in magic in Egypt; and to compare Jesus' practice in miracle-working with that of miracle-working magicians attested in the Hellenistic and Roman world. In its most extreme form this thesis is stated by Smith himself as follows: 'when such window-dressing (as evangelists' editing) is stripped away, what remains is an absolutely primitive figure: a magician-god who unites his followers to himself by giving them his body and blood to eat and drink'.[12]

Many features of the portrait thus derived are either convincing as they stand or at any rate highly plausible; the descent of the spirit in the baptism at the Jordan is construed in terms of magical initiation, where a bird is also involved as a 'carrier'; the idea of Jesus as 'Son of God' would be an allusion to similar and frequent titles in the magical papyri; while the dissatisfaction of Jesus' family with his odd behaviour would be consistent with 'possession'.[13]

But there are several problems of circularity: it is not entirely clear how much in imprecisely datable papyri of the later Empire can be attributed directly to the prestige of Jesus himself, frequently invoked by later magicians: does this prove his magical involvement, or does it merely suggest that the real impact and prestige of his personality and miracles made such an impression as to endow the name Jesus with magical efficacy?[14] Moreover, Smith's consistently ingenious identification of magical accusations in the very earliest strata of tradition does not in itself prove that such accusations were well founded: the ambiguous parameters of *mageia* and the lightness of the accusations against Apuleius can be countered just as easily with a 'they would say that, wouldn't they?'. A successful healer whom the local scribal establishment has good reason to wish to discredit would easily resort to such a charge.

Another nagging doubt hangs over the enormous amount of evidence that is quite properly dependent on inference. Having inferred that a charge of magic must have had *some* foundation, the questioner then finds that all the evidence coherently supports the charge. Yet the same kind of case could easily be made for Christ's being a homosexual on the basis of his being unmarried, 'loving John', and the general currency of such a charge against philosophers and holy men in general; and with as little hope of conclusiveness on current evidence.

A most important factual divergence from the New Testament accounts is Celsus' assertion that Jesus acquired magic in Egypt.[15] In the gospels the only reference to Jesus in Egypt is the infancy narrative in Matthew: to avoid Herod's revenge it is necessary to get this new King of the Jews out of Herod's way.[16] But this is contradicted in Luke, where Jesus is kept near Jerusalem for forty days for the presentation in the temple.[17] Matthew explains his story characteristically as the fulfilment of a prophecy ('From Egypt I have called my son'). Smith takes the prophecy as a cover-up: to counter a rabbinical rumour that Jesus learned magic in Egypt, he has to be put there at an age when he could not have learned it.

The best way to test the assertions and counter-assertions is to ask how and why they could have arisen. Smith does not note that in a sense Jesus does not need to go to Egypt: *magoi* are alleged to come to him and give him three gifts, of which the frankincense and myrrh are regular properties of magicians. On the other hand the temptation narratives put Jesus in the desert, refusing to do the kind of party tricks that Satan encourages him to do. In fact once the possibilities of magical practice are raised, both these episodes fit. It may not have been in a Palestinian, but in an Egyptian, desert that Jesus did the preparation which the gospels construe as testing but which Celsus and his sources might have seen as apprenticeship in magic. And the gospels themselves would then give substance to the idea that Jesus receives a royal horoscope from visiting Chaldaei; and that, perhaps as a result, he follows it up with a flirtation with desert asceticism, some of the disciplines of which are construed as magical (making bread out of stones, miraculously avoiding injury, worship of a demon).

It does not help Smith's case that he presses in great detail the analogy between the gospel narratives of baptism and the magical initiation of *PGM* I.54ff. He plausibly finds five points of resemblance in the two narratives (p. 100); but he fails to call attention to the significant difference that the hawk in the papyrus deposits a magical gemstone with the magician undergoing initiation. The implication for Smith would of course be that any such element would have been 'expurgated out' at an early stage; but be fails to indicate how far from decisive the analogies really are beyond the basic convergence of magical and religious norms.

A much more plausible analogy is offered by *PGM* IV.54–221 which Smith also quotes (p. 103). This time, after the approval represented by the bird, we find the would-be initiate burning grains of frankincense. Now the canonic Christ of Christian belief does possess such a potential magical attribute – given by Eastern sages in infancy. Smith takes the story as modelled on the embassy of Tiridates to Nero, a totally arbitrary association. By contrast, apocryphal gospels and acts convey much more material: the Jesus of Gnostic tradition can assume the mantle of the magician with ease; and it is in relation to this evidence that those defending an established Christian position are most vulnerable.

In short, Smith has not quite proved his case, but the circumstantial evidence as provided even by the canonic gospels is on occasion stronger than he actually acknowledges. There is nothing to suggest that Jesus Christ did not have some background of magical elements, or that after a flirtation with it as represented in the temptation narratives he still retained some techniques that could be construed by enemies or allies alike to be of that order.

On the other extreme from Smith stands Howard Kee, who attempts to use the same range of texts to defend the integrity of Jesus Christ. Kee usefully explores the Graeco-Roman and Jewish environments in a series of studies, but one has the strong impression still of management of evidence and, rather regrettably, the accusation levelled against almost anyone who approaches the subject of neglecting underlying assumptions and contexts, which Kee himself duly provides with unfortunately deceptive clarity. Underlying assumptions are stressed, but not always accurately reported: views of the Elder Pliny, Apollonius of Tyana, Aristides, or Apuleius are seldom reliable; and Jesus Christ emerges from Mark and 'Q' as an ancient forerunner of the sociological preoccupations of the 1960s and 1970s, 'redefining community' – a phrase which would fit much more comfortably on the lips of Dio Chrysostom one suspects. But there is a lack of balance here. Magic is denied the sort of neutral sociological analysis attempted for Jesus Christ, and presented as predominantly self-seeking and manipulative. Apocalyptic by contrast tends to be always seen in a good light, as the culmination of a conflict with cosmic forces in which Jesus Christ and Kee are obviously on the same side, instead of as the sort of scare-mongering and blackmail for which Celsus perceived it not without some justification. It is also stridently insisted by Kee that the thought-world of the first century is fundamentally different from that of the second and third, an assertion which turns out on closer inspection to rely heavily on Kee's preoccupation with apocalyptic. But this frame of mind is readily identifiable in the later centuries also, as the thirteenth Sibylline all too readily proves.

All in all we are no nearer the criteria which will extricate any given holy man from accusations of magic. The ambiguities of magic and holiness, and the deficiencies in our primary evidence, render such impasses unsurprising. And as I write I have just seen Vermes' *The Religion of Jesus the Jew*: the debates still continue.

NOTES

Full publication details of works by modern authors appear at the first citation within the Notes; thereafter, works are referred to by author and date only; full details are available in the Bibliography.

1 CONCEPTS:
THE HOLY MAN AND HIS MILIEUX

1 Josephus, *BJ* 6.300–9.
2 Dio 79(80).18.1ff.; F. G. B. Millar, *A Study of Cassius Dio* (Oxford, 1964) 214–18.
3 *Resp.* 2.359D.
4 For an extensive variorum study on the nature and functions of ancient sages from Sumer to the Roman Empire, J. G. Gammie and L. G. Perdue (eds), *The Sage in Israel and the Ancient Near East* (Winona Lake, 1990).
5 *Peregrinus (de Morte Peregrini)* 13; *Philopseudes* 16. For the term 'sophist', G. Anderson, *Philostratus: Biography and Belles-Lettres in the Third Century AD* (London, 1986), 8ff.; and in D. A. Russell (ed.), *Antonine Literature* (Oxford, 1990) 92ff.
6 *Actus Petri cum Simone* 9.32 (p. 83 Lipsius-Bonnet).
7 Apuleius, *Met.* 9.8.
8 E.g., Demonax, below p. 35f.; Dio Chrysostom, below p. 177.
9 As did Aelius Aristides; for his illness, C. Behr, *Aelius Aristides and the Sacred Tales* (The Hague, 1968) especially 18–86 passim.
10 For recent characterisation of Graeco-Roman paganism in the early Empire, R. Macmullen, *Paganism in the Roman Empire* (New Haven, 1981), R. Lane Fox, *Pagans and Christians* (Harmondsworth, 1986) especially 27–261; on a more narrowly Roman perspective, J. H. W. G. Liebeschuetz, *Continuity and Change in Roman Religion* (Oxford, 1979). For a somewhat later epicentre, J. Geffcken's classic *Der Ausgang des griechisch-römischen Heidentums*, 2nd edn (Heidelberg, 1929) has been translated and updated by S. MacCormack as *The Last Days of Graeco-Roman Paganism* (Amsterdam, 1978). There are also highly evocative surveys on a broad front by P. R. L. Brown, *The*

228

World of Late Antiquity (London, 1971) and *The Making of Late Antiquity* (Cambridge, Mass., 1978). Still important over the whole horizon of late antique religious experience is A. D. Nock's *Conversion: The Old and the New in Religion from Alexander the Great to Augustine of Hippo* (Oxford, 1933). The same author's collected papers, ed. Z. Stewart as *Essays on Religion and the Ancient World* (2 vols, Oxford, 1972) offer a constant stimulus in almost all the directions holy men are likely to lead.

11 For Judaism under the Empire, E. Schuerer's *A History of the Jewish People under Roman Rule* has been revised by G. Vermes, M. Black, F. Millar and M. Goodman in five volumes (Edinburgh, 1973–87); see also E. M. Smallwood, *The Jews under Roman Rule* (Leiden, 1976). M. Goodman, *The Ruling Class of Judaea: The Origins of the Jewish Revolt against Rome AD 66–70* (Cambridge, 1987) has much wider terms of reference than its title suggests. For the changing position of Judaism relative to the changing religious environment, see now J. Lieu, J. North and T. Rajak (eds), *The Jews among Pagans and Christians* (London, 1992).

12 For emerging Christianity, Lane Fox (1986) 265–681 (among much); R. Macmullen, *Christianizing the Roman Empire (AD 100–400)* (New Haven, 1984). W. H. C. Frend, *The Rise of Christianity* (London, 1984) presents an immense survey within manageable compass.

13 For such activities, R. Macmullen, *Enemies of the Roman Order: Treason, Unrest and Alienation in the Empire*, (Cambridge, Mass., 1966), 142–62; D. E. Aune, *Prophecy in Early Christianity and the Ancient Mediterranean World* (Grand Rapids, Michigan, 1983).

14 Lucian, *Alexander sive Pseudomantis* 23f. and passim.

15 On their identity, V. Georgi, *The Opponents of St. Paul in Second Corinthians* (1964; E.T. Edinburgh, 1987); E. Earle Ellis, 'Paul and his opponents, trends in research' in *Christianity, Judaism and other Graeco-Roman Cults, Studies for Morton Smith at Sixty*, ed. J. Neusner, Vol. 1 (Leiden, 1975) 264–98.

16 Cf. Artemidorus' *Oneirocritica*, *praef.* (p. 2 Pack).

17 For Roman priesthoods, M. Beard and John North (eds), *Pagan Priests* (London, 1990); for the *arvales*, R. Syme, *Some Arval Brethren* (Oxford, 1980).

18 As in the case of, e.g., Lucian, *Alexander* 23.

19 For dreams and oracles, e.g., Lane Fox (1986) 102–261 passim.

20 For examples, Nock (1933) 99–137.

21 For Platonism in the early Empire, J. Whittaker, 'Platonic philosophy in the early centuries of the Empire', *ANRW* 2.36.1 (1987) 81–123; J. M. Dillon, *The Middle Platonists* (London, 1977).

22 On philosophical schools in general in the early Empire, J.-M. André, 'Les écoles philosophiques aux deux premiers siècles de l'Empire', *ANRW* 2.36.1 (1987) 5–77. On Epicurean spirituality, A. A. Long, 'Epicureans and Stoics', in A. H. Armstrong (ed.), *Classical Mediterranean Spirituality: Egyptian, Greek, Roman* (New York, 1986) 138–45. On Pythagoreanism in particular, W. Burkert, *Lore and Science in Ancient Pythagoreanism* (Cambridge, Mass., 1972);

D. J. O'Meara, *Pythagoras Revived: Mathematics and Philosophy in late Antiquity* (Oxford, 1989). For the figure of the philosophic sage, G. B. Kerferd, 'The sage in Hellenistic philosophical literature, 399 BCE–199 CE' in Gammie and Perdue (1990) 319–28.

23 For the latter aspect, M. Griffin and J. Barnes, *Philosophia Togata, Essays on Philosophy and Roman Society* (Oxford, 1989); Macmullen, (1966) 46–94; M. T. Griffin, *Seneca: a Philosopher in Politics* (Oxford, 1978).

24 On Cynicism in general, D. R. Dudley, *A History of Cynicism from Diogenes to the Sixth Century AD* (London, 1937); M.-O. Goulet-Cazé, 'Le cynisme à l'époque Impériale', *ANRW* 2.36.4 (1990) 2720–833. For Heracles, see also D. L. Tiede, *The Charismatic Figure as Miracle-Worker* (Missoula, Montana, 1972), 71–100.

25 E.g., Matt. 10.9f.

26 Macmullen (1966) 95–100.

27 On the programme of Apollonius' Pythagoreanism, below p. 54.

28 On whom see Goodman (1987) 219f.

29 And still did; for the charismatic outsiders, cf. G. Vermes, *Jesus the Jew: A Historian's Reading of the Gospels*, 2nd edn (London, 1983), 69–82.

30 Cf. F. G. B. Millar, *The Roman Empire and its Neighbours*, 2nd edn (London, 1981) 197ff.

31 On the background of Galilee, S. Freyne, *Galilee from Alexander the Great to Hadrian* (Delaware, 1980).

32 On the citizenship, A. N. Sherwin-White, *Roman Society and Roman Law in the New Testament* (Oxford, 1963).

33 On whom see, e.g., J. Neusner, 'The formation of rabbinic Judaism: Yavneh (Jamnia) from AD 70 to 100', *ANRW* 2.19.2 (1979) 3–42.

34 E.g., Frend (1984) 230–66.

35 For the whole subject, A. D. Momigliano, *Alien Wisdom: The Limits of Hellenization* (Cambridge, 1975).

36 For the *Brachmanes*, Macmullen (1966) 97ff.; J. W. Sedlar, *India and the Greek World: A Study in the Transmission of Greek Culture* (New Jersey, 1980) 68–74 and passim.

37 For the gymnosophists, Anderson (1986) 216ff.

38 *Philopseudes* 13.

39 See now H. D. Rankin, *The Celts and the Classical World* (London, 1987) 270–94; Momigliano (1975) 50–73.

40 For this theme, A. Wardman, *Religions and Statescraft among the Romans* (London, 1982).

41 For the added implication of the Imperial cult, S. R. F. Price, *Rituals and Power: The Roman Imperial Cult in Asia Minor* (Cambridge, 1984).

42 For Athens, S. Follet, *Athènes au IIe et IIIe siècles* (Paris, 1976); J. H. Oliver, *The Athenian Expounders of the Sacred Law* (Baltimore, 1950).

43 *Metamorphoses* 9.8.

44 Porphyry, *Vita Plotini* 10.

45 Goodman (1987) 76–108.

46 For the climate of piety, H. D. Saffrey, 'The piety and prayers of

ordinary men and women in late Antiquity' in Armstrong (ed.) (1986) 195–213.

47 On the general repertoire of popular morality in the period, e.g., A. Oltramare, *Les Origines de la diatribe Romaine* (Lausanne, 1926); A. C. van Geytenbeek, *Musonius and Greek Diatribe* (Assen, 1963).

48 For Dives and Lazarus, Lk. 16.19–31, cf. Lucian, *Kataplous*.

49 Cf. still S. Dill, *Roman Society from Nero to Marcus Aurelius* (London, 1905) 289–333 (Seneca as 'the philosophic director').

50 Epict., *Diss.* 4.4.39; cf. 1 Cor. 9.19; Gal. 5.1. For this relationship in general, A. Bonhoeffer, *Epiktet und das Neue Testament* (Giessen, 1911).

51 Epict., *Diss.* 4.4.33; cf. Rom. 6.15–19.

52 E.g., Aelius Aristides, *Or.* 50.6f.

53 Ibid. *Or.* 51.48.

54 See especially the oracle text *P. Oxy.* 1477 (*c.* 300 AD); Lane Fox (1986) 214f.

55 Apuleius, *Met.* 11.15.

56 For demonology, F. Brenk, 'In the light of the moon: demonology in the early Imperial period', *ANRW* 2.16.3 (1986) 2068–2145; E. R. Dodds, *Pagan and Christian in an Age of Anxiety: Some Aspects of Religious Experience from Marcus Aurelius to Constantine* (Cambridge, 1968) 37–68. For some conceptual difficulties, J. Z. Smith, 'Towards interpreting demonic powers in Hellenistic and Roman Antiquity', *ANRW* 2.16.1 (1978) 425–39.

57 Dillon (1977) 46f.; for Plutarch, G. Soury, *La démonologie de Plutarque* (Paris, 1942); for Lucian, M. Caster, *Lucien et la pensée religieuse de son temps* (Paris, 1937) 214–24.

58 For the political ramifications of apocalyptic prophecy, see Macmullen (1966) 140–62.

59 Note especially Eusebius *PE* 4.5, with other passages usefully collected in G. Luck, *Arcana Mundi: Magic and the Occult in the Greek and Roman Worlds* (Baltimore, 1985) 218–25.

60 For claims of this kind in a magical context, e.g., H. D. Betz, *The Greek Magical Papyri in Translation, including the Demotic Spells* (Chicago, 1986) passim; M. Smith, *Jesus the Magician* (London, 1978) 96–104.

61 *Contra Celsum* 7.9.

62 On the Hellenistic and late antique world-view, Dodds (1968).

63 For two cases of overlap between sacred and secular, Polemo and Aristides, below pp. 156, 106f.

64 For Lucian's frequent satire on the subject, e.g., *Bis Accusatus* 2f.; *Juppiter Tragoedus* passim; Caster (1937) 123–211 passim.

65 *Annales* 15.44; Acts 17.21; Lucian, *Alexander* 9, 14.

66 Philostratus, *Vita Apollonii* 1.15.

67 Lucian, *Peregrinus* 4ff.

68 Cf. *Actus Petri cum Simone* 8.25ff.

69 *Iliad* 1.35–54.

70 Ibid. 68–108.

71 Lucian, *Alexander* 40.

72 Lk. 9.18–22.
73 For the tradition, Burkert (1972); Tiede (1972) 14–29; B. Blackburn, *Theios Anēr and the Markan Miracle Traditions* (Tübingen, 1991) 37–51.
74 On Apollonius' life, below p. 36.
75 On Porphyry and Iamblichus, Burkert (1972) 97–101; and now O'Meara (1989) 25–29; 35–40.
76 Iamblichus 91.
77 Porphyry 28; 29.
78 Iamblichus 142; 61.
79 Ibid. 135.
80 Ibid. 18f.
81 Ibid. 215–21.
82 Seneca, *Ep*. 108.17–22.
83 Plato, *Apology* 40AB. On the ideal wise man and divine men after Socrates, Tiede (1972) 30–70.
84 *In Vatinium* 14.
85 Suetonius, *Aug*. 94.5, cf. Dio 45.1.3ff.
86 Apuleius, *Apology* 52.
87 For a summary of Nigidius' work, E. D. Rawson, *Intellectual Life in the Late Roman Republic* (London, 1985) 310ff.
88 On Elijah, 1 Kings–2 Kings 2.11.
89 For the concept of Messiah in general, Vermes (1983) 129–56.
90 For the Moses myth as such, J. G. Gager, *Moses in Graeco-Roman Paganism* (Nashville, 1972).
91 Ex.2.5–10.
92 Ex.2.12–15.
93 Ex. 8.19–16.26.
94 Ex. 20–Deut. 34 passim; Deut. 34.6.
95 For this action, Josephus *AJ* 20.97.
96 Acts 21.38.
97 Gregory of Nyssa, *Vita Gregorii*, Migne PG 46 col. 913B.
98 For the latter, R. van Dam, 'Hagiography and history: the life of Gregory Thaumaturgus', *Classical Antiquity* 1 (1982) 272–308. For Gregory's handling of the *Life of Moses*, see now P. Cox, *Biography in Late Antiquity: A Quest for the Holy Man* (Berkeley, 1983) 102–33.
99 *Vita Gregorii* 908C, 907C, 925D, 949A.
100 *Vita Moesae* 1.27.

2 VIEWPOINTS:
PERCEPTIONS AND PERSPECTIVES

1 On the attitudes of Roman Imperial historians to religion, e.g., A. Wallace-Hadrill, *Suetonius, The Scholar and his Caesars* (London, 1983) 189–97; Millar (1964) 179ff.; A. D. Momigliano, 'Ancient biography and the study of religion in the Roman Empire' (= *On Pagans, Jews and Christians*, Middletown Conn., 1987, 159–77); H. C. Kee, *Miracle in the Early Christian World: A Study in Socio-Historical Method* (New Haven and London, 1983) 174–220; D. E. Aune,

'Graeco-Roman biography', in *Graeco-Roman Literature and the New Testament*, ed. D. E. Aune (Atlanta, 1988) 107–26.

2 *Annales* 15.44.

3 Ibid. 15.47.1; for other instances, ibid. 12.43; 12.64.1.

4 Ibid. 6.20.

5 On the significance of Thrasyllus and his family, below p. 155.

6 72.23.1.

7 Suetonius, *Vita Domitiani* 15.3; cf. Dio 67.16.3.

8 Ibid. 67.18.1f.

9 Ibid. 66.22.2, 23.1.

10 For an overall view T. Rajak, *Josephus: The Historian and his Society* (London, 1983).

11 See below p. 151.

12 For the problem of gospels and historicity, Sherwin-White (1963) 172–94.

13 For the problems of Apollonius' *Letters*, R. J. Penella's Commentary *The Letters of Apollonius of Tyana: A Critical Text with Prolegomena, Translation and Commentary* (Leiden, 1979) 23–9; Anderson (1986) 185–91.

14 Matt. 16.21; Mk 9.31; Lk. 9.22.

15 Matt. 8.28–34 (cf. Mk 5.1–20, Lk. 8.26–39).

16 Philostratus *VA* 4.10.

17 Matt. 15.21–28 (Mk 7.24–30).

18 Mk 6.6–13 (Lk. 9.1–6).

19 See in particular M. Smith, 'Prolegomena to a discussion of aretalogies, divine men, the gospels and Jesus', *JBL* 90 (1971) 174–99.

20 For a powerful argument in this direction, Kee (1983).

21 *Vita Antonii* 11 (*PG* 26 col. 860B-861A) 11.

22 Gregory of Nyssa, *Vita Gregorii* (*PG* 46 coll. 924C-929A).

23 Athanasius, *Vita Antonii* 14 (tr. R. C. Gregg).

24 *HE* 6.11.

25 E.g., Plato, *Apology* 40AB.

26 *Itinerarium Egeriae* 20.6f. For the background, E. D. Hunt, *Holy Land Pilgrimage in the late Roman Empire, A.D. 312–460* (Oxford, 1984).

27 Mk 6.14.29; *AJ* 18.109–19.

28 Josephus ibid. 116–19.

29 Mk 6.17–25.

30 Ibid. 17.

31 *Or.* 48.26ff.

32 *Or.* 49.21f.

33 For similar self-deception in Aristides, cf. below pp. 106f.

34 For the impasse between them, M. Dibelius, *Studies in the Acts of the Apostles*, tr. W. Greeven (London 1956) 93–101; E. Haenchen, *The Acts of the Apostles: A Commentary* (Oxford, 1971); M. Hengel, *Acts and the History of Earliest Christianity* (E.T. London, 1979) 111–26.

35 *Adv. Marcionem*, 2.20.1.

36 *Alexander* 4. For the conventions of ancient rhetorical invective and their bearing on Lucian's treatment, M. Caster, *Etudes sur Alexandre ou le Faux – Prophète de Lucien* (Paris, 1938) 79–93.

37 Ibid. 6–10.
38 For Dio's complex attitudinising, in particular J. L. Moles, 'The career and conversion of Dio Chrysostom', *JHS* 99 (1979) 79; C. P. Jones, *The Roman World of Dio Chrysostom* (Cambridge: Mass. and London, 1978) passim.
39 For Apuleius, the first excerpt of the *Florida* is particularly revealing.
40 See in particular *Alexander* 55.
41 On the nature and genre of Apollonius, E. L. Bowie, 'Apollonius of Tyana: tradition and reality' *ANRW* 2.16.2 (1978) 1652–99; Anderson (1986) 121–53, 227–39.
42 *IG* 4.951 = Dittenberger, *Sylloge*, 4th edn 1163.
43 *IG* 4.952 = Dittenberger, *Sylloge*, 4th edn 1164.
44 Note the puzzling references to the 'marks of Jesus', Gal. 6.17.
45 Acts 14.11f.
46 *Acta Pauli* PH 2–5.
47 2 Cor. 11.5, cf. 2.3.
48 Cf. 2 Cor.11.6.
49 2 Cor. 11.7–11; 12.14–18.
50 2 Cor. 12.1–10; 12.12.
51 *Oneirocritica* 3.66. On the man and his work, R. A. Pack, 'Artemidorus and his waking world', *TAPhA* 86 (1955) 280–90.
52 *Oneirocritica* 1 *praef.*
53 Ibid.
54 Ibid. 1 *praef.*; 4.72; 4.2; 4.22; 4.1.
55 16.222 Kühn.
56 *Oneirocritica* 4 *praef.*
57 For a general view, H. C. Kee, *Medicine, Miracle and Magic in New Testament Times* (Cambridge, 1986).
58 Kee (1986) 122ff.
59 For examples of the problems, F. Graf, 'Prayer in magic and religious ritual' in C. Faraone and D. Obbink (eds), *Magika Hiera: Ancient Greek Magic and Religion* (New York, 1991) 188–213.
60 For doctors and Asclepius, G. W. Bowersock, *Greek Sophists in the Roman Empire* (Oxford, 1969) 64–75; Kee (1986) 60ff.
61 Cf. Morton Smith (1978) 81–93 passim.
62 Kee (1983) 146–73. The best formulation I have seen for the problem overall is by H. Drivjers, 'Syrian Christianity and Judaism', in J. Lieu et al.(1992) 129: 'All people want to be healed from their illnesses and sorrows, and therefore go to the magician, whether he be a gentile sorcerer, a Jewish rabbi, or a Christian monk. Religious texts stress ideological differences; religious practice is often a shared experience of a basically social character'. What was true of Edessa in the fifth century AD would have held for the Near East in general throughout our period.
63 Suet. *Cl.* 25.
64 *Peregrinus* 13.
65 For Celsus' notice (Origen, *contra Celsum* 1.28); Smith (1978) 58ff.
66 *SHA* Marcus 13.6.
67 For the testimonia, below p. 86 and n. 3.
68 Caster (1938) 99–102.

69 L. Bieler, *Theios Anēr: Das Bild des 'Göttlichen Menschen' in Spätantike und Frühchristentum*, (2 vols, Vienna 1935/6; repr. as one, Darmstadt, 1967).

70 M. Hadas and M. Smith, *Heroes and Gods: Spiritual Biographies in Antiquity* (New York, 1965); C. H. Talbert, 'Biographies of philosophers and rulers as instruments of religious propaganda in Mediterranean Antiquity', *ANRW* 2.16.2 (1978) 1619–51.

71 P. R. L. Brown, 'The rise and function of the holy man in late Antiquity', *JRS* 61 (1971) 80–101, repr. in *Society and the Holy in Late Antiquity*, (London, 1982) 103–52.

72 See Appendix below p. 224–7.

73 Aune (1983).

74 Macmullen (1966) discusses magicians in one chapter, diviners in another, following a first chapter on philosophic opposition. But the materials run the risk of excessive schematisation, vulnerable on chronological grounds.

75 Lane Fox (1986) 99f.

76 Lucian, *Alexander* p. 10–24 passim.

77 Kee (1983) 290–6 and passim.

78 Kee (1986) 122–7 and passim.

79 *VA* 4.45; below p. 94.

80 For the *mélange*, e.g., F. G. B. Millar, 'Empire, community and culture in the Roman Near East: Greeks, Syrians, Jews and Arabs', *JJS* 38 (1987) 143–64.

81 For summaries of the *theios anēr* debate by recent participants, see, e.g., Tiede (1972) 242–92; Kee (1983) 297ff.; Blackburn (1991) 1–12 and 263: 'the "miracle-working *theios anēr*" is really a twentieth-century abstraction encompassing a wide array of figures, mythical and historical, whose diversity becomes apparent when one analyzes their social roles, the nature of their divinity, and the types and techniques of the miracles or miraculous powers ascribed to them'. Blackburn prefers to set the Markan Jesus tentatively within the Jewish perspective of the Jerusalem church. But the real problem is the degree of cultural assimilation which makes the task of separating Greek and Jewish elements in a Near-Eastern context so difficult at so late a date.

3 PATTERNS:
LIVES AND LIFESTYLES

1 On Peregrinus see now C. P. Jones, *Culture and Society in Lucian* (Cambridge, Mass., 1986) 117–32; M. J. Edwards, 'Satire and verisimilitude: Christianity in Lucian's *Peregrinus*', *Historia* 38 (1989) 89–98.

2 Lucian, *Peregrinus* 10f., cf. 14. For the spurious and over-general terminology, J. Schwartz *Lucien de Samosate, Philopseudès et de Morte Peregrini avec introduction et commentaire* (Paris, 1963), ad 11 (commixture of Bacchic and Judaeo-Christian overtones).

3 *Peregrinus* 11–14.

4 Ibid. 14ff. Cf. below p. 133.

5 Ibid. 16ff.
6 Ibid. 19. For a riposte of Herodes Atticus to Peregrinus, Philostratus, *VS* 563f. He was a natural target for Cynics: cf. Lucian's *Demonax* 24f., 33.
7 *Peregrinus* 36.
8 On Demonax see the monograph treatment by K. Funk, *Untersuchungen über die lucianische Vita Demonactis, Philologus* Suppl. 10 (1907) 558–674; Jones (1986) 90–8.
9 *Demonax (Vita Demonactis)* 3ff.
10 Ibid. 7.
11 Ibid.
12 Ibid. 8f.
13 Ibid. 11. Imitation also of Diogenes' refusal to be initiated, *DL* 6.39; Jones (1986) 93.
14 *Demonax* 25 (Herodes Atticus, Jones (1986) 94); 37. The soothsayer is unnamed. For an attack on a *magos*, ibid. 23.
15 Ibid. 63. (So Crates, Apuleius, *Flor.* 22, Julian *Or.* 6.201BC, Funk (1907) 619f.)
16 *Demonax* 65.
17 The fullest recent treatments are Bowie (1978) 1652–99; Anderson (1986) 121–239; M. Dielska, *Apollonius of Tyana in Legend and History* (Rome, 1986) (with little margin of agreement on the credibility of Philostratus); and now J.-J. Flintermann, *Politiek, Paideia & Pythagorisme* (Groningen, 1993), the most detailed overall study so far, which reached me too late to be taken fully into account.
18 For a systematic account of the sources, G. Petzke, *Die Traditionen über Apollonius von Tyana und das Neue Testament*, (Leiden, 1970) 19–157.
19 Philostratus, *VA* 8.26, cf. Dio 67.18.1.
20 See W. L. Dulière, 'Protection permanente contre des animaux nuisibles assurée par Apollonis de Tyane dans Byzance et Antioche: evolution de son mythe', *BZ* 64 (1970) 247–77.
21 Lucian, *Alexander* 5.
22 For the problems raised by these, Anderson (1986) 185–90.
23 Origen, *contra Celsum* 6.41.
24 On the general literary character of the work, Anderson (1986) 227–39.
25 For Apollonius' late antique *Nachleben*, below pp. 107f.; 193f.
26 Porphyry, *Vita Plotini* 10. On the episode, E. R. Dodds, 'Theurgy and its relationship to Neoplatonism', *JHS* 67 (1947),60f.; below p. 89.
27 Porphyry, *Vita Plotini* (Olympias of Alexandria).
28 Ibid.
29 Ibid. 2.
30 Ibid. 8; 7, 9.
31 Ibid. 16.
32 Ibid. 3; 7.
33 Commentary by Caster (1938).
34 *Alexander* 22ff.
35 Ibid. 56, 41f.; cf. *Peregrinus* 10, 9.
36 Ibid. *Alexander* 27, 48.

37 Ibid. 23f.; 8, 16.
38 On the Juliani, Macmullen (1966) 104, 106f.
39 Psellus, *peri tēs chrusēs haluseōs*, *Ann. Assoc. Grec.*, p. 216, 24ff.
40 For the problems of the attribution, H. Lewy, *Chaldaean Oracles and Theurgy*, 2nd edn (Paris 1978) 224 n. 195.
41 On the rain-making and its difficulties, below p. 153f.
42 For the problems of relating theurgy to Neo-Platonism, Dodds (1947) 55–69.
43 On Aristides, Behr (1968); B. P. Reardon *Courants Littéraires grecs dans la littérature des IIe et IIIe siècles après J.-C.* (Paris, 1971) 255–65; and now L. T. Pearcy, 'Theme, dream and narrative: reading the sacred tales of Aelius Aristides', *TAPhA* 118 (1988) 377–91; idem 'Diagnosis as narrative in ancient literature', *AJPh* 13 (1992) 595–616.
44 Cf. below p. 56.
45 For whom see W.S. G. Green, 'Palestinian holy men: charismatic leadership and rabbinic tradition', *ANRW* 2.19.2 (1979) 619–47.
46 *AJ* 14.2.22–5.
47 G. Vermes, 'Hanina ben Dosa: a controversial Galilean saint from the first century of the Christian era', *JJS* 23 (1972) 28–50; ibid. 24 (1973) 51–64.
48 Arav: yBer 7c, (Vermes (1983) 72); Gamaliel, bBer 34b (Vermes (1983) 30). Healing:bBer 34b; yBer 9d (Vermes (1983) 30f.).
49 tBer 3:20; yBer 9a (Vermes (1983) 34–7); queen of the demons, Vermes (1983) 55; rain: bTaan 24b (Vermes (1983) 39f.); poverty: cf. bTaan 24b-25a (Vermes (1983) 42); ritual issues, e.g., Vermes (1983) 36f.
50 Hillel, J. Neusner, *A Life of Rabban Yohanan ben Zakkai Ca. 1–80 CE* (Leiden, 1962) 18–24; Hanina, ibid. 27–32. Integrity of Torah, Avot 1.13; 2.9. Pharisees and Sadducees, Neusner (1962) 34–59 passim. Chariot-enigma:Neusner (1962) 97f.
51 Neusner (1962) 115–21.
52 *Vita* 1.2.
53 Ibid. 2.9, cf. Lk. 2.46f.
54 *Vita* 2.10–12.
55 Ibid. 7.28f.; *BJ* 3.399–407.
56 *Vita* 76.423; 76.425, 429.
57 Acts 8.9f.
58 Ibid. 8.8–23.
59 *Actus Petri cum Simone* 6.17.
60 Ibid. 2.4; 2.5.
61 Ibid. 4.8.
62 Ibid. 4.9–5.14.
63 Ibid. 8.23–29.
64 Ibid. 9.31f.; Hippolytus, *Refutatio* 6.20.
65 On whom see A. von Harnack, *Marcion. Das Evangelium vom fremden Gott*, 2nd edn (1924) 21–30.
66 Epiphanius, *Panarion* 42.
67 Ibid.
68 Ibid.
69 On Cerdo, Irenaeus, *Adv. Haer.* 1.27.1.

NOTES

70 For Tertullian's polemics, T. D. Barnes, *Tertullian: A Historical and Literary Study*, 2nd edn (Oxford, 1985) 124–9.

71 P. Rousseau, *Pachomius, The Making of a Community in Fourth-Century Egypt* (Berkeley, 1985) 32.

72 Eusebius, *HE* 7.24.

73 *Panarion* 67.

74 Eusebius, *HE* 6.9f.

75 Ibid.

76 Lucian, *Peregrinus* 11, 17–19; outside Athens, Aulus Gellius, *NA* 12.11.1.

77 On Dio's environment, Jones (1978).

78 Lucian, *Peregrinus* 14f.

79 Lucian, *Alexander* 9.

80 Tertullian, *adv. Marcionem* 1.1.

81 E.g., Mk 1.14–4.34.

82 On the journeys, below pp. 167ff.

83 Cf. Gal. 2.6ff.; 2.11f.

84 Lucian, *Alexander* 9, with Caster (1938) for the traditional rigorism of the Paphlagonians, readily susceptible to Montanism. For a useful conspectus of religious patriotism in Pontus, van Dam (1982) 296–300. One should also note the kind of alternatives that would have been available to Alexander's remedies: V. Nutton, 'The perils of patriotism: Pliny and Roman medicine' in R. French and F. Greenaway, *Science in the Early Roman Empire: Pliny the Elder, his Sources and Influence* (London, 1986) 45: 'woe betide the unwitting visitor to the Paphlagonian backwoods, for instead of receiving treatment for his illness he might be struck dead by the glance of an angry Palaeotheban' (cf. Plutarch *Quaest. Symp.* 7.1).

85 *Peregrinus* 17. For similar examples of Cynic 'indifference', Diogenes Laertius 6.2, 46; 69 (Diogenes).

86 *Demonax* 3.

87 Matt. 4.3f.; Lk. 4.3f.

88 Lk. 2.46f.; Matt. 2.11f.

89 See below p. 66.

90 Philostratus, *VA* 1.7 (Euxenus of Heraclea); magi: 1.26; Brahmans v. gymnosophists, 6.11.

91 On the distinctions, and the frequent blurring between them in practice, Lane Fox (1986) 102–67.

92 Lucian, *Peregrinus* 10f., cf. 14.

93 Ibid. 15ff.

94 Ibid. 30.

95 E.g., Mk 6.8ff.; Bethany, Mk 14.3ff.; Matt. 26.6–9.

96 2 Thess. 3.8–12.

97 1 Cor. 9.12–18.

98 E.g., Paul in 1 Cor. 16.5f.

99 Euphrates, accused of a social move through 'Imperial' cities to Italy by Apollonius of Tyana, *Ep. Apoll.* 3, cf. Pliny *Ep.* 1.10.8 (a 'good marriage').

238

100 Change: as emphasised by Philostratus' insistence that the sage always remains true to himself, *VA* 6.35.

101 Ejection: e.g., Peregrinus from Rome, *Peregrinus* 18. For philosophical opposition to the regime in general, Macmullen (1966) 46–94.

102 Lucian, *Alexander* 6f. The role of the Macedonian lady is perhaps misrepresented by Lucian: Caster (1938) compares the female associates of Simon Magus or Montanus.

103 For the important contrast between Egyptian and Syrian desert, Brown (1971) 82–5.

104 Mk 1.1–8; Matt. 3.1–12; Lk. 3.1–18.

105 *AJ* 20.97.

106 John of Gischala and Simon b. Gioras, *BJ* 6.351.

107 Above p. 2f.

108 For the site of Abonouteichos, Jones (1986) 134. On the material aspects of Alexander, see now especially L. Robert, *A travers l'Asie Mineure: poètes et prosateurs, monnaies grecques, voyageurs* (Paris, 1979) 393–421. On Qumran, Schuerer et al. 3.1 (1986) 380–469; M. A. Knibb, *The Qumran Community* (Cambridge, 1987), among much. For the Therapeutae, J. Riaud, 'Les Thérapeutes d'Alexandrie dans la tradition et dans la recherche critique jusqu' aux découvertes de Qumran', *ANRW* 2.20.2 (1987) 1189–1295.

109 See below pp. 168f; 172.

110 Lucian, *Alexander* 9; on the Byzantine tradition, Petzke (1970) 24–8.

111 *Nigrinus* 17f.

112 Philostratus, *VA* 7.10–15.

113 Aulus Gellius *NA* 12.11.1: Peregrinus is here presented as *virum gravem atque constantem*.

114 Cf. Philostratus, *VA* 1.13 and passim.

115 Acts 13.5 and passim.

116 As in, e.g., *Or.* 48.71–80.

117 Philostratus, *VA* 4.21; 22.

118 Mk 14.22–41; Matt. 27.33–56; Lk. 23.33–49; Jn 19.17–30.

119 *Peregrinus* 36. For the background, below p. 110f.

120 Philostratus, *VA* 8.30.

121 *Vita Demonactis* 66.

122 Athanasius, *Vita Antonii* 90f. (tr. R. C. Gregg).

123 On whom see now R. van Dam (1982) 272–308.

124 *Vita Gregorii* 897BC/900A; 905CD.

125 Ibid. 908BC; 913D–918A.

126 Ibid. 926D–927A; 924BC; 929A–932C.

127 Ibid. 940C–941C; 941C–944A.

128 Ibid. 945Df.; 953A–C; 944BD–948C.

129 In the canonical letter, *PG* 10.1020–48; *Vita* 956A. For the misconceptions surrounding Gregory's life, van Dam (1982) 274ff.

130 *Peregrinus* 1.

131 Ibid. 20.

132 1 Cor. 3.18.

133 E.g., Origen, *contra Celsum* 3.9.

134 Matt. 20.20–28; Mk 10.35–45; cf. Lk. 9.48b, 12.50, 22.24–27.

135 For the *topos* applied to heretics, note the accusations against Florinus and Blastus, Eusebius, *HE* 5.14. Against Marcion, above p. 41.

136 Lucian, *Peregrinus* 10, 14, 36.

137 See below p. 158f.

138 For Paul's protesting too much, 1 Cor. 15.8ff.

139 Matt. 26.57–75; Mk 14.53–72; Lk. 22.54–71.

140 *CMC* 20.11ff. (*ZPE* 1975 pp. 23f.).

141 Mk 1.10f.; Matt. 3.16f.; Lk. 3.21f.

142 Acts 9.3–6; 15ff.

143 Lucian, *Alexander* 11.

144 2 Thess. 2.10.

145 Lk. 12.49–56 (John preaching repentance, Matt. 3.7–10; Lk. 3.7–9).

146 *Contra Celsum* 7.9.

147 Athanasius, *Vita Antonii* 45 (tr. R. C. Gregg).

148 Ibid. 48.

149 Philippians 3.12ff.

150 On Zosimus, G. Fowden, *The Egyptian Hermes* (Cambridge, 1986) 120–6.

151 *Or.* 58.27.

4 WISDOM:
CRAFTS, CUNNING, CREDULITY

1 *Ep. Apoll.* 52. 'Divine prophecy' would serve to distinguish Apollonius' gifts from those of *goētes* (Olearius). For doubts about Apollonius' Pythagoreanism, Bowie (1978) 1690–4.

2 Lucian, *Alexander* 18. As Caster (1938) notes ad *Alex.* 40, 'Alexandre avait accumulé sur sa personne quatre fois plus de titres qu'il n'en fallait pour sanctifier un homme' (p. 65).

3 Origen, *contra Celsum* 7.9.

4 Acts 8.10; cf. Justin, *Apol.* 1.26.3; *Dial.* 120, where Simon's status continues into the mid-second century. For a 'Gentile' emphasis to Simon's activities, Haenchen (1971), with an appreciation of the considerable difficulties of the episode.

5 *Alexander* 11.

6 Genealogies, Matt. 1.1–17; Lk. 3.23–38. For the difficulties (and potential equivocation) of the title Son of God, Vermes (1983) 192–213; for the problems of defining Jesus Christ's claims, Blackburn (1991) 97–182; Christian scholarship sometimes wants it both ways, ibid. 179: 'all this, of course, does not entail the absurd notion that Jesus considered himself to be God: on the other hand, there is a real sense in which Jesus did assimilate himself to God'.

7 Philostratus, *VA* 1.4.

8 Lucian, *Peregrinus* 1, with Harmon and Schwartz ad loc.

9 On the problems, E. Norden, *Agnōstos Theos* (Berlin, 1913); M. Dibelius (1956) 26–77; P.W. van der Horst, 'The altar of the "unknown God" in Athens (Acts 17.23) and the cult of "unknown

gods" in the Hellenistic and Roman periods', *ANRW* 2.18.2 (1989) 1426–50.

10 Acts 17.23–31.

11 Justin, *Apology* 1.26 (in fact an extant statue base corresponding to the indications reads not *Simoni Deo Sancto* but *Semoni Sanco Deo Fidio* – a detail which might reflect on the state of literacy of some holy men or their informants as well as on that of their clients). There may be a like confusion between the plural θεοῖς ἀγνώστοις and some such phrase as θεοῖς ἁγιωτάτοις; but the tradition of the former in Athens is a strong one. Cf. Haenchen ad Acts 17.23 (p. 521, n.2).

12 Irenaeus, *Adv. Haer.* 1.25.1.

13 Philostratus, *VA* 4.11ff., 16.

14 Ibid. 4.23.

15 Ibid. 4.19f.

16 Ibid. 4.28.

17 Ibid. 5.20.

18 Ibid. 5.22.

19 *VA* 5.21.

20 Mk 14.58; Lk. 11.37ff.

21 For overall perspectives on Gnosticism, H. Jonas, *Gnosis und Spätantiker Geist*, (Göttingen, 1934–64); A. D. Nock, 'Gnosticism',(1972.2) 940–59; H. Puech, *En Quête de la Gnose* (Paris, 1978); E. Pagels, *The Gnostic Gospels* (London, 1980).

22 Irenaeus, *Adv. Haer.* 1.1.1ff.

23 Basilides after Hippolytus 7.25.7 (W. Foerster *Gnosis: A Selection of Gnostic Texts*, tr. R. McL. Wilson (Oxford, 1972) 70); Epiphanius, *Panarion* 24.7.6 (Foerster (1972) 62); Hippolytus 7.21.10 (Foerster (1972) 60); 7.21.14f.(Foerster (1972) 67).

24 Irenaeus, *Adv. Haer.* 1.24.4 (Foerster (1972) 60).

25 On opposition to Paul in Corinth, above p. 5n. 15.

26 *VA* 4.26. For the rest of his (allegedly) inglorious career, *Epp. Apoll.* 36f., 60, 74, 77, with Penella (1979) ad 36.

27 On medicine and holiness, E. J. and L. Edelstein, *Asclepius*, 2 vols (Baltimore, 1945). I accept in general the useful distinction of primary assumption between medicine, miracle and magic in Kee (1986) 122ff.; but I am sceptical about how far it can be pressed in practice (cf. above p. 28). If a doctor compels a disease to leave a patient by normal healing methods, he or his audience or his enemies can present the effect as one of magic or miracle depending on their initial assumptions; magic will appropriate to itself any kind of compulsion, some of which will have resulted from natural laws; and magicians and doctors alike can attribute their success to divine powers of one order or another. And the conjunction of any kind of effective healing to any particular skill may be suspected of being either naive or manipulative.

28 Cf. F. Kudlien, 'Galen's religious belief' in V. Nutton (ed.), *Galen: Problems and Prospects* (London, 1981) 117–30.

29 Aristides, *Or.* 52.2.

30 Philostratus, *VA* 6.43.

31 *VA* 4.10.

32 Pliny, *NH* 30.7.19f. For useful *aperçus* on Pliny's limitations, Nutton (1986).

33 Pliny, *NH* 30.8.21.

34 Ibid. 30.49.142.

35 Ibid. 30.14.43.

36 Ibid. 30.29.96–30.104.

37 *VA* 5.42.

38 *Actus Petri* 4.9, 11; 5.12; *Acta Thomae* 3.31ff.; 4.39ff.

39 Aelius Aristides, *Or.* 49.49f.

40 See, for example, J. Scarborough, 'The pharmacology of sacred plants, herbs, and roots', in Faraone and Obbink (1991) 138–74.

41 Philostratus, *VA* 2.3; 5.5.

42 Philostratus, *VA* 6.41.

43 Ibid. 6.38.

44 Aristides, *Or.* 49.38.

45 Gregory of Nyssa, *Vita Gregorii* (*PG* 46 col. 924BC).

46 On dreams in general, J. S. Hanson, 'Dreams and visions in the Graeco-Roman world and early Christianity', *ANRW* 2.23.2 (1980) 1395–1427. For Artemidorus, Pack (1955) 280–90; A. J. Festugière, *La Clef des Songes* (Paris, 1975); Reardon (1971) 247–55. Unfortunately too much trust is often placed on Artemidorus as a case-historian: he might just as readily be taken as an example of how little operators can be trusted in relation to their alleged material.

47 Artemidorus 2.65.

48 Ibid. 4 praef.

49 Ibid. 4.23.

50 On the whole subject of prophecy, Aune (1983); Macmullen (1966) 142–62; Luck (1985) 229–305. For the potent combination of prophecy and miracle-working, A. B. Kolenkow, 'Relationships between miracle and prophecy in the Graeco-Roman world and early Christianity', *ANRW* 2.23.2 (1980) 1470–1506.

51 Philostratus, *VA* 5.13.

52 Athanasius, *Vita Antonii* 82 (tr. R. C. Gregg) (*PG* 26 col. 957A–960B).

53 On Greek astrology in general, F. Bouché-Leclerq, *L'Astrologie grecque* (Paris, 1899); W. and H. G. Gundel, *Astrologoumena, Die astrologischen Literatur in der antike und ihre Geschichte* (Wiesbaden, 1966). For our period, F. Cramer, *Astrology in Roman Law and Politics* (Philadelphia, 1954) (speculative); Macmullen (1966) 128–42; Luck (1985) 309–58. On the Jewish dimension, J. H. Charlesworth, 'Jewish interest in astrology during the Hellenistic and Roman period', *ANRW* 2.20.2 (1987) 926–50.

54 Augustine, *Civ. Dei* 5.3.

55 Vettius Valens, *Anthologiae* 6.1 (p. 242 Kroll).

56 For apocalyptic in general as an anti-Roman phenomenon, Macmullen (1966) 142–62.

57 On Essene prophecy, Aune (1983) 145.

58 Text in H. Windisch, *Die Orakel des Hystaspes* (Amsterdam, 1929).

59 E.g., *SHA* Marcus 13.6; Epiphanius, *Panarion* 48.2, 49.1.

60 See D. S. Potter, *Prophecy and History in the Crisis of the Roman*

Empire: A Historical Commentary on the Thirteenth Sibylline Oracle (Oxford, 1990) 143.

61 On these elements in the New Testament Apocalypse, e.g., J. M. Court, *Myth and History in the Book of Revelation* (London, 1979) subject-index passim; and for the genre as a whole, A. Yavro Collins, 'Early Christian apocalyptic literature', *ANRW* 2.25.6 (1988) 4665–711.

62 Oenomaus: Eusebius *PE* 5,22 214A; Parke (1985) 142–5, with additional material; Diocletian and Saturn: Fuhrmann *Roem. Mitt.* (1938) 44; Lane Fox (1985) 111.

63 For the phenomenon in our period, E. C. Evans, 'The study of physiognomy in the second century AD', *TAPhA* 72 (1941) 96–108; Reardon (1971) 243–48. Texts in R. Foerster, *Scriptores Physiognomonici Graeci et Latini*, 2 vols (Leipzig 1893). For a suspected Essene physiognomy (4Q 561), R. H. Eisenman and A. Wise, *The Dead Sea Scrolls Uncovered* (Shaftesbury, Dorset, 1992) 264f.

64 Sallust, *Cat.* 15.5.

65 For Polemo's *aperçus* on his clients, J. Mesk, 'Die Beispiele in Polemons Physiognomik', *WS* 50 (1932) 51–67.

66 Polemo *SPG* 1.286–91; Heliodorus 3.5.5ff.

67 *Vita Plotini* 11.

68 On ancient magic, Macmullen (1966) 95–127; Luck (1985) 3–131. The Greek magical papyri are collected in K. Preisendanz, rev. A. Henrichs (2 vols, Stuttgart 1973–74); translation, with that of the Demotic papyri, in Betz (1986). For fourth-century survival, A. Barb, in A. D. Momigliano (ed.), *The Conflict between Paganism and Christianity in the Fourth Century* (Oxford, 1963) 100–25. For relations with medicine and miracle, Kee (1986) with the reservations expressed above p. 28. Kee is concerned to find a conception of magic which will dissociate Jesus Christ from the charges (123–6). But this will not do: the problem is that the casting out of demons is itself a form of compulsion, from which Jesus Christ can hardly be exonerated – miraculous to his supporters, potentially magical to his opponents. There is a much more satisfactory formulation in J. G. Gager (ed.), *Curse Tablets and Binding Spells from the Ancient World* (New York, 1992) 24f., rightly refusing to go beyond the subjective applications of the term itself. Faraone and Obbink (1991) is an excellent collection of papers across the whole subject; for early Christian magic, J. M. Hull, *Hellenistic Magic and the Synoptic Tradition* (London, 1974); D. E. Aune, 'Magic in early Christianity', *ANRW* 2.23.2 (1980) 1507–57; and the remarks on Smith (1978) in Appendix below. For the hardware of magic, C. Bonner, *Studies in Magical Amulets, chiefly Graeco-Roman* (Ann Arbor, 1950); R. Merrifield, *The Archaeology of Ritual and Magic* (London, 1987).

69 Pliny, *NH* 30.1.1f.

70 There is a useful survey of Pliny's magical chapters in Kee (1986) 99–107; but accompanied by questionable assumptions about the beliefs of their author, who is for the most part an uncritical compiler.

71 Pliny, *NH* 30.2.3–9.

72 Apuleius, *Apology* 25f. Kee (1986) is misled in his discussion by the assumption that the *Metamorphoses* is substantially autobiographical (95–9).
73 Apuleius, *Apology* 27. On this hallowed pantheon, J. Bidez and F. Cumont, *Les Mages Hellénisés* (Paris, 1938).
74 For his defence, A. Abt, *Die Apologie des Apuleius von Madaura und die antike Zauberei: Beiträge zur Erläuterung der Schrift de magia* (Giessen, 1908).
75 *Apology* 41.
76 Ibid. 45.
77 Lucian, *Alexander* 36. For the general atmosphere of Alexander's pronouncements, Caster (1938) ad loc., noting Perdrizet's publication of a fragment of the verse on an inscription from Syrian Antioch, *CRAI* (1903) 62, followed by the seven prophylactic vowels, from the base of a statuette of Apollo *Alexikakos*.
78 Petske (1970) 24–8.
79 F. Nau, *Biblos sophias kai suneseōs apotelesmatōn Apollōniou tou Tuaneōs*, *Patrologia Syriaca* 1.2 (Paris, 1907) 1363f.; for the magical tradition on Apollonius the fullest treatment is now Dielska (1986) 85–127.
80 Gregory of Nyssa, *Vita Gregorii* (*PG* 46 col. 916D).
81 *SHA* Marcus 13.6.
82 Lucian, *Alexander* 40.
83 On Oenomaus, see now J. Hammerstädt, 'Der Kyniker Oenomaus von Gadara', *ANRW* 2.36.4 (1990) 2834–65.
84 Hippolytus, *Refutatio* 4.37.
85 Ibid. 4.30f.
86 Ibid. 4.41.
87 Ibid. 4.28.
88 Apuleius, *Met.* 9.8.1–5.
89 For a similar trick, *Vita Aesopi* G78ff.
90 Eusebius, *PE* 5.22 214Aff.; H. W. Parke, *The Oracles of Apollo in Asia Minor* (London 1985) 142f.
91 Lucian, *Peregrinus* 1.
92 Philostratus, *VA* 1.4.
93 Hippolytus 9.8ff.
94 *NH* 30.6.18.
95 *Alexander* 5. Alexander's would-be successors included another physician, one Paetus (*Alex.* 60).
96 Ibid. 22.
97 1 Cor. 9.19–22.
98 Philostratus, *VA* 1.10.
99 Gregory of Nyssa, *Vita Gregorii* (*PG* 46.904A–C).
100 *Historia Monachorum* 22.3.
101 E.g., Mk 1.22–7.
102 Philostratus, *VA* 1.17.
103 Porphyry, *Vita Plotini* 10.

5 ACCLAMATION:
THE RHETORIC OF REVELATION

1 Philostratus, *VA* 4.31. For the *chreia* form, V. K. Robbins in Aune (1988) 1–24.

2 Lucian, *Alexander* 38. For suspicion of Lucian's reporting here, Caster (1938) ad 38–40 (p. 61) both on the terms of the exclusion (as too specific) and the hints of comparison to Eleusis.

3 Acts 19.34.

4 *Vita Secundi* qq. 8, 20 (pp. 82, 90 Perry).

5 *VA* 4.31; Cf. also 7.35 on Apollonius' brevity in letter-writing.

6 E.g., *VA* 1.15.

7 Mk 1.22.

8 *Dialogue with Trypho* 7 (prophets rather than philosophical demonstration as source of truth).

9 Lk. 6.39.

10 Lk. 6.39–45; cf. Matt. 15.14, 10.24f., 7.7f.; 12.33ff.

11 Lk. 14.15–24 (banquet); Matt. 25.1–13 (virgins); Neusner (1962) 84.

12 Lk. 8.4–18; ibid. 8.9f.

13 For the *Allegory of Prodicus*, J. Alpers, *Hercules in Bivio* (1912).

14 Paul's allegory of the Law: Gal. 4.21–31; Gnostic allegory of the labourers: Irenaeus, *Adv. Haer.* 1.13; Irenaeus on the four gospels: ibid. 3.11.11.

15 1 Cor. 1.19–23.

16 1 Cor. 2.7.

17 Lucian, *Philopseudes* 31.

18 Lucian, *Alexander* 13. Caster (1938) notes the possible magical overtones here; E. Babelon, *Revue Numismatique*, 4th series 4 (1900) 30, thinks of a Gnostic sect; time and place are certainly right for the latter.

19 Acts 2.4–13.

20 For the phenomenon in magical texts, e.g., the spell at *PGM* VII.505–28, including the words AŌ SATHREN ABRASAX IAŌAI AEŌ ĒŌA ŌAĒ IAO IĒO EY AĒ EY IE IAŌAI; for vowels in Gnostic belief, cf. the *Marsanes Tractate*, tr. B. L. Pearson in *The Nag-Hammadi Library in English* (Leiden, 1977) 422.

21 *Didachē* 11.

22 Hermas, *Vis.* 2.3.4; *Mand.* 4.4.

23 1 Cor. 12.8–10.

24 Ibid. 12.28–31.

25 Lucian, *Alexander* 11.

26 For the Troketta oracle, with its similar appeal, Parke (1985) 150ff., 155ff.

27 Tr. Morton Smith in Betz (1986). For the relationship between magic and rhetoric in general, J. de Romilly, *Magic and Rhetoric in the Ancient World* (Cambridge, Mass., 1975).

28 Lucian, *Peregrinus* 41; Rev. 1.4–3.22.

29 E.g., *Ep. Apoll.* 24 (despising the Olympic Games); 27 (veiled threat of misfortune to Delphi for blood sacrifices).

30 For the problem, Penella (1979) 3.

31 E.g., Col. 1.13–2.8. For a broad perspective, L. J. White, 'New Testament epistolary literature in the framework of ancient epistolography', *ANRW* 2.25.2 (1984) 1730–56.

32 Col. 2.16–19, cf. 2.9–15.

33 Isidore of Pelusium *Ep.* 1.99 (*PG* 78 coll. 249C-252A).

34 On the genre, Reardon (1971) 264f.

35 Pp. 8ff. Russell-Wilson.

36 *Or.* 38.7. For Aristides' case, D. A. Russell, 'Aristides and the prose hymn', in Russell (1990) 199–219; for his verse efforts, E. L. Bowie, 'Greek sophists and Greek poetry in the second Sophistic', *ANRW* 2.33.1 (1989) 214–21.

37 E.g., *Or.* 50.25, 31, 39–46 passim.

38 E.g., *Or.* 50.39; *Or.* 50.43.

39 *VA* 4.7.

40 *VA* 4.8.

41 In his *Borystheniticus* (*Or.* 36.39–61); see below p. 177.

42 Rom. 9.19–21.

43 Ibid. 9.16–24.

44 1 Cor. 4.10ff.

45 For bibliography see above, Chapter 4 n.9.

46 Acts 17.23.

47 Ibid. 17.24–31.

48 E.g., Dibelius (1956) 27–57.

49 Philostratus, *VA* 4.19–22.

50 Max. Tyr. *Or.* 2.1–3 Hobein.

51 Ibid. 2.4c. For the topos of Egyptian theriomorphic gods, see now K. A. D. Smelik and E. A. Hemelrijk, ' "Who knows not what monsters demented Egypt worships?" Opinions on Egyptian animal worship in Antiquity as part of the ancient conception of Egypt', *ANRW* 2.17.4 (1984) 1852–2000.

52 Ibid. 2.5–10a.

53 Ibid. 2.10cd.

54 *PG* 46.897BC.

55 Tertullian *adv. Marcionem* 1.1.

6 ACTION:
DISPLAY AND INTERVENTION

1 On the holy man's activities, Bieler (1935/6) 101–22; for late Antiquity, Brown (1971), especially 87–100 passim.

2 Apuleius, *Apology* 55.

3 Hippolytus, *Refutatio* 6.3; variants in Maximus of Tyre, *Or.* 29.4a Hobein; Aelian, *HA* 14.30, cf. Justin 21.4; Pliny, *NH* 8.16. The perpetrator's name is variously given as Psaphon, Apsephus, Absethus.

4 *Alexander* 10f.; Caster (1938) ad loc. The geographical implication of the choice of Chalcedon would have been crucial to the enterprise: so inaccessible a site as Abonouteichos would have been useless for the purpose.

5 *Alexander* 12.

6 Ibid. 13. For the gobbledegook, cf. above p. 77.

7 *Acta Archelai* 22f.

8 Mk 1.6ff.; 1.9; cf. Matt. 3.11–16; Lk. 3.15–21.

9 *VA* 8.15.

10 Lucian, *Peregrinus* 20, 3–6 at 4, 6; cf. Caster (1937) 237–55; J. Schwartz (1963); Jones (1986) 117–32.

11 *Epp. Apoll.* 24, 25, 26. For their considerable inconsistency, Penella (1979) ad 24, 26.

12 Lucian, *Alexander* 38ff. For reservations over the comparison, Caster (1938) ad 38–40 (p. 61). But its overall effect is calculated by Lucian to give Alexander's antics the flavour of a 'poor man's Eleusis'.

13 Porphyry, *Vita Plotini* 10.

14 See, e.g., Dodds (1947) 60f.; A. H. Armstrong, 'Was Plotinus a magician', *Phronesis* 1 (1955) 73–9.

15 *Philopseudes* 36.

16 Lk. 1.5–25; 57–66.

17 Jn 4.5–42 (at 18f., 28f., 39–42).

18 Kaibel 1034 (Callipolis).

19 See now Parke (1985) 152 with bibliography.

20 Lucian, *Alexander* 24.

21 Wiegand, *SB Berl. Akad.* (1904) 205a; Parke (1985) 76f. For the Apellas inscription, *IG* 4.955 (Dittenberger, *Sylloge*, 4th edn, 1170).

22 Philostratus, *VA* 4.1.

23 *Inscr. Did.*, Rehm 496; L. Robert, *Hellenica* 10/11 (1960) 544; Lane Fox (1986) 102f., 141ff. with bibliography.

24 On exorcism in general, K. Thraede, s.v. Exorzismus, *Lexicon f. Antike u. Christentum*; Brown (1971) 88f. Kee (1986) 71, stresses the apocalyptic element in Hellenistic Judaism for the concept of demonic control of the world which the exorcist will challenge; but the same concept is hardly alien to the pagan world, as the Apuleius' account of the healing of Lucius serves to show.

25 *VA* 4.20.

26 Mk 1.23–8. For parallels in Jewish material, M. J. Geller, 'Jesus' theurgic powers: parallels in the Talmud and incantation bowls', *JJS* 28 (1977) 141–55.

27 Mk 1.34. For the importance of miracle to the Markan tradition, Vermes (1983) 20–26, 58–82. For the social significance of the miracles in their Gospel setting, Kee (1986) 73: the miracles offend against the religious politics of Jesus Christ's opponents. But that has nothing to do with how exorcisms actually work in historical fact.

28 *VA* 3.38.

29 *Alexander* 55. Caster (1938) has doubts about the historicity of the whole incident; one must certainly bear in mind that Lucian is now unlikely to be contradicted from the quarter of Alexander's former power-base.

30 Mk 5.21–24, 35–43.

31 Apuleius, *Florida* 19. For Asclepiades, see now E. D. Rawson, 'The life and death of Asclepiades of Bithynia', *CQ* 32 (1982) 358–70. It is quite misleading to argue, as Kee does (1986) 78, that material on miracle

NOTES

from later Classical literature (Lucian, Philostratus, the late Magical Papyri) 'embodies basic shifts in the worldviews prevalent from the first part of the first century AD down to the second and third centuries'. What are these shifts, and how does he prove that 'the centre of interest in these (gospel) narratives has to do with participation in covenant community, not in medical skills'? Even if the evangelists are interested in the social consequences of curing outsiders – hardly relevant in the case of Jairus' daughter – that does not constitute proof of how or why they were done. Kee is particularly questionable in his use of Philostratus. He wants this author to be late and unreliable to undermine his opponents subscribing to a 'divine man' theology, and of course discredits Philostratus' alleged source 'Damis' to the same end. But the crucial episode in Apollonius has nothing to do with Damis, real or imaginary; and Kee misattributes to Apollonius Philostratus' own speculation that the sage recognised a spark of life in the patient. Time and again we find the slightest possibility of magical technique discounted in the case of Jesus Christ and given the greatest credence in the case of Apollonius. See further Appendix below.

32 TB Berahot 34b. Kee's argument (1986) 80–3, that rabbinical views of miracle are only to confirm the individual rabbi's authority, whereas those of Jesus Christ are not, might be allowed to stand; but there is a certain perversity in refusing to use miracles to confirm one's authority and then using one's authority to announce a new age.

33 *Demonax* 27. Edelstein (1945.1) 374–80 on the Athenian Asclepieion; S. Walker, *ABSA* 74 (1979) 256f.

34 Jn 4.52.

35 New evidence, albeit equivocal, has given us a possibility of looking again at the New Testament account of the raising of Lazarus. This episode is peculiar to John, where it forms a natural prefiguration of the resurrection of Jesus Christ himself. The absence of this material in the Synoptic tradition naturally weakened its claim to be considered a 'real' happening in the historical sense, as opposed to an edifying story akin to parable. A major turnup in recent biblical scholarship has been the emergence in 1973 of a fragment purporting to be from an Alexandrian revision of Mark (Morton Smith, *Clement of Alexandria and a Secret Gospel of Mark*, Cambridge, Mass., 1973); the quotation is connected by its context with Synoptic tradition and fills a gap in that tradition corresponding to the narrative in John. This is particularly illuminating because it contains a single tell-tale phrase missing in the Johannine account: 'and Jesus, being angered, went off with her to the garden where the tomb was, and straightway a great cry was heard from the tomb'. In John it is Jesus who calls to Lazarus after the tomb in opened. In the so-called 'Secret Gospel' fragment there is scarcely the basis for a miracle at all, although Lazarus has been in the tomb four days; he would simply in this account have woken from his coma and be trying to attract attention; such a detail would have been suppressed in the Johannine account to give Jesus the credit of another resurrection miracle. For the not inconsiderable problems of authen-

248

ticity, cf. S. Levin, 'The early history of Christianity, in light of the "Secret Gospel" of Mark', *ANRW* 25.6 (1988) 4370–92.

36 *Philopseudes* 14.

37 *Met.* 2.28ff.

38 *Aethiopica* 6.14f.

39 *Historia Monachorum*, Rufinus *PL* 21 coll. 449–52.

40 Cf. 'The tale of Judar' in the *Arabian Nights*, tr. N. Dawood (Harmondsworth, 1973) 341f.

41 Five thousand: Mk 6.30–44; Matt. 14.13–21; Lk. 9.10.17; four thousand: Mk 8.1–10; Matt. 15.32–9.

42 On the episodes in general, H. van der Loos, *The Miracles of Jesus* (Leiden, 1965) 619–37.

43 Lk. 9.12. There is the implication that although local supplies were available they were not sought.

44 Origen, *contra Celsum* 1.68; cf. Philostratus, *VA* 4.25, where the Lamia in Corinth is exposed as practising the same trick.

45 Irenaeus, *adv. Haer.* 1.13.

46 Lk. 9.28–36.

47 For discussion of the so-called 'Messianic Secret', W. Wrede, *Das Messiasgeheimnis in den Evangelien. Zugleich ein Beitrag zum Verständnis des Markusevangeliums* (Göttingen, 1901).

48 *Actus Petri cum Simone* 2.4 (pp. 48ff.); 4.9f. (pp. 57f.); 5.13 (pp. 60f.). For the relationship of miracle and prophecy in general, Kolenkow (1980) 1470–1506

49 *P. Westcar* (P. Berlin 3033) 8, tr. M. Lichtheim, *Ancient Egyptian Literature* (Berkeley, 1973) 1 p. 219 (joining the severed heads of animals and revitalising them).

50 Hippolytus, *Refutatio* 6.7.1; 4.51.3–14.

51 Mk 4.12f.; Matt. 4.1–11; Lk. 4.1–13.

52 *Apol.* 42.

53 Philostratus, *VA* 6.39.

54 Lucian, *Alexander* 50. But for doubts on its historicity, Caster (1938); cf. G. Anderson *Lucian: Theme and Variation in the Second Sophistic* (Leiden, 1976A) 126, on the oracles in general.

55 *Vita S. Theodori Sykeotae* 34.

56 Lucian, *Alexander* 44.

57 Porphyry in Eusebius, *PE* 5,6 190B; L. Robert, *CRAI* (1968) 579; Philostratus, *VS* 515f.

58 Foerster (1893) vol. 1, 282–5.

59 *Ep.* 2.20.2–6.

60 For Regulus' career, Sherwin-White (1963) on Pliny, *Ep.* 1.5.1; *PIR²* A1005.

61 Lk. 3.7–14.

62 Lucian, *Peregrinus* 19, cf. *SHA* Pius 5.

63 *Ep. Apoll.* 54, cf. 32 (with διοικηταῖς, not δικαιωταῖς as the heading) most probably addressed to procurators; cf. Penella (1979).

64 *Ep. Apoll.* 22, presumably to a wealthy recipient, though the Lesbonax in question cannot be satisfactorily identified; for the difficulties, Penella (1979).

65 Matt. 26.6–13; Mk 14.3–9.
66 *Ep. Apoll.* 11, with the possibility of anti-Semitic sentiment, cf. *VA* 5.27; L. Levine, *Caesarea under Roman Rule* (1975) 35, 170.
67 Philostratus, *VA* 4.1.
68 Ibid. 4.2.
69 Ibid. 4.27, cf. *Ep. Apoll.*63; *VA* 6.34.
70 Dio, *Or.* 32, 33f., 31.
71 Philostratus, *VA* 4.5.
72 Ibid. 4.22; Lucian, *Vita Demonactis* 57.
73 *Ep. Apoll.* 11.
74 *Ep. Apoll.* 11.2.
75 *Ep. Apoll.* 47. I agree with Penella (1979) against Petzke (1970) 43f., that Apollonius is not being recalled to receive an honour, but for some uncongenial purpose; we have rather the figure used by Socrates at Plato *Apol.* 36D, where an accused man suggests that an honour is more justified in his own case than a penalty.
76 *Epp. Apoll.* 38–41, *Ep.* 56.
77 Philostratus, *VA* 6.38.
78 Ibid. 6.37.
79 Acts 14.8–19. Lane Fox (1986) 99–101 gives a good counterblast to those who dismiss the incident as improbable (e.g. Haenchen (1971) 432ff.); the epiphany of Alexander of Abonouteichos is relevant as a corrective.
80 Lk. 10.10–15; 9.52–5.
81 Jones (1986) 140.
82 Eusebius, *HE* 5.18.
83 Gregory of Nyssa, *Vita Gregorii* Migne 46.908A.
84 *Alexander* 36.
85 *IGRRP* 4.1498; tr. Parke (1985) 152ff.
86 Parke ibid. 150–7 passim.
87 Philostratus, *VA* 4.10f.
88 Ibid. 1.15; *VS* 526.
89 *Or.* 49.38 Keil.
90 John Malalas, *PG* 97 col. 401AB; Dulière (1970) 254f.
91 Malalas ibid. 401C–404A; Dulière (1970) 255.
92 Athanasius, *Vita Antonii* 91 (tr. R. C. Gregg).
93 *Deut.* 34.6.
94 *VA* 8.30.
95 Ibid.
96 Ibid.
97 Ibid.
98 Lucian, *Peregrinus* 1.20 and passim. For motivation, cf. R. A. Pack, 'The volatilization of Peregrinus Proteus', *AJPh* 67 (1946) 334–45.
99 Tacitus, *Annales.* 15.60.
100 Lucian, *Peregrinus* 24f.
101 Ibid. 25 (with the well-attested precedent of Calanus under Alexander; and of Zarmonochegas under Augustus, Strabo 15.1.73).
102 *Peregrinus* 33. For this aspect, Pack (1946) p. 337f.
103 Cf. the case of Euphrates' suicide, 'authorised' by Hadrian, Dio 69.8.3.

104 Lucian, *Peregrinus* 32f.
105 *VA* 8.30.
106 Ibid. 8.31.
107 Lucian, *Peregrinus* 41.
108 Ignatius, *Epp. ad Smyrnaeos* 11; *ad Polycarpum* 7.
109 *VA* 1.3.
110 Appearances to the disciples: Lk. 24.34–52; Mk 16.14; Matt. 28.16; Jn 20.19–21; Acts 1.3–9.
111 Lk. 24.13–35.
112 See especially Lane Fox (1986) 102–67 passim.
113 *Od.* 6.20–4; 13.221f.

7 ALLIANCE:
DISCIPLES, CLIENTS, PATRONS

1 Josephus' family: *Vita* 1.2. Elagabalus as hereditary priest of the Baal of Emesa: Herodian 5.3.4, with Whittaker's note in *LCL* ad loc.; F. G. B. Millar , 'The Phoenician cities. A case-study of Hellenisation', *PCPS* (1983) 157f. on the god.
2 For the evidence, E. R. Dodds (1947) 56.
3 Artemidorus 4 praef.; Inscr. Did. II.277 (one of Ulpianus' uncles was Aelianus Poplas, on whom see below p. 122).
4 Marcion's father as bishop of Sinope, Epiphanius, *Panarion* 3.42.1; on Mani's father's sect of Elchaisites, Eusebius, *HE* 6.38; A. Henrichs, 'The Cologne Mani-Codex reconsidered', *HSCP* 83 (1979) 354–67.
5 Lk. 1.36.
6 Gal. 1.19 (in whatever sense); cf. Acts 15.13–21; Eusebius, *HE* 2.23.4.
7 Ibid. 3.11.
8 Mk 3.31–5.
9 Lucian, *Alexander* 6. Caster (1938) characteristically harbours suspicions about the treatment of Coconnas; cf. G. Anderson, *Lucian: Theme and Variation in the Second Sophistic*, (Leiden, 1976A) 76.
10 *Alexander* 8.
11 Ibid. 9f.
12 Lucian, *Peregrinus* 3–6.
13 Ibid. 4, 25; 29.
14 Ibid. 36.
15 Matt. 3.11.
16 Matt. 3.3.
17 Philipp. 2.19; 2.22.
18 Gal. 2.3.
19 Philostratus, *VA* passim; 1.3. For detailed – and as yet inconclusive – discussion of 'Damis', see now Bowie (1978) 1653–70; Dielska (1986) 19–49 (Damis as out-and-out fabrication by Philostratus); for qualified rescue of Damis, W. Speyer, 'Zum Bild des Apollonios von Tyana bei Heiden und Christen', *JAC* 17 (1974) (Neo-Pythagorean forgery) 47–63; Anderson (1986) 155–73; and now Flintermann (1993) 87–97.
20 *VA* 1.19.

21 Ibid. 5.13; 7.38.
22 Lucian, *Alexander* 23.
23 Ibid. 24; 38ff.
24 Matt. 10.1–15; Mk 6.7–13; Lk. 9.1–6; seventy-two, Lk. 10.1–16.
25 Philostratus, *VA* 4.17.
26 Ibid. 4.37; Origen, *contra Celsum* 6.41.
27 Jn 3.1–21; Mk 10.17–22: (a man in Mk 10.17, a ruler in Lk. 18.18, a young man in Matt. 19.20).
28 Lk. 7.36; 11.37.
29 Lk. 7.1–10 (at 5, 3).
30 Titus 3.13; Col. 4.14.
31 Rom. 16.24 (of Cornith; cf. H. J. Cadbury, *JBL* (1931) 42–58).
32 *Actus Petri cum Simone* (*Actus Vercellenses*) 6.17. On the whole subject of women's participation in cults, see now R. S. Kraemer, *Her Share of the Blessings: Women's Religions Among Pagans, Jews, and Christians in the Greco-Roman World* (New York, 1992).
33 Lucian, *Alexander* 6f.
34 Ibid. 42.
35 Lucian, *de Mercede Conductis* 40.
36 For Jerome's circle at Rome, J. N. D. Kelly, *Jerome: His Life, Writings, and Controversies* (London, 1975) 91–103.
37 *Actus Pauli* appendix (Hennecke-Schneemelcher 2 p. 389).
38 Eusebius, *HE* 5.16.9. On their role and the nature of Montanism, Kraemer (1992) 157–73.
39 Lk. 8.2f. On women and leadership in the early church, Kraemer (1992) 174–90.
40 Apuleius, *Apology* 48.
41 Ibid. 51.
42 Epiphanius, *Panarion* 33.3, 1–7, 10.
43 Ibid. 33.4.3–7.1–8.
44 Tr. G. Fowden (1986) 122. For the overall context, Zosimus Panopolitanus, Alch. gr. 239–46 (A. J. Festugière, *La Révélation* d'Hermes Trismegiste (3rd edn, Paris, 1981) vol. 1.363–8).
45 Lucian, *Alexander* 30f. For Rutilianus' background and career, Caster citing *CIL* 14.3601 (Dessau 1101); for reservations on his superstitious character, Caster (1938) 30 (pp. 54ff.)
46 Lucian, *Alexander* 33.
47 Lucian, *Alexander* 34. For the theological aspect, Caster (1938).
48 Ibid. 35.
49 Ibid. 32.
50 *SHA Sev.* 3.6.
51 Apuleius, *Apology* 94; PIR^{2}H40 (L. Hedius Rufus Lollianus Avitus).
52 *Alexander* 50.
53 Ibid.
54 For Severianus, *Alexander* 27, Bowersock (1969) 86f.; for *Sacerdos*, Alexander 43; cf. the Oenoanda inscription, C. W. Chilton, *Diogenes of Oenoanda* (Hull, 1971); with subsequent additions by M. F. Smith. On Trimalchio's murals, Petronius, *Sat.* 29.3–6.
55 H. Erbse, *Fragmente der griechischer Theosophien* (Hamburg, 1941)

22f., tr. Parke (1985) 206f.; Lane Fox (1986) 192, 219ff., 228. For the identification, L. Robert *CRAI* (1968/9) 513.

56 *Inscr. Did.* II.277; Robert *CRAI* (1968/9) 586; *Hellenica* 10/11 (1960) 543; Parke (1985) 87f.

57 *Ep. Apoll.* 58; for the identification problem, Penella (1979).

58 *VA* 4.40. On the problems relating to date and rank, Anderson (1986) 177f. There is nothing inherently implausible in a visit to Rome by Apollonius under Nero, nor in the problems in harmonising it with the sort of sophisticated historical background account postulated, e.g., by Bowie (1978) 1662 for the Flavian episodes.

59 *VA* 4.40; 4.43.

60 *VA* 8.7.14; 8.12.

61 *Actus Petri cum Simone (Actus Vercellenses)* 4.8–5.14.

62 *PIR*² E.84.

63 *Actus Petri (Actus Vercellenses)* 4.8.

64 Tacitus, *Annales* 13.33.

65 Lk. 3.14.

66 Lk. 7.3ff.

67 Ibid. 7.7f.

68 Acts 10.1f. For the probable identity of the cohort, Haenchen (1971).

69 Acts 10.7f.

70 Acts 10.45f.

71 *Vita Antonii* 48.

72 Lucian, *Alexander* 27. For considerable reservations on Lucian's presentation, Caster (1938): Severianus did not have a choice which the oracle could determine; and the quasi-Imperial insignia should not have been promised to a mere general.

73 See below pp. 51ff.

74 Acts 13.6–12.

75 Josephus, *AJ* 20.142.

76 Cf. Haenchen (1971) on *Acts* 13.8, who does not exhaust the possibilities. It is not quite necessary to render Hetoimos as 'Dr. Fix', an obviously disreputable nuance; in addition to comparison with Arabic *elim* 'wise', one might suggest Hebrew *Elohim* as a *nomen sacrum* which the magician would have taken on, rather like the godly titles of Simon Magus. Whatever the real solution, it would have been normal enough to have Greek and 'native' names, as in modern cross-cultural situations.

77 *Ep.* 1.10.9ff.

78 A standard Stoic view, e.g., Seneca, *Ep.* 20.2.

79 *Ep.* 7.27.3.

80 Ibid. 7.27.14.

81 Fowden (1986) 162–5 (Thessalus, *de virtutibus herbarum* I proem 1–28).

82 *VS* 552ff. I suspect a degree of affinity between this kind of 'wisdom' encounter and those of 'Midas and the Satyr' as attributed to Theopompus in Aelian *VH* 3.18.

83 On Agathion, see further J. F. Kindstrand, 'Sostratus–Hercules–

Agathion: the rise of a legend', *Annales Societatis Litterarum Humanarum Upsaliensis* (1979/80) 50–79.

84 *PGM* 1.97–103, 187–91, tr. E. O'Neil in Betz (1986) 5–8.

85 For 'libertine' Gnostic texts, Foerster (1893) 1.313–25.

86 Philostratus, *VA* 1.13; *VS* 570.

87 Jn 19.26; Rom. 1.26f.

88 In this connexion the so-called 'Secret Gospel of Mark' purportedly quoted by Clement of Alexandria may afford some further context for Jesus Christ's possible relationship with Lazarus. (For the problems, above pp. 248ff). In a fragment of Clement purportedly discovered by Morton Smith and published by him in 1973, we are told that Lazarus was rich, though we might also have inferred it from the tale of the precious jar of spikenard. We are told that as soon as Jesus arrives at Lazarus' tomb and raised him, 'the youth, looking upon him loved him, and began to beseech him that he might be with him' (Morton Smith (1973) III.4, p. 111). In the version of the raising of Lazarus by John, the Jews have already offered the scandalised aside 'see how he loved him' (Jn 11.36). It has always been tempting to identify Lazarus with the rich youth rejected by Jesus – as the man with great possessions who will not give them up. With or without that link, we can also note the possibility of a sexual connexion between master and pupil. It is stressed rather than suppressed by Clement's insistence that a sexual nuance did *not* occur in the 'Secret Gospel's' account of Lazarus' subsequent baptism at night, but that it obviously did occur in some other account. So much is immediately clear from the evidence as it stands. But one further question might well be asked. What is Lazarus doing shouting in a tomb, then loving Jesus and wanting him to be with him; then in one account lying naked with him for a night? What occasioned Lazarus' illness? Has he been pining from unrequited love, or indeed has he staged the whole event to attract the attention and sympathy of Jesus? In John what Jesus actually says is 'This sickness is not unto death, but for the glory of God, that the Son of God may be glorified by it' (Jn 11.4). He then stays away another two days, to be reproved by the sisters ('If you had been there, he would not have died'). A similar inference has been drawn against the passage in which the man in the white robe is found with Jesus in Gethsemane: Smith suggests an initiatory rite into the 'secrets of the kingdom'. Little can be securely inferred from either situation – except the near-certainty of their suppression by the second-century church. But they may still point to a credible human lifestyle for an associate of publicans and sinners – or anyone else for that matter.

8 OPPOSITION:
FALSE PROPHETS, CHEATS AND CHARLATANS

1 Philostratus, *VA* 4.10; Acts 7.58–8.1.

2 Philostratus, *VA* 4.18.

3 Ibid. 8.19. For the story as a likely part of pre-Philostratean tradition, Bowie (1978) 1672.

4 Lucian, *Vita Demonactis* 34.

5 Ibid. 11.

6 Gregory of Nyssa, *Vita Gregorii Thaumaturgi* (*PG* 46.916A–D).

7 Mk 13.5f., 21ff.; Matt. 24.4f., 23f.; Lk. 21.8; 1 Cor. 12.28, 14.

8 *Alexander* 10; 13; Eusebius, *HE* 5.14–19 passim.

9 On the general concept of pollution, R. Parker, *Miasma* (Oxford, 1983).

10 Philostratus, *VA* 4.12. Bowie (1978) 1680, suspects various 'Atticising' traces as the overlap of Philostratus, but cultural and religious purism may also be part of a continuous spectrum.

11 *Ep. Apoll.* 71, cf. *VA* 4.5 (the Ionians).

12 Matt. 15.21–8; Mk 7.24–30.

13 Gal. 2.11–13, cf. Acts 15.1. On the issue, W. A. Meeks, *The First Urban Christians: The Social World of the Apostle Paul* (New Haven, 1983) 97–100.

14 Lucian, *Peregrinus* 16 with Harmon and Schwartz ad loc.

15 *CMC* 80.18–83.19 (= *ZPE* 32, 1978, 101ff.).

16 On Jewish purity, e.g., Goodman (1987) 80–4, 103f., 106ff.

17 Neusner (1962) 77 (*Avot de Rabbi Natan* text A = AR Na 12, Schechter 28b, cf. eund. text B = ARNb27; repr. NY 1945 tr. Goldin, *The Fathers according to Rabbi Nathan*, (New Haven, 1955) 71).

18 Ibid. 49f. Mishnah Yadaim 4.6, cf. Tosefta Yadaim 2.9.

19 *P. Oxy.* 840.

20 Above p. 133.

21 Matt. 26.6–13; Mk 14.3–9.

22 Cf. Dudley (1937) 199.

23 E.g., Philostratus, *VA* 5.38f. On Euphrates' career, above p. 126f.

24 *Ep. Apoll.* 8.

25 E.g., *Ep. Apoll.* 7f.

26 Lucian, *Alexander* 21. For the problems of identification with Origen's opponent, Caster (1938) 1–5.

27 Aulus Gellius, *NA* 14.1.

28 Ibid. 14.1.2ff.

29 Ibid. 14.1.5–36.

30 Philostratus, *VA* 8.22.

31 Ibid. 5.39. For the plausibility of this association, Anderson (1986) 183f.; against, Bowie (1978) 1690; Dielska (1986) 42ff.

32 Ibid. 8.21; 22.

33 Philostratus, *VA* 6.41.

34 Ps. Clement, *Homiliae* 7.9.1.

35 Lucian, *Vita Demonactis* 37.

36 See G. E. R. Lloyd, *Science, Folklore and Ideology, Studies in the Life Sciences in Ancient Greece* (Cambridge, 1983).

37 For the tension in earlier Greek tradition, E. R. Dodds, *The Greeks and the Irrational* (Berkeley, 1951).

38 Lucian, *Philopseudes* 8ff. Cf. above p. 58f.

39 Ed. G. Hoffman in *SPG* 1.162.

40 Gellius, *NA* 12.1.

41 Philostratus, *VS* 490f.

42 For Polemo's showing in this field, above p. 100f.
43 Gellius, *NA* 14.1.32f.
44 *Ep. Apoll.* 1.
45 Cf. above p. 76. For an appreciation of Valentinus, see D. Dawson, *Allegorical Readers and Cultural Revision in Ancient Alexandria* (Berkeley, 1992) 127–82.
46 E.g., Irenaeus 1.1.1–12.
47 *Vita Antonii* 72 (tr. R.C. Gregg).
48 Ibid. 73.
49 Ibid. 74–80.
50 Philostratus, *VA* 4.30. For the tradition of Apollonius and the language of birds, Porphyry, *de Abstinentia* 3.3, cf. *VA* 4.3. But such a language is not imaginary: for an actual example, W. Lambert, 'An Akkadian birdcall text', *Anatolian Studies* 20 (1979) 111–17.
51 Cf. *VA* 5.22f.
52 1 Cor. 1.12; 3.6.
53 1 Cor. 4.16–20.
54 E.g., 2 Cor. 12.11ff.
55 Philipp. 1.15ff.
56 Cf. *Ep. Apoll.* 74. For Bassus, above 57, below 145.
57 Acts 15.36–9. For whatever reason Luke does not mention that John Mark and Barnabas are cousins (*Col.* 4.10).
58 Gal. 2.11–14.
59 Lk. 7.18–35.
60 Jn 3.23–36.
61 Lk. 5.17–26.
62 Lk. 5.27–32.
63 Lk. 6.1–5.
64 Lk. 7.36–50.
65 Lk. 8.35ff.
66 Lk. 9.52f.
67 On Dositheus, S. Isser, 'Dositheus, Jesus, and a Moses aretalogy' in Neusner (ed.) (1975) vol. 4, 167–89.
68 Isser ibid. 169 (from a tradition preserved in Abu'l Fath); Origen, *contra Celsum* 6.11.
69 For a good general evocation of an individual's dealing with early Imperial cities, Jones, (1978).
70 Cf. above p. 34.
71 Lucian, *de Morte Peregrini* 10–16. For an attempt to reconstruct the procedure, Schwartz (1963).
72 As implied by the situation found in Bithynia by Pliny, *Ep.* 10.96.
73 *Peregrinus* 15; but cf. the renunciations of property by Apollonius (*VA* 1.13) and Crates (*DL* 6.87).
74 Acts 13.44–14.5; 14.19f.
75 Ibid. 13.50.
76 Cf. also above p. 117f.
77 2 Cor. 10.10, cf. 10.8; on the whole subject, Georgi (1964).
78 2 Cor. 12.14.
79 For the general background of Athenian offices, Follet (1976).

80 *EM* 13366, ed. J. H. Oliver 'Marcus Aurelius: aspects of civic and cultural policy in the East', *Hesperia* Suppl. 13 (1970) 43f.; also W. Ameling, *Herodes Atticus* (1983) 1.139–49.

81 Plaque 2 lines 7–11.

82 On this aspect, cf. E. L. Bowie 'Greeks and their Past in the Second Sophistic' in M. I. Finley (ed.), *Studies in Ancient Society* (London, 1974) 195–203.

83 E.g., Philostratus, *VS* 559ff.

84 For Mamertinus' career, *PIR²* C802.

85 Acts 19.23–41. See further Sherwin-White (1963) 83–92.

86 Acts 19.34.

87 Philostratus, *VA* 5.20.

88 Hippolytus, *Refutatio* 9.12.1–26 passim.

89 Ibid. 9.11.1ff.

90 Ibid. 9.12.24.

91 Eusebius, *HE* 5.18.6, 9.

92 *Epp. Apoll.* 2, 4, 6.

93 *Ep. Apoll.* 5, cf. *Ep.* 51, *VA* 5.38. On Imperial gifts in such a context, F. G. B. Millar, *The Emperor in the Roman World* (London, 1977) 491–506.

94 *Ep. Apoll.* 7, 14, cf. *VA* 8.7.11 (including *captatio*); cf. Juvenal 3.70–8; Lucian, *Nigrinus* 24, *de Mercede conductis* passim. But such letters are scarcely at variance with the pro-Roman lines of the *VA*, pace Bowie (1978) 1682: holy men will castigate cities or societies and still be conciliatory with their rulers.

95 *Ep. Apoll.* 14.

96 *Ep. Apoll.* 16, cf. 17. On the ambiguity of *mageia*, above p. 65–8.

97 *VA* 4.26, *Ep. Apoll.* 74 (with characteristic innuendo over a philosopher's pupil): cf. Lucian, *D. Meretr.* 10, among much.

98 *Ep. Apoll.* 36, with Penella (1979).

99 Ibid.

100 Cf. *Ep. Apoll.* 37.

101 *VA* 4.31.

102 See above pp. 92ff.

103 Acts 19.13–20. A high priest of the name Scaeva is unknown.

104 Ibid. 15.

105 Ibid. 16–20.

106 Acts 13.6–12.

107 See further A. D. Nock, 'Paul and the magus' (= Nock (1972) 308–30). Alternative explanations of the blindness might include hypnosis or simple fear of a curse by Paul. But such interpretations would only have served to elicit (very properly) a charge of magic instead of violence against Paul.

108 Porphyry, *Vita Plotini* 10.

109 Lucian, *Alexander* 25.

110 On Lepidus, Caster (1937) *Alexander* 25; *PIR²* C910.

111 Hegemonius, *Acta Archelai*, ed. C. H. Beeson (Leipzig, 1906).

112 *VA* 4.10.

113 Acts 5.1–12. Some overingenious attempts to expurgate the story in

some way are exposed by Haenchen (1971) who none the less tries his own hand at just such a ploy.

114 *Vita Gregorii Thaumaturgi, PG* 46.940C–941C (explicitly citing the case of Ananias and Peter as a precedent).

115 Acts 13.44–14.14; above p. 141.

116 Acts 13.50.

117 Acts 14.19.

118 Acts 21.27–22.24.

119 On Oenomaus, above p. 69f.

120 Cf. in general Caster (1937) especially 225–67 on oracles.

121 For the work, Lucian, *Alexander* 21.

122 The context that relays the fragment of the so-called 'Secret Gospel' of Mark (Smith 1973) may offer a fascinating eavesdrop on how rival sects could conduct their relationships. Clement of Alexandria is presented as writing to one Theodore about the menace posed by the Carpocratians, whom he regards as libertarian heretics. On no account must the true authorship of the 'Secret Gospel of Mark' be divulged to them. In fact it must be denied under oath. Various scriptural justifications for falsehoods are then put forward ('to the pure all things are pure', the Carpocratians of course being for these purposes 'impure'). The practical motives of Clement would not be hard to see. The Carpocratians have got hold of this 'Secret Gospel', and they will doubtless be able to use it, if only by way of unauthorised interpolation, as authentic justification of their libertarian practices. It will become in effect a gay gospel. Only by denying Markan authorship, which Clement acknowledges, can the Carpocratians be checked or discredited. One notes that Clement's text of the 'Secret Gospel' is actually unexceptionable, in so far as it does not according to Clement contain a tell-tale phrase that would imply homosexual relations with Lazarus. But who can now trust Clement or his sources, given their bare-faced sanctioning of an official lie of this magnitude? Either way, Clement would stand convicted of a cover-up, and one must ask how many more of the kind there could have been in so many sectarian wars. Once more these views will of course depend on the authenticity of the fragment: see Levin (1988).

9 AUTHORITY: CAESARS, PRINCIPALITIES AND POWERS

1 Josephus, *BJ* 4.623–9.

2 Philostratus, *VA* 5.31.

3 On the rest of Apollonius' encounters with Vespasian, Bowie (1978) 1660; Anderson (1986), 178f.; Flintermann (1993) 152–61.

4 Neusner (1962) 115–20.

5 Tacitus, *Historiae* 4.81; with Chilver-Townend (Oxford, 1985) ad loc.; Suetonius, *Vesp.* 7.2f.; Dio 65.8.1.

6 On the incident, P. Derchain and J. Hubaux, 'Vespasien au Serapeium', *Latomus* 12 (1953) 38–52; A. Henrichs, 'Vespasian's visit to Alexandria', *ZPE* 3 (1968) 76f.; Bowie, (1978) 1660ff.

7 Dio-Xiphilinus 72.8ff.; Harnouphis, 72.8.4. We know of an Arnouphis, an Egyptian *hierogrammateus* as a contemporary dedicator to Isis at Aquileia: details in G. Fowden, 'Pagan versions of the rain-miracle of AD 172', *Historia* 36 (1987) 83–95 at 87f. As he goes on to show (ibid. 89) the propaganda was quick to drop the Egyptian attribution of the episode, in favour of a more patriotic explanation.

8 Dio-Xiphilinus 72.9; cf. already Tertullian *Apol.* 5.6; *ad Scap.* 4. For the 'thundering legion', Eusebius, *Chron.* 1.206f., 2.619ff. Helm; in the latter passage Jupiter is actually credited with the miracle – of course representing the God of the Christians. On the episode as a whole, see now Fowden (1987).

9 On the role of Marcus, included in Tertullian but not in the Column of Marcus, Fowden (1987) 84ff. On the date, O. Salomies, 'A note on the establishment of the date of the rain miracle under Marcus Aurelius', *Arctos* 24 (1990) 107–12.

10 Lucian, *Alexander* 48. Caster (1937) suspects that Lucian invented Alexander's defence.

11 On imperial consultation of seers, Cramer (1954) 81–231.

12 For the anecdote, Tacitus, *Annales* 6.21; Suetonius, *Tib.* 14.4; Dio 55.9.2f.; Cod. Paris. gr. Suppl. 607A f.44v ed. cat. 8, 4; 99f.

13 For the career of Thrasyllus and his family, Cramer (1954) 92–144 (largely speculative, however).

14 Pliny, *NH* 30.5.14f.

15 Ibid. 30.6.16f.

16 Dio 78.17.2.

17 Matt. 2.1–12.

18 For further religious aspects of Polemo, G. Anderson, *The Second Sophistic: A Cultural Phenomenon in the Roman Empire* (London, 1993) 200.

19 Polemo, *SPG* I (Leipzig, 1893) 140ff.

20 *VA* 6.34.

21 Lucian, *Peregrinus* 18; Schwartz (1963) compares Vespasian's deportation of the Cynic Demetrius (Dio 66.13); see also Jones (1986) 124.

22 *Ep. Apoll.* 30.

23 Lucian, *Demonax* 50.

24 *PGM* 4.244ff.

25 Lucian, *Philops.* 34ff. For the identity of Pachrates, K. Preisendanz s.v., *RE* 18.2 (1942) coll. 2071–74; A. D. Nock, *Essays on Religion in the Ancient World*, ed. Z. Stewart (Oxford, 1972) 1.183f.

26 *AJ* 8.44f. The root was the Baaras, described in *BJ* 7.180–4.

27 Apollonius in Parthia: V. A. Smith, 'The Indian travels of Apollonius of Tyana', *ZDMG* 68 (1914) 329–44; J. Charpentier, 'The Indian travels of Apollonius of Tyana', *Skrifter utgivna av. K. Humanistika Vetenskaps-Samfundet i Uppsala* 29.3 (Uppsala, 1934) 1–66.

28 For the affair and its consequences, Eusebius, *HE* 1.12; J. B. Segal, *Edessa, The Blessed City* (Oxford, 1970) 62–109.

29 Edition of the Greek text and burgeoning medieval tradition in B. E. Perry, *Secundus the Silent Philosopher* (Ithaca N.Y., 1964).

30 E.g., Dio 69.3.3–6 (Favorinus, Dionysius of Miletus).

31 Pliny, *Ep.* 10.96, with its stress on the punishment of *pertinacia* and *inflexibilis obstinatio*, 3.

32 Perry (1964) 78–90.

33 Bowersock (1969) 118f.

34 Secundus the Gnostic: Irenaeus adv. Haer. 1.11.1f. (Foerster (1893) 1.194f.).

35 M3 recto tr. L. J. R. Ort, *Mani, A Religio-Historical Description of his Personality* (Leiden, 1967) 52f.

36 M3 verso, ibid. 53.

37 Epiphanius, *Panarion* 56.1.5. For the general background of Bardesanes, H. Drivjers, *Bardaisan of Edessa* (Assen, 1966).

38 Dio 78.12.1.

39 *VA* 1.3.

40 Ibid. 3.41.

41 Ibid. 4.40, 44. For the chronological problem, Anderson (1986) 176ff.

42 *VA* 5.28–37 passim (consultation with Apollonius and others); 5.41 (repudiation of Vespasian's policy).

43 *VA* 6.29, 30; 6.31, cf.33; 6.34.

44 Ibid. 6.34.

45 Ibid. 6.32.

46 Ibid. 7.5.

47 Ibid. 7.4.

48 Ibid. 7.6.

49 Ibid. 6.42.

50 Ibid. 7.7.

51 *Epp. Apoll.* 20, 21.

52 For the apologetic and missionary viewpoint of Luke, e.g., H. C. Kee, *Good News to the Ends of the Earth: The Theology of Acts* (London, 1990).

53 Sherwin-White (1963) passim, esp. 120ff. (in contrast to the gospel handlings of Galilee, 122).

54 Acts 18.12–17. For the whole episode, H. W. Tajra, *The Trial of St Paul: A Juridical Exegesis of the Second Half of the Acts of the Apostles* (Tübingen, 1989) 51–60, somewhat arbitrarily arguing for a hearing late rather than early in Gallio's proconsulship (i.e. early 52 rather than 51), ibid. 55; cf. Sherwin-White (1963) 99f.

55 Acts 21.27–36; Tajra (1989) 63–9. The significance of Trophimus as a provocateur to the Diaspora Jews is lost to us: presumably he was identified as an uncircumcised Gentile Christian.

56 Ibid. 21.37–40; 22.1–21. For difficulties, Haenchen (1971) 618; note Tajra (1989) 72: 'Luke has consciously intertwined the legal and theological (kerugmatic) dimensions in carrying out his apologetic strategy in this last part of Acts'.

57 Acts 22.1–29. See n.66 below.

58 Ibid. 22.30–33.10, Tajra (1989) 90–7; on the Sanhedrin's status and powers, ibid. 98–103.

59 Acts 23.12–35; Sherwin-White (1963) 48–70 on this and the following procedure.

60 Acts 24.1–27.
61 Ibid. 25.1–12.
62 Acts 25.13–27, with Tajra (1989) 152–63.
63 Acts 26.1–23, with Tajra (1989) 163–8.
64 Acts 26.26–32.
65 Ibid. 23.29; 25.19f.
66 Ibid. 21.39; 22.26; 23.6. Tajra (1989, 76) well stresses the theological implication: Paul's 'primary identity is religious not legal'; and his Roman citizenship has been effectively contrasted with the (bought) citizenship of his interrogator (22.28); and again 'Acts is prompt to show that except in very perilous circumstances the apostle neither invokes its protection nor avails himself of his rights'. For the basic plausibility of Paul's Roman citizenship, Tajra (1989) 81–9.
67 Haenchen (1971) on Acts 26.32 ('this imaginary acquittal'). Haenchen notes the Luke-author's unwillingness to allow Agrippa to blame Paul for his not being released.
68 Pliny, *Ep.* 10.96.1.
69 Matt. 26.57–68; 27.1f., 11–18. For an overall view of the problem, E. J. Bickerman, 'Utilitas Crucis', *RHR* (1935) 169ff., = *Studies in Jewish and Christian History* 3 (1986) 82ff.; Sherwin-White (1963) 24–47; O. Betz, 'Probleme des Prozesses Jesu', *ANRW* 2.25.1 (1982) 565–647; R. Lane Fox, *The Unauthorized Version: Truth and Fiction in the Bible* (London, 1991) 283–310. The real difficulty is not the Roman trial, which is convincingly presented as a *cognitio extra ordinem*; but the hearing before the Sanhedrin. See Sherwin-White (1963) 32–43 against Lietzmann's old view (*Das Leben des Heiligen Symeon Stylites* (Leipzig, 1908)) that this latter was a fabrication. It seems reasonable enough that the Sanhedrin conducted a blasphemy trial, but that a charge of sedition was also raised in view of the reluctance of Roman officials to execute on a theological offence; but Sherwin-White (46f.) notes the blackmail element ('You are not Caesar's friend', Jn 19.12) applicable as a pressure whichever charge had to be made to stick.
70 Lk. 23.6–11. For possible explanations, Sherwin-White (1963) 28–31. These comprise the possibility of trial in the jurisdiction of one's area of domicile; a remnant of courtesy extradition as under Herod the Great; or a personal trade-off with Herod. The convenience of a specialist Jewish consultant for a supposedly Jewish religious offence should also be entertained.
71 Jn 19.6; 16.
72 *The Trial of Jesus of Nazareth* (London, 1968).
73 *Ep.* 10.96.3–8. Cf. Sherwin-White (1963) 35: 'Pliny . . . did not understand the charges against the Christians in Pontus, but he condemned them to a Roman execution without hesitation'.
74 Cf. 10.96.5.
75 Ibid. 10.96.10.
76 P. Roussel and F. de Visscher, 'Les inscriptions du temple de Dmeir', *Syria* 23 (1942–3) 173, with *SEG* 17.259 and N. Lewis, *TAPhA* 99 (1968) 255; Millar (1977) 455f.

10 TRAVEL:
HOLY MEN ON THE MOVE

1 On travel in the ancient world, L. Casson, *Ships and Seamanship in the Ancient World* (Princeton, 1971); L. Casson, *Travel in the Ancient World* (London, 1974).

2 Marcion as *nautēs*: Rhodon in Eusebius *HE* 5.13; as *nauclerus*, Tertullian *adv. Marcionem* passim. Christ and the fishermen, Matt. 4.18–22; Mk 1.16–20, affording at least two boats. Thomas' voyage to India, *Acta Thomae* 1.1ff. (2.2 pp. 100–4 Lipsius-Bonnet).

3 Acts 13.4–14.25. On St Paul's journeys in general, W. M. Ramsay, *St. Paul the Traveller and the Roman Citizen* (London, 1895) is still useful; and now Haenchen (1971) ad Acts 13–28 passim.

4 Acts 15.36–16.6.

5 Acts 16.8–12; 17.1, 10.

6 Acts 16.11–17.13.

7 Acts 17.14–18.23.

8 Acts 19.23–41.

9 Acts 20.16.

10 Acts 21.1–17.

11 Acts 19.22; 20.6f.

12 On the historical geography of Galilee, Freyne (1980); Vermes (1983) 42–57.

13 For the political and cultural aspect, Sherwin-White (1963) 120–43.

14 Matt. 11.20ff.

15 Mk 1.29.

16 Freyne (1980) 287–93.

17 On Galilee and the Gospels, Freyne (1980) 380.

18 On Mani's missionary activity, P. Brown, 'The diffusion of Manichaeism in the Roman Empire', *JRS* 59 (1969) 92–103; S. N. Lieu, *Manichaeism in the Later Roman Empire and Medieval China: A Historical Survey* (Manchester, 1985) 60–90.

19 W. Henning, 'Mani's last journey', *BSOAS* 10 (1942) 941–53.

20 Preface to the *Sabuhragan* dedicated to Shapur, cited apud al-Biruni, *Chronology* tr. Sachau; Lieu (1985) 60.

21 Keph. 154 (tr. J. Stevenson, *A New Eusebius* (London, 1957) 282); Lieu (1985) 61.

22 13941 + 14285 V/5 MMTKGI (546) 3.1 p. 36 (Lieu (1985) 64). R 12 (173) p. 26 (Lieu ibid.); M 2 R1 9–11, MM ii p. 301.

23 For the background of Ignatius' letters, W. R. Schoedel, *A Commentary on the Letters of Ignatius of Antioch* (Philadelphia, 1985) 10–15.

24 On pilgrims and tourists, no more easily separable than today, Casson (1974) 229–329 passim.

25 Lucian, *Philopseudes* 33f., 38.

26 See above p. 157f.

27 *VA* 6.35.

28 For an aspect of Apollonius' Indian journey, below p. 206f; for the Ethiopian episode, Anderson (1986) 215–20.

29 Giannini, *Paradoxographici graeci* (1966) 208; *VA* 4.13.

30 *VA* 4.13.

31 *Heroicus* p.41 Lannoy.

32 On Aristides' Egyptian journey, *Or.* 36. Unfortunately the loss of his notebooks prior to writing render this piece much less informative than it might otherwise have been.

33 On Pausanias, C. Habicht, *Pausanias' Guide to Ancient Greece*, (Cambridge, Mass., 1985).

34 Keph. I p. 11, lines 18–20 (Lieu (1985) 71).

35 Epiphanius, *Haer.* 66.1.8f.

36 On Julianus of Laodicea, C. P. Jones 'A Syrian at Lyon', *AJPh* 100 (1978A) 336–53; G. Anderson, 'Julianus of Laodicea, trader or rhetor?', *JHS* 102 (1982) 202.

37 *Ep. Apoll.* 3; 7.

38 Philostratus, *VA* 5.20.

39 Ibid. 1.20. For similar misunderstanding of Jesus Christ as slave-master of Thomas, *Acta Thomae* 1.2 (pp. 101f. Lipsius-Bonnet).

40 Mk 4.35–41; cf. Lk. 8.22–5.

41 Philostratus, *VA* 5.18; 3.23.

42 Aristides, *Or.* 48.12ff.

43 Acts 27.9f.

44 Acts 27.22f.

45 Lucian, *Peregrinus* 43.

46 Aulus Gellius, *NA* 19.1.

47 Dio *Or.* 36.1. Commentary by D. A. Russell, (Cambridge, 1992); see also Anderson (1993) 216–20.

48 Ibid. 22f. For the 'celestial dance' commonplace, Russell (1992).

49 Ibid. 39–61, with Russell (1992) 39, who is realistic about the numerous difficulties; but we cannot acquit Dio totally of some Iranian elements in the myth, or some coincidence or conflation with what he understood to be such.

50 Ibid. 25. See now G. Hedreen, 'The Cult of Achilles in the Euxine', *Hesperia* 60 (1991) 13–31.

11 REPRESENTATION:
THE HOLY MAN IN FICTION

1 On ancient fiction in general: B. E. Perry, *The Ancient Romances: A Literary-Historical Account of their Origins*, (Berkeley, 1967); Reardon (1971) 309–403; G. Anderson, *Ancient Fiction: The Novel in the Graeco-Roman World* (London, 1984). T. Hägg, *The Novel in Antiquity*, 2nd edn (Oxford, 1983) and N. Holzberg, *Der Antike Roman* (Munich, 1986) are popular accounts, cf. R. F. Hock, 'The Greek novel', in Aune (1988) 127–46. For Christian fiction, R. Söder, *Die Apokryphen Apostelgeschichten und die romanhafte Literatur der Antike* (Würzburg, 1932); Hägg (1983) 154–65; Averil Cameron, *Christianity and the Rhetoric of Empire* (1991) 89–119; note also Kee (1983) 252–89 ('Miracle as propaganda in pagan and Christian romances'). For a wider literary perspective on the image of the sage,

B. Fiore, 'The sage in select Hellenistic and Roman literary genres', in Gammie and Perdue (1990) 329–42.

2 Plutarch, *de defectu oraculorum* 421AB; *Itinerarium Egeriae* 20.5f.; Lucian, *Dionysus* 7.

3 Apuleius, *Metamorphoses* 7.27–7.28.2.

4 Ibid. 8.28.5f.; 30.5.

5 Commentary by Schwartz (1963); for the character of the work, Caster (1937), 315–34; G. Anderson, *Studies in Lucian's Comic Fiction* (Leiden, 1976b) 23–33.

6 *Philopseudes* 29–39.

7 Ibid. 34. On Pachrates, above p. 157f.

8 Petronius, *Satyrica* 60.8; 71.12 (with the commentaries of L. Friedlaender (Leipzig, 1906) and M. Smith (Oxford, 1975).

9 *Sat.* 44.16f.; 61.6–64.1.

10 *Sat.* 77.4; 29.5.

11 *Sat.* 76.10–77.4.

12 Perry (1964); above p. 158f.

13 *Acta Thomae* 2.17–24 (Lipsius-Bonnet 2.2 pp. 124–38). See also J. J. Collins, 'The sage in the Apocalyptic and Pseudepigraphic literature' in Gammie and Perdue (1990) 343–54.

14 W. Sundermann, *Mitteliranische Manichaische Texte Kirchengeschichtlichen Inhalts* (Berlin, 1981) 102ff.

15 Lane Fox (1986) 566f.

16 On the nature of the *Thomas-Acts*, Hennecke-Schneemelcher II, 428–41.

17 *Acta Thomae* 2.17; 3.30–5; 6.51–4; 7.62–7.

18 Ibid. 3.31ff. (serpent); 4.39f. (colt).

19 On the character of the *Pseudo-Clementines*, Perry (1967) 285–93; M. Edwards, 'The *Clementina*: a Christian response to the pagan novel', *CQ* n.s. 42 (1992) 459–74.

20 Lucian, *Icaromenippus* and *Necyomantia*.

21 For Calasiris, J. Winkler, 'The mendacity of Kalasiris and the narrative strategy of Heliodoros' *Aithiopika*', *YCS* 27 (1982) 93–158; M. F. Pinheiro, 'Calasiris' story and its narrative significance in the "*Aithiopika*" of Heliodoros', in H. Hofmann (ed.) *Groningen Colloqia on the Novel* 4 (Groningen, 1991) 69–83.

22 For the religious dimension of the *Aethiopica* as a whole, Reardon (1971) 385f., with the reservations of G. Anderson, *Eros Sophistes* (California, 1982) 33ff.

23 In particular *Aethiopica* 2.24.5–7.8.7.

24 Commentary on Book XI by J. Gwynn Griffiths (Leiden, 1975).

25 See above p. 127. But that is a very far cry from the assertion of Kee (1986) 95, that '[Apuleius'] story in the *Metamorphoses* . . . is almost certainly in large part autobiographical'(!). Kee does not distinguish an author's interest in magic from his character's enthusiasm for it (95f.).

26 *Met.* 9.27.

12 PRESTIGE:
THE ENHANCEMENT OF HOLINESS

1 Lucian, *Peregrinus* 27f. For the variety of strands in the future cult of Peregrinus, Schwartz (1963) 28. For the enhancement of holy men in general, P. Brown, *The Cult of Saints* (London and Chicago, 1981).

2 Athenagoras, *Legatio de Christianis* 26.

3 Lucian, *Peregrinus* 39f. For Lucian's proclivities to falsehood, cf. G. Anderson 'Lucian, a Sophist's Sophist', *YCS* 27 (1982) 69–74.

4 Athanasius, *Vita Antonii* 60 (tr. R. C. Gregg).

5 *Historia Monachorum* 22.7.

6 9.35–11.46 (Hennecke-Schneemelcher I, 185f.).

7 Vermes (1972) 29f.

8 Hanina and the snake, ibid. 34–7. For the intrusion of snake-handling in Christian tradition, Mk 16.18. For the rain-miracle, Fowden (1987); I have doubts only on the role of Julian the thaumaturge; rather than accept his late inclusion in the story, I suspect he himself would have been associated with the business at the time, whether present or not; such an event draws sacred propaganda, as did the accession of Vespasian.

9 Vermes (1972) 40f.

10 W. S. G. Green 'Palestinian holy men: charismatic leadership and rabbinic tradition', *ANRW* 2.19.2 (1979) 619–47.

11 Lk. 5.19; Mk 2.4.

12 Mk 6.48f; Matt. 7.24–7.

13 Lk. 6.20f.; Matt. 5.3, 6.

14 Lk. 5.35.

15 Matt. 15.14.

16 Matt. 7.18f.

17 Lk. 6.39; 6.43.

18 *P. Labib* pl. 87.5ff. (Hennecke-Schneemelcher I, 109).

19 *P. Oxy.* 1.9–14 recto (Hennecke-Schneemelcher ibid.).

20 Ibid. 11–22 verso at 11–17 (Hennecke-Schneemelcher 106f.); *P. Labib* pl. 86, 20–31 (Hennecke-Schneemelcher 107). A rather longer Coptic version expands the saying still further.

21 Jerome, Commentary on Matt. 12.13 (tr. R. McL. Wilson, Hennecke-Schneemelcher 147f.).

22 Commentary on Matt. 15.14/19 (Lat. 16ff.) (Hennecke-Schneemelcher 148f.).

23 Ibid. (Hennecke-Schneemelcher 149).

24 Neusner (1962) 115–20.

25 Jn 4.46–53.

26 Lk. 7.1–10; Matt. 8.5–13.

27 *HE* 7.18.

28 Athanasius, *Vita Antonii* 91 (tr. R. C. Gregg).

29 For the tradition surrounding Pachomius' death, Rousseau (1985) 184.

30 For relics and the religious tourist, E.D. Hunt (1982) 128–35.

31 *VA* 8.20.

32 *VA* 1.3.

NOTES

33 For an inscription on Apollonius in the Adana Museum, and probably of local Cilician provenance, Bowie (1978) 1687f.; Dielska (1986), 64–72.
34 *In Hieroclem 7.*
35 Ibid. 29.
36 Ibid. 25.
37 Ibid. 35.
38 For the Apollonian traditions, Petzke (1970); Dulière (1970).
39 *PG* 89.524D-525B; R. J. Penella, 'An unnoticed Testimony of Apollonius in Anastasius Sinaita', *Traditio* 34 (1978) 414f. Nock (1933) 129. For pertinent questions about the Younger Julianus' involvement in the rain-miracle, Fowden (1987) 90–4; though here the configuration of evidence either way is more difficult.
40 *VPS* 454.
41 *VPS* 455ff.
42 *VPS* 458f.

13 PROGRESS:
CONTINUITIES AND COMPARISONS

1 On the late pagan holy man, G. Fowden, 'The pagan holy man in late antique society', *JHS* 102 (1982) 33–59. Geffcken (1929) is still important. On Christian asceticism, A. Vööbus, *A History of Asceticism in the Syrian Orient* (2 vols, Louvain, 1958–60); Brown (1971) 83–91 (Syria); on Egypt, Rousseau (1985) 1–36 passim.
2 On Eunapius, above p. 195f.
3 Nor is their superstition merely a matter of Eunapius' perspective; on the case of Libanius, cf. *Or.* 1.244–50, with C. Bonner, 'Witchcraft in the lecture room of Libanius', *TAPhA* 63 (1932) 34ff.
4 *VPS* 464f.
5 On Aedesius and his pupils, R. J. Penella *Greek Philosophers and Sophists in the Fourth Century AD* (Leeds, 1990) 63–78.
6 Above p. 68f.
7 Eunapius, *VPS* 466.
8 Ibid.
9 474f.
10 Ibid. 476f.
11 Ibid. 478–81.
12 Cf. above p. 137.
13 Above p. 66f.
14 Migne *PG* 26 coll. 835–976.
15 Athanasius, *Vita Antonii* 16–43 (tr. R. C. Gregg).
16 Ibid. 69.
17 Ibid., e.g., 61–4 (healing); 84 (judges).
18 Ibid. 61f.; 62ff.; 74–80; 84; 81.
19 Theodoretus *PG* 82 col. 1404C.
20 *Historia Monachorum in Aegypto*, ed. A. J. Festugière, *Subsidia Hagiographica* 34 (Brussels, 1961) 1.4.
21 Ibid. 1.13ff.

22 Ibid. 1.1.
23 Ibid. 1.2.
24 Ibid. 1.4–9.
25 Ibid. 1.12, 16.
26 On Martin and Sulpicius Severus, C. Stancliffe, *St. Martin and his Hagiographer: History and Miracle in Sulpicius Severus* (Oxford, 1983).
27 Sulpicius Severus, *Vita Martini* 9f.
28 Ibid. 12.
29 Ibid. 13.
30 *Carm.* 2.13.
31 *Vita S. Danieli* 14f., 18 (following the example of Antony's struggle with demons, 14); *Vita Gregorii, PG* 46.913D–920A; Lucian, *Philopseudes* 31.
32 *Vita S. Danieli* 65; Lucian, *Alexander* 27.
33 E.g., *Vita Theodori Sykeotae* 35, 43; 52.
34 E.g., defence of demons, *Vita S. Danieli* 18; defeat of a prostitute on a trumped-up charge, 39; column survives swaying in a storm, 47.
35 For Apollonius' *Nachleben*, above p. 193f.
36 *Vita Theodori* 36.
37 E.g., Lucian, *Philopseudes* 34 (Pancrates).
38 *Vita Theodori* 19.
39 Brown (1971) 92.
40 Ibid. n.143, citing *VA* 1.15.
41 Brown (1971) 96; Lucian, *Alexander* 8.
42 Heliodorus 3.5.4ff.; 4.5.1–4.
43 B. Spooner, 'The evil eye in the Middle East', in C. Maloney (ed.) *The Evil Eye* (New York, 1976) 76–84.
44 So Funk and Wagnall, *Standard Dictionary of Folklore, Mythology and Legend* (London, 1975) ed. M. Leach, s.v.
45 Heliodorus 4.7.13.
46 For others, J. Winkler (1982).
47 Philostratus *VA* 3.15, 17.
48 C. Harper, 'The Witches' flying ointment', *Folklore* 88 (1977) 105f.; Apuleius, *Met.* 3.21.4.
49 Harper (1977) 105.
50 J. Morier, *The Life of Hajji Baba of Ispahan* (London, 1895) vol. 2 pp. 102ff.
51 Lucian, *Alexander* 24.
52 Dodds (1951) 139.
53 Ibid.
54 On Shamanism in general, M. Eliade, *Shamanism, Archaic Techniques of Ecstasy* (Paris, 1951; E.T. Princeton, 1972).
55 On whom see J. P. D. Bolton, *Aristeas of Proconnesus* (Oxford, 1962) 156ff., 164f.
56 Bolton (1962).
57 For the site, Jones (1986) 134.
58 Cf. *Philostratus, VA* 1.4.
59 Ibid. 1.13.

60 Cf. Lk. 9.28–36.
61 For a claim for Apollonius, Philostratus *VA* 8.25.
62 See, e.g., Pagels (1980) 70–101 passim.
63 Lucian, *Alexander* 12.
64 Philostratus, *VA* 3.17.
65 17.714.
66 *Religion and the Decline of Magic: Studies in Popular Beliefs in Sixteenth and Seventeenth Century England* (London, 1971).
67 For our theme, see especially 'Cunning men and popular magic', Thomas (1971) 212–52.
68 Thomas (1971) 381–93; 638–52.
69 Ibid. 417.
70 Ibid. 414f.
71 For Roman examples, above pp. 154ff; cf. Thomas (1971) 405–9 on political predictions.
72 Lactantius, *de Mortibus Persecutorum* 11.7.
73 Mk 3.23–30; Matt. 12.25–37.
74 Thomas (1971) 282f.
75 *Alexander* 9 with Harmon ad loc.
76 Betz (1986) passim.
77 (1971) 211.
78 Ibid. 213.
79 Cf. Thomas (1971) 212.
80 Cf. Thomas (1971) 247.
81 Ibid. 220.
82 Ibid. 227f.
83 Ibid. 228.
84 Cf. Thomas (1971) 244, after Marc Bloch.
85 Ibid. 231.
86 *Philopseudes* 10 (with the preceding discussion of 'sympathetic' cures, 7ff.); *Alexander* 36.
87 Idries Shah, *Tales of the Dervishes: Teaching-stories of the Sufi masters over the past thousand years* (London, 1967) 56.
88 Ibid. 103–6.
89 *Legends of the Sufis: Selected Anecdotes from the Work Entitled The Acts of the Adepts*, tr. J. W. Redhouse, 3rd edn (London, 1976) 86f.
90 Ibid. 74.
91 Qur'an 18.59–81.
92 Redhouse (1976) 83f.; 85.
93 Matt. 17.1–8; Mk 9.2–8; Lk. 9.28–36.
94 *The Subtle Ruse, The Book of Wisdom and Guile*, tr. R. R. Khawam (London, 1980) 326ff.
95 Ibid. 329f.
96 Ibid. 330f.
97 Ibid. 334.
98 *Witchcraft, Oracles and Magic among the Azande*, abridged edn (Oxford, 1976).
99 E.g., *Alexander* 19–24,
100 *Magic and the Millenium* (London, 1973).

101 Ibid. 136–41.
102 Ibid. 142.
103 Ibid. 500.

APPENDIX:
JESUS THE JEW; JESUS THE MAGICIAN

1 The basic doxographical surveys of the New Testament and pre-Constantinian Christianity in *ANRW* 23 alone run to six volumes of approaching 5,000 pages.
2 For the Jewish dimension in a Christian context prior to Vermes, M. Black, *An Aramaic Approach to the Gospels*, 3rd edn (Oxford, 1967).
3 Vermes (1983) 69–79.
4 Ibid. 129–213.
5 Ibid. 42–82.
6 For Honi, Green (1979).
7 Above p. 140.
8 Vermes (1983) 153f.
9 Ibid. 200; 160–91.
10 Lk. 22.54–61.
11 Smith (1978).
12 Smith (1978) p. 146. The idea of magical practice is not, however, a new one: for previous contributions, cf. Geller (1977) 141–55 with previous bibliography.
13 Smith (1978) 96–104; 125f.; 24.
14 As suggested as early as the encounters between apostles and Simon Magus, Acts 8.13, 19–24.
15 Origen, *contra Celsum* 1.28.
16 Matt. 2.13–21; Smith (1978) 48.
17 Lk. 2.21–4.

SELECT BIBLIOGRAPHY

Abt, A. (1908): *Die Apologie des Apuleius von Madaura und die antike Zauberei: Beiträge zur Erläuterung der Schrift de magia* (Giessen)

Alderink, L. J. (1989): 'The Eleusinian Mysteries in Roman Imperial times', *ANRW* 2.18.2, 1457–98

Anderson, G. (1976A): *Lucian: Theme and Variation in the Second Sophistic* (Leiden)

—— (1976B): *Studies in Lucian's Comic Fiction* (Leiden)

—— (1982): 'Julian of Laodicea, trader or rhetor?', *JHS* 102, 202

—— (1986): *Philostratus: Biography and Belles-Lettres in the Third Century AD*, (London)

—— (1989): 'The *Pepaideumenos* in action: sophists and their outlook in the early Roman Empire', *ANRW* 2.33.1, 79–208

—— (1993): *The Second Sophistic: A Cultural Phenomenon in the Early Roman Empire* (London)

Armstrong, A. H. (1955): 'Was Plotinus a magician?', *Phronesis* 1, 73–9

—— (ed.) (1986): *Classical Mediterranean Spirituality: Egyptian, Greek, Roman* (New York,)

Aune, D. E. (1980): 'Magic in early Christianity', *ANRW* 2.23.2, 1507–57

—— (ed.) (1983): *Prophecy in Early Christianity and the Ancient Mediterranean World* (Grand Rapids, Michigan)

—— (1988): *Graeco-Roman Literature and the New Testament* (Atlanta)

Barigazzi, A. (1966): *Favorino di Arelate: Opere* (Florence)

Barnes, T. D. (1985): *Tertullian: A Historical and Literary Study*, 2nd edn (Oxford)

Baur, F. C. (1832): 'Apollonius von Tyana und Christus', *Tübinger Zeitschrift für Theologie* 4, 111ff.

Behr, C. (1968): *Aelius Aristides and the Sacred Tales* (The Hague)

Bell, H. I. (1924): *Cults and Creeds in Graeco-Roman Egypt* (Oxford)

Bell, H. I., Nock, A. D. and Thompson, H. (1933): *Magical Texts from a Bilingual Papyrus in the British Museum* (Oxford)

Belloni, L. (1980): 'Aspetti dell'antica sophia in Apollonio di Tiana', *Aevum* 54, 140–9

Berg, B. (1976): 'Dandamis: an early Christian portrait of Indian asceticism', *C&M* 31, 269–305

Berthelot, M. and Ruelle, C. E. (1988): *Collection des anciens alchimistes grecs* (Paris)

Betz, H. D. (1961): *Lukian von Samosata und das Neue Testament* (Berlin)

—— (1980): 'Fragments from a catabasis ritual in a Greek magical papyrus', *HR* 19, 287–95

—— (1986): *The Greek Magical Papyri in Translation, including the Demotic Spells* (Chicago)

Betz, O. (1982): 'Probleme des prozesses Jesu', *ANRW* 2.25.1, 565–647

Bickerman, E. J. (1986): *Studies in Jewish and Christian History* 3

Bieler, L. (1935/6): *Theios Anēr: Das Bild des 'Göttlichen Menschen' in spätantike und frühchristentum* (Vienna, repr. Darmstadt, 1967)

Blackburn, B. (1991): *The Theios Anēr and the Markan Miracle Tradition* (Tübingen)

Blau, L. (1898): *Das Altjüdische Zauberwesen* (Strassburg)

Bolton, J. P. D. (1962): *Aristeas of Proconessus* (Oxford)

Bonner, C. (1950): *Studies in Magical Amulets, chiefly Graeco-Egyptian* (Ann Arbor)

Bowersock, G. W. (1969): *Greek Sophists in the Roman Empire* (Oxford)

Bowie, E. L. (1978): 'Apollonius of Tyana: tradition and reality', *ANRW* 2.16.2, 1652–99

Bowman, A. J. (1950–2): 'A lost work of Apollonius of Tyana', *Proceedings of the Glasgow Oriental Society* 14, 1–10

Brenk, F. E. (1986): 'In the light of the moon: demonology in the early Imperial period', *ANRW* 2.16.3, 2068–145

Brock, S. (1973): 'Early Syrian asceticism', *Numen*, 20, 1–19 (= *Syriac Perspectives in Late Antiquity* (London, 1984) Paper 1

Brown, P. R. L. (1970): 'Sorcery, demons and the rise of Christianity from late Antiquity into the Middle Ages' in M. Douglas, (ed.), *Witchcraft Confessions and Accusations (Association of Social Anthropologists Monographs* 9), 17–45

—— (1971): 'The rise and function of the holy man in late Antiquity', *JRS* 61, 80–101

—— (1969): 'The diffusion of Manichaeism in the Roman Empire', *JRS* 59, 92–103

—— (1972): *Religion and Society in the Age of St. Augustine* (London)

—— (1981): *The Cult of the Saints* (Chicago)

—— (1982): *Society and the Holy in Late Antiquity* (London)

—— (1988): *The Body and Society* (New York)

Brunt, P. (1973): 'Aspects of the social thought of Dio Chrystostom and the Stoics', *PCPS* n.s. 19, 9–34

Burkert, W. (1972): *Lore and Science in Ancient Pythagoreanism* (Cambridge, Mass.)

Casson, L. (1974): *Travel in the Ancient World* (London)

Caster, M. (1937): *Lucien et la pensée religieuse de son temps* (Paris)

—— (1938): *Etudes sur Alexandre ou le Faux-Prophète de Lucien* (Paris)

Charlesworth, J. H. (1987): 'Jewish interest in astrology during the Hellenistic and Roman period', *ANRW* 2.20.2, 926–50

Charpentier, J. (1934): 'The Indian travels of Apollonius of Tyana', *Skrifter utgivna av. K. Humanistika Vetenskaps-Samfundet i Uppsala* 29.3 (Uppsala) 1–66

Clinton, K. (1989): 'The Eleusinian Mysteries: Roman initiates and benefactors, second century BC to AD 267', *ANRW* 2.18.2, 1499–539

Collins, A. Y. (1984): 'Numerical symbolism in Jewish and early Christian apocalyptic literature', *ANRW* 2.21.2, 1221–87

Conley, Th. M. (1983): 'Philo's rhetoric: argumentation and style', *ANRW* 2.21.1, 343–71

Cox, P. (1983): *Biography in Late Antiquity: A Quest for the Holy Man* (Berkeley)

Cramer, F. H. (1954): *Astrology in Roman Law and Politics* (Philadelphia)

Cumont, F. (1929): *Les religions orientales dans le paganisme romain*, 4th edn (Paris)

Dam, R. van (1982): 'Hagiography and history: the life of Gregory Thaumaturgus', *Classical Antiquity* 1, 272–308

Derchain, P. and Hubaux, J. (1953): 'Vespasien au Serapeium', *Latomus* 12, 38–52

Dielska, M. (1986): *Apollonius of Tyana in Legend and History* (Rome)

Dihle, A. (1956): *Studien zur griechischen Biographie* (Göttingen)

—— (1964): 'The conception of India in Hellenistic and Roman literature', *PCPS* 10, 15–23

Dill, S. (1905): *Roman Society from Nero to Marcus Aurelius* (London)

Dodds, E. R. (1947): 'Theurgy and its relationship to Neoplatonism', *JHS* 67

—— (1951): *The Greeks and the Irrational* (Berkeley)

—— (1968): *Pagan and Christian in an Age of Anxiety: Some Aspects of Religious Experience from Marcus Aurelius to Constantine* (Cambridge)

Drivjers, H. (1966): *Bardaisan of Edessa* (Assen)

Dudley, D. R. (1937): *A History of Cynicism from Diogenes to the sixth century AD* (London)

Dulière, W. L. (1970): 'Protection permanente contre des animaux nuisibles assurée par Apollonius de Tyane dans Byzance et Antioche: évolution de son mythe', *BZ* 63, 247–77.

Edelstein, E. J. and L. (1945): *Asclepius*, 2 vols (Baltimore)

Edwards, M. (1989): 'Satire and verisimilitude: Christianity in Lucian's *Peregrinus*', *Historia* 38, 89–98

Eitrem, S. (1929): 'Philostrats *Heroikos*', *SO* 8, 1–56

Ellis, E. E. (1975): 'Paul and his opponents: trends in research' in Neusner (1975.1) 264–98

Faraone, C. A. and Obbink, D. (eds) (1991): *Magika Hiera: Ancient Greek Magic and Religion* (New York)

Fairweather, J. A. (1974): 'Fiction in the biographies of ancient writers', *AS* 5, 231–75

Festugière, A. J. (1942/3): 'Trois rencontres entre la Grèce et l'Inde', *RHR* 125, 35–57

—— (1975): *La Clef des Songes* (Paris)

—— (1981): *La révélation d'Hermès Trismegiste*, 3rd edn, 4 vols (Paris)

Flinterman, J.-J. (1993): *Politiek, Paideia, & Pythagorisme, Griekse identiteit, voorstellingen rond de verhouding tussen filosofen en alleenheersers en politieke ideeën in de Vita Apolloniia van Philostratus* (Groningen) in Dutch, with English summary, 307–21

Foerster, R. (1893): *Scriptores Physiognomonici Graeci et Latini*, 2 vols (Leipzig)

Foerster, W. (1972): *Gnōsis: A Selection of Gnostic Texts*, tr. R. McL. Wilson, 2 vols (Oxford)

Fowden, G. (1982): 'The pagan holy man in late antique society', *JHS* 102, 33–59

—— (1986): *The Egyptian Hermes: A Historical Approach to the Late Pagan Mind* (Cambridge)

—— (1987): 'Pagan versions of the rain miracle of AD 172', *Historia* 36.1, 83–95

Frede, M. (1989): 'Chaeremon der Stoiker', *ANRW* 2.36.3, 2067–103

Frend, W. H. C. (1976): *Religion Popular and Unpopular in the Early Christian Centuries* (London)

—— (1984): *The Rise of Christianity* (London)

Freyne, S. (1980): *Galilee from Alexander the Great to Hadrian* (Delaware)

Funk, K. (1907): 'Untersuchungen über die Lucianische *Vita Demonactis*', *Philologus* Suppl. 10, 558–674

Gager, J. G. (1972): *Moses in Graeco-Roman Paganism* (Nashville)

—— (ed.) (1992): *Curse Tablets and Binding Spells from the Ancient World* (New York)

Gammie, J. G. and Perdue, L. S. (eds) (1990): *The Sage in Israel and the Ancient Near East* (Winona Lake)

Geffcken, J. (1929): *Der Ausgang des griechisch-römischen Heidentums*, 2nd edn (Heidelberg), tr. with suppl. by S. MacCormack as *The Last Days of Graeco-Roman Paganism* (Amsterdam, 1978)

Geller, M. J. (1977): 'Jesus' theurgic powers: parallels in the Talmud and incantation bowls', *JJS* 28, 141–55

Georgi, V. (1964): *The Opponents of St. Paul in Second Corinthians* (E.T. Edinburgh, 1987)

Ginzberg, L. (1909–38): *The Legends of the Jews*, 7 vols (Philadelphia)

Gnuse, R. (1990): 'The Jewish dream interpreter', *Journal for the Study of the Pseudepigrapha* 7, 29–53

Goodman, M. (1987): *The Ruling Class of Judaea: The Origins of the Jewish Revolt against Rome AD 66–70* (Cambridge)

Goulet-Cazé, M.-O. (1990): 'Le cynisme à l'époque Impériale', *ANRW* 2.36.4, 2720–833

Green, W. S. G. (1979): 'Palestinian holy men: charismatic leadership and rabbinic tradition', *ANRW* 2.19.2, 619–47

Gundel, W. and H. G. (1966): *Astrologoumena. Die astrologischen Literatur in der Antike und ihre Geschichte*, (Wiesbaden)

Haenchen, E. (1971): *The Acts of the Apostles: A Commentary*, 14th edn rev. and tr. R. McL. Wilson (Oxford)

Hammerstädt, J. (1990): 'Der Kyniker Oenomaus von Gadara', *ANRW* 2.36.4, 2834–65

Hanson, J. S. (1980): 'Dreams and visions in the Graeco-Roman world and early Christianity', *ANRW* 2.23.2, 1395–1427

Helgeland, J. (1979): 'Christians and the Roman army from Marcus Aurelius to Constantine', *ANRW* 2.23.1, 724–834

Hempel, J. (1920): *Untersuchungen zur Ueberlieferung von Apollonius von Tyana* (Leipzig)

Hengel, M. (1971): *Acts and the History of Earliest Christianity* (London)

Hennecke, E. (1974): *New Testament Apocrypha*, 2 vols ed. W. Schneemelcher, tr. E. Best et al. (London)

Henrichs, A. (1968): 'Vespasian's visit to Alexandria', *ZPE* 3, 51–80

—— (1973): 'Mani and the Babylonian baptists: a historical confrontation', *HSCP* 77, 23–59

—— (1979): 'The Cologne Mani-Codex reconsidered', *HSCP* 83, 339–67

Henrichs, A. and Koenen, L. (1970): 'Ein griechischer Mani-Codex', *ZPE* 5.2, 97–216

Hoerig, M. (1984): 'Dea Syria – Atargatis', *ANRW* 2.17.3, 1536–81

Holladay, C. (1977): *Theios Anēr in Hellenistic Judaism* (Missoula)

Hopfner, T. (1921): *Griechisch-aegyptischer Offenbarungzauber*, 2 vols, revised 1924 (Leipzig)

—— (1931): 'Apollonius von Tyana und Philostratos', *Seminarium Kondakovianum* 4, 135–64

—— (1934): 'Die Brachmanen Indiens und die Gymnosophisten Aegyptens in der Apolloniosbiographie des Philostratos', *Archiv Orientalni* 6, 58–67

Horst, P. W. van der (1989): 'The altar of the "unknown God" in Athens (Acts 17.23) and the cult of "unknown gods" in the Hellenistic and Roman periods, *ANRW* 2.18.2, 1426–56

Hull, J. M. (1974): *Hellenistic Magic and the Synoptic Tradition* (London)

Hunt, E. D. (1984): *Holy Land Pilgrimage in the Late Roman Empire, AD 312–460* (Oxford)

Isser, S. (1975): 'Dositheus, Jesus, and a Moses aretalogy' in Neusner (1975.4) 167–89

Jaeger, W. (1961): *Early Christianity and Greek Paideia* (Cambridge, Mass.)

Jones, C. P. (1978): *The Roman World of Dio Chrysostom* (Cambridge, Mass. and London)

—— (1980): 'An epigram of Apollonius of Tyana', *JHS* 100, 190–4

—— (1982): 'A martyria for Apollonius of Tyana', *Chiron* 12, 137–44

—— (1986): *Culture and Society in Lucian* (Cambridge, Mass.)

Juttner, H. (1898): *De Polemonis rhetoris vita operibus arte* (Breslau), repr. Hildesheim 1967

Kee, H. C. (1977): *Community of the New Age: Studies in Mark's Gospel* (London)

—— (1983): *Miracle in the Early Christian World: A Study in Socio-Historical Method* (New Haven and London)

—— (1986): *Medicine, Miracle and Magic in New Testament Times* (Cambridge)

—— (1990): *Good News to the Ends of the Earth: The Theology of Acts* (London and Philadelphia)

Kelly, J. N. D. (1975): *Jerome: His Life, Writings, and Controversies* (London)

Kiefer, O. (1929): *Aretalogische Studien* (Freiburg)

Kindstrand, J. F. (1980): 'Demetrius the Cynic', *Philologus* 124, 83–98

—— (1979/80): 'Sostratus–Hercules–Agathion: the rise of a legend', *Annales Societatis Litterarum Humanarum Upsalienis*, 59–79

Kolenkow, A. B. (1980): 'Relationships between miracle and prophecy in the Graeco-Roman world and early Christianity', *ANRW* 2.23.2, 1470–506

Koster, R. E. (1990): 'Ephesus as a religious center under the Principate I. Paganism before Constantine', *ANRW* 2.18.3, 1661–728

Kraemer, R. S. (1992): *Her Share of the Blessings: Women's Religions Among Pagans, Jews, and Christians in the Greco-Roman World* (New York)

Labriolle, P. de (1912): *La Crise Montaniste* (Paris)

—— (1950): *La réaction paienne. Etude sur la polemique antichrétienne du Ier au VIe siècle* (Paris)

Lane Fox, R. (1986): *Pagans and Christians* (Harmondsworth)

—— (1991): *The Unauthorized Version: Truth and Fiction in the Bible* (London)

Lenz, F. (1964): 'Die Selbstverteidigung eines politischen Angeklagten, Untersuchungen zu der Rede des Apollonios von Tyana bei Philostratos', *Altertum* 10, 95–110

Levin, S. (1988): 'The early history of Christianity, in light of the "Secret Gospel" of Mark', *ANRW* 2.25.6, 4370–92

Levy, M. I. (1926): *Recherches sur les sources de la légende de Pythagore* (Paris).

—— (1927): *La Légende de Pythagore de Grèce en Palestine* (Paris)

Liebeschuetz, J. H. W. G. (1972): *Antioch: City and Imperial Administration in the later Roman Empire* (Oxford)

—— (1979): *Continuity and Change in Roman Religion* (Oxford)

Lietzmann, H. (1908): *Das Leben des Heiligen Symeon Stylites* (Leipzig)

Lieu, J., North, J., and Rajak, T. (eds) (1992): *Jews Among Pagans and Christians* (London)

Lieu, S. N. C. (1985): *Manichaeism in the later Roman Empire and Medieval China: A Historical Survey* (Manchester)

Lipsius, A. and Bonnet, G. (1891–1903): *Acta Apostolorum Apocrypha*, 2 vols (Berlin-Leipzig)

Lo Cascio, F. (1974): *La forma letteraria della Vita di Apollonio Tianeo* (Palermo)

—— (1978): *Sulla autenticità delle epistole di Apollonio Tianeo* (Palermo)

Long, A. A. (1986): 'Epicureans and Stoics' in Armstrong, 135–53

Luck, G. (1985): *Arcana Mundi: Magic and the Occult in the Greek and Roman Worlds* (Baltimore)

Lutz, C. E. (1947): 'Musonius Rufus, the Roman Socrates', *YCS* 10, 3–147

Macmullen, R. (1966): *Enemies of the Roman Order: Treason, Unrest and Alienation in the Empire* (Cambridge, Mass.).

—— (1981): *Paganism in the Roman Empire* (New Haven)

—— (1984): *Christianizing the Roman Empire* AD 100–400 (New Haven)

Magie, D. (1950): *Roman Rule in Asia Minor*, 2 vols (Princeton)

Mantero, T. (1966): *Richerche sull' Heroikos di Filostrato* (Genoa)

Meeks, W. A. (1983): *The First Urban Christians: The Social World of the Apostle Paul* (New Haven)

Mesk, J. (1898): 'Ein unedierte Tract *peri lithōn*', *WS* 20, 309–21

—— (1921): 'Die Damisquelle des Philostratos in der Biographie des Apollonios von Tyana', *WS* 49, 121–38.

Meyer, E. (1917): 'Apollonius von Tyana und die Biographie des Philostratos', *Hermes* 52, 371–424 (= *Kleine Schriften* 2 (Halle 1924) 131–91)

Millar, F. G. B. (1971): 'Paul of Samosata, Zenobia and Aurelian: the Church, local culture and political allegiance in third-century Syria', *JRS* 61, 1–17

—— (1977): *The Emperor in the Roman World* (London)

—— (1981): *The Roman Empire and its Neighbours*, 2nd edn (London)

—— (1987): 'Empire, community and culture in the Roman Near East: Greeks, Syrians, Jews and Arabs', *JJS* 38, 143–64

Miller, J. (1892): 'Die Beziehungen der *Vita Apollonii* des Philostratos sur Pythagorassage', *Philologus* 51, 137–45

—— (1892): 'Zur Frage nach der Persönlichkeit des Apollonios von Tyana', *Philologus* 51, 581–4

—— (1907): 'Die Damispapiere in Philostratos Apolloniosbiographie', *Philologus* 66, 511–25

Miller, P. (1986): 'In praise of nonsense', in Armstrong, 481–505

Moehring, H. R. (1984): 'Joseph Ben Matthia and Flavius Josephus: the Jewish prophet and Roman historian', *ANRW* 2.21.2, 864–944

Momigliano, A. (1975): *Alien Wisdom: The Limits of Hellenization* (Cambridge)

—— (1987): *On Pagans, Jews, and Christians* (Middletown, Conn.)

Moles, J. L. (1979): 'The career and conversion of Dio Chrysostom', *JHS* 99, 79–100

Musurillo, H. (1954): *The Acts of the Pagan Martyrs* (Oxford)

Neusner, J. (1962): *A Life of Rabban Yohanan ben Zakkai Ca. 1–80 CE* (Leiden)

—— (ed.) (1975): *Christianity, Judaism and Other Graeco-Roman Cults: Studies for Morton Smith at Sixty 1–4* (Leiden)

—— (1979): 'The formation of rabbinic Judaism: Yavneh (Jamnia) from AD 70 to 100', *ANRW* 2.19.2, 3–42

Nilsson, M. (1960): 'Die Religion in den griechischen Zauberpapyri' in *Opuscula Selecta* 3 (Lund), 129–66

—— (1961): *Geschichte der griechischen Religion*, 2 vols (Munich) revised 1967

Nock A. D. (1933): *Conversion: The Old and the New in Religion from Alexander the Great to Augustine of Hippo* (Oxford)

—— (1933): 'Paul and the magus' in Jackson and Lake, *The Beginnings of Christianity*, 164–88 (= Nock 1972.1, 308–30)

—— (1934): 'A vision of Mandoulis Aiōn', *HTR* 27, 53–104 (= Nock 1972.1, 357–400)

—— (1972): *Essays on Religion in the Ancient World*, ed. Z. Stewart, 2 vols (Oxford)

Norden, E. (1898): *Die Antike Kunstprosa vom VI Jahrhundert v. Chr. bis in die Zeit der Renaissance* (Leipzig)

—— (1913): *Agnostos Theos: Untersuchungen zur Formengeschichte religiöser Rede* (Berlin)

Norris, F. W. (1990): 'Antioch-on-the-Orontes as a Religious Center, I: Paganism before Constantine', *ANRW* 2.18.4, 2322–79

Oliver, J. H. (1970): 'Marcus Aurelius: aspects of civic and cultural policy in the East', *Hesperia* suppl. 13

Pack, R. A. (1946): 'The volatilization of Peregrinus Proteus', *AJPh* 67, 334–45

—— (1955): 'Artemidorus and his waking world', *TAPhA* 86, 280–90

Pagels, E. (1980): The Gnostic Gospels (London)

Palm, J. (1976): *Om Filostratos och hans Apollonios-Biografi* (Uppsala)

Parke, H. W. (1985): *The Oracles of Apollo in Asia Minor* (London)

Pearcy, L. T. (1988): 'Theme, dream, and narrative: reading the sacred tales of Aelius Aristides', *TAPhA* 118, 377–91

Pearson, B. A. (1983): 'Philo and Gnosticism', *ANRW* 2.21.1, 295–342

Penella, R. J. (1975): 'An unpublished letter of Apollnius of Tyana to the Sardians', *HSCP* 79, 305–11

—— (1978): 'An overlooked story about Apollonius of Tyana in Anastasius Sinaita', *Traditio* 34, 414f.

—— (1979): *The Letters of Apollonius of Tyana: A Critical Text with Prolegomena, Translation and Commentary* (Leyden)

Perry, B. E. (1964): *Secundus the Silent Philosopher* (Ithaca , N.Y.)

Petzke, G. (1970): *Die Traditionen über Apollonius von Tyana und das Neue Testament* (Leiden)

Place, E. des (1984): 'Les oracles chaldaiques', *ANRW* 2.17.4, 2299–335

Potter, D. S. (1990): *Prophecy and History in the Crisis of the Roman Empire: A Historical Commentary on the Thirteenth Sibylline Oracle* (Oxford)

Price, S. R. F. (1984): *Rituals and Power: The Roman Imperial Cult in Asia Minor* (Cambridge)

Priessnig, A. (1929): 'Die literarische Form der spätantiken Philosophenromane', *BZ* 30, 23–30

Rajak, T. (1983): *Josephus: The Historian and his Society* (London)

Rawson, E. D. (1982): 'The life and death of Asclepiades of Bithynia', *CQ* 32, 358–70

—— (1985): *Intellectual life in the Late Roman Republic* (London)

Raynor, D. H. (1984): 'Moeragenes and Philostratus: two views of Apollonius of Tyana', *CQ* 34, 222–6

Reardon, B. P. (1971): *Courants littéraires grecs des IIe et IIIe siècles après J.-C.* (Paris)

Redhouse, J. W. (tr.) (1976): *Legends of the Sufis: Selected Anecdotes from the work entitled The Acts of the Adepts*, 3rd edn (London)

Reitzenstein, R. (1906): *Hellenistische Wundererzählungen* (Leipzig) repr. Stuttgart, 1963)

—— (1913): 'Die Areopagrede des Apostels Paulus', *NJKA* 31, 393–422

Riaud, J. (1987): 'Les Thérapeutes d'Alexandrie dans la tradition et dans la recherche critique jusqu'aux découvertes de Qumran', *ANRW* 2.20.2, 1189–1295

Rohde, E. (1871): 'Die Quellendes Iamblichus in seiner Biographie des Pythagoras', *RhM* 26, 554–576; ibid. 27 (1872), 23–61 (= *Kleine Schriften*, Tübingen 1901) vol. 2 102ff.)

Rose, V. (1874): 'Damigeron, *De Lapidibus*', *Hermes* 9, 471–91

Rousseau, (1978): *Ascetics, Authority and the Church in the Age of Jerome and Cassian* (Oxford)

—— (1985): *Pachomius, the Making of a Community in Fourth-Century Egypt* (Berkeley)

Russell, D. A. (1972): *Plutarch* (London)

—— (1990): 'Aelius Aristides and the Prose Hymn' in D. A. Russell (ed.) *Antonine Literature* (Oxford), 199–219

Saffrey, H. D. (1986): 'The piety and prayers of ordinary men and women in late Antiquity', in Armstrong, 195–213

Scarborough, J. (1991): 'The pharmacology of sacred plants, herbs, and roots' in Faraone and Obbink, 138–74

Schuerer, E. (1979–87): *The History of the Jewish People in the Age of Jesus Christ*, rev. and ed. G. Vermes and F. G. B. Millar, 5 vols (Edinburgh)

Schwartz, J. (1963): *Lucien de Samosate, Philopseudès et de Morte Peregrini avec introduction et commentaire* (Paris)

Sedlar, J. W. (1980): *India and the Greek World: A Study in the Transmission of Greek Culture* (New Jersey)

Segal, J. B. (1970): *Edessa, the Blessed City* (Oxford)

Segal, A. F. (1980): 'Heavenly ascent in Hellenistic Judaism, early Christianity and their environment', *ANRW* 2.23.2, 1333–94

Settis, S. (1972): 'Severo Alessandro e i suoi lari', *Athenaeum* 50, 237–51

Sherwin-White, A. N. (1963): *Roman Society and Roman Law in the New Testament* (Oxford)

—— (1966): *The Letters of Pliny* (Oxford)

Smith, J. Z.: 'Good News is no news: aretalogy and Gospel' in Neusner (1975.1) 21–38

—— (1978): 'Towards interpreting demonic powers in Hellenistic and Roman Antiquity', *ANRW* 2.16.1, 425–39

Smith, M. (1971): 'Prolegomena to a discussion of aretalogies, divine men, the gospels and Jesus', *JBL* 90, 174–99

—— (1973): *Clement of Alexandria and a Secret Gospel of Mark* (Cambridge, Mass.)

—— (1978): *Jesus the Magician* (London)

Smith, V. A. (1914): 'The Indian travels of Apollonius of Tyana', *ZDMG* 68, 329–44

Soeder, R. (1932): *Die apokryphen Apostelgeschichten und die romanhafte Literatur der Antike* (Würzburg)

Speyer, W. (1971): *Die literarische Fälschung im heidnischen und christlichen Altertum, Ein Versuch ihrer Deutung* (Munich)

—— (1974): 'Zum Bild des Apollonios von Tyana bei Heiden und Christen', *JAC* 17, 47–63

Stancliffe, C. (1983): *St. Martin and his Hagiographer: History and Miracle in Sulpicius Severus* (Oxford)

Syme, R. (1980): *Some Arval Brethren* (Oxford)

Tajra, H. W. (1989): *The Trial of St. Paul: A Juridical Exegesis of the Second Half of the Acts of the Apostles* (Tübingen)

Talbert, C. H. (1978): 'Biographies of philosophers and rulers as instruments of religious propaganda in Mediterranean Antiquity', *ANRW* 2.16.2, 1619–51

Thomas, K. (1971): *Religion and the Decline of Magic: Studies in Popular Beliefs in Sixteenth and Seventeenth Century England* (London)

Tiede, D. L. (1972): *The Charismatic Figure as Miracle-Worker* (Missoula, Montana)

—— (1984): 'Religious propaganda and the Gospel literature of the early Christian mission', *ANRW* 2.25.2, 1705–29

Vermes, G. (1972/3): 'Hanina ben Dosa, a controversial Galilean saint from the first century of the Christian era', *JJS* 23, 28–50; 24, 51–64

—— (1983): *Jesus the Jew: A Historian's Reading of the Gospels* (London)

—— (1993): *The Religion of Jesus the Jew* (London)

Vööbus, A. (1958–60): *A History of Asceticism in the Syrian Orient*, 2 vols, (Louvain)

White, J. L. (1984): 'New Testament epistolary literature in the framework of ancient epistolography', *ANRW* 2.25.2, 1730–56

Wilson, B. M. (1973): *Magic and the Millenium* (London)

Winkler, J. J. (1982): 'The mendacity of Kalasiris and the narrative strategy of Heliodoros' Aithiopika', *YCS* 27, 93–158

INDEX

Apollo 37, 55, 90f., 100, 116, 149, 173

Apollonides, son of Aphrodisius 104

Apollonius, Christian opponent of Montanus 144

Apollonius of Tyana 6, 7, 12, 17, 19, 30, 32, 36, 38, 47, 54ff., 114ff., 130, 151, 194f., 205, 227; and ascetism 135; associations 44; at Antioch 107f., authority of 72, 131; as civic consultant 103f., and cure of dog-bite 58; death of 109ff.; and exorcism 93; expertise of 71; and forensic orators 136; impact 106; interest in nature 60; and Lamia at Corinth 97; letters of 79, 83; and magic 68; moral initiative 102; movements of 172f., opposition to 150; and patrons 122f.; and prophecy 62; and purism 113; quarrels with Euphrates 137–40, 144f.; and raising of the dead 94; reputation 193ff.; rhetoric of 73f.; and royal encounters 156ff., 160ff.; self-advertisement 89; ship-travel 174f.; trance 209; and treasure 98f.; violence of 148

Apostolic Council 24

Apuleius 8, 25, 66f., 86, 96, 98, 117, 187, 194f., 200, 227; *Apology* 118; and charlatans 69; *Metamorphoses* 178ff., 186, 207

Arabia 167

Arav 38

aretalogy, term defined 20

Arethas 23

Arians 201

Aricia, in Italy 41

Arignotus the Pythagorean 204

Aristeas of Proconnesus 209

Aristides, Aelius 23f., 27, 37f., 48, 52f., 58f., 106, 172, 174; hymns of 80f.; *Sacred Tales* 9, 26, 81; ship-travel 175

Aristobulus II 38

Aristogeiton 161

Aristotle 64

Artemidorus 61, 113; *Oneirocritica* 27

ascensions 189

Asclepiades 32; and raising of the dead 94f.

Asclepius 4, 8, 23f., 26, 28, 30, 38, 53, 55, 58, 81, 91f., 127, 132, 172, 213

Asia Minor 27, 37, 42f., 46f., 86, 127, 168, 174, 205

Askletarion 17

Aspendus 172

Assos 169

Assyria/n 14

astrology 62, 101, 135f., 155, 184, 210

astronomy 62

Atargatis, Syrian goddess 4, 8, 179

Athanasius 62, 109, 193; *Life of Antony* 20f., 189

Athenagoras, Ulpius 91

Athene 112

Athens 11, 43, 46f., 82f., 103, 129, 142, 159, 168, 171, 174

Atomos (Simon) 125

Attalus, Sentius 142

Augustus 13, 154

Aulus Gellius 47, 135, 137, 176

Aune, David 31

Avitus, Lollianus 121f.

Azande 215

Baal 13

Baalzebub 13

Babylon/ian 12, 44

Bahram I, Persian king 159f.

Balbillus, Tiberius Claudius 155

Barabbas 165

Bardesanes of Edessa (Bardaisan) 160

Barnabas 31, 104, 114, 133, 139, 141, 145f., 149, 168

Basilides 57, 153

Bassus of Corinth 57, 139, 145

Beamish, Henry, character in *The History Man* 218

Beroia 168

Berytus 137

Bet Ramah 134